THE BACKGROUND
OF THE REVOLUTION
IN MARYLAND

BY

CHARLES ALBRO BARKER

ARCHON BOOKS
1967

Library of Congress Catalog Card Number: 67-19512
Printed in the United States of America

TO

LOUISE COTTLE BARKER

PREFACE

THE present study falls in a field of history which has been intensively examined, and which has been interpreted with vision and with force. The American Revolution, its origins and meanings, has inevitably attracted scholars; it is so central in our history. But the case of Maryland has not been widely studied. Maryland was the fourth most populous British colony during the generation before the Revolution, and its authoritarian proprietary government was met and matched by a vigorous movement toward provincial autonomy. Yet little has been known about the tensions and impulses, the conditions and ideas, which prepared the colony for independence from Great Britain. In undertaking to discuss these questions, I have attempted to hold the large problem of the Revolution in view, to express the rising movement while speaking in provincial terms.

I was attracted to this investigation partly by chance and partly by taste. Early in the course of graduate study, a haphazard assignment of a seminar topic directed my attention to some of the eighteenth-century records of Maryland. Later, as I came to the writing of a doctoral dissertation, I formed a plan to use the Maryland materials for a new case-study in the provincial backgrounds of the Revolution. Maryland affairs seemed manageable enough for a thorough investigation. Social condition, economic trend, and institutional development could all be related to political event, local and intercolonial, and to the familiar great crises after 1763 which led directly into the War of Independence. Such early plans have often seemed too ambitious, the task too capable of indefinite extension. But I have never seriously altered the original aim and purpose; I hope now as I did then that I may make some contribution to the understanding of the Revolution.

At every stage of the investigation and writing there has recurred a tendency to search further back in time for the deeper impulses toward independence. My dissertation emphasized the two decades before the Revolution. The present work, largely based on additional investigation, combines a rewriting of the old with much that is entirely new. Certain trends are traced back into the seventeenth century; much importance is attributed to the political and economic crises of the years between 1725 and 1740. Besides the search backwards in time, there has been an equal tendency to investigate more widely and deeply into the conditions of mid-eighteenth-century life, to find more that is important and little-understood in social and intellectual condition, in economic life, and in financial arrangement. This tendency explains the structure of the book. The first six chapters are more topical than chronological; only the last four are more chronological than topical.

As my problem has grown, in writing and rewriting, I have felt an increasing need to express the intimacy of connection which I find to have existed among conditions, not always recogized as connected, in the coming of the Revolution. Political events, especially those in the long struggle between the proprietors and the "country party," are plainly kin to such political habits as insistence on parliamentary rights and privileges. But political protest is also kin, on the economic side, to crop regulation, and on the philosophical side, to the literary tastes of the province. The confidence of the House of Delegates is hardly to be understood apart from either the economic security of the members or the legal training of the leaders in protest. Likewise the conservatism of the "court party" conforms nicely with the financial privileges and the social prestige which emanated from the power of the lord proprietor. There is relatively little material for biography about colonial leadership in Maryland, except

in the case of Charles Carroll of Carrollton; this deficiency itself suggests a study of movements rather than
individuals, of traditions and ideas rather than parties.

My obligations, extending over a decade, are very many
and very great. I owe thanks to members of the staffs of
the Yale University Library, the Johns Hopkins University Library, the Peabody Library, the Stanford University Library, the Historical Society of Pennsylvania,
the New York Public Library, the New York State Library, and to the librarian of the Maryland Diocesan
Library. For great and repeated assistance, I am especially indebted to members of the staffs of the Library of
Congress, the Maryland Historical Society, the Maryland State Library, the Maryland Hall of Records, and
the Maryland Land Office. Without the kind personal
attention of Miss Florence Kennedy and of the late Mr.
Charles Fickus, I could never have managed the cardinal
materials of the Maryland Historical Society; and I am
under a similar obligation to Mr. Arthur Trader of the
Maryland Land Office. The late Dr. James A. Robertson, the first archivist in charge of the Hall of Records,
gave me generously of his time; and his successor, Dr.
Morris L. Radoff, has kindly helped me with the Bibliographical Note.

I have had financial assistance on generous terms.
The award of a Sterling Fellowship at Yale University
made it possible to put this study in its preliminary form,
as a doctoral dissertation, in 1932. Grants by the Stanford University Council of Research in the Social Sciences have made possible an extra summer of investigation in eastern libraries and the services of a secretary in
the preparation of the manuscript. The volume has been
published on the Frederick John Kingsbury Memorial
Fund of Yale University, and the portion of the expense
of publication not met from that source has been generously covered by a final grant from the Council of Research in the Social Sciences at Stanford. I wish especially to express my gratitude for these awards.

My great and lasting obligation is to Professor Charles M. Andrews of Yale. In the year of his retirement he encouraged me to go forward with the dissertation; in his first year as professor emeritus he supervised my work; he has continued his interest in the book. To Professor Andrews' successor in colonial studies at Yale, Professor Leonard W. Labaree, I owe gratitude for help in preparing the manuscript for the press, and for a long period of encouragement and patience in bringing this book toward readiness for the series of which he is the editor. At Yale I have also been advised and helped in particular ways by the late Professor Ulrich B. Phillips, and by Professors Ralph H. Gabriel and Ralph V. Harlow, the latter now of the University of Syracuse. At Stanford I have many obligations to my colleagues, especially to Professor Max H. Savelle, a specialist in colonial history. Many other friends and associates have helped me by letter or in consultation. Three especially, Professor Louis Hunter, of American University, and Mrs. Hunter, and Professor Merle E. Curti, of Columbia University, have helped in unique ways of their own. My wife, Louise Cottle Barker, has read the whole manuscript critically, chapter by chapter, and has made dozens of valuable suggestions for revision and for the development of ideas.

C. A. B.

Bristol, Connecticut
October 12, 1940

CONTENTS

THE BACKGROUND OF THE
REVOLUTION IN MARYLAND

I

THE STRUCTURE OF SOCIETY IN
PRE–REVOLUTIONARY MARYLAND

IN THE final decade of colonial history the proprietary government of Maryland almost collapsed. The
two houses of the legislature deadlocked, normal
processes of administration were abandoned, and the established church was demoralized. In its every aspect government was confused by the contradiction between the
authority of the lower house of assembly, conceived as
parliamentary, and the authority of the lord proprietor,
conceived as viceregal.

The movement for self-government matured and
became aggressive and ready for revolution when Maryland society matured, when the social order became complex and vigorous. The habit of attack on the prerogatives
and privileges of the lord proprietor had begun when the
colony began, and in the seventeenth century had led to
more violence and outbreak than in the eighteenth. But
there had been little staying power in the early anti-
proprietary thrusts. Resistance to Lord Baltimore was
then factional, but factions had no stable society in which
to root; it was religious, but religious antagonism was
already being dissolved by tolerance and indifference; it
was already constitutionalist and parliamentary in claim,
but constitutional forms had not yet become traditionalized nor parliamentary privileges well recognized in the
assembly. Liberalism still waited the phrasing of John
Locke and acceptance in principle throughout the English world. Not until the quieter eighteenth century were

the deeper conditions of colonial independence gradually fulfilled.

Such a fulfillment was only partly a matter of the differentiation of Maryland life, and American life, from English. The way in which the great planters of the eighteenth century lived was, like the architecture of their splendid brick houses, consciously patterned on the English model. If there were relatively few Marylanders of English birth in the eighteenth century, and not many who had intimate and nostalgic feeling for the mother country, society was nevertheless more English—more complex, more established and cultured—than in the seventeenth century. In making the combination which produced a vigorous and confident provincial society, the English things in Maryland—the classical education of young gentlemen, the rise of literary journalism, the parliamentary ideal, and the pursuit of trade—were no less prominent than the American things—the tobacco-staple economy, the increase of slavery, the settlement of the west, and speculation in land. The roots of Maryland activities and policies must, indeed, be traced to the soil, where the planting of tobacco and wheat and the digging of iron made fortunes and broke them. But political fruit is not to be understood without the parent stem, and the movement for colonial self-government would not have developed as it did without the influence of English and foreign attitudes and ideas. The two must be equally borne in mind as we approach the revolutionary movement.

Certain statistical aspects of the growth and division of Maryland society can be determined from the figures on population.[1] Such meager counts and estimates as were

1. The essential figures, with one exception, are conveniently assembled in Evarts B. Greene and Virginia D. Harrington, *American Population Before the Federal Census of 1790* (New York, 1932), pp. 123–134. I have considered invaluable the detailed table of the census of 1755 in *The Gentleman's Magazine and Historical Chronicle*, XXXIV (1764), 261. Stella Sutherland, *Population Distribution in Colonial America* (New York, 1936) is useful, especially for the population map and the discussion of factors in distribution (pp. 158, 178 ff.), but many of the figures are a decade too late for use here.

made and have remained of record show that the population of the province approximately doubled three times between the opening of the eighteenth century and the Revolution. In 1704 an official report estimated the population at just less than 35,000; in 1719 another estimate gave 80,000; in 1755 the most thorough census of the period gave 153,505; and various and evidently unreliable estimates for 1774 and 1775 ranged from 114,332 to 320,000. The most likely figures for the end of the colonial period are the middle ones, at 220,000 and 250,000, but none of them come well certified. The rapid expansion of numbers which Maryland shared with the entire colonial world, is interestingly attested by the census of 1755. It shows that there were more children younger than sixteen than there were adults of that age or older. Large families with many children prevailed at every social level of colonial life.

The census of 1755 also supplies information about the distribution of the people, both as to social status and geographic location. In that year there were 53,390 persons, or more than 35 per cent of the population, who belonged to unfree—the slave and servant—classes. Of these, 44,539, or more than 29 per cent of the population, were Negro and mulatto slaves, a steadily increasing class. As all the colored people, including the very few who were free, had numbered only 20 per cent of the population at the opening of the century, it appears that they were increasing more rapidly than the whites. Indentured white servants, with their freedom sold for various periods of years, numbered 8,851 in 1755, or a fraction less than 6 per cent of the population. One in four or five of the servants belonged to the class of transported convicts, who were sent out regularly from England and sold into servitude, and who comprised the most wretched group of people in Maryland.[2]

2. Even after considerable investigation, the history of servitude is none too clear. The census of 1755 gives figures for "hired or indented" servants without distinction, and I have used the figures as descriptive

Life in Maryland has always been vastly influenced by Chesapeake Bay. This deep inlet affects millions today, far and near, because it makes possible the great port of Baltimore. In the colonial period, however, the bulk of the population was in the lower and not the upper bay; and the expanse of water, stretching north about one hundred twenty miles through Maryland, from the mouth of the Potomac to the mouths of the Susquehanna, Elk, and North East rivers, effected a real separation between the Eastern and Western Shores. Families tended to intermarry and to own property on one shore or the other, rather than on both, and certain requirements of provincial administration led to the appointment of pairs of officials, one for each shore. Yet the bay which made some separations was also a convenient highway for immigrants and traders, so that through the whole colonial period settlement advanced about equally, and patterns of life developed similarly on the two shores. At the close of the seventeenth century there were eleven counties in Maryland, five on the Eastern Shore and six on the Western; and between that time and the Revolution four were added, two on each shore.[3] The census of 1755 shows that the

of indentured servitude; but "hired servants" may include members of the small and little-known class of free laborers. Because the transportation of convicts became a public issue, there is study, both contemporary and historical, of their number and status. See "A. B.," *Maryland Gazette* (Annapolis), July 30, 1767; the statement of the contractor for transportation to the House of Commons, *Maryland Historical Magazine,* XXVII, 265; and Basil Sollers, "Transported Convict Laborers in Maryland During the Colonial Period," *ibid.,* II, 17–47. The only large-scale treatment of white servitude in Maryland is Eugene I. McCormac, *White Servitude in Maryland, 1634–1820,* Johns Hopkins University Studies in Historical and Political Science (Baltimore), XXII (1904), nos. 3–4. Later citations from this series will be indicated by JHUS.

3. From south to north the seventeenth-century counties were: on the Western Shore, St. Mary's, Charles, Calvert, Prince George's, Anne Arundel, and Baltimore; and on the Eastern Shore, Somerset, Dorchester, Talbot, Kent, and Cecil. In the eighteenth century, Queen Anne's and Worcester counties were subdivisions of old counties on the middle and lower Eastern Shore; and Frederick and Harford counties, in the outlying west and northwest, mirrored the settlement of the Maryland frontier.

population of old Maryland, on the navigable tidewater of the Chesapeake, the Potomac, and the lesser rivers, was about equally divided between the two shores. There were then 67,509 inhabitants in the Eastern Shore counties; and there were 72,029 in those of the Western Shore, not counting Frederick county, which centered on the valley of the Monocacy, above the fall line.

Population was denser in the lower and middle counties than in those higher up the bay; and likewise the ratio of the unfree slaves and servants to the free inhabitants was higher to the south than to the north. These conditions were results of early settlement and a century and more of growth on the southern shores of the Chesapeake, and of the more successful cultivation of tobacco there, with unskilled labor, than to the north. In three adjoining counties of the lower Western Shore, Anne Arundel, Charles, and Calvert, nearly one-half of the population was unfree, for the most part slave. On the Eastern Shore opposite, in Queen Anne's and Talbot counties, similar conditions obtained. Of all the southern counties, only one had a small number of slaves and servants; this was Worcester, in the extreme southeast of the province, the one county which faced east on the Atlantic and away from the tobacco trade of the bay and rivers, and which with its sandy soil and extensive settlement by Scots was in every way a special case. In Cecil county, at the head of the bay on the Eastern Shore, less than 30 per cent of the population was unfree and less than 20 per cent was slave. Baltimore county, on the upper Western Shore, had somewhat larger proportions of the unfree than Cecil, but it too fell below the average of the province.[4]

North and west of the tidewater of the Western Shore lay the frontier settlements of the province, which comprised Maryland's share of the "Old West," described by Frederick Jackson Turner. The settlements lay in an area

4. For the figures of 1782, showing an absolute and proportional increase in the Negro population, see Sutherland, *Population Distribution*, p. 174.

roughly triangular in shape, bounded on the north by the Pennsylvania line, on the south and west by the course of the Potomac from its northernmost bow, near Hagerstown, to the site of Washington, and on the south and east by a line from that point to Baltimore and on to the northeastern corner of the province. This triangle was about as great in area as all of southern Maryland of both shores; it included the settled part of Frederick county, the back part of Anne Arundel, and most of Baltimore and Cecil counties. According to the census of 1755 it was about one-third as populous as lower Maryland. Its development was everywhere affected by nearness to Pennsylvania and Delaware. Immigration from the north and east, particularly in the second quarter of the eighteenth century, brought new and foreign influences of nationality, religion, and trade into Maryland.[5] But the section was not very homogeneous within itself. Although we shall see that the commercial settlements at the head of the bay had features in common with the outlying west which distinguished both from the lower tidewater, there were also important differences which distinguished Frederick from Baltimore county, and Baltimore from Cecil.

Frederick county included all there was in Maryland of the exposed French and Indian frontier of the eighteenth-century wars. Compared to the wide frontiers of Pennsylvania and Virginia, it was a very small area of conflict. Settlement advanced to the Conogocheague and a little beyond, where Fort Frederick guarded the narrow entrance to Maryland between the bow of the Potomac and the Pennsylvania line. Beyond that point, Frederick county—the truly western Maryland, after independence to be divided into Washington, Allegheny, and other counties—was more an area of land speculation and Indian fighting than of occupation and settlement in the

5. On the trade of the northeast, see Mary A. Hanna, *The Trade of the Delaware District before the Revolution,* Smith College Studies in History (Northampton), II (1917), 243, 261–262.

colonial period.[6] The part of Frederick county east and south of Fort Frederick was itself considerably larger than any other county entire, except Baltimore; and, with nearly 14,000 inhabitants in 1755, Frederick had a larger population than any other county, with the same exception. The census also shows that only 17.5 per cent of the population belonged to the unfree classes, and that 12.5 per cent were slaves. These ratios were only half as large as for the province as a whole and hardly one-third as large as for the southern tidewater counties.

Many of the ordinary characteristics of frontier life prevailed in Frederick county. Various reports of conditions in the seventeen-forties, the second decade of settlement, speak of the threat of wild animals from the forest, of poor inhabitants clothed like Indians and living in cold and discomfort, and of the vagrancy of hunters and other footloose people.[7] Even as late as 1772, William Eddis, a customs official, said that habitations were rude and life was plain. The people frequently lived in log houses of two rooms and an adjoining storehouse; and corn, beaten and baked into hominy, was the principle article of diet.[8]

Aside from its frontier location and character, the distinguishing feature of social life in Frederick county derived from the mixed settlement there of immigrant Germans with the English from the tidewater. The Ger-

6. On the career of Thomas Cresap, Yorkshireman and early settler of western Maryland, see Lawrence C. Wroth, "Thomas Cresap, a Maryland Pioneer," *Md. Hist. Mag.,* IX, 1–37.

7. See the description of standards of living in William J. Hinke and Charles E. Kemper, "Moravian Diaries of Travels through Virginia," *Virginia Magazine of History and Biography,* XI (1903-1904), 116-117; mention of bears and other animals in western Maryland, *Pennsylvania Gazette,* November 30, 1749; and a proclamation of Governor Thomas Bladen about vagrancy, October 10, 1745 (three years, however, before Frederick county was erected), *Archives of Maryland* (Baltimore, 1883-), XXVIII, 348-349. Later citations from this series will be given as *Archives.*

8. William Eddis, *Letters from America, Historical and Descriptive, comprising Occurrences from 1769, to 1777, inclusive* (London, 1792), p. 131.

mans, in Maryland as elsewhere, clung tenaciously to native language, customs, ideals, and traditions. Some, especially those from the Palatinate, came to Maryland direct, but the great number came by way of the old Lancaster road out of Pennsylvania into the fertile valley of the Monocacy, and many crossed the Potomac and went on into Virginia or farther south.[9] Important German settlement in Maryland commenced in 1729; and in 1732, after Lord Baltimore had offered especially favorable terms for the taking up of land, communities began to spring up rapidly. The town of Monocacy, situated on the stream of the same name, was the first, and Frederick, ten miles to the south, the second. By mid-century the Germans had established an outlying settlement at Conogocheague; and a Moravian center had sprung up at Graceham, in the splendid hilly country north of Frederick. In 1762, Jonathan Hagar, the best known of the early German settlers and the only one to become prominent in provincial politics, founded the flourishing agricultural and trading center since called Hagerstown.[10]

The non-Germans who shared the task of opening the new western lands are a group almost lost to history. The very earliest settlers in the back country, indeed, came from the lower Potomac, from St. Mary's, Charles, and

9. How the Germans occupied the back country is a tale more than twice told by admiring descendants and fellow nationals. Much the same ground is covered in Louis P. Hennighausen, "Early German Settlements in Western Maryland," *Sixth Annual Report of the Society for the History of the Germans in Maryland* (Baltimore, 1892); in Daniel Wunderlich Nead, *The Pennsylvania-German in the Settlement of Maryland* (Lancaster, Pa., 1914); in J. Thomas Scharf, in sections of his *History of Western Maryland* (Philadelphia, 1882), I; in Edward T. Schulz, *First Settlements of Germans in Maryland* (Frederick, Md., 1896); and in Thomas J. C. Williams, *History of Frederick County, Maryland* (Hagerstown, 1910), I. Of these local studies the most useful is that by Nead, but none displaces the treatment in Albert B. Faust, *The German Element in the United States* (Boston, 1909), I, 161–176. Most of these books lean heavily on Eddis, *Letters from America,* and Henry Harbaugh, *The Life of Rev. Michael Schlatter* (Philadelphia, 1857).

10. Basil Sollers, "Jonathan Hagar, the Founder of Hagerstown," *Second Annual Report of the Society for the History of the Germans in Maryland* (Baltimore, 1888).

Prince George's counties; and, as their plantations extended up the river from the fall line, they met the Germans coming from the north and merged with them around Frederick. Five Quaker meeting-houses indicate the transit of English dissenters to the Frederick county frontier.[11] While it is true that the Scotch-Irish element, so characteristic of the frontiers of Pennsylvania and Virginia, was not conspicuous in Frederick county, nor even as prominent there as in Cecil county and on the lower Eastern Shore, neither was it altogether lacking. A half dozen or more Presbyterian churches testify to its presence.[12] The best indication of the importance of the non-Germans in the occupation of the west appears in the provincial land records. A trial sampling of the rent rolls of Frederick county for the years from 1767 to 1775 shows that about five-sixths of the freeholds were held by English or Scotch-Irish, and about one-sixth by Germans.[13] Such figures as these, although they suggest the presence of a great majority of English-speaking inhabitants, actually give little indication of the relative numbers of the different nationalities, because many of the Germans were lessees and not owners and so were not listed in the proprietary records. The lists do show two conditions, nevertheless, which have not always been

11. Williams, *Frederick County*, I, 1; Clarence P. Gould, "The Economic Causes of the Rise of Baltimore," *Essays in Colonial History presented to Charles McLean Andrews* (New Haven, 1931), pp. 229-230; Charles O. Paullin, *Atlas of the Historical Geography of the United States* (New York, 1932), pl. 82e. Through the courtesy of Mr. Paullin and of Mr. C. K. Wright, the writer saw some of the materials used in compiling the *Atlas*.

12. Charles A. Hanna, *The Scotch-Irish, or the Scot in North Britain, North Ireland, and North America* (New York, 1902), II, 108; Paullin, *Atlas*, pl. 82 b.

13. Four groups of freeholds, selected at random, were counted as follows:

	Group I	II	III	IV	Total
English or Scotch-Irish holders	61	64	68	55	248
German holders	12	17	12	9	50

Rent Rolls, 32-36 (Frederick County, 1767-1775), Maryland Land Office, Annapolis.

clearly recognized: first, that a considerable number of settlers of the same British nationality and type as on the tidewater took up land and established themselves in the Maryland west; and, second, that a fair number of Germans became not leaseholders but the owners of land, some of them of several hundred acres, in the fullest freehold title of the day.[14]

Whatever the balance of numbers, it was the Germans rather than the English who caught the eye of such observers as Eddis, and who did in fact add something new and important to the culture and economy of the province. Religious discontent had been a powerful force in bringing Germans to America, and in Maryland their presence was marked by sectarian institutions and culture. The earliest congregation at Monocacy was Lutheran and at Frederick, German Reformed; and at Conogocheague, as during the seventeen-fifties at Baltimore, the two denominations, Lutheran and Calvinist, worshiped in unison. These two, strongest of the German sects, spread simultaneously and about equally in the back country. On the eve of the Revolution there were fifteen Lutheran and fourteen German Reformed congregations. The churches were poor, however, and the services of ministers and teachers had to be spread thin. The memorandum of the Reverend John Conrad Steiner, of the Reformed church of Frederick, gives a remarkable account of 2,960 miles of travel to hold services during a period of a little more than a year, between late 1757 and early 1759. A minister of the Dutch Reformed Church, Michael Schlatter, was commissioned by the synods of north and south Holland to examine the destitute congregations of his own and the German Reformed Church in America. After preaching in western Maryland he reported tender and moving scenes at his services, and he declared that he had never

14. Hagar, known as the greatest German landholder, had 2,488 acres, patented in parcels between 1739 and 1765. Sollers, "Jonathan Hagar," p. 19.

seen the Reformed faith more pure than in the Monocacy valley.[15]

In many ways the picture of German Protestantism in the Maryland west is a pleasing and romantic one. Besides the Lutherans and Calvinists, there were a few congregations of radical sectarians, such as the Dunkers, Moravians, and Mennonites. They also were free and active in the work of their respective faiths.[16] The names of the leaders among the Germans which have come down to us are chiefly those of teachers and preachers, such as John Conrad Steiner, Thomas Schley, the founder of a distinguished American family, and Theodore Frankenfeld. Under such guidance there was probably more group solidarity and sentiment than in any other social or geographical element in the province. When twenty-five Germans subscribed to a declaration, evidently to be used by promoters to attract new settlers to Maryland, they could truly say that they enjoyed full liberty of conscience in their new home.[17]

On the economic side, Frederick county enjoyed natural advantages of fertility and climate which the tidewater did not have. After a westward excursion from Annapolis, Eddis wrote that it was impossible to conceive a more rich and fruitful country, and he truly prophesied that when the population had grown Frederick county agriculture would at least equal any in America. In a similar vein Michael Schlatter, the missionary, declared that the soil of western Maryland produced splendid corn, ten-foot stalks without the use of fertilizer. In Eddis' judgment,

15. Henry Harbaugh, *Fathers of the German Reformed Church in Europe and America* (Lancaster, Pa., 1857), II, 35–37; Harbaugh, *The Life of Rev. Michael Schlatter*, pp. 154, 176–177.

16. In addition to the references above, p. 8, n. 9, the following give material on the radical sects: Martin Brumbaugh, *A History of the German Baptist Brethren in Europe and America* (Mount Morris, Ill., 1899); Augustus W. Drury, *History of the Church of the United Brethren in Christ* (Dayton, Ohio, 1924); and J. Taylor Hamilton, *A History of the . . . Moravian Church . . .* (Bethlehem, Pa., 1900).

17. Calvert Papers, n.d., *Archives*, XLIV, 697.

however, it was the German character rather than benefits of soil and climate which "chiefly tended to the advancement of settlements" in the west. He found the sectarians industrious, frugal, patient, and in everything well fitted for such pioneer tasks as felling timber and clearing and working the land.[18] The Germans came, moreover, without the tradition of slave labor and tobacco planting which was so firmly established on the tidewater. This difference, combined with the excessive cost and risk of carrying the leaf overland before shipment to England, tended to discourage tobacco culture in the west. Thus Frederick county became a grain-raising area, like the "bread colonies" to the north; and crop diversification came to Maryland partly as a result of the German immigration. Here was a sound reason, as will appear, for the enthusiasm of provincial officials, such as Eddis and Governor Eden,[19] at the success of the Germans in winning and working the soil of Frederick county.

Where the Germans settled, trade soon sprang up. In the period between the French and Indian War and the Revolution, the town of Frederick grew to be larger than Annapolis and any of the tidewater towns except Baltimore; and Hagerstown, too, expanded rapidly. In Frederick, Eddis found warehouses and stores, and he noticed that not only "woollens, linens, and implements of husbandry" and other such essentials were offered for sale, but "elegancies" as well. He speaks of "one large and convenient church" for Anglicans and of several chapels for Germans and English dissenters. Though the buildings were mostly of wood, he thought them "neat and regular," and he declared that Frederick had, "by imperceptible degrees, from an humble beginning . . . arisen to its present flourishing state." [20] Eddis visited Hagerstown, too, but a more particular description than his

18. Harbaugh, *The Life of Rev. Michael Schlatter,* p. 172; Eddis, *Letters from America,* pp. 99, 129–131.

19. Governor Robert Eden to the Earl of Dartmouth, January 29, 1773, *Md. Hist. Mag.,* II, 302.

20. Eddis, *Letters from America,* p. 101.

comes from Philip Vickers Fithian, a young New Jersey dissenter and tutor who traveled in the back country in 1775. He described the town as "a considerable village." In his own words:

It may contain two hundred houses—some of them are large and neat, built with stone or brick; but the greater part are built with logs neatly squared, which, indeed, make a good house. There are many stores here. And many mechanics, and it is a place of business. The inhabitants are chiefly Dutch. . . . There is here a Dutch-Lutheran church, and they are now building an English church. Frederick is the county town, so they have no court house.[21]

All who recorded impressions of the Maryland west spoke of essentially the same phenomena: fertility, industry, growth of population, and the importance of the German settlers.

In the northern counties, Baltimore and Cecil, as in Frederick, agriculture did not closely imitate the pattern of tobacco planting traditional in the lower counties. The rivers and streams entering the head of the bay did not open out into such navigable inlets as those of the Potomac and the Patuxent. The landholders, accordingly, did not frequently have the advantage of direct overseas shipping to the British ports, the opportunity which was so common and so valuable to planters facing on the southern rivers. The region was affected, moreover, by the tendency of the eighteenth century for wheat to appreciate in value and for tobacco to depreciate, due to an increasing overseas demand for American foodstuffs.[22] Under such stimulation grain culture sprang up around the head of the bay as it did in the west. Before the middle of the century there

21. Robert G. Albion and Leonidas Dodson, editors, *Philip Vickers Fithian Journal, 1775–1776* (Princeton, 1934), pp. 9–10.

22. For a scholarly analysis of economic trends in the Baltimore area, see Gould, "The Economic Causes of the Rise of Baltimore," *Essays in Colonial History*, pp. 225–251. See also Anne Bezanson, Robert D. Gray, and Miriam Hussey, *Prices in Colonial Pennsylvania* (Philadelphia, 1935), p. 84.

was a surplus for exportation, and it was being shipped both down the bay and east into the Delaware area.[23] At the same time the production of iron was being successfully undertaken. The two iron companies of the provincial period in Maryland, the Principio and the Baltimore, were launched between 1715 and 1730, the first near the mouth of the Susquehanna and the second in the lower Patapsco region.[24] The establishment of this industry and that of the cultivation of grain had effected a marked economic differentiation between northern and southern Maryland as early as the middle of the century.

In Cecil county, in the northeastern corner of the province, the influence of intercolonial trade and population movement was especially marked. A number of new towns, genuine if small centers of business and enterprise, sprang up there during the half-century before the Revolution. Elkton was the furthest east, located at the convergence of roads connecting the Eastern and Western Shores of Maryland with Philadelphia, Newcastle, and Wilmington. Fithian described the vicinity as "fertile and well cultivated" and the "village" itself as "small but containing some large elegant houses." [25] Charlestown was only a few miles to the west, at the mouth of the North East River and very near to the Principio iron works and the mouth of the Susquehanna. It is said to have had about sixty houses at the end of the colonial period.[26] Here a semiannual fair was established in 1744, only two years after the erection of the town. Held for three-day periods in April and October, it became a real commercial event and was continued for about a century. According to the county historian, the fairs attracted merchants from Baltimore and Philadelphia and buyers from Chester and Lancaster counties, Pennsylvania, as well as from the

23. Besides Gould, see Hanna, *Trade of the Delaware District,* pp. 261–262.

24. See below, pp. 106–107.

25. *Fithian Journal, 1775–1776,* pp. 5–6.

26. Chalmers Papers, Maryland, II, New York Public Library. Later citations from manuscripts in this Library will be indicated by NYPL.

immediate vicinity. They were effective outposts of British mercantilism, for they introduced coffee and tea drinking into the community. The fairs were also festive occasions, with fiddling and dancing for all.[27]

Of the lesser villages, which Burnaby describes as "built for the accommodation of strangers and travellers," and which stretched along the upper Western Shore from the Patapsco to the Susquehanna, there is little record. Dr. Alexander Hamilton, the Annapolis physician who passed through in 1744, speaks, however, of a good tavern in a large brick house in Joppa, and of a less attractive one ten miles north. There, he tells us, the only intelligible thing in a conversation of drunken club members was a string of "oaths and God-damnes; the rest was an inarticulate sound like Rabelais frozen words a-thawing, interlaced with hickupings and belchings." Dr. Hamilton found few elegant accommodations anywhere in northern Maryland. At the ferry house at Bohemia he was obliged to sleep in the same room with his landlord and the landlord's wife and daughters.[28]

In respect of nationality and religion as well as economic activity, the people of Cecil county had characteristics of their own. When, in 1661, Augustine Herrman, a Bohemian soldier of fortune, established Bohemia Manor on the Elk, and when, a quarter-century later, his son encouraged the foundation of a Labadist community there,[29] there had been settled in Cecil county only the earliest of many who were foreign born and religiously radical. English, Dutch, Swedish, Finnish, Danish, Welsh, Irish, and Scottish settlers all came to the county. In many cases they were emigrants from the Dutch and Swedish settlements on the Delaware or from the Quaker colonies,

27. George Johnston, *History of Cecil County, Maryland* . . . (Elkton, Maryland, 1881), pp. 269–271.

28. Alexander Hamilton, *Hamilton's Itinerarium, being a Narrative of a Journey from Annapolis* . . . *through* . . . *New Hampshire,* edited by Albert B. Hart (St. Louis, 1907), pp. 3, 5–6, 9–10.

29. Bartlett B. James, *The Labadist Colony in Maryland,* JHUS, XVII (1899), no. 6, chs. IV-V.

and came without contact or connection with southern Maryland.

The great variety and the small numbers of the foreign national groups, however, prepared the way for assimilation. In the eighteenth century it was English and Scottish sectarianism which, more than foreign descent, was prominent in Cecil county. Meeting-houses, the earlier ones built of logs and the later of stone, represented a substantial element of Quakerism at Nottingham, near Rising Sun. In the same community there were also Presbyterian churches, attended by poverty-ridden Scotch-Irish farmers; they were poorly constructed and uncomfortable houses of worship. Many of the Scotch-Irish, in fact, were mere temporary residents, and preferred to move on into Virginia and the Carolinas.[30] Yet some remained, and Presbyterianism exercised a real influence in the religious life of the community. In 1739 a Cecil county rector wrote the Society for the Propagation of the Gospel that dissent was a serious threat to the established church, and he begged for a library to help him meet the arguments of the Pennsylvania deists, Quakers, and Presbyterians.[31] He declared that the dissenters were "cunning" in catching ignorant and "licentious" people. Evangelical feeling ran strongest at the time of the Great Awakening. In 1741 the Presbyterian congregation at Nottingham was divided into factions by the preaching of Whitefield; and the "new sides," who built a new church, obtained as their minister a recent graduate of the Tennents' Log College, Samuel Finley. Finley established and operated a Presbyterian academy, the only one of its kind in Maryland, and he was called, after seventeen years, to be president of the College of New Jersey at Princeton.[32]

30. Johnston, *History of Cecil County*, pp. 28, 93, 155, 161, 169, 289–294.

31. Letter of Hugh Jones, July 30, 1739, William S. Perry, *Historical Collections Relating to the American Colonial Church* (Hartford, 1870–1878), IV, 321.

32. Bernard C. Steiner and others, *History of Education in Maryland* (Washington, 1894), p. 36; William B. Sprague, *Annals of the American Pulpit* . . . (New York, 1858), III, 96–97.

There also appeared in Cecil county, in the five years before the Revolution, a number of Methodists, not quite as early as those in Baltimore county but among the earliest in America.[33]

Between the mixed population of Cecil county and the German and English one of Frederick lay the most varied and dynamic section of Maryland society. In Baltimore county, and particularly in the area around the lower Patapsco River, there were many economic advantages. The profitable cultivation of wheat was established there before the middle of the century; the Baltimore iron works were there; and, especially around Elkridge, tobacco was successfully cultivated and exported. These local advantages gave rise to small commercial villages, such as Baltimore and Elkridge, in the seventeen-thirties and -forties. But there were other local factors at work before the mid-century. The exhaustive investigation of Professor Clarence P. Gould shows that the unparalleled expansion which transformed Baltimore from an undistinguished center to a small commercial city, the only one of its kind in the Maryland economy, derived from the rise of overland trade between the mouth of the Patapsco and the Monocacy valley. The road between, which was opened in the seventeen-forties, connected a rich and increasing hinterland with a good harbor, and the result was unique in Maryland history.[34]

William Eddis, writing with first-hand information in 1771, saw the situation accurately, and described it as follows:

Within these few years some scattered cottages were only to be found on this spot, occupied by obscure storekeepers, merely for the supply of the adjacent plantations. But the

33. Johnston, *History of Cecil County*, pp. 440–442.
34. Gould, "The Economic Causes of the Rise of Baltimore," pp. 236–238; Gould, *Money and Transportation in Maryland, 1720–1765*, JHUS, XXXIII (1915), no. 1, pp. 126–129; Paul H. Giddens, "Trade and Industry in Colonial Maryland," *Journal of Economic and Business History*, IV (1931–1932), 514–515.

peculiar advantages it possesses, with respect to the trade of the frontier counties of Virginia, Pennsylvania, and Maryland, so strongly impressed the mind of Mr. John Stevenson, an Irish gentleman, who had settled in the vicinity in a medical capacity, that he first conceived the important project of rendering this port the grand emporium of Maryland commerce. He accordingly applied himself, with assiduity, to the completion of his plan. The neighboring country being fertile, well settled, and abounding in grain; Mr. S—— contracted for considerable quantities of wheat, he freighted vessels, and consigned them to a correspondent in his native country: the cargoes sold to great advantage, and returns were made equally beneficial. The commencement of a trade so lucrative to the first adventurers, soon became an object of universal attention. Persons of a commercial and enterprising spirit, emigrated from all quarters to this new and promising scene of industry . . . . Within forty years, from its first commencement [1729], Baltimore became not only the most wealthy and populous town of the province, but inferior to few in this continent, either in size, number of inhabitants, or the advantages arising from a well-conducted and universal connexion . . . . Soon after the appointment of Mr. Eden to the government of Maryland [1768], Sir William Draper arrived in that province, on a tour throughout the continent. He contemplated the origin of Baltimore, and its rapid progress, with astonishment; and when introduced, by the governor, to the worthy founder, he elegantly accosted him by the appellation of the American Romulus.[35]

In a sense, Sir William's salute to Dr. Stevenson involved no exaggeration, for a great city had been founded; but the comparison with Rome was not apt, for Baltimore was far from being a dominating metropolis and a center of authority. One of the striking things about its rise is that during the first period of expansion it never stood, for all the breadth of its commercial contact, in

35. Eddis, *Letters from America,* pp. 96–98, quoted in Gould, "The Economic Causes of the Rise of Baltimore," pp. 238–239.

intimate connection with the dominant interests of southern Maryland and of the province as a whole. Although Baltimore merchants handled a great amount of wagon freight to and from Frederick county and received heavy shipments of wheat from the upper bay, they did not tap the tobacco trade in any important degree. That remained in the hands of the merchants and planters to the south. Similarly, those merchants and planters of the lower counties, though the wealthiest men in the province, do not seem, except in the case of the iron industry, to have invested in the commercial enterprises of Baltimore.

Migratory business, seeking the opportunities of a boom town, came from the north rather than the south, from commercial Pennsylvania more than from the aristocratic and agrarian tidewater.[36] This trend, indicated by advertising in the Baltimore newspaper, is particularly marked in the printing business itself. Printing began in Baltimore with the work of Nicholas Hasselbach, a German immigrant who is said to have learned his trade in Philadelphia from Christopher Saur, the ablest of the colonial German printers. All four or five of the other printers of pre-revolutionary Baltimore came from Philadelphia, too; not one came up the bay from the well established *Maryland Gazette* of Annapolis. Nor did the *Gazette* carry more than a bare minimum of news and advertising from either Baltimore or the back country.[37]

In 1754, when Baltimore was less than a decade along in its period of rapid growth, Governor Horatio Sharpe made a comment which reveals the contemporary sense of the difference between the Baltimore area and southern Maryland. In writing to England, Sharpe said that Baltimore was "the most increasing town in the province," and

---

36. Gould, "The Economic Causes of the Rise of Baltimore," pp. 231, 242–246. For a parallel case of dissociation between town life and plantation life, see Thomas J. Wertenbaker, *Norfolk, Historic Southern Port* (Durham, N. C., 1931), pp. 26–27.

37. *Maryland Gazette, passim;* Lawrence C. Wroth, *A History of Printing in Colonial Maryland, 1686–1776* (Baltimore, 1922), pp. 112–117, 122, 128.

he mentioned the commercial advantages of "the extensive country beyond." But he saw a real deficiency. The town needed, he said, "a few gentlemen of fortune to settle there and encourage the trade," because, "while few beside Germans (who are in general masters of small fortunes) build and inhabit there, I apprehend it cannot make any considerable figure." The governor's tone of condescension did not reappear ten years later, when he again wrote of Baltimore. He then spoke of its business leadership as recognized in the province, and predicted that it would soon "get the start" of Annapolis as to number of inhabitants.[38]

There were many social differences between Baltimore town and county and the plantation country to the south. As in the other outlying communities, but more markedly, settlement was by a various mixture of foreigners and British—by merchants, artisans, and dissenters, many of whom had entered from the north, through the back door of the province, rather than through the main entrance, between the capes. There were five or six Church of England parishes, as many or more than in other counties, and they were matched by several German churches, Lutheran and Reformed, and by Quaker and Presbyterian congregations. Methodism was particularly successful in and near Baltimore. The environment was right for a movement recently sprung from the Church of England: Anglicanism was there but the most conservative elements in the church were not, German pietism added to the evangelical spirit, and dissent was common. The Methodists benefited, moreover, from the local leadership of Robert Strawbridge, a vigorous Irishman, and from occasional visits by Francis Asbury, the leader of the movement in America.[39]

38. Letter to Lord Baltimore, May 2, 1754; to C. Calvert, August 22, 1764; *Archives,* VI, 57; XIV, 173.

39. William W. Sweet, *Methodism in American History* (New York, 1933), pp. 50–52, 66–68; Nathan Bangs, *The Life of the Rev. Freeborn Garrettson* (New York, 1829), pp. 21–31.

Especially in the decade before the Revolution, Baltimore grew rapidly. New lands were acquired, Jones Town was absorbed, and swamps were drained. Commerce and industry required the building of a market, of public and private wharves, of warehouses, a shipyard, a lumberyard, a brewery, a pottery, and many stores.[40] Domestic building was modest, in the early years at least, wooden houses prevailing over brick, as fitted the means and status of the people. There was not time in the colonial period for Baltimore to attain to architectural distinction. In 1771 Eddis spoke of "elegant and convenient habitations," but there was not enough elegance or convenience five years later, when the Continental Congress moved there for a few weeks, for the members to speak of Baltimore as anything but dirty and expensive and a "Tryal" to all concerned.[41]

Colonial Baltimore showed many signs, however, of civic enterprise and of a cosmopolitanism fitting to its location. There was a variety of churches, English and German, and a number of buildings for public use. In the half-dozen years before the Revolution a small theater, a "Mechanical Company," maintaining a fire engine, and a printing-house were all established. Practical science was represented by inoculation against small pox; [42] and popular interest in electricity, so typical of the age, was appealed to as early as 1764 by a commercial lecturer at the market-house. The lecturer, a William Johnson, announced that he would prove that electricity is "a simple, homogeneous, subtle fluid, lodged in the vacuities of all

40. On the appearance of Baltimore, see the following: Thomas W. Griffith, *Annals of Baltimore* (Baltimore, 1824) ; J. Thomas Scharf, *The Chronicles of Baltimore* . . . (Baltimore, 1874) ; Scharf, *History of Baltimore City and County from the earliest period to the present day, including biographical sketches of their representative men* (Philadelphia, 1881) ; Gould, "The Economic Causes of the Rise of Baltimore," pp. 240–242, 249–250.

41. Letters of William Ellery, Benjamin Harrison, and Oliver Wolcott, December 25, 1776–January 8, 1777, Edmund C. Burnett, editor, *Letters of Members of the Continental Congress*, II (Washington, 1923), 187, 188, 208.

42. *Maryland Gazette*, September 18, 1764.

bodies, and that it is the same as lightning, but not for that reason inconsistent with the principles of natural or revealed religion." [43] In 1773 literature and journalism came to Baltimore on a commercial basis. In that year William Goddard launched the first Maryland newspaper outside Annapolis, the *Maryland Journal and Baltimore Advertiser*, a paper in the Franklin tradition which printed literary as well as business and general items.[44] In the fall Goddard advertised both the launching of a circulating library in the city, and a proposal to bring out a five-volume edition of the works of Lawrence Sterne, provided that two hundred subscriptions could be obtained in advance.[45] Commercial, expansive, and beginning to participate in the intellectual life of the age, Baltimore quickly took place as a representative provincial city of the mid-eighteenth century.[46]

The whole frontier area of the province, from the upper Potomac to the Elk, stood in a kind of colonial relationship to the old Maryland of the proprietary government and the tobacco plantations. If the two sections lived much apart, the newer without many of the traditions and characteristics of the older, they were nevertheless bound in a political whole, they shared in population movements, they had certain economic connections, and a common military problem. The greatest interest in the settlement and economic development of the west and north was naturally that of the lord proprietor and the inner circle of higher officials at Annapolis. It was their task and function to encourage the settlement of new land, to see that fees were paid, titles established, and quit-rents collected, and that the administrative and judicial machinery of the province extended to all the people.

43. *Maryland Gazette,* July 26, 1764.

44. *Maryland Journal,* August 20, 1773; Wroth, *Printing in Maryland,* p. 122.

45. *Maryland Journal,* October 23, 30, 1773.

46. This and some of the other cultural phenomena mentioned in this book are discussed, in a different orientation, in the writer's article, "Maryland before the Revolution: Society and Thought," *American Historical Review,* XLVI (1940), 1–20.

Both Charles, the fifth, and Frederick, the sixth Lord Baltimore, gave some personal attention to this interest. In the thirties and forties, the former several times made or had made fresh arrangements—reducing quit-rents, modifying purchase-money charges, and the like—to smooth the way for western settlement.[47] "I pray learn again," wrote Lord Baltimore's secretary to Governor Sharpe, as late as 1764, "about reserved land in and around cities and towns." The Penns, he said, had been strict about holding for their own benefit the land around Philadelphia, but he feared that proprietary officials in Maryland had not been "assiduous" to secure similar profits from the rise of land values in Baltimore. The governor replied that the Calverts had, indeed, never planned or fostered a town, as the Penns had promoted Philadelphia, and that Maryland towns had always grown on lands earlier patented to individuals.[48] In Baltimore and elsewhere, therefore, the increment of rent went to the private holder; but the rise of the proprietor's income shows that he gained extensively, from quit-rents and from other sources, as a result of the increase in population.[49]

All through Maryland, but especially in Frederick county, where the great number of German farmers settled, many private holders took the profits of speculation and leasing. In the west Daniel Dulany, the elder, was the principal speculator. A man of humble immigrant beginnings, Dulany secured large grants in the twenties and thirties, the period of his rise into the inner circle of government. He established the town of Frederick, and, with the advice and consent of Lord Baltimore, he arranged transportation for German immigrants and sometimes made them advances of money.[50] What he did on a large

47. See below, pp. 135–136, 138.
48. Cecilius Calvert to Sharpe, February 29, 1764, Sharpe to Calvert, August 22, 1764, *Archives*, XIV, 137–138, 173.
49. See below, pp. 140–141.
50. Biographical materials for the Daniel Dulanys, the elder and the younger, are slender, for the Dulany Papers in the Maryland Historical Society are disappointing. See, however, St. George L. Sioussat, *Economics and Politics in Maryland, 1720–1750, and the Public Service of*

scale, others did on a lesser. Members of the important Snowden and Wolstenholme families also promoted immigration; Charles Carroll of Doughoregan held large estates and let much land in Frederick county; and his distant cousin, Dr. Charles Carroll, who once urged the governor to build roads and advance settlement for the sake of military protection,[51] owned about twenty thousand acres in the west. Shortly before the Revolution, such proprietary office holders and favorites as Dr. Upton Scott and John Morton Jordan, such merchants as Thomas Ringgold of the Eastern Shore and Launcelot Jacques of Annapolis, and such lawyers and later revolutionary leaders as Thomas Johnson, Samuel Chew, and Samuel Chase were all holders of western grants. Their estates uniformly ran into the thousands of acres, and more often were greater than five thousand acres than smaller.[52]

There is only a little evidence of protest or resentment in the "Old West" against the institutions, the officialdom, and the speculation which reached out from lower Maryland. According to a report which the governor laid before the provincial council in 1748, the newcomers of the back country, especially the Germans, were sometimes cheated by unscrupulous officials. Quit-rents ordinarily caused no trouble, but overdue accounts, known as "black lists" and collected by the sheriff, were occasionally overcharged. Such abuses caused a few settlers to leave Maryland, and

Daniel Dulany the Elder, JHUS, XXI (1903), nos. 6–7; and Richard H. Spencer, "Hon. Daniel Dulany, 1685–1753," *Md. Hist. Mag.,* XIII, 20–28. On the conditions of speculation, see Clarence P. Gould, *The Land System in Maryland, 1720–1765,* JHUS, XXXI (1913), no. 1, pp. 61–62.

51. Letter to Governor Samuel Ogle, February 17, 1731, *Md. Hist. Mag.,* XIX, 291–293. In this letter Carroll also advised, as Dulany later did, that the west be settled at once, lest Maryland soil be taken by grantees from Pennsylvania and Virginia. Dulany to Baltimore, July 21, 1744, Dulany Papers, II, 26, Maryland Historical Society. Materials in the Society's library will hereafter be designated by MHS.

52. Debt Books, Frederick county, 1771, Maryland Land Office. There is some information about the size of holdings in Gould, *Land System,* pp. 86–87; and in Kate M. Rowland, *The Life of Charles Carroll of Carrollton* (New York, 1898), I, 5–7.

certain Germans were reported to grumble that they had left home to escape oppression, and they had hoped not to find it in Maryland.[53] But there was little recurrence of this sort of complaint.

The Germans were unfamiliar with the ecclesiastical and the representative institutions of Maryland, and they made little effort to participate in them. Dulany recognized that church taxes, in support of the Church of England parishes, ran contrary to the convictions of the German Protestants and other dissenters, but he said that there was no great "obstruction" in the matter.[54] As to politics, Frederick like all the counties elected four representatives to the lower house. But the Germans, who were often averse to an oath of loyalty to the government, participated hardly at all. Not until 1773, with the election of Jonathan Hagar, was the question of seating a naturalized German as a delegate in the assembly so much as raised.[55] In one of the few communications from a German ever printed in the *Maryland Gazette*, the writer indicated the natural part of the German in provincial politics. "I am a Dutchman," he said, "but I have land, and the English come and give me newspapers for my vote, and I get the schoolmaster to read them. . . . If you publish such things in your paper as I can understand, I will buy it." [56] The Germans remained politically unassimilated to the end of the colonial period.

They and the other settlers of the west and north none the less effectively performed the services which the lords proprietors, the governors, the Dulanys, the Carrolls, and the others of the provincial great wanted. They formed outposts against enemy state and rival province, they expanded the institutions and administrative system of Maryland, they paid quit-rents, fees, and rents for great

53. June 7, 1748, *Archives*, XXVIII, 421–424.
54. Letter to Cecilius Calvert, September 10, 1764, *Calvert Papers*, II (Maryland Historical Society, *Fund-Publications*, no. 34, Baltimore, 1894), 240.
55. Sollers, "Jonathan Hagar," p. 21.
56. "N. U. R.," *Maryland Gazette*, April 2, 1767.

tracts of land. If they suffered the hazards and the charges which their position involved, they were not for that reason losers. They had new homes in a productive and promising country; they paid a price, the sort of price which builders of empire had everywhere to pay.

II

LIFE AND THOUGHT IN THE
SOUTHERN COUNTIES

THE generation after 1730, which saw so much new settlement and expansion in the outlying counties, also marked great developments in the condition of society in the tidewater counties of the lower bay and the Potomac. Advance from frontier conditions to those of security and from a population of less than 35,000 to more than 100,000 wrought many changes in the manner of living of every class.

Early in the century standards had been low enough. A visitor on a tobacco vessel from England in 1705 and 1706 spoke of half-naked Indians, bears, and wolves as familiar to the lower settlements. He observed a great plenty of venison and wild turkeys, but described the ordinary diet as composed of hominy, pork or beef, and sometimes vegetables.[1] Only two years after this description, Ebenezer Cooke, a satirist who had had an intimate view of life in the province, brought out in London his first Maryland poem, *The Sotweed Factor*. He too spoke of Indians, wild animals, and crude diet; and, with some malice, he described a rough and squalid way of life well in accord with location on the edge of the wilderness. The poem tells of two households, one of a poor planter and one of a well-to-do, in both of which the writer was hospitably received. They differed in respect of comfort, servants, and standard of diet, but both were slatternly and the people were coarse. Maryland, in the sardonic view of Cooke, was a roistering and cheating place, everywhere

1. "Narrative of a Voyage to Maryland, 1705–1706," *American Historical Review*, XII (1906), 327–340.

ridden with laziness, drunkenness, and seasonal malaria.[2]

From the decade of the seventeen-forties have survived the impressions and judgments of two immigrant physicians, Dr. Charles Carroll, an Irishman, and Dr. Alexander Hamilton, a Scot. In their eyes Maryland was only a tolerable place. Dr. Hamilton, who lived in Annapolis in association with the wealthy and the educated, said, after extensive travels in the north, that he found "little difference in the manners and character of the people of the different provinces," but that the "air and living to the northward is . . . much preferable, and the people of a more gigantic size and make. . . . The northern parts I found in general much better settled than the southern. As to politeness and humanity they are much alike, except in the great towns, where the inhabitants are more civilized, especially at Boston." Dr. Hamilton's chief objection to Maryland was that of many a newcomer, the unhealthiness of the summers. As he returned home from his journey he would have known without being told, he said, that there had been much sickness and heat, "by only observing the washed countenances of the people, . . . for they looked like so many staring ghosts. In short I was sensible I had got into Maryland, for almost every house was an infirmary, according to ancient custom." [3] Dr. Carroll spoke somewhat less specifically, but the tone of a letter, written in 1748 to a distant cousin in London, was nostalgic and touched with bitterness. The history of the fall of the ancient empires comforted him, he said, for the personal misfortunes which had driven him from his native land. He endeavored "to get a livelihood in this wild part

2. For the identity and character of Cooke, see Lawrence C. Wroth, "The Maryland Muse by Ebenezer Cooke," *Proceedings of the American Antiquarian Society*, New Series, XLIV (1935), 267–278. On the various editions of the *Sotweed Factor*, see *ibid.*, pp. 278–291, 293–298; and for a reprint of the 1731 edition, pp. 327–335. The 1708 edition is reprinted in *Early Maryland Poetry*, edited by Bernard C. Steiner, Maryland Historical Society, *Fund-Publications*, no. 36 (1900), pp. 11–31. See also James T. Poole, "Ebenezer Cooke and *The Maryland Muse*," *American Literature*, III (1931), 296–302.

3. Hamilton, *Itinerarium*, p. 244.

of the globe," but if he were young and unattached he would not remain in Maryland, for the West Indies offered more.[4]

For the last two decades before the Revolution the most informing judgments of Maryland come from the letters of Charles Carroll and his son, Charles Carroll of Carrollton, and from the writings of William Eddis, the customs official and friend of Governor Eden. About 1760, when young Carroll was completing his education at the Inns of Court, he exchanged ideas with his father about the advantages of living in Maryland. The father was embittered by the anti-Catholicism of the province during the French and Indian War, and thought of removing to a Catholic country. But the son, who had recently studied in France, longed for Maryland. Removal, he said, would involve not only a sacrifice of fortune but also living under a system of civil persecution such as that of Louis XV; such a choice he could not prefer. In England he observed that Catholics enjoyed "great peace and tranquility," and he hoped and believed that the same tolerance would come to Maryland. Young Carroll felt no desire, however, to reside in England; he had failed to arrange a marriage there because his colonial fortune did not satisfy as a dowry, and distaste for what he thought of as the artificialities and affectations of the law prevented his enjoying even a period of legal study. What he desired was the life of a country gentleman in Maryland—the enjoyment of solitude, rural pleasures, and the study of philosophy. Carroll's ideas reveal a wealthy Marylander to whom a colonial destiny not only looked better than any other immediately open to him, but also the best he could desire.[5] Thinking of American life in romantic terms, such as his acquaintanceship with French thought may well have

4. Letter to Daniel O'Carroll, September 9, 1748, *Md. Hist. Mag.*, XXII, 376–377.

5. Carroll to Carrollton, October 6, 1759, Rowland, *Life of Charles Carroll of Carrollton*, I, 38–39; Carrollton to Carroll, January 29, 1760, January 1, May 15, July 15, 1761, *Md. Hist. Mag.*, X, 251, 332; XI, 67–68, 71.

encouraged, he came home with a great consciousness of native land. His revolutionary career was soon to prove it abundantly sincere.

From a widely different—and ultimately loyalist— angle, William Eddis also thought of Maryland as an advantageous place in which to live. Nature, he said, provided bountifully for the people, and the people were liberal in both hospitality and sentiment. As a successful placeman, he moved in the circle of the official and the well-to-do; he found their living on quite as generous and pleasant a plane as that of wealthy Englishmen. Yet he did not fail to observe poverty nor omit to complain at the exorbitance of certain costs, particularly of fuel and labor. Even with such things in mind, he was persuaded that "by prudent management, a respectable appearance may be supported in Maryland on terms infinitely more reasonable than in most parts of the mother country; and that greater opportunities are afforded to the industrious and enterprising, to lay the foundation of a comfortable provision for a succeeding generation." [6] Further, Eddis thought that Americans were especially keen in recognizing their interests and in pursuing them. "Even those," he said, "who move in the humbler circles of life discover a shrewdness and penetration not generally observable in the mother country. . . . [The people] discriminate characters with the greatest accuracy; and there are few who do not seem perfectly conversant with the general and particular needs of the community." [7]

The complacence of Carroll and Eddis conforms nicely with the prestige and privilege of such landed wealth and official rank as they themselves enjoyed. Through the century as a whole the fortunes of all but a few of the people were determined by their connections with the tobacco-producing land. A thorough statistical analysis, if it could be made, would probably show that a diminishing propor-

6. Eddis, *Letters from America*, pp. 34–35.
7. *Ibid.*, p. 128.

tion of the land was being held in large estates.[8] The aristocratic ideal was nevertheless deeply entrenched. Such a tradition derived from the early manors, which the first proprietor had established on a feudal pattern; it remained inherent in the proprietary system; and in the eighteenth century it was encouraged by new considerations and factors. Great wealth in land took on fresh advantages as slavery increased, and as the produce of the colony multiplied the commercial and cultural contacts of Maryland with the mother country and the other colonies. In the last generation before the Revolution, economic differentiation between social classes was a dominant aspect of life in the tobacco counties.

At the base of the social pyramid was a large class of small landholders. At the time of the census of 1755 there were about two-fifths as many landholders as free adult white males on the Western Shore; and there were more than two-thirds as many landholders as free white adult males on the Eastern Shore. From 5 to 12 per cent of the populations of the various counties were owners.[9] As families were large, and as ownership tended to be in the names of the men, not the women and children, freeholding seems to have been widely spread. Probably more than half of the free whites of Maryland belonged to families of the landholding class.

The careful studies of Professor Gould show that at the middle of the eighteenth century the average individual landholding varied from about 250 or 300 acres in St. Marys', Kent, and Worcester counties, to about 350 in Charles and Calvert counties, and 475 in Anne Arundel.[10] Such averages are of course raised by the inclusion of the greatest estates in the calculation, and Professor Gould

8. For indications of such a trend, see Vertrees J. Wyckoff, "The Sizes of Plantations in Seventeenth-Century Maryland," *Md. Hist. Mag.*, XXXII, 331–339, and the data below on the sale of the proprietary manors, pp. 264–266.

9. Table I, in the appendix, shows the situation in such detail as available figures make possible. See below, p. 379.

10. See Table I, *idem.*

has estimated that "the average plantation of the middle class landholder was somewhere between 150 and 200 acres." [11] He thinks that perhaps "nearly one fourth of all the land in the older counties was held in parcels of from 50 acres to 250 acres by men who owned no other land, and who either by their own labor or by that of a few slaves cultivated all their clearing." [12] As the cleared and cultivated area of the small plantation ran from about 30 to 100 acres, the small owners had little surplus with which to take up losses caused by soil exhaustion.

The class of small planters, though numerically large and politically enfranchised, is elusive in the record. Lacking a peculiar nationality or religious faith to give them mark, or a servile status to be written in the statutes of the province, the small planters were everywhere taken for granted and only in the event of tobacco legislation or political turmoil much spoken of in newspaper or public record. Their lowly economic position suggests that there must have been truth in the lines of Ebenezer Cooke, who spoke of planters gathering to watch when he put ashore at Piscattaway, on the Potomac:

> Where soon repaired a numerous Crew,
> In Shirts and Draw'rs, of *Scotch*-cloth blew,
> With neither Stocking, Hat, nor Shoe:
> These *Sot-Weed* Planters crowd the Shore,
> In hew as tawny as a *Moor;*
> Figures, so strange, no GOD design'd
> To be a Part of Human-kind:
> But wanton nature, void of Rest,
> Moulded the brittle Clay in Jest.[13]

This refers to the opening of the century, but in the seventeen-forties another verse-maker described the common lot, also to satirize it:

11. Gould, *The Land System in Maryland*, p. 78.
12. *Ibid.*, p. 81.
13. Cooke, *The Sot-Weed Factor*, in *Proceedings of the American Antiquarian Society*, N.S., XLIV, 327.

Our fires are wood, our houses as good,
Our diet is Sawney and Homine,
Drink, juice of the Apple, Tobaccoe's our Staple
Gloria tibi Domine.[14]

These evidences of poverty are supported, from a totally different point of view, by a controversy in the *Maryland Gazette* in 1770. A writer, who signed himself a "Friend to Liberty," complained that a few people with lands fronting on the Potomac were trying to monopolize the herring fishing there, and he questioned what would happen to the price of fish. The "poorer sort," he said, had gotten fish cheap or free, and by means of it had been able to provide for their children even though their lands were poor. God made the fish like the fowls of the air, free to all men, and "Friend to Liberty" urged that the law of nature and the charter of the province opposed a special property right in fish.[15] This argument drew replies in the *Gazette*, and it may have been the ensuing controversy which inspired Eddis to speak of the shrewdness of the humble in defending their interests. Eddis certainly had the poor planters in mind when he wrote that, "An idea of equality seems generally to prevail, and the inferior order of people pay but little external respect to those who occupy superior stations." [16]

On the estates of average and more than average size resided in mutual dependence the moderately well-to-do or wealthy and the lower classes of the landless, free and servile. The numbers of the landless free tended to grow as population increased and the available lands were taken. Through the whole eighteenth century the practices of leasing to members of this class and of employing them as slave overseers were widespread. All the great land-

14. Quoted from the papers of Henry Callister in Lawrence C. Wroth, "A Maryland Merchant and His Friends in 1750," *Md. Hist. Mag.*, VI, 219. The word there printed as "Sawng" should be "Sawney," which means "bacon."

15. *Maryland Gazette*, June 7, 1770.

16. Eddis, *Letters from America*, p. 128.

holders leased plantation tenements, some on an elaborately organized basis; the lord proprietor maintained his manors with leaseholders; and even small owners frequently leased one or more tracts outside the clearing which they themselves cultivated. The variety of terms which were written into the leases, involving now many and now few acres, rates at all levels, and periods of tenure from a few years to three lives, indicates a class of farmers whose livings were more or less secure and who depended entirely on individual fortune in obtaining favorable contracts.[17] Socially the leaseholders seem to have been on about the same level as the overseers, whose contracts occasionally involved menial work but whose supervisory duties, as they required dependability, sometimes brought favorable terms in the form of a salary or a share of the crop.[18] Doubtless many leaseholders and overseers made better livings than the poorer freeholders, but the mark of landlessness was an unfavorable one. It left them politically powerless and economically attached to the interest of an upper class. Their status was one which the diminishing supply of free land made it difficult to escape.

The growth of the class of landless freemen was paralleled in the eighteenth century by the increasing numbers and more and more rigidly fixed status of the slaves and indentured servants. The slaves were increasing even in proportion to the growth of the general population, as we have seen, and at mid-century they were approaching numbers equal to the whites on the lower Western Shore. By that time, too, a considerable body of law had been passed limiting manumissions, restricting slave meetings, and otherwise elaborating and fixing the slave status.[19] In

17. Gould, *The Land System in Maryland*, pp. 68–69, 71, 81, 83, 91–95.
18. *Ibid.*, pp. 72–75.
19. Jeffrey R. Brackett, *The Negro in Maryland, a Study of the Institution of Slavery*, JHUS, Extra Volumes, VI (1889), 34, 39, 55, 76, 79, 93, 100, 116, 149. Stephen Bordley, the leader in the lower house, wrote a friend, M. Harris, January 30, 1740, that there had been a slave conspiracy to murder all the whites except the young women. A "fifteen minute militia" had organized to quell any disturbance. Stephen Bord-

an opinion of 1767, written to establish that slaves were legally incapable of marriage, Daniel Dulany said that in Maryland they were more mildly treated than in several colonies to the south, particularly the West Indies, but more severely treated than in the northern colonies.[20]

In the thirty years before the Revolution the indentured servants as a class also suffered a fixing of status, even a degradation. This was not so much the result of legal enactment as of adverse condition. In that period there was a considerable transportation of felons from the English jails, and an unusual number of them came to Maryland.[21] This brought an element into the province which was economically useful, for it was the chief source of immigrant artisan labor. According to the advertisements there came such types as tailors, weavers, shoemakers, carpenters, painters, bricklayers, plasterers, smiths, and even jewelers and silversmiths. Yet resentment of the system of transportation was inevitable, the convicts were distrusted, and the servant class became identified with the criminal class in the province. Nearly all the crimes mentioned in the newspaper were committed by or blamed upon convict servants, and at the time of a crime wave in 1751, special legislation was enacted against them.[22] Limited even in hope for the future by the diminished opportunity to take up free land after the period of indenture, the lot of the servant, whether convict or "free willer," was everywhere spoken of as hard.[23] What the evangelist Whitefield said

ley's Letterbook, 1738–1740, MHS. There was little Christian education for negroes in Maryland.

20. Thomas Harris and John McHenry, *Maryland Reports, being . . . law cases . . . in the Provincial Court and Court of Appeals . . . Maryland . . . 1700 . . . to the American Revolution* (New York, 1809), pp. 560, 563.

21. As to numbers, see above, p. 3.

22. *Pennsylvania Gazette,* September 15, 1743, April 26, July 25, August 22, 1751; "An act to make the testimony of convicted persons legal against convicted persons," 1751, *Archives,* XLVI, 616.

23. McCormac, *White Servitude in Maryland,* pp. 73–76; Father Mosley to his sister, 1772, Thomas Hughes, *History of the Society of Jesus in North America, Colonial and Federal* (Cleveland, 1908), Text, I, 342; Eddis, *Letters from America,* pp. 67–78.

of the southern slaves might well have been said of both of the unfree classes in Maryland. They "had neither convenient food to eat or proper raiment to put on, notwithstanding most of the comforts [the well-to-do] enjoyed were solely owing to their indefatigable labors." [24]

The great beneficiaries of the land system and social order of Maryland were those individuals and families whose large estates raised them far above the fortunes of the many. As in England landed wealth was the one essential mark of power, prestige, and gentility. Every county had its gentry, a class in Maryland similar in life and ideal to the squirearchy of the mother country. The Taskers, Hammonds, Carrolls, and Dulanys of Anne Arundel county, the Keys and Platers of St. Mary's, the Mackalls and Fitzhughs of Calvert, the Hansons and Lees of Charles, and the Lloyds, Goldsboroughs, Chamberlaines, Bennetts, and Tilghmans of Talbot and Queen Anne's, on the Eastern Shore, all represent this class. In the period before the Revolution such families were usually in the third or fourth Maryland generation, and connected by marriage with other families of the same class.

The very greatest estates in Maryland, those of the Bennetts, the Lloyds, the Dulanys, the Carrolls, and their kind, varied from about twenty thousand to forty thousand acres.[25] Such holdings, though hardly comparable with those of noblemen in England or with the enormous grants familiar in New York, placed the owners in an unrivaled position in Maryland. They were composed of plantations scattered through several counties. For example, Edward Lloyd, the greatest landowner of the Eastern Shore, held thousands of acres in each of four counties, Queen Anne's, Kent, Talbot, and Dorchester, and a few hundred acres in Cecil county. Similarly Charles Carroll of Carrollton, with a home in Annapolis, held

24. *Pennsylvania Gazette,* April 17, 1740.
25. For the materials from which these names and the figures below are taken, see Gould, *Land System of Maryland,* pp. 81–85; and below, pp. 180–182.

many thousands of acres in Anne Arundel, Baltimore, and
Frederick, each, and other estates in St. Mary's and
Prince George's counties.[26] Less wealthy members of the
gentry ordinarily held estates in no more than one county,
but they were frequently spread about and rarely contiguous. There were a good many holdings ranging from
one thousand to five thousand acres, at least a few in
every county and many in the rich tobacco counties of the
lower Western Shore.

There are a few documents remaining to tell us something of the extensive equipment and amount of capital
which went with great landholding. In 1764 Charles Carroll sent his son, Charles Carroll of Carrollton, an abstract
of their estate, as follows: 40,000 acres of land, estimated
to be worth twenty shillings sterling per acre, £40,000;
a fifth share of the Baltimore iron works, which Carroll
owned jointly with other great landholders of the Western
Shore, £10,000; [27] lots in Annapolis, with two houses,
£4,000; 285 slaves, each worth about £30, £8,550; cattle,
horses, other stock, and tools, £1,000; silver household
plate, £600; and loans, out at interest, as of 1762, £24,-
230 9s. 7d. The total value of the estate was £88,380 9s.
7d.; but Carroll warned his son that his annual income did
not equal a normal interest return on such a value.[28] He
added, however, that land values were steadily increasing,
and that he had a clear income of at least £1800—an
amount which, whether he knew it or not, was larger than
the salary of the governor of the colony. This large estate
may be compared with that of Carroll's distant cousin,
the moderately well-to-do Dr. Charles Carroll of Annapo-

26. Charles Carroll of Carrollton, Account Book, 1765–1829, Library
of Congress. Later citations of manuscripts or transcripts in the Manuscripts Division of this Library will be indicated by LC.

27. In 1765, a year of low values and general depression, Colonel
Tasker's fifth sold for £5,200. *Maryland Gazette*, March 14, 1765. The
original owners were Charles Carroll, Benjamin Tasker, Daniel Dulany,
Daniel Carroll, and Dr. Charles Carroll. Indenture, 1732, Portfolio no.
6, MHS.

28. Letter of January 9, 1764, Rowland, *Charles Carroll of Carrollton*,
I, 60; *Md. Hist. Mag.*, XII, 27.

lis. In 1754, Dr. Carroll estimated that his estate was worth £10,000 sterling plus £5,000, provincial currency, and that his son's estate, though at the moment depressed, would be worth £2,000 whenever tobacco should gain a proper price. He did not itemize in sufficient detail even to indicate that he, like his cousin, was a part owner of the Baltimore iron works. He simply said that his wealth consisted of land, slaves, and loans by "bond mortgages."[29]

The visible signs of wealth and dignity in Maryland, as almost everywhere in the British world, were the splendid residences which appeared so rapidly in the third quarter of the eighteenth century.[30] The new houses most characteristic of the place and period were built of brick and designed with that excellence of proportion which distinguishes Georgian architecture in all its varieties. They loomed up grand and isolated in a landscape where other building was low and utilitarian, and where town building was almost unknown. They were composed of three masses, a great central structure of two or three stories with high chimneys set in the end walls, and two flanking and equal wings, built lower but sufficient for domestic servants and office space. The interiors were often elaborately decorated in fine wood and plaster work; the exteriors, as in England, were usually simple, depending on symmetry and balance and on the dull salmon color of brick to produce the effect of beauty. Governor Sharpe's splendid Whitehall was somewhat exceptional, for its elegant Corinthian portico on the front and white painted bull's eyes on the

29. Letters of May 8, 1754, to his son, Charles Carroll (later known as "the Barrister"), and to William Black, *Md. Hist. Mag.*, XXVII, 218–221.

30. For discussions of Maryland architecture and for many excellent pictures, see: Lewis A. Coffin and Arthur C. Holden, *Brick Architecture of the Colonial Period in Maryland and Virginia* (New York, 1919); Swepson Earle, *The Chesapeake Bay Country* (Baltimore, 1923), and *Maryland's Colonial Eastern Shore* (Baltimore, 1916); Henry C. Gorman, *Early Manor and Plantation Houses of Maryland* (Easton, Maryland, 1934); John M. Hammond, *Colonial Mansions of Maryland and Delaware* (Philadelphia, 1914); Katharine Scarborough, *Homes of the Cavaliers* (New York, 1930); Paul Wilstach, *Potomac Landings* (Garden City, 1921), and *Tidewater Maryland* (Indianapolis, 1931).

rear were daring bits of design. Lovely doorways, such as
those at the Galloways' Tulip Hill, or large and beautiful
windows, such as at Belair, were more often the means of
lightening the exteriors.

How much these provincial mansions and the life within
them could impress a newcomer from England is elaborately testified by Eddis' letters. Shortly after his arrival,
in 1769, he wrote of the many pleasant "villas" near
Annapolis; Whitehall he found especially delightful. He
spoke at length of an estate, rich in tobacco and grain
lands and well stocked with cattle and game, which occupied an island across the bay. He described the owner
as "the monarch of his little fertile territory," and as
lavish in the feeding and entertainment of his guests.
Traveling by schooner, Eddis went with Governor Eden
for a Christmas visit at Rousby Hall, the estate of Colonel
Fitzhugh, a councilor, seventy miles south of Annapolis.
They were entertained with excellent and various wines,
cheerful fires, and good conversation; and they were barely
allowed to depart after staying several weeks. They went
on to visit most of the principal families in the five lower
counties of the Western Shore, and Eddis said that all of
the estates were "disposed with the utmost regularity." [31]
A year or so later, indeed, Eddis began to speak a little
critically of the sumptuous living of the wealthy. "In
this remote region," he wrote, "the phantom pleasure is
pursued with as much avidity as on your side of the Atlantic." He found the "affluent" quick to import fashions,
adopting them perhaps earlier than in England, and displaying them at parties, "in the race of vain and idle competition." He thought that lavishness was often mistaken
for generosity, and that the great planters impaired their
health and fortunes by splendor of appearance and mag-
nificence of entertainment. [32]

Aside from the concentration of wealth and profuse
living, the most striking thing about the position of the

31. Eddis, *Letters from America*, pp. 20–30.
32. *Ibid.*, pp. 106, 112–113.

gentry was their relationship with the common people of the province. On the economic side, the power to lend on mortgages created connections which increased the prestige and power of the wealthy. The death notice of Richard Bennett, a great landholder and trader of the Eastern Shore, tells as much about the power of money as about the benevolence of the individual. Bennett, it says, always used his fortune for the general good, he strove to prevent difficulties among his neighbors, he never deprived widows and orphans who were his debtors of the means of their support, and in his will he forgave one hundred fifty debtors.[33] The more ordinary tone of business relationships was stated by a Maryland lawyer, Stephen Bordley, in a letter to a London client, a merchant trading in the colony: "A man may write his heart out by way of dun to the people here, and scarce collect enough to bear the expense of pen, ink, and paper. . . . So with me in my private affairs, sue is the word, though the only possible advantage I can have by it is to know within what time I shall have my money." [34] Many cases of ejectment and bankruptcy in the courts, of debtors thrown into prison, or, occasionally, sold into servitude, and of laws passed and administered for poor relief, all testify to small men broken by debt in the half-century before the Revolution.[35]

The social and economic superiority of the gentry goes far to explain a peculiar characteristic of the provincial mind of Maryland, and one which survives in the records to plague the student to the present day. Some degree of legal knowledge was taken for granted among the wealthy; hardly an issue came before the legislature, or even before the public in the *Maryland Gazette*, which was not debated with a flair for the most involved and legalistic terms. Charles Carroll of Doughoregan Manor made explicit

33. *Pennsylvania Gazette*, December 5, 1749.
34. Letter to William Hunt, November 26, 1756, Stephen Bordley's Letterbook, 1756–1759, MHS.
35. Newton D. Mereness, *Maryland as a Proprietary Province* (New York, 1901), pp. 136, 255, 256, 403. For cases of ejectment see Harris and McHenry, *Maryland Reports, passim.*

what was more often implicit when he urged his son, as a landowner, to persist in his studies in the Inner Temple:

It is a shame for a gentleman to be ignorant of the laws of his country and to be dependent on every dirty pettifogger. . . . On the other hand, how commendable it is for a gentleman of independent fortune not only [not] to stand in need of mercenary advisers, but to be able to advise his friends, relations, and neighbors of all sorts. . . . Suppose you would be called on to act in any public character, what an awkward figure you would make without the knowledge of the law either as legislator, judge, or even an arbitrator of differences among your neighbors and friends. . . . Apply as if your whole and sole dependence was to be on the knowledge of the law.[36]

Knowledge of the law, in short, was worth the expense and effort of foreign study for a Carroll, or for any son of the wealthiest class in Maryland.

Yet the legalism of the province spread wider than the small circle of those who studied in London. As we shall see more fully in a later chapter, the class of large landholders dominated the offices of the provincial government, executive, legislative, and judicial. Particularly was the usage established that the justices of the peace, numbering about fifteen or twenty in a county, should be appointed from the gentry, and that members of even the greatest families should serve in the county offices.[37] Such men were lay justices, not professionally trained in the law; yet in the nature of their position, which called for judgment in petty civil and criminal cases, they achieved experience in and familiarity with the law. They were in-

36. Letter to Carroll of Carrollton, October 6, 1759, Thomas M. Field, editor, *Unpublished Letters of Charles Carroll of Carrollton* (New York, 1902), pp. 33–34. Compare with Carroll's argument the comment of Harris and McHenry, the editors of the earliest printed volume of Maryland court decisions, that it was important "to every landholder that the principles by which he holds his property should be familiarized to him." *Maryland Reports*, p. iv.

37. See below, p. 179.

structed to have the English statutes at hand and to use Dalton's *Country Justice*.[38] Speaking of England, Maitland says that "a history of the eighteenth century which does not place the justice of the peace in the very foreground of the picture will be known for what it is, a caricature. . . . It is so purely English, perhaps the most distinctively English part of our governmental organization."[39] The national trait to which Maitland refers, the freedom of local government from the Crown, applied in Maryland as well. The provincial landholder was appointed county justice by the governor, but his exercise of authority was not supervised or regulated from above.[40] His local office added something of the feudal to his position, for wealth in land was joined to public authority according to the old English tradition. Thus the justices of the peace combined the mentality of free government and knowledge of the common law with the condition of social superiority and economic security.[41] Secular thought offers no more favorable soil for the growth of political independence.

The prominence of legal-mindedness grew with the growth of speculation and business during the three decades before the Revolution. There was so much litigation, most of it over rights in land, that a professional class of lawyers appeared, and its members achieved wealth and distinction in both private and public life.[42] Its early leaders were the two Daniel Dulanys, whose fortune was built on western leasing and speculation, and Stephen

38. Carroll T. Bond, *The Court of Appeals of Maryland, a History* (Baltimore, 1928), p. 14.

39. Quoted by Bond, *ibid.,* pp. 9–10.

40. A lower house address of 1725 indicates that appointments were made with the advice of the council and sometimes of both houses of assembly. *Archives,* XXXV, 360.

41. A corresponding situation in England had stood a bulwark against Charles I during the "Eleven years Tyranny." J. R. Tanner, *English Constitutional Conflicts of the Seventeenth Century, 1603–1689* (Cambridge, 1928), p. 78.

42. See Sharpe to Baltimore, July 25, 1768, *Archives,* XIV, 522–523. Eddis comments on the "litigious spirit" in Maryland, *Letters from America,* pp. 127–128.

Bordley, the merchant, planter, and assemblyman. Of the thirty-five seventeenth and eighteenth-century Maryland-ers known to have been admitted to the Inns of Court, about two-thirds entered during the generation before the Revolution.[43] Many of their names, such as those of four Dulanys, two Tilghmans, two Carrolls, a Goldsborough, and a Hammond, are at once to be recognized as those of the great landed families. A few others, notably Thomas Johnson and William Paca, both to be revolutionary lead-ers and state governors of Maryland, were the sons of less distinguished families. But all stood far above the common lot, where training, association, and opportunity placed them.

Much that is significant about the temper of thought and feeling appears in the state of religion in the province. The tolerance granted to all Trinitarians by the first lord proprietor had from the beginning thrown the colony open to all manner of people: Roman Catholics, Angli-cans, Presbyterians, and Quakers had been quick to settle in the lower counties. During the eighteenth century there were at least a few of each of these types remaining on both shores. Members of the Church of England, bene-fited by the permanent law of establishment of 1702, were naturally the most widespread. The other churches showed some tendency to concentrate in certain localities.

The Catholic descendants and successors of the found-ers of the colony were strongest in St. Mary's, the oldest county, where they perhaps outnumbered the Protes-tants.[44] But their position there and everywhere was de-fined by statutory restrictions and disabilities. As if to wipe out the imprint of Catholic dominance during the seventeenth century, the eighteenth-century assembly

43. Bond, *The Court of Appeals of Maryland,* pp. 48–49; E. Alfred Jones, *American Members of the Inns of Court* (London, 1924).

44. The number of Catholics is often estimated to have been one in twelve or fourteen of the population, but there is little evidence. The Anglican rector of a St. Mary's county parish said that the Catholics were three to one against him. If so, this described a very local situation. Arthur Hall to the Bishop of London, May 20, 1734, Perry, *Collections,* IV, 316.

passed the severest anti-Catholic laws in America, forbidding the erection of churches and the employment of Catholic teachers, and prohibiting Catholics to hold office or to vote.[45] Private worship, however, was not denied, and the disability laws were not literally enforced. Under conditions of "tacit tolerance" and with the benefit of the wealth of the old and established Catholic families, such as the Darnalls, Roziers, Youngs, Sewalls, Carrolls, and Brookes, the faith was maintained in Maryland. Before the Revolution there were about twenty Jesuit priests in the province, with a half-dozen or more residences, such as Whitemarsh in Prince George's county. From these centers the priests moved about, conducting services and administering the sacraments in private homes and chapels. The wealthy were able to hire Catholic tutors secretly and without disturbance; and for a period, beginning about 1744, the Jesuits maintained a fugitive school at Bohemia Manor, now open and now closed. Here they prepared the sons of wealthy Catholics, notably Charles Carroll of Carrollton, for higher education at St. Omer, the English Jesuit college in Flanders.[46]

The other non-Anglicans, the Presbyterians and the Quakers, did not have the connections with the upper class which the Catholics enjoyed, but neither did they suffer from the disabilities. The Presbyterians were strongest on the lower Eastern Shore, especially in the area of Snow Hill in Worcester county. Francis Makemie, "the pioneer

45. Lawrence H. Gipson, *The British Empire before the American Revolution* . . . , II, *The Southern Plantations* (Caldwell, Idaho, 1936), 67–69.

46. The most recent and scholarly treatment of eighteenth-century Catholicism in Maryland is to be found in Peter Guilday, *The Life and Times of John Carroll, Archbishop of Baltimore* (New York, 1922), ch. I. See also Hughes, *History of the Jesuits,* Text, II, chs. XVI–XVII; and, among the older treatments, John G. Shea, *Life and Times of the Most Rev. John Carroll* . . . (*History of the Catholic Church in the United States,* II; New York, 1888), pp. 27–30; and B. U. Campbell, "Memoirs of the Life and Times of the Most Rev. John Carroll, First Archbishop of Baltimore," *The United States Catholic Magazine,* III (1844), 171. See also H. S. Spalding, S. J., *Catholic Colonial Maryland* (Milwaukee, 1931), chs. VIII–XIII.

Presbyterian missionary of the New World," had labored there in the sixteen-eighties; and from that decade dates the vigorous nucleus of four or five congregations which were coöperating among themselves and supporting such intercolonial activities of their church as mission schools and synod meetings during the quarter-century before the Revolution.[47] Quakerism had strength on both shores, chiefly around West River, near Annapolis, where the Galloway family of Tulip Hill gave it prestige, and in the neighborhood of "Third Haven," near Easton, across the bay. There had been Quaker belief in Maryland since 1660 or a little earlier; in 1672 George Fox himself visited the province and commented in his journal on the number of worshipers and on the high social position of the Quaker leaders. On the eve of the Revolution there were about thirty meetings in all.[48]

The predominance of Anglicanism in Maryland was a product of the Glorious Revolution. That crisis led to three decades of political transformation and reform; Catholicism was lowered from power and favor to special disability, and Protestantism assumed its regular preferred place, as elsewhere in the British world. The legal establishment of the Church of England, which before 1692 had been as weak as the presence of only four clergymen indicates,[49] was the thing which, more than any other change, distinguishes the eighteenth century as a period of normal colonial existence in Maryland, and contrasts it

47. Manokin Presbyterian Church, Somerset County, Maryland, Sessional Record, 1747–1858 . . . , photostat volume, MHS. See also J. William McIlvain, *Early Presbyterianism in Maryland,* JHUS, VIII (1890), no. 3, supplement, 15–25; and Hanna, *The Scotch-Irish,* II, 7, 14, 107–108.

48. Rufus M. Jones, *The Quakers in the American Colonies* (London, 1911), pp. 276–282. Details are to be found in the following: John S. Norris, *The Early Friends (or Quakers) in Maryland* (Baltimore, 1862), pp. 12–13; B. C. Steiner, "Maryland's Religious History," *Md. Hist. Mag.,* XXI, 6–7; D. L. Thornbury, "The Society of Friends in Maryland," *ibid.,* XXIX, 101–115.

49. H. F. Thomson, "Maryland at the End of the Seventeenth Century," *ibid.,* II, 166.

with the seventeenth century, when the influence of Catholicism gave the province a unique character in British America.

In the nature of the case, the aim and purpose of the established church was in every way conservative. The clergymen received their appointments by the authority of the lord proprietor and often were personally selected by him; they were required to pray for him and for the governor and council of the province at every service.[50] In the mind of the fifth Lord Baltimore, the church was expected to serve as a kind of moral cement, binding the loyalty of the people of Maryland to himself and to his government. At the time of a political crisis he promised his "care and protection" to the church, and wrote the clergy that he "made no doubt of [their] good offices toward promoting a perfect understanding between the proprietor and his servants; peace and harmony being the great characteristics of our mother Church." [51] In respect of teaching, the one duty of the clergy was to persuade to conformity and to resist dissent and unbelief.

The very establishment of the church in law gave it advantages of a kind which no other faith could rival. Besides prestige the clergy had assured incomes from a poll tax fixed in the permanent act of establishment. In this respect they were better off than the clergy in England, for the poll-tax system of payment freed them from the common difficulties in collecting the tithe at home.[52] After thirty years as the state religion, the Church of England in Maryland had increased sixfold, to about twenty-five parishes; and, by the end of the colonial period, to forty-four.[53] Such growth was rapid, but less than in proportion to the population. Since the product of the poll tax varied in exact ratio with the number of people in the parishes, the rectors were in the happy position of receiv-

50. Council Proceedings, April 10, 1733, *Archives,* XXVIII, 30.
51. Baltimore to the clergy, [c.1730], Calvert Papers, no. 295½, MHS.
52. Eddis, *Letters from America,* pp. 47–48.
53. Lists, 1722, 1775, Perry, *Collections,* IV, 128–129, 345–347.

ing steadily increasing salaries. According to an official estimate of 1767, three parishes yielded more than £300 sterling yearly, a large income in Maryland; seventeen yielded more than £200; and fourteen, from £150 to £200. Such substantial salaries made the clergy livings in Maryland the most attractive in America, and they were much sought after.[54]

At the opening of the century the condition of the church in Maryland must have seemed favorable to those most concerned. Figures in the possession of the newly established missionary society, the Society for the Propagation of the Gospel in Foreign Parts, estimated 20,000 Anglicans in Maryland, the same number as in the larger colony of Virginia and many times more than in any other colony.[55] While the society had no direct control over the churches of the province, it did assist the ministers there, and it commanded the respect and coöperation of Governor Hart, who went to Maryland in 1714.[56] The governor assembled the clergy immediately on his arrival, and made a series of inquiries about the state of the church. The replies were by and large favorable: services and sacraments were regularly administered, the church buildings were adequate and the libraries nearly so, and a due sense of authority of the Bishop of London prevailed. The clergymen found little at fault except a deficiency of glebe lands and the need for better masters for the schools.[57]

Their complacence, however, did not satisfy Governor Hart, who wrote the bishop that, while some of the clergy deserved well, he was amazed at the illiteracy and immoral-

54. Lists, 1767, 1775, *ibid.*, IV, 336–337, 343–344; Jonathan Boucher (Maryland) to Rev. M. James, March 9, 1767, *Md. Hist. Mag.*, VII, 339–340; address of 21 clergymen to Governor Eden, October 5, 1771, Letters, I, Maryland Diocesan Library (hereafter indicated as Md. Dioc. Lib.). See below, pp. 148, 365–366.

55. C. F. Pascoe, *Two Hundred Years of the S.P.G.* (London, 1901), p. 87.

56. Bishop of London to S.P.G., November 2, 1711, S.P.G. Transcripts, Series A, vol. 6; John Hart to S.P.G., July 20, 1714, *ibid.*, Series B, vol. 1, pt. ii, LC.

57. Maryland clergy to Hart, 1714, Perry, *Collections*, IV, 75–77.

ity of others, and that the Jesuits were profiting by their sins and winning many converts.[58] The governor's letter, though possibly excessive, is significant, because it was among the earliest of an unhappy series of protests, to continue to the Revolution, about the evil conditions of the established church in Maryland. Some of the complaints arose from the practical difficulties with which the clergymen had to contend. One such complaint, a typical one, had to do with the size of the parishes, which were far too large for a minister to manage single-handed. An area of from four to eight hundred square miles was not unusual. Where curates were rare, services at the outlying chapels had to be infrequent, said one rector, and could be conducted only at the cost of much traveling "through uninhabited woods and marshes and many other discouragements." [59] Another fault, which brought protests from the parishioners themselves to the Bishop of London, derived from long delays in the induction of new ministers. Periods without leadership, they said, opened the field for the activities of dissenters and discredited the established church.[60] But no grievance was so serious or so frequently mentioned as the unsavory character of many of the clergymen. In a full report of 1722, apparently compiled by Commissary Henderson, one minister was described as an "idiot," a second as "a rake," a third as "a horrid preacher and a good liver"; and in 1730 Henderson wrote to the bishop of the induction in Maryland of two clergymen "drove from" Virginia because of their bad char-

58. Letter of July 10, 1714, *ibid.,* IV, 78. For an account of Hart, and an adverse judgment, see Mereness, *Maryland,* pp. 442–446.

59. "Queries to be Answered by every Minister," 1724, Perry, *Collections,* IV, 190–231; Alexander Adams to S.P.G., July 2, 1711, S.P.G. Transcripts, Series A, vol. 6, LC; George Murdock to Bishop of London, June 17, 1730, John Lang to same, August 14, 1731, May 29, 1735, Thomas Fletcher to same, June 18, 1740, Fulham Palace Transcripts, Maryland, nos. 188, 16, 52, 193, LC.

60. Six parishioners, North Elk River, to Bishop of London, 1716; Vestrymen, Allhallows, to same, August 1, 1719, Perry, *Collections,* IV, 84–85, 116–117.

acters.[61] Drunkenness was a frequent sin, sometimes reported to the bishop. One of the most scandalous clergymen, Thomas Phillips of Kent Island, was charged with a number of delinquencies: he failed to visit the sick; he did not care to bury the dead except for wealthy families, where there were funerals to be paid for; he failed to wait long enough after ringing the church bell for the people to come together and hear the service; and he was the father of a bastard by a transported convict servant.[62]

The appearance and reappearance of scandal among the clergy led to various plans of reform. In 1725, the vestrymen of a parish in Somerset county, perhaps influenced by the example of the Presbyterians of their vicinity, demanded to select their own minister.[63] At about the same time the assembly considered a bill providing for a lay court with power to discipline the clergy.[64] But both proposals, the parochial and the statutory, would have infringed upon the prerogative of Lord Baltimore, and both failed. Proprietary rights were opposed even to the authority of a commissary representing the Bishop of London. The last man to hold that appointment was able to conduct no visitations after 1731, and resigned the office in 1734.[65] From that time until the decade before the Revolution, when a new reform movement achieved some headway, the Maryland church was thoroughly the lord proprietor's own.

61. "A Character of the Clergy of Maryland," 1722, *ibid.*, IV, 128–129; Henderson to Bishop of London, October 27, 1730, Fulham Palace Transcripts, Maryland, no. 6, LC.

62. Four vestrymen and six "people," Kent Island, to Bishop of London, July, 1726, Perry, *Collections*, IV, 257–258.

63. Seven vestrymen, Somerset parish, to Bishop of London, 1725, Fulham Palace Transcripts, Maryland, no. 206, LC.

64. Assembly Journals, October 27, 31, 1724, March 23, 1725/6, *Archives*, XXXV, 39–40, 66, 482.

65. Ethan Allen, "Synodalia, Or Records of Clergy Meetings in Maryland between 1695–1773," photostat of MS., p. 164, LC. See Mereness, *Maryland*, pp. 442–444; Arthur L. Cross, *The Anglican Episcopate and the American Colonies* (New York, 1902), pp. 72–78.

All the serious difficulties of the church, however, were not comprehended in the irresponsible exercise of power by proprietor and governor. Those most anxious for the welfare of the church traced spiritual feebleness to the rationalism and deism which was having such a devastating effect on the Church of England everywhere. Commissary Lang urged the clergymen of the Eastern Shore to insist on belief in divine revelation as the foundation stone of morality, for without the fear of God there would be no fear of punishment. He instructed the ministers in resisting the arguments of the deists, and begged them to preach the restoration of family worship and to be exemplary in their own lives.[66] In 1750 Thomas Bacon, the most scholarly of the Maryland clergy, wrote that

Infidelity has indeed arrived to an amazing and shocking growth in these parts. And it is hard to say whether 'tis more owing to the ignorance of the common people, the fancied knowledge of such as have got a little smattering of learning, or the misconduct of too many of the clergy. . . . Religion among us seems to wear the face of the country, part moderately cultivated, the greater part wild and savage.[67]

Bacon and the Reverend Hugh Jones both thought that the reading of the English deists encouraged infidelity. Tindal's *Christianity as Old as Creation,* Bacon said, had gotten into most houses where anyone read; though poorly understood, it gave people the conceit to believe that there was a convincing case against revelation. He considered the *Independent Whig,* the English magazine some issues of which were reprinted in Philadelphia, to be more widely read and a greater source of deist strength.[68] Nor was the clergy itself immune to rationalism. Jonathan Boucher

---

66. Sermon, June 24, 1730, Perry, *Collections,* IV, 288–295.

67. Letter to Bishop of London, August 4, 1750, Perry, *Collections,* IV, 324.

68. Jones to S.P.G., July 30, 1739, S.P.G. Transcripts, Series B, vol. 7, part 1, LC; Bacon to Bishop of London, August 4, 1750, Perry, *Collections,* IV, 325.

admits that, after reading first Clarke and Whiston, with disturbing effects, and then more radical works, he nearly lost his belief in the Trinity; he confesses to having omitted the Athanasian creed from his services for about a year. In his experience the American environment, so far removed from the old centers of authority and traditionalism, seemed to favor heresy and religious indifference.[69]

From a different angle, however, Maryland Anglicanism presents a more pious aspect. The distinguished Reverend Dr. Thomas Chandler, who was very critical of the establishment as a whole, reported to the Bishop of London that he had visited a community on the lower Eastern Shore, "The most sober and orderly, the least vicious, and the most religious, and at the same time the freest from enthusiasm, of any people I have ever met with." [70] Chandler might also have spoken with respect of other parishes, where honorable and attractive men carried on their ministries in the best tradition of the church. Such a man was Thomas Cradock, of Baltimore county, who translated the Psalms, and who gave long and loving service to his people.

Some of the clergymen did what they could, moreover, to compensate for the many deficiencies in education in Maryland. Provincial statute provided for free schools in every county, but the law was poorly executed, and even the private teaching was largely done by indentured servants.[71] The Reverend Thomas Bacon, accordingly, launched a Charity Working School, and expressed the hope that others would follow his example. "God only knows," he said, "the necessity of such a work in this province, where education is hardly to be attained to, at any

69. Jonathan Bouchier, editor, *Reminiscences of an American Loyalist, 1738–1789, being the Autobiography of the Rev'd Jonathan Boucher* (Boston, 1925), pp. 43–45. See R. W. Marshall, "What Jonathan Boucher Preached," *Virginia Magazine of History and Biography,* XLVI (1938), 1–12.

70. Letter of October 21, 1767, Perry, *Collections,* IV, 334–335.

71. Steiner, *History of Education in Maryland,* pp. 19–34, 38.

rate, by the children of the poor. Many poor white children I have found (I speak from sad experience), and many more undoubtedly there are, as ignorant as the children of the poor benighted negroes." [72] Bacon's school failed from lack of money; [73] it was a humanitarian effort in an age and place where humanitarianism was all but absent. Two or three other clergymen succeeded, however, in conducting private schools for young gentlemen. The most prominent of these schoolmasters, the Reverend Henry Addison, a relative of the Dulanys, promoted his school by a patriotic plea for American education. Both economy and love of native land, he said, should encourage parents to educate their children at home not overseas.[74] Thus the Anglican clergymen achieved their best as servants of the community. There was little theological-mindedness in lower Maryland; the Great Awakening did not evoke a single work of doctrinal controversy.

In the development of cultural activities generally, Maryland was placed at a disadvantage, compared to the northern colonies. To the north, where the colonial colleges were rising and growing, and where libraries and scientific and printing activities were most considerable, cultural achievement was associated with the concentration of people and wealth in towns. All of the colonial colleges, save one, were promoted, moreover, by the zeal of one or another of the Protestant churches. Maryland was lacking in such dynamics of culture as these. Not only did the decentralization of the plantation economy discourage town development; but the impulses toward it, exhibited in the growth of Annapolis and Baltimore, drove in two directions, not one. In the north, Boston, New York, and Philadelphia, as commercial cities, each focused the economic resources of a great area; and as colonial capitals, each enjoyed the prestige and the associations of power.

72. Quoted in Oswald Tilghman, *History of Talbot County Maryland, 1661–1861* (Baltimore, 1915), I, 286.
73. Sharpe to Baltimore, May 23, 1760, *Archives,* IX, 415.
74. *Maryland Gazette,* September 4, 1760.

In Maryland, on the other hand, Baltimore, the one true commercial town, was still young before the Revolution, and it stood apart, as we have seen, from the traditional way of life in the colony and from its greatest fortunes. Annapolis, though it shone in the light of official life and display, was forever prevented by location and mediocre roadstead from becoming a great port. Neither town was in a position to concentrate the surplus of a whole people —economic, social, and intellectual—in any such way as the prominent northern cities.

Yet the decentralization of life was not altogether a disadvantage for the transit of English culture to Maryland. Every small port where tobacco ships entered was in some degree a line of communication with the intellectual as well as the material resources of the mother country. The factor, Henry Callister, who came to the Eastern Shore in 1742 as a representative of the firm of Foster and Cunliffe, of Liverpool, spent two decades in small tobacco ports; he ended a business failure, unhappy and isolated in his American home. Yet he brought to Maryland something of the enthusiasm for science, the acquaintanceship with the new literature of history and geography, and the taste for ideas which were the life of eighteenth-century thinking. He owned until bankruptcy a microscope, a botanical thermometer, and a library which included a volume of Newton, other scientific and philosophical works, histories, and French books "of elegant language and good subjects." He wrote to England for seeds for his flower garden, and he begged for English birds—linnets, larks, and goldfinches—that he might turn them loose for breeding. He wrote sensitive letters: his descriptions of reading the *Phaedo* to a dying friend and of his sense of loss, when he sacrificed his musical instruments, are still moving.[75] Not many tobacco ports could have had

75. Nearly all that is known about Callister is to be found in the Callister Papers, Md. Dioc. Lib. There are sketches in Tilghman, *History of Talbot County*, I, 84–98, and Wroth, "A Maryland Merchant and His Friends in 1750," *Md. Hist. Mag.*, VI, 213–240.

a Callister, although there were occasional tokens of art and taste. The fine houses of Upper Marlborough impressed Philip Fithian when he crossed the province in 1774, and so did the charm of Chestertown, where his eye was caught by the clock in the handsome courthouse.[76] Generally speaking the tobacco ports were small, a matter of only a few warehouses, stores, inns, a ferry-house, and one-story residences.[77] Life was more nearly on the level of the small plantation than on that of an active commercial town.[78]

The gayety and the cultivation of life at Annapolis derived entirely from its standing as the capital city. Commercially it had no special advantages. Nor did its appearance impress strangers; Burnaby, who passed through in 1760, had no more than faint praise for the two hundred houses, the handful of public buildings, and the one church, which comprised the town.[79] Even Eddis found more to admire in the situation of the town, swept around by the Severn River, than in its buildings. He noticed that many lots were being held for future building, and that a spirit of improvement prevailed; he was persuaded that, with the wealth concentrated by the residence of the principal families, Annapolis would soon increase. Of the statehouse, he had only to say that it had been erected in the infancy of the colony, "when convenience was the directing principle, without attention to the embellishment of art." [80] In 1769, indeed, the very year in which he set down

76. John R. Williams, editor, *Philip Vickers Fithian, Journal and Letters* (Princeton, 1900), pp. 152–154, 169.

77. George Chalmers listed the number of houses in the Eastern Shore towns, as of about 1774, as follows: Charlestown, 60; Chestertown, 200; Cambridge, 50; Vienna, 30; Princess Anne, 50; Snow Hill, 50; Georgetown, 60, Chalmers Papers, Maryland, II, NYPL. There is an account of Oxford in Tilghman, *History of Talbot County*, II, 351–353, 357. See H. J. Berkley, "Extinct River Towns of the Chesapeake Bay Region," *Md. Hist. Mag.*, XIX, 125–141.

78. See Boucher's comment on life in a Virginia port, *Reminiscences*, pp. 26–27.

79. Rufus R. Wilson, editor, *Burnaby's Travels Through North America* (New York, 1904), p. 81.

80. Eddis, *Letters from America*, pp. 13–14, 18–19. T. Henry Randall,

these impressions, the assembly appropriated money for
a new statehouse, a handsome building with exterior lines
much like those of the larger mansions. It was destined to
be completed just when the provincial government collapsed, and it was to see first service for the revolutionary
government.[81]

The presence of the governor and of the surrounding
circle of high officials and men of wealth and station carried with it a spirited social life. The most mentioned affair
of the year was the celebration of the lord proprietor's
birthday; cannon were fired, the town was illuminated, a
huge bonfire set, and a hogshead of punch opened for "the
populace." In the evening the governor entertained the
ladies and gentlemen of the community, and this was the
occasion for elaborate displays of fashionable dress and
for the repeated drinking of loyal healths.[82] Beginning in
1752 there, was occasional drama in Annapolis, and in
1772 a permanent theater building was erected, the second in the colonies. The capital enjoyed a wide variety of
entertainment: English troupes played Shakespeare, the
Beggar's Opera, and the now forgotten farces of the eighteenth century; there were lectures on science, "interspersed," according to one announcement, "with reflections moral and philosophical, suited to every capacity." [83]
The official set were the leaders of Maryland horse-racing,
a favorite sport throughout the province.[84] During the

"Colonial Annapolis," *Architectural Record*, I (1891), 309–343, is in-
forming about the appearance of the capital. See also William O.
Stevens, *Annapolis, Anne Arundel's Town* (New York, 1937), chs.
V–VI.

81. Society of Colonial Wars in the State of Maryland, *The Maryland
State House* (n.p., 1931); David Ridgely, *Annals of Annapolis* (Baltimore, 1841), pp. 145–146.

82. *Maryland Gazette*, February 22, 1753; *Pennsylvania Gazette*,
March 5, 1754; Ridgely, *Annals of Annapolis*, pp. 116–117.

83. *Ibid.*, p. 127; *Maryland Gazette*, January 15, 1770, and *passim;*
Arthur Hornblow, *A History of the Theater in America from its Beginnings to the Present Time* (Philadelphia, 1919), I, 47, 78, 106–108,
140–142.

84. There were races, according to announcements in the *Maryland
Gazette*, at Upper Marlborough, Pomonkey, and Frederick, as well as
Annapolis, on the Western Shore, and at Georgetown and Chestertown,
on the Eastern.

half-dozen years before the Revolution, Governor Eden and ex-Governor Sharpe founded and promoted the Jockey Club, which offered large prizes and encouraged intercolonial as well as local racing. Their horses were as good as the best in England; Man o' War is descended from one of the racers of colonial Maryland.[85]

All these social and sporting activities charmed the people who organized and enjoyed them. After one of the celebrations of the proprietor's birthday, Eddis wrote with enthusiasm that not a town in England the size of Annapolis could boast a greater number of handsome and fashionable women. The theater pleased and surprised him with its excellence; and the racing, with which he was connected as secretary of the Jockey Club, gratified him not only because of the horses but also because it brought out a brilliant and fashionable company.[86] The Reverend Mr. Boucher, who also belonged to the official circle, declared with equal satisfaction that Annapolis was "the genteelest town in North America." [87]

The most sophisticated element in the social life of the upper class of Maryland flourished in the gentlemen's clubs, established between the opening of the century and the Revolution. Such clubs, with a literary and political bias, were common to the age, at home and in the provinces. The oldest in Maryland was the Ancient South River Club; another old one was the Royalist Club, founded about 1715 by George Neilson, a deported Scottish Jacobite. Schism and new organization produced a series of clubs: Neilson, when ejected from the Royalist, founded the Redhouse Club; the Redhouse afforded a building, but it did not last long; it was followed by the Ugly Club and by the famous Tuesday Club, founded in 1745. This, the most interesting of the clubs, was considered to be authorized by an old commission, which Neilson had held, from

85. William Woodward, "The Thoroughbred Horse and Maryland," *Md. Hist. Mag.,* XVII, 146.
86. Eddis, *Letters from America,* pp. 31, 93–94, 106–108.
87. Boucher, *Reminiscences,* p. 65.

the Tuesday Club of Lannerie, Scotland. Many Scots belonged to the club, but in the long run it drew its fifteen members from the various types of cultivated men, evidently without much preference for Scottish blood. There were members of the assembly, such as Michael Earle and Edward Dorsey; officials of high place, such as Dennis and Walter Dulany; clergymen, such as Thomas Bacon and John Hamilton; merchants, such as Robert Morris; and people of various distinction, such as Stephen Bordley, the lawyer, and Jonas Green, of New England ancestry, the printer and postmaster.[88]

The full and witty records of the Tuesday Club preserve an open window into the spontaneous attitudes and pleasures of the upper class. A group of pen and ink sketches show the members seated around a table, smoking and drinking; one of them has slipped entirely under the table.[89] The record makes much mention of Jamaica rum and of the combined office of the "Poet, Printer, Punster, Purveyor and Punchmaster-general," the office held by Jonas Green. And yet the pleasure of cultivated wit was the object of the club; the drinking was incidental. The members amused themselves with puns, conundrums, speech-making, and, most of all, with mock trials, which elaborately caricatured the procedure of the law. They wore badges and performed certain none too serious ceremonials, which included a procession, two by two, through the streets of Annapolis, when they celebrated the anniversaries of the club. An important regulation forbade the discussion of local politics. When anyone spoke of such matters there was to be no response, but all members were to wait the end of the discourse and then laugh loudly. After the manner of the age, the members loved satire, and

88. For accounts of the clubs, see "The Tuesday Club of Annapolis," *Md. Hist. Mag.*, I, 59–65; Ridgely, *Annals of Annapolis*, p. 117 and *passim;* Frank B. Mayer, "Old Maryland Manners," *Scribner's Monthly,* XVII (1878–1879), 327–331; Walter B. Norris, *Annapolis, its Colonial and Naval Story* (New York, 1925), ch. V; Stevens, *Annapolis*, pp. 51–57.

89. Sketches in Dulany Papers, II, 18, MHS.

a fondness for Butler's *Hudibras* rings through the mock-heroics of their own rhyming. They were very clever, too, in ornamenting what they had to say with reference and allusion to Greek and Roman history and mythology. Their erudition was derived from Latin schooling and from a knowledge of contemporary literature.

An occasional item in the papers of the Tuesday Club shows that the members, however light their ordinary mood, did not fail to appreciate and to share the biting and critical cynicism, which, as well as the amusing, was a part of the literary age in which they were living and in their own way participating. "There is really but a trifling difference between the histories of the smallest clubs and those of the greatest empires and kingdoms," wrote Dr. Alexander Hamilton in his manuscript history of the Tuesday Club, about 1755.

We find in the latter, a parcel of mortals denominated, emperors, kings, potentates, and princes, contending and scrambling, about little parcels and portions of this terrestrial ball; we find state politicians racking their invention to bring about certain schemes, and still like a parcel of earth moles countermining and undermining one another. We find generals, or rather licensed banditti, leading forth great armies, pillaging and laying waste vast countries, burning towns, and cutting throats, and all to acquire for themselves or master a certain perishable power, eminence or grandeur, or certain sonorous title. . . . Can anything worse be said of . . . clubs, whose members being men, in a lower rank of life, have the same affections and passions, with those of the great, and go upon pursuits and schemes of a parallel and like insignificant and ridiculous nature, for the bringing about purposes equally vain and transitory, though under a different class and denomination.[90]

These lines must have been written at about the time when Voltaire was setting down his own satire of war and perse-

90. "History of the Tuesday Club," in the handwriting of Dr. Alexander Hamilton, Dulany Papers, V, 16, MHS.

cution in the pages of *Candide*, a book soon to be known in Maryland. They are sufficient to indicate that something of the spirit of Voltaire, in its irony and in its will to freedom, flourished in the Tuesday Club.

In the two decades between the distintegration of the Tuesday Club and the Revolution, a number of new "clubbical" organizations arose and flourished in and around the capital. A lodge of Free Masons was established about 1750; eight others were set up in Baltimore and the smaller ports in the following quarter-century. The Annapolis Masons are mentioned in the *Gazette* as marching, "all properly clothed," at the time of special sermons and celebrations, from their lodge room to a coffee house.[91] Maryland also shared with the other colonies the legend and organization of St. Tammany. According to Eddis, who probably knew nothing of Tammany's origin in Pennsylvania, Marylanders celebrated "Tamina" on May Day; young men dressed as Indians broke in on the Maypole dance, whooped and did a war dance, took a collection, and departed satisfied. A "Society" is mentioned, but it is not clear that a formal body ever existed in Maryland.[92] In 1759 was founded the Forensic Club, the members of which included the lawyers and future patriots, Samuel Chase, William Paca, and Thomas Stone. This club continued active at least through the period of the Stamp Act; quite different from the Tuesday Club, it encouraged rather than suppressed the discussion of public events and political principles. In 1761 Paca debated the question "whether aristocracy be a better form of government than a democracy"; later in the same year the question, "whether it is lawful to keep slaves," was resolved in the negative; and in December, 1765, the club voted that it was right and proper to "take up arms to deliver sub-

91. *Maryland Gazette,* June 25, 1761, December 29, 1763; J. Hugo Tatsch, *Free Masonry in the Thirteen Colonies* (New York, 1929), ch. XII; Edward T. Schulz, *History of Freemasonry in Maryland* . . . (3 vols., Baltimore, 1884).

92. Eddis, *Letters from America,* p. 115; Ridgely, *Annals of Annapolis,* p. 148.

jects from the yoke of a strange prince who is become a tyrant." [93]

Yet the final word in the provincial clubs was social, not political. The Hominy Club, presided over by Jonathan Boucher and having Governor Eden as an honorary member, was the most prominent of the later clubs; and it carried on the literary and dilettante spirit of the Tuesday Club. The meetings were devoted to "innocent mirth" and "ingenious humor." "Courtiers," such as the Dulanys, Eddis, and Boucher, enjoyed themselves in company with the lawyer-leaders of the "country party": they received applications for membership in verse, they dined with the younger men of the Independent Club, and they staged mock trials. So things went, at least, until political strain became too great. According to President Boucher, the Hominy continued active until the preliminaries of the Revolution "put an end to everything that was pleasant and proper" in Maryland. [94]

In what ways and how far the attitudes and moods of the rationalist age penetrated from the level of the education and wealth of the upper class into the common consciousness of the people of Maryland is a question hardly capable of a satisfying answer. There are a good many indications, however, that the irony, the satire, and the interest in the classical and secular, so common in the period everywhere, were not confined to the cultivated gentlemen of the Annapolis clubs. Gibbon said that eighteenth-century literature breathed "the spirit of reason and liberty" in England; so, in miniature, many a brief comment in newspaper and in personal correspondence shows that the abrasives of contemporary thought cut wide and deep in Maryland. The province had its minor writers, and they all shared the rationalist spirit.

93. Maryland MSS. (Miscellaneous), Box I, NYPL.

94. Boucher, *Reminiscences*, p. 67. There are miscellaneous documents referring to the Hominy Club in the Gilmor Papers, III, 1, and in the Dulany Papers, V, 20, MHS. There are an attack on and a defense of the Hominy and Independent Clubs in the *Maryland Gazette*, December 12 and 19, 1771.

Printing, and therefore literature, owed its origin in Maryland to the patronage of the government. From small beginnings in the seventeenth century to the extensive work of William Parks, between 1726 and 1737, and of Jonas Green and members of his family, from 1738 until the Revolution and after, the printer at Annapolis ordinarily held an official appointment and was paid by legislative appropriation for services rendered.[95] Accordingly a great share of the printing of the Annapolis press was for the government; but there were also two periodical issues, the weekly *Maryland Gazette* and the annual *Maryland Almanack*, and a certain number of occasional imprints—political pamphlets and broadsides, sermons preached for ceremonial events, long poems, particularly those of Ebenezer Cooke and Richard Lewis, and at least one treatise, *The Farmer's Companion, directing how to Survey Land after a new and particular Method*, by Abraham Milton.[96]

The *Maryland Almanack*, like the more famous almanacs by Ames and Franklin, was intended for wide circulation and utility among farmers and mariners. Unfortunately only a very few numbers have been preserved; but it is clear that, like almanacs elsewhere, those printed in Maryland carried an interest over and beyond practical tables of astronomical and commercial information. They bore the mark of Newtonism:

> God gave to man an upright Heart, that He
> Might view the Stars and learn Astronomy.

There was also a romantic touch, decrying cities, where

95. On the official connections of the provincial printers, see Wroth, *Printing in Colonial Maryland*, pp. 3–4, 17–18, 22–23, 28, 33–34, 50, 55–57, 60–62, 77–79, 90–91, 100–105, 149–153; see also, by the same author, *William Parks, Printer and Journalist of England and Colonial America* (Richmond, Va., 1926), and "The St. Mary's City Press; a New Chronology of American Printing," *Md. Hist. Mag.*, XXXI, 91–111.

96. Wroth's invaluable "Maryland Imprints . . . from 1689 to 1776," in his *Printing in Colonial Maryland*, pp. 157–256, is a record of the literary product of the province.

"self-cankering Envy dwells," and praising the independent farmer, the man who is

> Pensive to Rove, not meditating Harm,
> And live in Affluence at his Country Farm.

And most prominently, the *Almanack* displayed the worldly wisdom of Addisonian epigram, essay, and comment.[97] In the *Almanack*, then, the liberal mind, imbued with the scientific and the secular, achieved expression for the widest body of readers in Maryland.

The same contemporary spirit penetrated the *Maryland Gazette*. William Parks, the founder of the paper, was almost certainly born and trained to his craft in England; in any case, the *Gazette*, as he made it, became one of the earliest American papers to imitate Addison and Steele.[98] Some of the most representative and vigorous of this sort of essay-writing appeared in the issues of December, January, and February, 1728 and 1729, when the paper was a little more than a year old. A writer, who signed himself as "Plain-Dealer," began with an essay entitled "Philosophical Doubting," pleading the importance of an independent mind in making judgments. "An honest man," he said, "cannot be too much upon his guard, by accustoming himself to a habit of doubting. . . . Common sense requires we should not neglect the proper and ordinary methods of information: how all information comes by enquiry; and all enquiry comes by doubting." [99] In his next essay "Plain-Dealer" proceeded to compare and to evaluate the arts of poetry and painting. He found

97. The present writer has seen and here quoted from the *Maryland Almanack* for 1762 and 1765, LC, and for 1764, MHS. See Wroth, *Printing in Colonial Maryland*, pp. 183, 215; and Chester E. Jorgenson, "The New Science in the Almanacs of Ames and Franklin," *New England Quarterly*, VIII (1935), 555–561.

98. Wroth, *William Parks,* and *Printing in Colonial Maryland*, pp. 59–60, 63–68. See also Elizabeth C. Cook, *Literary Influences in Colonial Newspapers, 1704–1750* (New York, 1912), ch. VI; and M. C. Howard, "The *Maryland Gazette:* an American Imitation of the *Tatler* and the *Spectator*," *Md. Hist. Mag.*, XXIX, 295–298.

99. *Maryland Gazette*, December 17, 1728.

them both important, saying that in the one art words and numbers, and, in the other, lights and shades were "equally wonderful" and "under the conduct of a Superior Genius." He judged poetry to be more instructive than painting, however, and declared that in that "point alone the poet justly claims preëminence over the painter." A few weeks later "Plain-Dealer" wrote on the subject of religion. He began with the proposition that "Religion has three great adversaries, atheism, superstition, and enthusiasm," and he proceeded, using the language and the ideas of the English deists, to attack each of these attitudes as extreme and unreasonable. In the final essay of his series, the writer turned to government, taking the stand of the advanced Whig of his day. "In popular and mixed governments," he said, "men have always been more watchful and solicitous for the public weal, than in absolute and unlimited monarchies." On the premise of constitutionalism, "Plain-Dealer" ended with an attack on the dangers of war and passion to the well-being of the state.[100]

Literary beginnings were interrupted in 1734, when Parks abandoned the *Gazette*, but they were taken up again in 1745 when Jonas Green reëstablished the newspaper. In an early issue a contributor, who signed himself "Philo-Eleutherius," wrote urging the readers of the *Gazette* to study history for the sake of the moral lessons it taught. The writer recommended, for example, a study of Codrus, Timoleon, and Leonidas, for their virtues, and of Catiline, and Caesar, for an understanding of the dangers of treachery and tyranny. "History," he declared,

describes the various changes and vicissitudes of fortune, with the causes from which they flow; and exhibits the several characters and scenes of human life. . . . To know history truly is *to know mankind*, which is indeed the subject-matter of it; it is *to study the motives, opinions, and passions of mankind;* and carefully to observe how they operate upon

100. The three essays are in the *Maryland Gazette,* December 24, 1728, January 7, February 11, 1728/9.

their various tempers and dispositions; and to draw useful and instructive conclusions from these observations.[101]

Thus for a generation and more before the pamphlets and arguments of the revolutionary period, the provincial mind produced its own minor literature of moral judgment and historical comparison.

As with writing, so, in the large, with reading: the standards of the Enlightenment prevailed.[102] The local sale of books in Maryland, as elsewhere in America, was closely connected with the printing business.[103] In a notable advertisement of 1762, William Rind, who for a period of years was the partner of Jonas Green, listed something over one hundred fifty titles as the basis for establishing a circulating library.[104] Except for the writings of John Locke, who was quoted and named everywhere, the list includes most of the works which the writer has seen mentioned as known and read in Maryland. There were several works of modern history, referring, for the most part, to Great Britain and to recent national and overseas affairs. Such were the histories of England by Rapin, Hume, and Smollett; Robertson's important works on *Scotland* and on *Charles the Fifth;* and books on Canada, Cape Breton, and California. There were also small histories for children. Of equal prominence were the ancient classics and works in classical history; and these were more extensively represented on the Roman side than on the Greek. The list contained Rollin's big Roman history,

101. *Maryland Gazette,* June 7, 1745. This naturalistic view of history may be profitably compared with the theological view taken by Jonathan Edwards in his *Work of Redemption.* See Osgood, *American Colonies in the Eighteenth Century* (New York, 1924), III, 413–414.

102. This section was written without the benefit of Joseph T. Wheeler's informing articles, "Booksellers and Circulating Libraries in Colonial Maryland," "Thomas Bray and the Maryland Parochial Libraries," and "The Laymen's Libraries and the Provincial Library," *Md. Hist. Mag.,* XXXIV, 111–137, 246–265; XXXV, 60–73. His treatment of the circulating libraries includes many interesting book lists; the later ones conform nicely with the lists given here.

103. Wroth, *Printing in Colonial Maryland,* pp. 40, 71, 85.

104. *Maryland Gazette,* August 26, 1762.

Montesquieu's *Causes of the Greatness and Decadence of the Romans*, Dryden's *Vergil*, Pope's *Homer*, and various of the writings and editions of Cicero, Livy, Pliny, Quintilian, and Seneca. The list also included a number of the still recognized works on political thought of the seventeenth and eighteenth centuries, namely, Harrington's *Oceana*, Vattel's *Law of Nations*, Voltaire's *Letters on the English Nation*, and Montesquieu's *The Spirit of the Laws*. Theoretical science was represented by titles now remembered as in the early rationalist current, such as Fontenelle's *Plurality of Worlds*, Burnet's *Theory of the Earth*, and Derham's *Physics and Astro-theology*. A number of handbooks, compendia, and guides were listed, notably Postelthwayt's *Dictionary of Trade*, Child's *Discourse of Trade*, a *Merchants Directory*, gazetteers, and works on surveying and medicine, all with evident appeal to the practical interests of the colony. Literature was represented by many of the great English works of the two centuries before the American Revolution, and these were supplemented by translations of certain foreign literature, such as *Don Quixote* and the letters of Ninon l'Enclos. The older English writings included the works of Shakespeare, the epics of Milton, *The Pilgrim's Progress*, and the poetry of Dryden and of Butler—the advertised edition of *Hudibras* was illustrated by Hogarth. From the eighteenth century there was much more: eight volumes of the *Spectator; Robinson Crusoe;* twelve volumes of Swift, ten of Pope, ten or more of Smollett; Richardson's *Clarissa Harlowe* and *Pamela; Tom Jones, Joseph Andrews*, and other works by Fielding; the *Dictionary* and other volumes, including the *Rambler* essays, by Samuel Johnson. There were also listed Steele's *Ladies Library* and such guide books as *The Young Lady Conducted* and *Conversation on Polite Life*, offerings to appeal to the gentility of the upper class. Altogether Rind's list was made in perfect accord with the tastes exhibited in the *Almanack* and the *Gazette*, and with the interests of the educated element of lower Maryland.

Yet this first circulating library in Maryland soon proved a commercial failure. Neither Rind's enterprise, nor the launching of two or three other libraries between 1762 and the Revolution, gives much support to the boast of Franklin, that the circulating libraries of the colonies, of which his own was the original, "made the common tradesmen and farmers as intelligent as most gentlemen from other countries. . . ." [105] On the other hand, commercial failure does not cast doubt on the popularity and appeal of the books offered. Henry Callister wrote Rind, within a month of the announcement, that the plan was good and certain to be useful in a "young country" where there was a considerable "want of cultivation." Callister knew certain gentlemen on the Eastern Shore who would subscribe, and he himself would recommend the library; the real difficulty, as he saw it, lay in the fact that "several" of his friends imported books directly from London and that there was hardly a book on Rind's list which they had not read.[106] In 1773, moreover, when William Aikman advertised a new library in Annapolis, he offered exactly the same sort of books. He announced twelve hundred volumes, and declared that his library would equal or excel any in America.[107]

The private libraries, purchased, as Callister said, largely by planters dealing directly with London, offer the most satisfying evidence of purposeful reading and intellectual taste. Stephen Bordley, for example, owned all five volumes of Bayle's *Dictionary;* he read Rollin's history and found it excellent. In an intellectual correspondence with a friend, he expressed critical judgments of the Roman statesmen, he quoted Swift, and he asked for copies of Polybius and the *Oceana.*[108] While abroad Charles Carroll

105. *Autobiography,* Albert H. Smyth, editor, *The Writings of Benjamin Franklin* (New York, 1905–1907), I, 312.
106. Letter to Rind, September 20, 1762, Callister Papers, Md. Dioc. Lib.
107. *Maryland Gazette,* November 11, 1773.
108. Many letters to M. Harris, 1740–1745, Stephen Bordley's Letterbooks, 1738–1740, 1740–1747, MHS.

of Carrollton asked the permission of his father to make extensive purchases of French works, certainly to include those of Boileau, Voltaire, and Rousseau.[109] Similarly, Charles Carroll, Barrister, asked a merchant in London to send him "15 or 20 shillings of the best political and other pamphlets, especially any that relate to the colonies, . . . but none of religious controversy. It is some amusement to learn from your authors and their works of wit how things pass with you." At other times Carroll ordered many books, including, as titles representative of his taste, Tindal's continuation of Rapin's history of England, Clarendon's *History of the Rebellion*, the works of Tacitus and Sallust, the memoirs of Madame Pompadour, Montesquieu's *The Spirit of the Laws*, and d'Alembert's commentary on the same.[110]

In any final estimate of the thinking of southern Maryland, the prominent thing is the unresisted dominance of the upper class. The science and secularism implicit in the *Almanack*, the worldly wisdom of the essays in the *Gazette*, the philosophical works in the circulating and private libraries, all conform to the liberal pattern—the pattern which was the modern product and taste of upper and middle-class England, and which was the normal intellectual import of planters of wealth and education. There is no record to establish in any large way that the inarticulate small planters understood or accepted such a pattern of thought; the suggestive thing is that the record shows no opposite thrust. The Great Awakening may have thrown a few Annapolitans into "the vapors," as Bordley said,[111] but there was no division of class from class, no schism within church congregations, in lower

109. Letter of January 17, 1759, *Md. Hist. Mag.*, X, 231.
110. Letters to William Anderson, October 4, 1764, October 9, November 2, 1765, February 24, 1767, Papers of Dr. Charles Carroll and Charles Carroll, Barrister, MHS.
111. Letters to J. George and M. Harris, December 11, 1739, Stephen Bordley's Letterbook, 1738–1740, MHS. For a cynical description of a convert of the Great Awakening, from the back country, see Hamilton, *Itinerarium*, pp. 8, 10.

Maryland as in the outlying areas and in other colonies. The testimony of the Anglican ministers that rationalism reached deep in the parishes indicates a real conformity of thought between the lower classes and the educated essayists of the *Gazette*.[112]

For the time being, at least, lower Maryland had achieved a stable social order. The unfree classes had no idea or thought of emancipation. The inferior free, the planters of small estate, were in a position, as we shall see, to demand reforms; but, as the middle members of a stratified society, they had neither opportunity nor language to speak for changes in the social system. The well-to-do enjoyed rising standards and increasing hopes: plantation life could be amply arranged and ideally conceived; families could grow; speculative fortunes could be made; their whole way of life encouraged a sense of superiority. The educated knew the advantage of professional training, the stimulus of fresh currents of literary and philosophical ideas; they spoke the language of high moral and historical judgment. Their legalism, their rationalism, and their literary interests formed a body of tradition and thought without internal contradictions. If the common life presented perplexities—commercial conditions which were adverse, or political differences not easily reconcilable—the Maryland of Bordley and the Carrolls knew no order of men better able to solve those perplexities than the Bordleys and the Carrolls themselves.

112. In 1773 Francis Asbury came to Annapolis "with some desire to preach." When he discovered, however, that the tavern-keeper, who offered his house, was a deist, Asbury says that "I did not feel free to open my mouth." In 1777 he did preach in Annapolis; but it was to a "deistical audience" in the playhouse, and he discovered that "many people openly deny the Holy Scriptures, as well as the power of inward religion." *Journal of Francis Asbury* (New York, 1852), I, 58, 60–61, 93, 179, 181, 182.

III

EXPANSION AND DEPRESSION IN ECONOMIC LIFE

IN THE eighteenth century the influence of the tobacco staple was felt at every level and in every area of Maryland life. Slaves and servants cultivated it; landholders had their fortunes in it; officials received their salaries in it; it was widely, although not exclusively, used as a medium of exchange. In the last quarter-century of the colonial period its old predominance was somewhat reduced by the growing diversity of agriculture and commerce,[1] but tobacco remained the core and center of the Maryland economy. Prosperity and depression followed on the state of the tobacco market.

Almost from the beginning that dependence had produced its difficulties. Tobacco planting began in the seventeenth century as an easy crop for settlers and as the occasional maker of great fortunes. Yet, after the first rush of Virginia tobacco to the British market, when the profits were high, prices had quickly dropped close to the cost of production; and there were sharp depressions in the course of the century. Returns were sufficient and market conditions good enough, however, to encourage tobacco to the exclusion of other surplus products for overseas shipping, and tobacco planting conformed excellently to the special requirements of colonial life. Unskilled labor, such as that of immigrants from the cities, white servants, and slaves, was adequate; and one man could produce a greater value in tobacco than in other crops. If the cultivation of the staple were extravagant in one respect—the depletion of the soil—that was the point where extravagance seemed most easily borne. There was an abundance of free land,

1. See Gould, *Money and Transportation in Maryland,* pp. 48, 52–53, 70–73.

and men of influence could secure it in large grants.[2]

With the opening of the eighteenth century, and particularly during the fifty years before the Revolution, a condition of chronic depression and discontent settled upon the tobacco planters of Maryland. The market now declined and now improved a little, but it was at no time expanding and there were years of acute depression in every decade before the Revolution. Through the period as a whole the returns from provincial tobacco duties show that the annual exportation tended to be fairly constant or to increase a little,[3] and of course tobacco shared in the generally rising price level.[4] But trends of such apparent buoyance were far from being in proportion with the rapid increase of the population or with the demand for imported commodities. From 1739 to 1761 tobacco exportation was subjected, moreover, to interruption and loss caused by the wars with Spain and France. A multitude of complaints and of proposed remedies shows that adverse conditions were recognized and strongly resented in Maryland.

The great prominence in the record of depressed conditions after 1726 is partly to be ascribed to the coming to Annapolis of William Parks, the printer. As he launched and managed the *Maryland Gazette*, Parks assigned much space to open letters and discussions of the commercial affairs of the province, and in 1729 he also printed the pamphlet of Henry Darnall, *A Just and Impartial Account of the Transactions of the Merchants in London, for the Advancement of the Price of Tobacco*. This pub-

2. On the economics of early tobacco culture, see Lewis C. Gray, *History of Agriculture in the Southern United States to 1860* (Washington, 1933), I, 218, 259–268; and Avery O. Craven, *Soil Exhaustion as a Factor in the Agricultural History of Virginia and Maryland*, University of Illinois Studies in the Social Sciences (Urbana), XIII (1925), no. 1, pp. 29–32.

3. The periods of acutest depression were from 1703 to 1713, from 1724 to 1734, from 1740 to 1747, from 1754 to 1760, and from 1763 to 1765. See Gray, *Agriculture in the Southern United States*, I, 268–274; Craven, *Soil Exhaustion*, pp. 51–53; and below, pp. 295–297, 341–342, 381.

4. Bezanson, *Prices in Colonial Pennsylvania*, pp. 294, 422.

licity mirrored a wide general interest in improving the staple. The economic problem became a political problem because reform of the staple, either in production or in marketing, would inevitably affect the income from export duties, the fees of officials, the salaries of clergymen, and all the revenues of the lord proprietor.[5]

None was more conscious of the relationship of these affairs than Governor Benedict Leonard Calvert, whose report of 1729 to the proprietor, his brother, gives a summary of economic adversity:

Tobacco, as our staple, is our all, and indeed leaves no room for anything else. It requires the attendance of all our hands, and exacts their utmost labor, the whole year round; it requires us to abhor communities or townships, since a planter cannot carry on his affairs, without considerable elbow room within his plantation. When all is done, our tobacco sent home, it is perchance the most uncertain commodity that comes to market, and the management of it, there, is of such a nature and method, that it seems to be of all other, most liable and subject to frauds, in prejudice to the poor planters. Tobacco merchants, who deal in consignments, get great estates, run no risk, and labor only with the pen; the planter can scarce get a living, runs all the risks, attendant upon trade, both as to his Negroes and tobacco, and must work in a variety of labor. I write not this in malicious envy to the merchants, nor do I wish them less success in business but I heartily wish the planters' lay was better.[6]

Governor Calvert's view, and that of any provincial, naturally tended to overlook such a long-range influence as the exhaustion of the soil. What he saw as the immediate crux of the matter, and what provincials saw as subject to legislation, argument, and rearrangement, was the problem of marketing.

5. This connection was discussed in a one-shilling leaflet printed by Parks in 1726, *Proposals for a Tobacco-Law . . . offered to the Consideration of the Legislature, and all Lovers of their country.*
6. October 26, 1729, *Archives,* XXV, 602–603.

Under the British policy of "enumeration," enacted in the great law of trade of 1660, Maryland tobacco could be sold only in British or colonial markets; and it could be sold to a foreign purchaser only after being sent to Great Britain in the first instance. It could not be exported directly to the continent of Europe. Yet Maryland tobacco was mostly of the "oronoko" type, which did not command the best prices and was not purchased by British consumers. According to long usage it was reëxported from the mother country to European buyers, much of it to the Farmers-General of the Revenue of France, who monopolized the French market.[7] From the early years of the colony the assembly had debated methods of improving the staple and getting good prices. A number of laws for the regulation of the trade had been written into the statute books, but none had been very extensive or effective.[8] Up to 1747, provincial law left the tobacco producers and merchants little controlled and little protected; they had to compete with Virginia, and they were dependent on the uncertain fortunes of the international market.

In the practice of eighteenth-century Maryland, the planter with a crop for sale did exercise a certain choice as to the way in which he sent his product to the British market. He shipped direct to the mother country, or he sold in the locality, either to the representative of a British firm or to an independent merchant of the province. He chose according to his wealth and bargaining power.

If he were the producer of many hogsheads, he was in a position to command the correspondence and the services of a merchant in London or one of the outports, to send consignments of tobacco direct, and to order commodities and enjoy credit facilities in the metropolis. If his plantation faced deep water and he had a landing of his own, he had as an added benefit the most convenient access to over-

7. *Virginia Gazette,* August 5, 1737.
8. Vertrees J. Wyckoff, *Tobacco Regulation in Colonial Maryland,* JHUS, Extra Volumes; New Series, no. 22 (1936), pp. 51, 102, 124–125, 128.

seas shipping. With several of these privileges of location and wealth, he could, if he wished, handle consignments and arrange importations for his neighbors, and in this way enter trade as an independent planter-merchant, such as Richard Bennett and Dr. Charles Carroll.

Provincials who shipped their own product did not sell directly to their correspondent merchants in England. They consigned tobacco to them in the capacity of commission agents rather than as purchasers for resale. Thus the ownership of tobacco and the risks and expenses of bringing it to market remained with the shippers until the time of purchase for processing and consumption in Europe. The British merchants managed, supervised, and extended credit for the provincials, and made their charges for each individual consignment. The process of bringing to sale was a long one; even at the colonial end, where the planters could participate, it was slow. Weeks and months were consumed in the fall and winter of each year by vessels and lighters moving in and out of the small ports, dropping consignments of imported goods and picking up tobacco shipments. Ship captains sometimes advertised their sailings and their destinations for such business as they could pick up while in the colony. The value to the Marylander of handling his own business was that of independence of local middlemen and of personal access to the British buying market.

There are few figures on the point, but the great amount of tobacco selling must have been handled by middlemen rather than by producers independently.[9] Small planters, with only one or a very few hogsheads for annual exportation, could hardly manage an overseas correspondence; they needed local credit and trading facilities. They chose, according to convenience and prejudice, between the factors, on the one hand, the representative buyers and store-

9. The following figures appeared in the newspaper: number of hogsheads exported from Maryland annually, 36,000; "crop tobacco," sent on consignment, 16,000; "purchase tobacco," bought in the colony, 20,000. The figures were excessive but the proportion between them may well have been just. "Mercator," *Maryland Gazette,* April 7, 1747.

keepers for great British firms, established in the province, and, on the other hand, the independent merchants of Maryland who shipped to the British market. Either type of middleman led to British commercial houses of wealth and name: in London to those of Micajah Perry, William Hunt, Samuel Hyde, Robert Cruickshanks, John Hanbury and Company, later Capel and Osgood Hanbury, Sylvanus Grove, Jordan and Maxwell, Anthony Bacon, William Black, John Stewart and Company, and William and James Anderson. The London trade was handled through provincial planters and merchants, rather than through factors; it overshadowed that of all the outports. Foster Cunliffe and Sons of Liverpool, however, maintained several Maryland stores up to the time of the French and Indian War;[10] and there was trade with firms in Whitehaven and Bristol. The Scottish traders, who seem to have done business exclusively through their own stores and factors, had come to the province early in the century; after about 1750 they became very prominent in the Potomac and Patuxent areas. The Glasgow firms of James Brown and Company, Jamieson, Johnstone, and Company, John Glassford, Shortridge and Gordon, and others maintained stores, a dozen or so, in Bladensburg, Upper Marlborough, Leonardtown, Piscattaway, Port Tobacco, and Nottingham.[11]

The factors well represented the established interests and purposes of the old British mercantilism. As employees rather than free correspondents of the British firms, their status was inferior and their attention consistently devoted to the conventional exchange of finished products from the mother country for colonial tobacco. Their contracts required them to keep in regular communication with the chief factor of the firm in the colony or with the firm itself, and they were required periodically to go before a judge and swear to the accuracy of their

10. See Wroth, "A Maryland Merchant and His Friends in 1750," *Md. Hist. Mag.*, VI, 216, 238, and *passim*.
11. Firm Accounts, Virginia and Maryland, LC.

books. They received salaries of from five to ten pounds sterling monthly, and were given allowances for maintenance and the hire of some assistance. They were sometimes allowed to import and sell on their own accounts, but under restrictions which were calculated to prevent injuring the interest of their principals.[12]

The factors' stores represented a large British investment in Maryland trade. An inventory of 1772 gives a picture of a Scottish store: it was equipped with a mahogany desk and bookcase, copies of the collected laws of Maryland and of Virginia, pictures of the king and queen, a miscellany of furniture and utensils, some broken; and there were a slave and three horses. This capital was valued at £132 15s. 6d.,[13] more than any provincial not of the wealthy class could have readily assembled. The goods held in stock by the factors were often extensive. Cunliffe's store at Oxford, on the Eastern Shore, in 1756, carried a great variety of textiles, most of them inexpensive; but there were plushes, velvets, and linens as well as India goods such as chintzes, calicoes, cambrics, and ginghams, and such coarse goods as German and Irish osnaburg and sail canvas. There were also finished items such as petticoats, draperies, counterpanes, blankets, and rugs. In the same store, aside from dry goods, there was a great variety of hardware and other manufactures, such as hats, shoes, gloves, saddles for men and women, paint, rope, rum, stationery, mariners' equipment, window glass, ammunition, and dozens of miscellaneous items for life on the plantations and on the inland waters. The value of the goods in this particular store, which was quite typical and was one of three operated on the Eastern Shore for Cunliffe, was about £2500 sterling plus £1000, Maryland currency.[14] Such stores operated largely on credit, trading in

12. This statement is generalized from evidence in the Firm Accounts, LC; the Callister Papers, Md. Dioc. Lib.; and particularly from a letter of Robert Mendell, a Glassford factor, November 4, 1766, Hamilton Papers, MHS.

13. Firm Accounts, Inventories and Invoices, 1769, LC.

14. Inventory of October, 1756, Callister Papers. Inventories in the Firm Accounts, LC, show similarly large stocks of goods.

expectation of tobacco payment, and they tried to secure settlements by the end of each calendar year.

The rôle of the independent merchant is not fully recorded; but there is much information in the letters of Dr. Charles Carroll and his son, Charles Carroll, Barrister; in the correspondence of Samuel Galloway of West River, a large part of it with Thomas Ringgold, a merchant on the Eastern Shore; and in the letter books of Wallace, Davidson, and Johnson, of Annapolis.[15] Most of their business naturally, like that of the factors, had to do with the normal exchange of tobacco for manufactured goods. Like the factors, they bought and sold with the planters on a credit basis; and, like the planters who exported directly, they corresponded with British merchants as agents and bankers. Yet the distinguishing feature of their activities was a new and different element in trade: they played vigorous parts as commercial adventurers and innovators. When tobacco was depressed they were forced, if they were to survive, to essay new directions and new commodities in trade. Under pressure they sought out new markets for iron, foodstuffs, and lumber, and some of them established wide connections. Dr. Carroll, for example, corresponded at various times with eight or more merchants in London, with three or four in Liverpool, Bristol, and Whitehaven, and with an English firm in Madeira. Wherever Maryland exports besides tobacco were shipped, that was likely to be the business of the independent merchants. This particular interest probably explains the tendency of these merchants to displace the factors on the Eastern Shore, where grain culture was increasing,[16] while the Glasgow factors

15. The Carroll papers are extensively printed as "Extracts from the Account and Letter Books of Dr. Charles Carroll of Annapolis," *Md. Hist. Mag.*, XVIII–XXVII, and as "Letters of Charles Carroll, Barrister," *ibid.*, XXXI—; see also W. S. Holt, "Charles Carroll, Barrister: the Man," *ibid.*, XXXI, 112–126. The Galloway and Ringgold letters are in the Galloway, Maxcy, Markoe Papers, LC, and the Galloway Papers, NYPL; and the Wallace, Davidson, and Johnson Letterbooks, 1771–1777, are in the Maryland Hall of Records, Annapolis (later citations from this depository will be identified by MHRecs).

16. Tilghman, *History of Talbot County*, II, 352–353; Gould, "The Economic Causes of the Rise of Baltimore," p. 246.

remained strongly entrenched in the tobacco country across the bay.

The two types of traders were everywhere thrown into rivalry with each other. Both bought tobacco outright from the planters, giving the benefit of immediate credit and themselves assuming the responsibilities and delays of shipping and selling in the British market. The factors had the considerable advantage of their large stocks of goods, while the country merchant had that of being closer to local sentiment and of greater adaptability. There is evidence, too, that the very size of the factor's establishment could involve a disadvantage. A detailed statement by Henry Callister, in 1747, while he was a factor for Cunliffe, shows that his firm stood heavy outlays, amounting to one-fifth or even one-third of the purchase price, for transporting tobacco already bought from the plantations to the store.[17] The expenses which he listed, such as rolling, lighterage, storage, the factor's salary, and the hire of horse and boy, were such as would have been less heavy in the case of a smaller establishment and one dealing with a less extensive area; and they were such as would have been largely avoided by a planter shipping his own tobacco. But the more widely recognized difficulties of the factor were of a different order. According to an anonymous letter printed in the *Gazette*, the factors were held in general disrespect and were spoken of "by the ill fitting epithet of foreigners." [18] Early in his Maryland career, Callister wrote his principal that the factors suffered two disadvantages in buying tobacco, namely, that the planters who shipped independently could not be brought to low terms, and that the "poor indigent fellows" were much too closely entangled with the country merchants. Again, nearly twenty years later, when he was about to go bankrupt after an attempt in independent trade, Callister declared that he suffered unpopularity which derived from

17. "Calculation of the Costs of 100 hhds. Tobo. ready for Shipping, Maryland, 1747," Callister Papers, Md. Dioc. Lib.
18. "X," *Maryland Gazette,* December 21, 1758.

his old connection with a British firm, and that it had done much to ruin him.[19]

In 1765 so wealthy and distinguished a landholder as Charles Carroll of Carrollton vigorously expressed the sentiment of the country against the factors: "Our factors are closely combined: tho' hating and hated by each other they confederate to oppress us; conscious of their iniquity they will be desirous of concealing it or at least willing and united to oppose anyone who attempts to detect or put a stop to their illicit practices." He also said that his father did not consign tobacco to Great Britain direct, but found it more advantageous to sell to the merchants of the province.[20] The evidence is indirect, and none of it is statistical, but the tendency is plain that, for a long period, before the non-importation agreements of 1769 and later clamped down so drastically on the trade of the tobacco areas, the British firms were losing strength in Maryland, and the independent merchants were gaining over their powerful and entrenched rivals.

The transfer of colonial tobacco into purchasing power for British goods, whether accomplished at a factor's desk in Port Tobacco or in an office in London, everywhere involved long-term debtor and creditor relationships. In the overseas trade, the credit standing of the provincials, planters and independent merchants alike, was indicated to them by the accounts rendered by their correspondents in Great Britain. There were general accounts, or "accounts current," summarizing debits and credits for a year or other given period; and there were special accounts or bills, sent for each consignment of tobacco as it was sold and itemizing the charges incurred from the time of shipment from Maryland. These special accounts reached Maryland many months or even a period of years

19. Letters to C. Craven (Liverpool), July 28, 1745, to Cunliffe and Sons, 1747, to Mr. Lachlan, September 30, 1763, Callister Papers, Md. Dioc. Lib.

20. Letter to Henry Graves (London), September 15, 1765, *Unpublished Letters*, p. 91.

after the tobacco had been sent, and they usually reported a disappointingly small net credit to the shipper. Naturally the provincials conceived their financial embarrassments in terms of the charges made against their tobacco sales, as itemized in the accounts. Whether the accounts represented just or unjust dealing, they certainly pictured transactions which were complicated and prolonged in ways far out of the control of the shippers. They were an inevitable focus for controversy and resentment.

A full list and a discussion of the costs and complexities of marketing tobacco was addressed to the planters of Virginia and Maryland in the *Virginia Gazette* in 1737.[21] It was written by a representative of the Farmers-General of France in support of a proposal to prearrange tobacco sales in the colonies and so reduce the charges on handling and marketing by way of London. For illustration of the ordinary difficulties he gave an estimated account of the sale of one hogshead of tobacco weighing 790 pounds at the time of shipment and 732 pounds at the time of sale, at two pence one farthing per pound. The estimated charges follow:

	£	s.	d.
Old subsidy	2	5	1½
Other British duties	14	13	0½
Freight (at £7 per ton)	1	15	0
Maryland duties, per hogshead	0	2	9
Primage and entry charges, do.	0	2	1
Entry inwards, etc., do.	0	1	6
Entry out, etc., do.	0	2	0
Cooperage, etc., do.	0	2	0
Porterage, etc., do.	0	1	0
Warehouse rent, etc., do.	0	3	6
Brokerage, do.	0	2	0

21. *Virginia Gazette,* August 5, 12, 1737. At the time, the *Virginia Gazette* had recently been established by Parks, who had moved from Maryland. As the *Maryland Gazette* had lapsed there was no route of more direct presentation to the people of Maryland.

	£	s.	d.
Postage, etc.	0	1	0
Drafts (4 lbs. tobacco)	0	0	9
Loss of weight (allowing 14 lbs. for natural loss on shipboard) 44 lbs. tobacco	0	8	3
Commission, 2½% on duties and selling price	0	12	0
	20	12	0

Against these many charges the estimate showed three credits, as follows:

	£	s.	d.
Drawback, old subsidy	2	5	1½
Drawback, other British duties	14	13	0½
Sale, one hogshead, suttle 732, drafts 4, trett 28, net 700 lbs. at 2¼d. per lb.	6	11	3
	23	9	5

This calculation showed net proceeds to the colonial exporter of £2 17s. 5d. for the hogshead,[22] an amount equal to little more than 12 per cent of the entire account and to 43½ per cent of all items except the British duties, which were drawn back.

Representative documents from the actual trade show that the estimates of the French agent, though referring to tobacco of low price and quality, offered a fair picture of the situation. Ordinarily about half or, as in the estimate, less than half of the selling price of a consignment of tobacco was credited, net, to the account of the Maryland shipper. The selling price was reduced, moreover, by allowances for shrinkage in weight and for tret and draft; these were items which the provincials viewed with habitual suspicion. The share of the selling price which the mer-

22. *Virginia Gazette*, August 5, 1737.

chant charged the shipper for marketing was divided among a dozen or more items. In the round, one-half went to freight, ordinarily for shipment in the merchant's own vessel; one-fourth went to a miscellaneous group of charges on moving the tobacco, namely, provincial duties, fees for entry in and out, and such services as cooperage, cartage, warehouse rent, watching, wharfage, and lighterage; and one-fourth went to what may be called financing charges—insurance, a brokerage fee, and the British merchant's commission.

This last category of charges, expressing the profits of the British merchants, was a natural focus for controversy. The normal commission rate was 2½ per cent, but this was charged not on the selling price but on the whole account as it was enlarged to an amount equal to three or four times the selling price, by the inclusion of British duties—the "old subsidy," the "new subsidy," and other customs payments. Yet most of the duties were never paid: although the merchants had to assume responsibility for full payment if the tobacco were held in Great Britain beyond the time limit of the law, this requirement amounted in practice to a statutory limitation on the period of holding the tobacco for export, not to the necessity of advancing large sums. The law required cash payment on only one duty, the penny per pound of the "old subsidy," which was itself drawn back when the tobacco was sold and exported. This was enough, indeed, to involve a considerable outlay when large consignments were brought through the customs; a penny a pound represented from one-third to one-half or more of the expected selling price.[23] Yet it amounted to no more than four times the expected commission. If the commission be regarded largely as interest on this deposit, as it justly may, the merchant had a very favorable position as money-lender—the return was large and he himself controlled the sale of the tobacco from which payment was

23. For a careful analysis of the incidence of the British duties, see Gray, *Agriculture in the Southern United States*, I, 243–246.

made. What the provincial shipper and owner saw was
that his British correspondent received 2½ per cent
which was actually about 10 per cent of the selling price.[24]

Whether or not the services of transportation across the
Atlantic and bringing tobacco to market gave the British
merchant a just claim to make charges equal to the returns
to his Maryland correspondent, for land and labor, is a
moot question not subject to decision.[25] The occasional
withdrawal of the merchants from the trade is sufficient to
show that the commission business was not always profitable. Yet the division of credits from the tobacco sales
makes Governor Calvert's jealousy for the planters seem
inevitable. "[Tobacco] exacts their utmost labor. . . . It
is perchance the most uncertain commodity that comes to
market; and the management of it . . . is of such a
nature and method, that it seems to be of all other, most
liable and subject to frauds, in prejudice to the poor
planters." [26]

An elaborate bill of complaint in the same mood was
printed in the *Maryland Gazette* in 1729. A writer, who
signed himself "J. S.," submitted a list of the "legal
charges" for which Maryland was annually debtor for
the exportation of 20,000 hogsheads, and he set over
against that list another of "unreasonable" charges for
which the exporters were actually billed. He admitted as
valid the full charge on freight at £7 per ton, and he took
no exception to the brokerage fee or to the provincial
duties. He estimated the smaller charges, however, such as
entry in and out, primage, cooperage, and porterage, as
overcharged from 100 to 300, or even 600 per cent. But
the great difference between what was "legal" and what
was "unreasonable" appeared in the charges for loss of

24. This discussion is based on representative commercial documents,
especially those in the Hill Papers, Shipping Accounts, 1764–1793; and
in the Hamilton Papers, MHS. See Gipson, *The British Empire Before
the American Revolution*, II, 129–139.

25. See Craven, *Soil Exhaustion*, p. 53.

26. Letter to Lord Baltimore, October 26, 1729, *Archives*, XXV, 602–
603.

weight, for samples taken and "sold by the merchants," and for commission charged on money credited to the British duties. "J. S.'s" concluding figures indicated that Maryland tobacco exports might properly be charged £49,000 for transportation and sale, but that they were actually charged more than three times that amount, with an overcharge of £109,000.[27] The French agent in 1737 did not propose amendments quite in proportion to "J. S.'s" complaints, but his criticisms of the trade pointed to the same charges. He specified that eight shillings per hogshead could be saved the shipper on the deductions commonly made for loss of weight and by the elimination of sampling and the "ordinary kinds of pilfering," that an equal amount could be saved on the merchant's commission, and that about eleven or twelve shillings more could be saved on freight, cooperage, primage, wharfage, lighterage, and the like.[28]

Such criticisms and complaints do not establish the fact of serious or personal dishonesty on the part of the British merchants, but they must have increased the prejudice of the colony. At about the time of "J. S.'s" analysis, the newspaper printed an estimate of the low profits of a typical two-slave planter who exported three hogsheads of tobacco. According to the calculation such a man received £12 credit, he deducted £5 for the maintenance of his slaves, and with £7 net had hardly enough to justify his investment of £56 in slaves, an investment peculiarly subject to loss and depreciation.[29] Every printed discussion of the tobacco trade was penetrated with the feeling of objection and resentment.

The most convincing evidence of actual bad faith on the part of the British merchants is found in occasional letters of Maryland exporters, men whose long and continuing connection with the business should have prevented them from accusing too freely. Leonard Holliday, for

27. "J. S.," *Maryland Gazette,* May 20, 1729.
28. *Virginia Gazette,* August 5, 1737.
29. "P. P.," *Maryland Gazette,* March 25, 1729.

example, complained to Hyde of London that his tobacco was liable to plundering while stored in London; and Stephen Bordley on different occasions protested that he was overcharged for warehouse rent and that the merchants were exporting to Maryland "anything that might be patched up for the plantations." [30] Both Bordley and Dr. Carroll wrote to London merchants that they had been charged for insurance which had never been placed. Bordley declared that insurance rates had been too high, for that reason he had specially asked that a certain cargo be not insured; he had nevertheless been charged for it, and he was convinced that if the ship had been lost he would have been told that he had no recourse. He knew this practice to be common in the tobacco trade and regarded it as a scandal. On one occasion Dr. Carroll wrote his son, the barrister, that he thought that Black of London had received payment for some of his iron earlier than it was credited in the account, but that there was no necessity for a "squabble" about it.[31] The younger Carroll had his own difficulties with the sale of iron in England, though he spoke of discrimination rather than of dishonesty. In consecutive years, 1756, 1757, 1758, and 1759, he complained to the Hanburys that he had been unable to send iron, and so balance his account, because the captains of their ships had refused or failed to take his iron. No captain in the Maryland trade would carry iron consigned to another merchant than his owner.[32]

The embarrassments and difficulties of the relationship of the debtor to the creditor, however, occupy more space in the letters of Maryland merchants to British than do

---

30. John Hyde to Leonard Holliday, December 5, 1729, Hill Papers; Bordley to Richard Molineux, March 21, 1747, to Flowerdewe and Norton, December 13, 1751, Stephen Bordley's Letterbooks, 1740–1747, 1749–1752, MHS.

31. Bordley to Molineux, March 21, 1747, *ibid;* Carroll to Samuel Hyde, April 11, 1747, to Carroll, Barrister, July 9, 1754, December 6, 1757, *Md. Hist. Mag.,* XXII, 293; XXVII, 227.

32. Letters of July 30, 1756, August 31, 1757, January 2, 1758, September 15, 1759, *Md. Hist. Mag.,* XXXI, 318; XXXII, 40, 178, 356.

their complaints about dishonesty or discrimination. Many aspects of the Maryland situation tended to increase the commercial debt to British merchants: the low price of tobacco and the persistent hope of better, the credit arrangement which made the British merchant at once the banker and the selling agent of the provincial, the increasing needs of a growing population, and the colonial deficiency in sterling, all pointed to lagging balances. The irritation which was natural to such a situation is well illustrated in the long correspondence, otherwise friendly, between Samuel Galloway and Sylvanus Grove of London. Grove wrote bitterly of having taken Galloway's advice about investment in the Maryland trade, and regretting it. He complained of having made large advances and having received small remittances, of being put out of cash and embarrassed in his affairs, and of being driven to the merchant's resort of protesting rather than paying colonial drafts.[33]

Yet long credits were expected, and the provincials did not entirely lack bargaining power. In 1754, when tobacco was especially low, the assembly passed a bankruptcy law which the great merchants attacked as discriminatory against themselves.[34] Henry Callister must have felt that the custom of the trade was on his side when as an independent merchant he wrote a vigorous letter to a correspondent in London, defending himself against charges of breach of contract. He explained that, though a date of payment was always named in the obligations of colonial merchants to British, it was understood that interest should begin at that time and not that full payment should be made.[35] The strongest words, on the subject of credit, came from Dr. Carroll: "Unless you gentlemen at

33. Letters to Galloway, April 10, 1760, July 11, October 1, 1761, January 21, 1762, March 9, April 16, 1763, Galloway, Maxcy, Markoe Papers, LC.
34. See Sharpe to Cecilius Calvert, August 8, 1754; Calvert to Sharpe, April 17, December 10, 1754, *Archives*, VI, 82–85, 44–45, 131.
35. Callister to Mr. Maclane, September 12, 1762, Callister Papers, Md. Dioc. Lib.

the head of trade," he wrote to William Black, "will so order and conduct with respect to the interest of the people in the plantations, that they may live and be supported by their industry and remittance, it will fall out with ye as it did with the man in the fable who had a hen that laid golden eggs." [36]

As between the colonial exporters and the British merchants in their long connections, so entirely within the colony, the planters were customarily the debtors of the merchants, especially of the stores operated by factors. The evidence is not full, but here too it shows economic friction and strain. In the depressed war years of the middle seventeen-forties, a number of the factors were withdrawn from the trade altogether;[37] and others, in an effort to improve their business, in the absence of a tobacco inspection law took private measures to secure the best product for themselves. The receivers of tobacco employed by Cunliffe were instructed to inspect all that was brought to them, except by the most dependable planters, and to reject the bad. They did this to the point of refusing one-third, and the factors of other firms at least tried to do likewise. Such use of the factors' bargaining power, refusing tobacco and keeping prices down, made the planters particularly angry and resentful.[38] Callister as factor thought and spoke of the planters as "knaves," ever trying to sell trash tobacco. He could not, he said, deal openly and frankly with men who would neither admit that the shippers of good "heavy" tobacco deserved extra prices, nor recognize their own disadvantage in living on distant and barren lands, the disadvantage which cost the factor in terms of long hauls and low quality. So he met the situation as he could. Much "dissimulation if not downright lying," he declared, "is sometimes the way to

36. January 1, 1747, *Md. Hist. Mag.*, XXII, 366–367.

37. Governor Thomas Bladen and others to Lord Baltimore, February 1, 1743, *Archives*, XXXVIII, 307–310.

38. Callister to Cunliffe and Sons, August 13, 1744, July 10, 1745, October 2, 1750, to Charles Craven, November 20, 1746, Callister Papers, Md. Dioc. Lib.

hook 'em, and since reason will not do, they must be deceived into a fair distinction." [39] Another factor wrote his principal that a lawsuit was the most effective way he knew to rid himself of an undesirable customer.[40] "A man of business must have a good share of devil in him," wrote Callister, when years of experience had given him hindsight, "he must not be obstinately just; he must be subtile as well as supple; he must rob Peter to pay Paul, without the wiles of the serpent, the innocence of the dove would be betrayed and crushed. I believe for all this, that a steady perseverance would in the end be crowned with success; but while the grass grows the stud starves." [41]

The three decades between the severely felt depression of the seventeen-twenties and early thirties and the period of economic and political crisis preliminary to the Revolution saw considerable effort to improve the economic situation of Maryland. Tension in commercial life was matched by discussion and activity directed toward improving the tobacco trade by regulation and toward the production of new goods and selling them wherever a market could be found. The period ended with important advances made: by the seventeen-sixties Maryland had an economy considerably more diversified than in 1730, and it had in working order a public system for the regulation of tobacco. Although the gains were all too small, in terms of credit and stability, to spare Maryland economic stress and strain in the decade before the Revolution, there did appear many signs of an increasing degree of self-management and self-sufficiency. This was perhaps quite as significant, in the staple economy, as the brave and independent words of the delegates in the provincial assembly.

In a way which was fitting to the aristocratic tradition

39. Letter to Cunliffe and Sons, December 28, 1747, *ibid.*

40. Alexander Hamilton to James Brown and Co., December 4, 1773, Letters, 1773, Firm Accounts, Virginia and Maryland, LC.

41. Letter to John Jackson, February 11, 1762, Callister Papers, Md. Dioc. Lib.

of Maryland, the most sweeping and in some respects the most promising early efforts to reform the tobacco trade were made and supported by members of the provincial gentry. The protagonist in the matter was Henry Darnall, a member of a prominent family and a large landholder. When in London, early in 1728, Darnall privately negotiated a kind of trade agreement with the merchants trading to Maryland. On his return to the colony he enlisted the support of eighty or more gentlemen, and discussion of the matter was prominent in the *Gazette* for nearly a year.

Darnall told the history of the whole affair in the fifty-three page pamphlet, *A Just and Impartial Account*, printed by Parks. He said that the merchants themselves admitted to him that their own competition to sell in the foreign market was one of the causes for the low price of tobacco. They acknowledged what the French agent was later to say in the *Virginia Gazette*, that they had no bargaining power against a monopolist purchaser for France. With the help of one of their number, Darnall managed to meet the merchants as a group; he secured a preliminary agreement that they would make a practice of meeting once a month to discuss the affairs of the trade, that they would constitute an organization on a permanent basis, and that they would establish a fund to carry their common expenses, particularly that of bringing petitions before Parliament. They set up a committee of twelve, six representing the Maryland trade, Samuel Hyde, Robert Cruickshanks, Joseph Adams, John Hanbury, William Hunt, and John Falconar, and six representing the Virginia trade, to make specific recommendations at the next meeting. The great reforms proposed to the committee, some of which were recommended and some withheld, all indicate a sense of urgency. Such proposals were made as the establishment of a permanent organization with a steering committee, the employment of a secretary to keep records on the trade and to maintain the most open and friendly correspondence with exporters in the colonies, the fixing of minimum prices for oronoko and other low grades of tobacco, the setting up of a credit pool for the trade, and even the boycott of any merchant not conforming with such agreements as should be made permanent. A full meeting of twenty-nine merchants, in April, 1728, considered recommendations on the point of organization, adopted seven out of eight proposals, but dropped the one involving a boycott against non-conformers; they all signed their names in support of a permanent arrangement.[42]

At this stage of organization, as yet without the determination of policies, Darnall left London. In the province he must have been very hopeful and active in support of the plan, for within three or four months prominent men were speaking and combining among themselves in behalf of it. Charles Calvert, Daniel Dulany, and eighty-one other gentlemen sent a letter to the merchants; they expressed gratitude at the prospect of improving the trade, and they added an element of compulsion by saying that they would regard any merchant not conforming to minimum prices as an enemy of the country, and they would boycott him.[43] Yet the reply to the gentlemen, signed by seventeen merchants of London, said that price agreements had already failed and that none could be made in the face of the competing and growing importations of Glasgow.[44] This letter, and others from individual merchants to Darnall, indicate that the London merchants were able neither to agree upon a strong policy nor to effect one. The letters admitting failure to control the market in England ended with advice about controlling production and exportation in the colony. They proposed restricting the amount of tobacco planted, coöperation rather than competition between Maryland and Virginia, handling tobacco without rolling or otherwise damaging it, and

42. Darnall, *Just and Impartial Account* (Annapolis, 1729), pp. 3–28.
43. "P. P.," referring to September, 1728, *Maryland Gazette,* March 25, 1729.
44. Letter of November 7, 1728, *ibid.,* April 15, 1729.

shipping in the spring and summer rather than in the winter.[45] The British merchants, in short, threw the responsibility for economic reorganization and improvement directly on the province.

The one other serious attempt to reform the trade by private action was the proposal which followed the analysis of the representative of the Farmers-General, made in 1737. The essence of this plan was that the French maintain a permanent agent in America to inspect and to arrange consignments before shipping. The tobacco was of course to be shipped through Great Britain as the law required, but it was to proceed immediately to France, and sampling, petty charges, and the long delays were all to be eliminated.[46] The proposal was not put into effect; if it had been it would have been soon cut short by the outbreak of war with France. Yet, unnatural as foreign operation within the old colonial system would have been, it found support in Maryland, most explicitly from Henry Darnall. He wrote to the *Virginia Gazette* that, "I confess that at present I am very fond of the scheme, and am solicitous for the execution of it. . . . I can with the strictest honor say, that within the circle of my acquaintance, which is not very confined, the proposal is always talked of with the warmest expression of wishes for its success." [47]

The French scheme and Darnall's earlier proposal had in common the advantage and appeal of directness. To the provincial tobacco shippers, they offered programs of reform at the point which, in their minds, most needed reform, the tobacco market in Great Britain. If such a proposal had succeeded, action would have been accom-

45. Darnall, *Just and Impartial Account*, pp. 43, 47, 51–52; *Maryland Gazette*, April 15, 1729.
46. *Virginia Gazette*, August 5, 1737.
47. *Virginia Gazette*, April 21, 1738. In the preceding issue another Marylander had expressed an opposite view with favorable reference to a Maryland letter in the *Pennsylvania Gazette* of March 7, 1737/8. Still another Maryland writer supported the proposal in the *Pennsylvania Gazette*, April 13, 1738.

plished without much change in the situation at home, which was on the whole satisfactory to the great landholders like Darnall. On the other hand, when the proposals failed, reliance had to be put on political action, if strong steps were to be taken; and legislation was certain to involve a long chain of conflicts and delays. A tobacco law in Maryland required the determination of a policy which the great landholders seated in both houses would enact, which the lesser landholders, with their votes and their power of violence, would accept, and which the nonresident proprietor, Lord Baltimore, would approve. Tobacco rioting in Prince George's county, by men in "despair of any relief from the legislature," brought a grim reminder that the very peace of the community hung on the condition of the staple.[48]

The possibility of tobacco legislation as a way out of prevailing difficulties was in the minds of the supporters of Darnall's plan on both sides of the Atlantic. In a letter written after the merchants' scheme had begun to disintegrate, John Falconar, who had seconded Darnall in London, wrote to urge that the Maryland legislature might force the merchants after all to conform to a "strict and steady" union. He suggested that a provincial law could require ship captains in the trade to have certificates showing that their owners were bonded to conform to agreed marketing regulations.[49] But the Marylanders were not hopeful; prominent members of both houses of assembly, such as Charles and Edward Henry Calvert of the council, and the delegates Holliday, Jennings, and Dulany, all expressed their doubts. In their closing letter on the business, the provincials spoke of the possibility of a law controlling exports, but dwelled for the most part on counter-suggestions about what could be done in England, especially in the way of eliminating commission charges on the amount of the British duties and reducing compe-

48. Address of Governor Samuel Ogle, July 11, 1732, *Archives*, XXVII, 370.
49. Darnall, *Just and Impartial Account*, pp. 51-52.

tition between London and the outports.[50] Darnall's final suggestion for improving marketing conditions was that the Maryland exporters of tobacco maintain an agent to represent them in London. The best arrangement, he said, would have been the appointment of a colonial agent, named and supported by the legislature; failing that, he proposed an agent supported by subscription.[51] Nothing came of the idea, however, and Maryland went without an agent, public or private, in this as at later hours of serious need.

While great merchants and exporters were attempting and failing at the private negotiation of large-scale reform, the Maryland legislature approached the tobacco problem in what ways it could.[52] In 1727 it regulated the cutting, packing, and handling of tobacco in terms which reached considerably deeper into the operation of the industry than did the traditional laws to fix the gauge and tare of hogsheads. But, like other arrangements demanding a standard of quality rather than a limitation of quantity, the act of 1727 was taken as favorable to the great planters with good land and unfavorable to the small planters; it was largely repealed in 1728. In that year a new measure was passed, favorable to the small landholders. The number of tobacco plants which a planter might set out was restricted in proportion to the number of workers on his land; slight differentials were made in favor of planters without slaves or servants and of those with less than six; and a machinery for supervision was set up.[53] But Lord Baltimore disallowed the law, after two years of indifferent enforcement. The proprietor seems to have acted without considering the merits

50. Letter of May 21, 1729, *Maryland Gazette,* June 3, 1729.

51. Darnall to Inhabitants of Maryland, *ibid.,* February 4, 1728/9. The policy of sending an agent was supported by "P. P.," *ibid.,* March 4, 1728/9.

52. For a brief treatment and comparison with Virginia, see Gray, *Agriculture in the Southern United States,* I, 228–229.

53. The preference of small planters for crop limitation is spoken of in a letter of Governor Ogle to Lord Baltimore, February 12, 1748, Calvert Papers, no. 1139, MHS.

of the tobacco policy involved, and chiefly with a purpose to defend his appointees, the Anglican clergymen, whose tobacco incomes the law reduced by twenty-five per cent. The same sort of plan of crop restriction was enacted again in 1730, however, this time with compensation provided the clergy, and the proprietor approved the law.[54] But in that year Virginia enacted a much more thorough tobacco law, and one based on contrasting principles. It required that tobacco to be exported must be brought well and uniformly packed to a public warehouse under the supervision of public officers, and that it must pass inspection for sound quality. Thus the Maryland law of 1730 was outmoded from the beginning and the Maryland tobacco trade was subjected to the further strain of increased competition. The law brought no recognized improvement in the trade, and it was permitted to lapse.

The laws of 1727, 1728, and 1730 left no permanent mark on the Maryland economy; they must be regarded as experimental and half-hearted. And yet these laws indicate a compulsion to act in regard to tobacco, and small steps taken when private business could achieve no reform. The enactment of an important paper-money law, in 1733, moreover, shows another kind of attack on the economic problem. In his report of 1729, Governor Calvert had connected the deficiencies of Maryland money with the limitations of the staple economy, as follows:

When our tobacco then is sold at home, whatever is the produce of it, returns not to us in money, but is either converted into apparel, tools or other conveniences of life, or else remains there, as it were dead to us. For where the staple of a country, upon foreign sale, yields no return of money, to circulate in such a country, the want of such circulation must leave it almost inanimate; it is like a dead palsie on the

54. The laws referred to are Acts, October, 1727, ch. 7; October, 1728, ch. 2; and May, 1730, ch. 7, *Archives,* XXXVI, 86–89, 266–275; XXXVII, 138–151. For the fullest account, see Wyckoff, *Tobacco Regulation,* pp. 143–151; see also Sioussat, *Economics and Politics in Maryland, 1720–1750,* pp. 20–24.

public, since it can never exert its members or faculties, in the pursuit of trade and commerce.[55]

Governor Calvert therefore favored an emission of paper money as a way out of the difficulties of the trade; and the same idea was written into the act of 1733. The preamble said that paper money offered "the most probable means to enable the people to discharge their taxes, and other engagements now payable in tobacco, and . . . to put the people in a condition to carry on the tobacco trade." [56] How well the law served this particular purpose there is no way to know, but it is clear enough that it had a sound and stimulating effect on the life of the province. Years after enactment Governors Ogle and Sharpe expressed satisfaction with the paper, and modern students of Maryland money agree that the law was a useful one.[57] So viewed, the law of 1733 marks the legislature as the one authority competent for economic reform, and as in some degree ready and able to act.

The depression and discussion of the years around 1730 also promoted a sense of need for diversifying and expanding Maryland production. Governor Calvert, speaking with envy of the northern colonies, hoped that paper money would promote industry; and Dr. Carroll, anticipating westward expansion, spoke of the advantage of new crops.[58] With a similar thought, both houses of the

55. Letter to Baltimore, October 26, 1729, *Archives,* XXV, 603.
56. Acts, 1733, ch. 6, *ibid.,* XXXIX, 92.
57. Ogle to Board of Trade, April 20, 1740, House of Lords Library, LC, item 166, indicated in Charles M. Andrews and Frances G. Davenport, *Guide to the Manuscript Materials for the History of the United States to 1783, in the British Museum, in minor London Archives, and in the Libraries of Oxford and Cambridge* (Washington, 1907), p. 214; Ogle to Duke of Bedford, December 13, 1749, *Archives,* XXVIII, 466–467; Sharpe to Cecilius Calvert, August 8, 1754, and to William Sharpe, October 24, 1755, *ibid.,* VI, 85–86, 300. For modern discussion and approval, see Gould, *Money and Transportation in Maryland,* ch. V; and Kathryn L. Behrens, *Paper Money in Maryland, 1727–1789,* JHUS, XLI (1923), no. 1.
58. Calvert to Baltimore, October 26, 1729, *Archives,* XXV, 602, 603; Carroll to Ogle, February 17, 1731, *Md. Hist. Mag.,* XIX, 291–293.

assembly urged the governor that the resources of the province were such as to make possible escape from over-dependence on tobacco. Soil and climate, they said, were favorable to livestock, timber, and fruit; and a limited domestic manufacture of woolen and linen goods had sprung up among the people.[59] Perhaps the fullest bill of particulars, and certainly one close to common knowledge and feeling, came from the rhyming pen of Ebenezer Cooke, in his *Sotweed Redivivus*, of 1730. After comment on the frauds and difficulties of the tobacco trade, Cooke advised the planters to drain the swamps and marshes, to plant hemp and grain, and to raise sheep and cattle. His most extreme proposals, that Marylanders try cotton and rice culture, were extravagant; but in some respects, especially when he urged shipbuilding, he was prophetic.

> Materials here, of every kind
> May soon be found, were Youth inclin'd,
> To practice the Ingenious Art
> Of sailing by Mercator's Chart. . . .
> Nothing is wanting to compleat,
> Fit for the Sea, a trading Fleet
> But Industry and Resolution,
> Wou'd quickly heal our Constitution,
> Were we unanimously bent
> Impending Evils to prevent.[60]

Maryland did not build a great fleet; but the materials for shipbuilding, timber, iron, flax, and hemp, were to be somewhat produced, and used as the poet suggested.

A series of laws, passed in a period when political strain and controversy made legislation very difficult to accomplish, well testify to the prevailing interest in economic diversification. In October, 1727, the assembly provided a bounty of one hundredweight of tobacco for each lot of hemp of equal weight certified by the county judges; and

59. September 4, 1731, *Archives*, XXXVII, 291–292.
60. Ebenezer Cooke, *Sotweed Redivivus: or the Planter's Looking-Glass*, Bernard C. Steiner, editor, *Early Maryland Poetry*, pp. 48, 49.

in 1731 the same sort of encouragement was provided for the manufacture of linen cloth from flax or hemp. The preambles of both laws mentioned the inadequacy of the tobacco trade to support the people of the province and referred to the particular and general benefits of producing new commodities.[61] Under the title of "An Act for the Benefit of the Poor and Encouragement of Industry," the linen law was carried forward in 1740 and again in 1744.[62] In the same period mining enterprises were encouraged: white men working at iron production were released in 1732 from obligations to attend the musters or to assist in building highways or roads, and ten years later a petitioner undertaking a copper works secured a statute releasing such experienced workers as he would bring to the colony from tax payment, and from militia and road duty.[63]

This legislation plainly indicates widespread interest in economic diversification, but the actual gains in that direction, especially in their influence on trade balances, are difficult to trace. A comparison of the periodic "answers to queries" returned to the British Board of Trade, nevertheless, gives a picture of a provincial economy slowly increasing in variety and self-sufficiency. The "answers" of 1697 declared that the "sole and only manufacture or rather production of this province for merchants' and shippers' supply is tobacco." The barest exceptions were made of small exportations of sassafras and furs to England, and of food and timber to Barbados.[64] A report of 1732, based on information supplied by the legislature, however, mentioned new and different items in the trade. Besides tobacco it spoke of iron, furs, staves, lumber, and such foodstuffs as grain, flour, bread, beef, and pork,

61. Acts, October, 1727, ch. 3; July, 1731, ch. 3, *Archives*, XXXVI, 83–84; XXXVII, 248–249.

62. Acts, July, 1740, ch. 11; May, 1744, ch. 19; *ibid.*, XLII, 144–146, 613.

63. Acts, July, 1732, ch. 17; September, 1742, ch. 20, *ibid.*, XXXVII, 540–541; XLII, 430–431.

64. June 9, 1697, *Archives*, XIX, 581.

goods which were exported in occasional shiploads to the West Indies, Madeira, and Lisbon. The same report spoke of the depression in tobacco driving people to make their own textiles, and of nineteen Maryland-owned vessels in the trade, most of them built in the province.[65] Two years later a special report on naval stores and other products, requested by the Board of Trade, said that the "great wages" required by free labor, namely, two shillings a day and "diet," seriously discouraged the working of hemp and the overland transportation of lumber; that British restrictions on the importation of salt from Europe prevented the natural development of fishing for exportation; and that British import duties combined with high labor costs placed a heavy burden on the iron industry.[66] In 1749 Governor Ogle described the trade to the sugar islands, Lisbon, and Madeira as though non-staple exports were not much different from 1732, but he specified 50 Maryland vessels manned by about 400 seamen, or an increase of 300 per cent or more in the sixteen-year interval.[67] The only further diversification marked by Governor Sharpe, in 1756 and 1761, was the exportation of a few cargoes of flaxseed to Ireland. He noted in approximate figures that there were 60 Maryland-owned vessels, totaling around 2,000 tons and employing 480 men, but that the war reduced these figures by one-half. His figures on the British tobacco trade from Maryland, which he said employed about 180 vessels of a burden of 10,000 tons and about 3,600 men, give a rough suggestion of the balance between the tobacco trade and the non-staple trade of the province.[68]

65. "Short Account of the Province of Maryland," 1732, Calvert Papers, *Archives*, XXXVII, 588–589.

66. Ogle to Board of Trade, October 16, 1734, Board of Trade Papers, Proprieties, 1697–1776, Historical Society of Pennsylvania, Transcripts from the Public Record Office, XIII. Later citations from these transcripts will be indicated by HSP.

67. Report to Board of Trade, December 13, 1749, *Archives*, XXVIII, 468.

68. Sharpe to Board of Trade, February 8, 1756, January 14, 1762, Board of Trade Papers, Proprieties, XIX, XXI(1), HSP; see *Archives*, XXXI, 145; XXXII, 23.

The many trade ventures and enterprises discussed in the merchants' correspondence support the official reports of diversification, and they convey a sense of urgency and makeshift in the trade. On the Eastern Shore, where, according to an account of 1746, planters "in great numbers have turned themselves to the raising of grain and livestock, of which they begin to send great quantities to the West Indies," [69] a minor commercial revolution was taking place. Oxford, the leading tobacco port of the first half of the century, was declining, and even Cunliffe of Liverpool, whose store focused the trade of the town and section, was forced to retrench and experiment, and then to withdraw. In the opening years of the French and Indian War the firm instructed Callister as its factor to buy pork, wheat, Indian corn, and lumber, to use old debts and goods in stock for purchasing, to ship the goods to Jamaica in a colonial vessel, not expecting the firm to send one from England, and to remit in bills or in shipments of sugar or cotton. In this way Cunliffe was trying to balance accounts in preparation for retiring from the Maryland trade.[70] Callister in setting up as a country merchant announced himself as in the tobacco trade, but at the same time he proposed sending grain to New York.[71] Similarly Thomas Ringgold of Chestertown, an established planter-merchant and a delegate from Kent county, dealt extensively in the West India and Portuguese trade. He sometimes combined with Galloway, and like him carried on such financial arrangements, including insurance, as in the tobacco trade would have been managed in London, through correspondents in Philadelphia.[72]

In the tidewater country of the Western Shore there

69. *London Magazine,* quoted in Gray, *Agriculture in the Southern United States,* I, 167; see Wyckoff, *Tobacco Regulation,* p. 186.

70. Cunliffe and Sons to Callister, September 9, 1756, Callister to Ellis Cunliffe and Company, April 16, 1759, Callister Papers, Md. Dioc. Lib.

71. Callister to Mr. White, July 22, 1760, *ibid.*

72. Letters in Galloway Papers, NYPL.

was no such agricultural change as on the Eastern Shore; but the settlement of the back country and the rise of iron production around the head of the bay made it possible for some of the independent merchants to trade in other products than tobacco. Dr. Charles Carroll, who had the benefit of one-fifth ownership of the Baltimore iron works, was corresponding all through the decade of the forties with other than British merchants. He invited and carried on at least some trade with Boston, asking Thomas Hutchinson, the future governor, to send him shoe lasts in return for wheat, and suggesting to Edmund Quincy that he accept Maryland tobacco, iron, or grain for such "never failing" commodities as rum, sugar, and molasses, or New England made "joynery," "turnery," and pots. At the same time he was exporting iron, flour, bread, and peas to Barbados, and ordering in return sugar, molasses, limes, ginger, chocolate, and pineapples.[73]

The extensive correspondence of Samuel Galloway with Sylvanus Grove of London testifies to long perseverance in the tobacco trade and to difficulties with it; but it also shows new enterprise in relief of the old. Besides Ringgold, Galloway sometimes combined in business with Joseph Galloway of Philadelphia, he corresponded with merchants of Boston and Charleston, and he operated along every line of Maryland trade. He exported lumber, corn, and pork to Jamaica, Barbados, and other West India islands, "mixed cargoes" of grain and cask staves to Madeira, grain to the variable market at Lisbon, and staves to Cork. The West India and Irish trade seem to have been successful; the Portuguese trade less so. A large credit transferred from Benson of Cork to Grove in 1762 helped restore an account more than £2000 out of balance.[74] In the period of the French and Indian War, both Galloway and Carroll undertook building ships for

73. Letters to C. Carrington (Barbados), December 25, 1742, May 16, 1743, to Hutchinson, April 20, 1743, to Quincy, July 9, 1748, *Md. Hist. Mag.*, XX, 174–175, 268–269, 267; XXII, 375.

74. Grove to Galloway, October 21, 29, 1762, Galloway, Maxcy, Markoe Papers, LC.

sale in London; Carroll had attempted the same thing during King George's War as well. Grove reported little demand or liking for Maryland vessels on the London market, but Carroll's persistence would indicate some degree of success in the venture.[75]

In the forties, while the independent merchants were trying various enterprises, the members of the assembly turned anew to the question of tobacco regulation. For ten years after 1736 the relations between the houses of assembly were so strained that few laws of any sort were passed and tobacco legislation was largely disregarded.[76] But the war period brought hard times and fresh pressure to take such action as would place Maryland's trade on an equal footing with Virginia's. Two or three enemy privateers around the capes in the summer of 1744 set the trade all "acrook," and even well-to-do officials were embarrassed by inability to get credit for their mounting reserves of tobacco.[77] There was a poor crop the next year, and in 1746 Dr. Carroll explained to a London merchant that he could not remit because it was impossible to collect debts in the province. At the close of the year he declared that, "I am too old to run away nor do I know well where to run to, the rice trade is as bad as ours, and I shall want more clothes if I go northward; therefore I hope you will contribute to keep me here a little longer till better times." [78]

In 1743 Daniel Dulany wrote to Lord Baltimore urging tobacco regulation on the pattern of the Virginia inspection system. Such a provision, he said, would prevent the present large crop from depressing the market too much,

75. Dr. Carroll to William Black, January 21, 1746, Carroll, Barrister, to John Hanbury, November 15, 1755, *Md. Hist. Mag.*, XXII, 194–195; XXXI, 307–308; Grove to Galloway, February 28, 1760, Galloway, Maxcy, Markoe Papers, LC.

76. Wyckoff, *Tobacco Regulation*, pp. 160–163.

77. Benjamin Tasker to John Browning, November 20, 1744, Edmund Jennings to Lord Baltimore, August 23, 1744, Calvert Papers, no. 1128, MHS; Callister to Cunliffe, to Charles Craven, August 13, 1744, Callister Papers, Md. Dioc. Lib.

78. Letter to Black, December 4, 1746, *Md. Hist. Mag.*, XXII, 191.

and it should be enacted even though tobacco fees and salaries for officials and clergymen be cut. "Without sound effectual regulations," wrote Dulany, "I am afraid that a great many will be under the unhappy necessity of deserting their habitations, and very few, if any, will come into a country which is on the brink of ruin." [79] By the beginning of the next year Dulany's colleagues in the council had come to agree with him. In a formal petition to Lord Baltimore, which rehearsed the evils of the trade and the competitive disadvantage of Maryland with Virginia, Governor Bladen, Dulany, and the other members of the council urged that concessions be made to the lower house to secure an inspection law.[80] This was the political step which opened the way for passing the inspection law of 1747.

On the side of the lower house and of popular sentiment, the revival of the *Maryland Gazette* by Jonas Green in 1745 must have had much to do with promoting the law. The hard year of 1746 saw the tobacco trade subjected to public discussion, as it had been in 1728 and 1729; but now every statement was penetrated with the thought that Maryland was losing to Virginia. The case for an inspection system was argued in terms of the disadvantage Maryland suffered by producing and marketing low quality tobacco and so being compelled to accept the terms of foreign purchasers. The best, at least, of Virginia tobacco could be sold to British retailers even at the high prices which the import duties required. Earlier shipping, and more careful handling, curing, and pressing were all urged.[81] There was a little opposition to inspection in the newspaper. Opponents said that the expense involved would take up possible advances in price, and particularly that small planters would suffer. One writer calculated that a man with an annual crop of 1,500 pounds

79. Wyckoff, *Tobacco Regulation*, p. 165.
80. February 1, 1744, *Archives*, XXVIII, 308–311.
81. "A. B." *Maryland Gazette*, April 1, October 28, 1746; "Z. Z.," *ibid.*, August 12, 1746; "Mercator," *ibid.*, April 7, 1747; "An Essay on . . . Improving the Trade . . . ," *ibid.*, December 17, 1747.

of tobacco ordinarily had 1,000 pounds of good quality and 500 of second rate, and that he paid about 800 pounds for "rent." Such a planter would have only 200 pounds to sell after an inspection act, or an annual credit of £1 13s. 4d. with which to provide for his family.[82] The predominance of newspaper expression, however, naturally coming from the educated and articulate classes, strongly favored adopting the system.

In keeping with the title of the law as it was finally passed, "An Act for Amending the Staple of Tobacco, for preventing Frauds in his Majesty's Customs, and for the Limitation of Officers' Fees," the launching of an inspection system marked a combined economic and political achievement. The concessions of the upper house represented by the last part of the title show the close connection between economic reform and the political balance of power in Maryland. With some degree of solidarity attained between the houses and indeed compelled by the necessity for reform, the legislature put into effect a stronger measure than merchants and planters acting privately could have accomplished; it was able at last to place the Maryland staple under requirements equal to those of Virginia. The law provided for a system of eighty public warehouses in charge of official inspectors. All tobacco for exportation was required to be brought to one or another of the warehouses, where the inspectors were to give notes for such as they approved, and to have the rest repacked or burned. The notes were to be negotiable instruments, acceptable in all tobacco payments, and they were to serve as money until retired by the final purchaser for exportation. The parish officials, vestrymen and churchwardens, were to make nominations for the positions of the inspectors; and the justices of the peace were to have supervisory authority.[83] Thus the machinery of the law as well

---

82. "Q-in-Corner," *ibid.*, April 28, 1747. The newspaper discussion of the law is reported in Wyckoff, *Tobacco Regulation*, pp. 169–171.

83. Acts, July, 1747, ch. 1, *Archives*, XLIV, 595–638. The law is analyzed in detail in Wyckoff, *Tobacco Regulation*, pp. 174–177; and in Sioussat, *Economics and Politics in Maryland, 1720–1750*, p. 73.

as its enactment involved a new step in self-government, with new and important authority placed in local hands. The original law was reënacted at expiration, in 1753, and was continued until 1770, when, under especially disturbed political conditions, it lapsed for three years.[84]

The continuation of the law is the best indication of its worth, with tobacco inspection and fee limitation considered together. Its economic value in advancing the prosperity of Maryland, however, is far from clear. Tobacco prices rose immediately after the enactment, but they soon declined again.[85] Bad weather in 1752 and 1754, the continued preference for Virginia tobacco in London, and the hazards of the war years all operated against the trade; commercial letters of the middle years of the decade of the seventeen-fifties were quite as troubled as those of the forties.[86] The independent merchant, Dr. Carroll, spoke of the law at the time of enactment as an "ill timed experiment," which might "serve as a South Sea job with some";[87] and Callister, the factor, declared that it operated as it had been conceived, without regard for the merchants or the small planters who came to their stores. It benefited, he said, the people in the assembly: those in the upper house because, although the tobacco fees of

84. See below, pp. 340–358.

85. Wyckoff, *Tobacco Regulation*, pp. 177–179, 194–197, makes a full statement of the evidence for rises shortly after 1747. This accords with tobacco and general price trends in Philadelphia, as does the decline beginning about 1753. See Bezanson, *Prices in Colonial Pennsylvania,* pp. 294, 422.

86. The effects of bad weather are spoken of in the *Virginia Gazette,* August 21, 1752; in letters to Galloway from H. Hall, December 9, and Richard Snowden, December 13, 1754, Galloway Papers, NYPL; in one from Joseph Gowman, December 22, 1754, Galloway, Maxcy, Markoe Papers, LC. Grove made a specific point of English preference for Virginia tobacco in a letter to Galloway, September 11, 1753, *ibid.;* and his letters between 1752 and 1758 speak repeatedly of low prices and depression. Robert Lloyd wrote to James Hollyday, October 20, 1755, of a great scarcity of both corn and tobacco, and of "people almost naked and destitute of money and credit," *Pennsylvania Magazine of History and Biography,* VII (1883), 432. The Callister letters make equal point of hard times.

87. Letter to Black, August 29, 1747, *Md. Hist. Mag.,* XXII, 297.

officers had been reduced, they were also rendered more salable;[88] and those in the lower house because the members were mostly planters selling on consignment to England. Callister added that the inspectors connived with influential planters to let their tobacco of low quality pass.[89] When reënactment was being discussed in the *Gazette* in 1753, the principal difference of opinion fell along the line of advantage and disadvantage between the great planters and the small.[90] The law was continued, but there was much doubt and criticism from many points of view, a condition which war and depression could have done little to allay.[91]

The records do not permit a full statistical view of Maryland trade, but by the middle of the century there are enough figures, from provincial and British sources, to throw some light on the situation. They make plain, first of all, that through the century there was an absolute increase in shipping. Between the period of royal government and the middle of the century, the number of vessels engaged in the carrying trade with the mother country doubled or more than doubled: about 1715, from 70 to 100 vessels were engaged,[92] and in 1749 Governor Ogle

88. Governor Sharpe spoke of the officials' advantage from the tobacco law in a way which supports Callister's opinion. Letter to Calvert, March 12, 1755, *Archives*, VI, 183.

89. Letters to Cunliffe and Sons, July 7, 1751, to Craven, September, 1752 (?), Callister Papers, Md. Dioc. Lib. Stephen Bordley expressed ideas similar to Callister's, in respect both of the disadvantage of small planters and of dishonesty among the inspectors. Letters to William Hunt, 1749, and to Flowerdewe and Norton, October 31, 1750, Stephen Bordley's Letterbook, 1749–1752, MHS.

90. The difference appears in the newspaper controversy between "George Meanwell" and "A Planter," *Maryland Gazette,* April 5, June 7, June 13, 1753.

91. See Sharpe to Calvert, October 20, 1755, *Archives*, VI, 294.

92. Margaret S. Morriss, *Colonial Trade of Maryland, 1689–1715,* JHUS, XXXII (1914), no. 3, p. 87. This chapter was written before the publication of Vertrees J. Wyckoff's series of articles, "Ships and Shipping of Seventeenth Century Maryland," *Md. Hist. Mag.,* XXXIII, 334–342; XXXIV, 46–63, 270–283, 349–361. Wyckoff's figures for the end of the seventeenth century are somewhat larger than Miss Morriss's (see XXXIV, 273), but his materials do not alter the larger aspects of trade as they are discussed here.

reported that 200 vessels, totaling about 12,000 tons and manned by 4,000 seamen, were in the tobacco trade.[93] Governor Sharpe's lower estimates, showing 180 vessels, 10,000 tons, and 3,600 (1,600?) men in 1756, and 120 vessels, 18,000 (?) tons, and 1,700 (1,900?) men in 1760, reflect the hard times beginning in 1753, the damages of war and the costs of depression. Both Ogle and Sharpe reported great increases in Maryland-owned shipping, as we have seen, the largest estimate, that of 1756, showing 60 vessels, 2,000 tons, and 480 seamen.[94] The returns from the provincial duty of fourteen pence per ton, charged on all vessels not owned in the province, show about 17,000 tons in British and other-colony trade, the same at the middle of the century as in 1733, but this figure increased almost 50 per cent in the years shortly before the Revolution.[95]

The record of the export trade in tobacco approximates that of shipping, though with an appreciable lag. The increase from a normal exportation of about 25,000 hogsheads early in the century to 30,000 in the early thirties was small;[96] and for three decades after that the trade seems hardly to have held its own. Slightly over 30,000 hogsheads were exported in 1753,[97] but there were

93. To Board of Trade, December 13, 1749, *Archives,* XXVIII, 468.

94. Sharpe's figures (1756, 1761) do not well agree with Ogle's (1749) or with each other. His estimate of 3,600 seamen in the tobacco trade in 1756, as transcribed in the Board of Trade Papers, is close enough to Ogle's figure of 4,000; but the Maryland copy of the record shows 1,600 seamen, close to his estimate of 1761. Again, Sharpe estimated 10,000 tons for 180 vessels in 1756, but 18,000 tons for 120 vessels for 1760. See Sharpe to Board of Trade, February 8, 1756, January 14, 1762, Board of Trade Papers, Proprieties, XIX, XXI (1), HSP; compare Council Proceedings, August 23, 1756, December 21, 1761, *Archives,* XXXI, 145; XXXII, 23.

95. See Table III, in the appendix, below, p. 381.

96. An increase in the size of hogsheads may have been sufficient to signify an increase in the export which is not indicated by the figures. For figures see Morriss, *Colonial Trade of Maryland,* p. 89; and Table III, in the appendix, below, p. 381.

97. Calvert Papers, no. 596, MHS, quoted by Paul H. Giddens, "Trade and Industry in Colonial Maryland, 1753–1769," *Journal of Economic and Business History,* IV, 521.

fewer than 27,000 in 1756 (in a fiscal year ending at Michaelmas and hardly affected by the war), and in 1762 Sharpe reported 28,000 as normal. The detailed reports on the income from tobacco duties by official "ports" show that the Eastern Shore exported less than one-sixth of the total for the province: only 3,779 hogsheads in 1733, and 4,218 in 1756. On the Western Shore, there were great decreases in the upper bay and the Patuxent areas, in the second quarter of the century; there was an increase in the Potomac area alone. The port of Potomac, where the Scottish factors were so strong, exported 7,615½ hogsheads in 1733, or about one-quarter of the total; and in both 1759 and 1760, the lowest years of record for the province as a whole, it exported more than 8,000 hogsheads, or at least two-fifths of the total. The port of Annapolis, embracing the upper Western Shore, dropped from 13,168½ hogsheads in 1733 to 10,745 in 1753 and 6,720 in 1756; and the port of Patuxent, from 7,105 in 1733 to 5,814 in 1756.[98] The purchasing power of these exportations of course depended on selling prices in England. Governor Sharpe in 1762 selected £5 sterling as the average value, to a Marylander, of a hogshead of tobacco. Thinking of his estimate of 28,000 hogsheads as normal, he reported to the Board of Trade that the staple returned £140,000 annually to the province.[99]

Iron is the only export besides tobacco on which there is any detailed statistical evidence. Figures reported to the House of Lords show that iron was exported from Maryland and Virginia for the first time in 1718, a matter of a few tons only, and that from 1724 to 1731, the annual shipments mounted rapidly, to more than 2,000 tons.[100]

98. All figures in this paragraph not attributed to other sources are taken from accounts rendered by naval officers, in charge of the provincial duties, for the ports and years discussed. Calvert Papers, nos. 912, 914, 947, 948, 949, 950, 951, MHS.

99. Letter to Board of Trade, January 4, 1762, Board of Trade Papers, Proprieties, XXI (1), HSP; see *Archives*, XXXII, 24.

100. Account of iron imported from America, 1710–1749, House of Lords, Manuscripts, LC, Andrews and Davenport, *Guide*, p. 218, item 185.

The Principio Company, the first to produce iron in Maryland, began operations in the lower Susquehanna region in 1715. The company was an association of English investors, apparently Quakers, and it included among its members Joshua Gee, the mercantilist pamphleteer and merchant of Boston, and Stephen Onion, who seems also to have operated privately in Maryland.[101] Before 1729 the Baltimore iron works, owned in partnership by five men prominent in the colony, Benjamin Tasker, Charles Carroll, Daniel Dulany, the elder, Daniel Carroll, and Dr. Charles Carroll, had begun to compete with the Principio Company.[102] Between that time and the Revolution iron works were set up in all the northern counties. The names of the Hampton Furnace on the Monocacy River, Richard Snowden's works on the Patuxent, Onion's works on the Gunpowder, and a Bush River iron works, all survive, but little is known of their history.[103]

Shortly before the British Iron Act of 1750, which prohibited the colonial manufacture of the ore, Dr. Charles Carroll said that there were no laborers able to make even skillets; at the time of the passage of the act, Governor Ogle reported that there was only one plating forge with tilt hammers and that there were no slitting or rolling mills, of the kind forbidden by the statute, in Maryland.[104] The large number of mines and works, how-

---

101. There are 21 documents on the Principio Company in a bound volume, Principio Company, Letters and Deeds, 1723–1730, MHS. They were used by James M. Swank for his treatment in *History of . . . Iron in All Ages* (Philadelphia, 1884), pp. 240–250. The fullest treatment of the subject is Henry Whitely, "The Principio Company," *Pennsylvania Magazine of History and Biography*, XI (1887), 63–68, 190–198, 288–295.

102. Letter of William Smith (?), March 17, 1729, British Museum, Additional MSS. 29,600, LC. An indenture of partnership for the Baltimore Works, 1732, is in Portfolio no. 6, MHS; the operation of the company—the chairmanship of Charles Carroll of Doughoregan, the clumsiness of the five-man partnership, the administrative task of a salaried "clerk"—is to be studied in the Charles Carroll Letters, 1684–1771, LC.

103. Giddens, "Trade and Industry in Colonial Maryland," *Journal of Economic and Business History*, IV, 522–523.

104. To Board of Trade, September 24, 1750, *Archives*, XXVIII, 485.

ever, were now producing considerable iron for exportation. In a special report to the Board of Trade in 1758, Governor Sharpe said that there were eight furnaces and ten forges in Maryland, a few of them built in the last four years. He submitted a summary of production, by tons, as follows:

Year	Pig Iron	Bar Iron
1750	1424	578
1751	3005	622
1752	1390	635
1753	3076	573
1754	1978	534
1755	3331	640[105]

Such amounts equaled one-seventh of the annual production of England; and, as this iron was known for its superior malleable quality, Maryland was able to export 1500 tons annually, or about half the total from all the colonies.[106] At £6 or £7 per ton for pig iron and £15 for bar, profits were attractive enough to invite investment. Individual Marylanders were willing to invest several thousand pounds in capital goods,[107] and they liked to trade in iron. Dr. Carroll greatly preferred it to tobacco, and his son continued with it after he had abandoned the tobacco trade altogether.[108] The figures on production tell little, however, about the net returns of the iron business to Maryland. It may have come to £5,000 annually, but there is too little information about carrying charges and selling prices for a dependable estimate. Whatever

105. Sharpe to Board of Trade, March 16, 1758, Board of Trade Papers, Proprieties, XX, HSP.
106. Giddens, "Trade and Industry in Colonial Maryland," *Journal of Economic and Business History,* IV, 523.
107. Col. Tasker's fifth share in the Baltimore iron works sold for £5200 in 1765, a depression year. *Maryland Gazette,* March 14, 1765. Aside from land, the capital in the Hockley forge and adjacent furnace was valued at £20,755, in "utensils," "improvements," and slaves. Daniel Dulany to George Fitzhugh, 1784(?), Dulany Papers, II, 82, MHS.
108. Carroll, Barrister, letters of 1758, *Md. Hist. Mag.,* XXXII, 179–190, 348–357.

the return, it could have affected only a few individuals, particularly the partners in the Baltimore company, and could have done little to improve the credit of the people of the province.

With respect to the branches of trade leading not to Great Britain but to the other continental colonies, the British West Indies, Madeira, and Lisbon, there are few figures, and none are comprehensive. The "port of entry books," or naval officers' records, which supply a cargo-by-cargo record for the limited periods and place for which they have been preserved,[109] do confirm the impression of a large and growing non-staple trade. Early in the century occasional exchanges, either with the West Indies directly or through New England, brought minor imports of tropical goods to Maryland,[110] but by the seventeen-fifties such exchanges were more than occasional on both shores. For the years 1759, 1761, and 1762, the following number of vessels, which entered at the port of Oxford, indicate the high proportion of diversified trade on the Eastern Shore:

From	1759	1761	1762
Great Britain	5	8	4
New England and New York	14	30	46
West Indies	1	2	4

Similar figures for the port of Annapolis, including Baltimore, for the first six months of 1758 and for the six months following April, 1762, show the following entries:

From	1758	1762
Great Britain	19	7
New England and New York	4	15
West Indies	7	15

Even the port of Patuxent, in the southern tobacco-

109. In the Maryland Historical Society and the Hall of Records. See below, pp. 386, 388.
110. Morriss, *Colonial Trade of Maryland*, pp. 82–83.

raising section, cleared twenty-five or more cargoes of grain each year between 1757 and 1763.

A document of 1753 supplies a summary of the goods exported from Maryland that year, as follows: [111]

Tobacco	30,634 hogsheads
Wheat	110,567 bushels
Corn	154,741 bushels
Pig iron	2,500 tons
Bar iron	600 tons
Bread and flour	6,327 barrels
Pork	430 barrels
Peas and beans	420 barrels
Flaxseed	100 hhds. / 100 bags
Herring	170 barrels
Staves	1,095,500
Shingles	2,000,000

The "port of entry books" show that non-staple products were sent both north and south, principally to New England and the British West Indies, and that there was trade at one time or another with all the continental colonies, possibly excepting Connecticut and Georgia. To those colonies with which trade was light, such as New York, New Jersey, and the Carolinas, the exports were usually grain and lumber, as they were also to Madeira, Lisbon, and Ireland.

The commodities imported by Maryland in the non-staple trade are also indicated in the "port of entry books." The Portuguese trade, including Madeira, returned salt and wine; the West Indies returned a little of

111. Calvert Papers, no. 596, MHS, quoted in Giddens, "Trade and Industry in Colonial Maryland," *Journal of Economic and Business History,* IV, 521. Materials in the Chalmers Papers, Maryland, II, NYPL, give a statistical view of the swing from tobacco to foodstuffs on the Eastern Shore, about 1774. The exports of the section were: tobacco, 8–10 thousand hogsheads; wheat, in grain and flour, 5–6 hundred thousand bushels; Indian corn, 200–250 thousand bushels; oats, 150,000 bushels. Chalmers said that this grain was exported by way of Philadelphia and Chestertown as well as Baltimore.

the same, but chiefly tropical products, namely, sugar, molasses, rum, coffee, cocoa, and chocolate. There were irregular shipments of rice and citrous fruits from South Carolina, of tar, pitch, and turpentine from North Carolina, and of imported manufactures from Virginia. The New England and middle colonies, especially Massachusetts, New York, and Pennsylvania, sent many cargoes of reëxported West India goods, chiefly molasses, sugar, and rum. Such trade had long been practiced, but now New England sent, as it had not early in the century,[112] a variety of colonial goods and British and East India commodities. Shipments from Boston and Rhode Island included fish, blubber, salt, apples, cranberries, cheese, iron ware, wooden ware, pottery, furniture, chaises, axes, brandy, cordials, allspice, gunpowder, and miscellaneous items. The New England and other northern trade was sometimes carried, as occasional entries show, in Maryland vessels, but more frequently in New England vessels or those of the colony in the trade. In the southern and West India trade, on the other hand, Maryland was on the way to be independent of out-of-colony carriers. The entries show that vessels of Maryland build and ownership carried the great share of the south-bound coasting trade.

Totals and values are far from clear in such a widely dispersed and diversified trade, but the estimates of the governors made about the middle of the century amply testify to its growing proportions. In 1748 Governor Ogle estimated that, aside from tobacco, the annual exports of Maryland were worth £16,000 sterling; in 1756 and 1761, Governor Sharpe estimated respectively, £40,000 and £80,000 for the same trade.[113] These estimates include, of course, iron and the minor exports to Great Britain, and a certain transfer of credit from the

112. Morriss, *Colonial Trade of Maryland*, pp. 82–84.
113. Ogle to Board of Trade, December 13, 1749, *Archives*, XXVIII, 469; Sharpe to Board of Trade, February 8, 1756, January 4, 1762, Board of Trade Papers, Proprieties, XIX, XXI (1) HSP; see *Archives*, XXXII, 24.

Portuguese and Irish trade to the British. But most of the non-staple trade is shown in the "port of entry books" to have operated on an intercolonial, not a transatlantic basis. The correspondence of Dr. Carroll with the Boston merchants, and letters to Samuel Galloway from correspondents in Boston, Charleston, Barbados, and Jamaica, moreover, indicate that intercolonial trade in Maryland lumber and foodstuffs took the form of fairly direct exchange. It was arranged according to immediate and local considerations of supply and demand, and it seems to have involved neither long-term credit nor the ultimate movement of purchasing power to the mother country.[114] Such trade supplemented the tobacco trade, making possible increasing importations from other sources than Great Britain. If Governor Sharpe's estimate of £80,000 as the value of non-staple exports is in correct proportion to his estimate of £140,000 as the value of the annual crop of tobacco, the intercolonial trade must have come to be worth about half as much as the tobacco trade at the close of the French and Indian War.

The statistical balance between the credits created by tobacco, iron, the minor exports, and bills of exchange sent to Great Britain, on the one side, and the colonial debts deriving from purchases and charges, on the other, is, like other large aspects of the Maryland trade, a matter of tentative estimate at best. Maryland and Virginia are listed together in a report to the House of Lords to show the value of exports from England to the North American colonies for the period between 1739 and 1764. The figures indicate a rapid expansion of purchasing which accords far better with the growth of the colonial population and civilization than with the state of the tobacco trade. The figures for the two colonies, to the

114. Carroll to Edmund Quincy, July 9, 1748, *Md. Hist. Mag.*, XXII, 374-375; and letters to Galloway from Samuel Hughes, Boston, December 13, 1757, William Potts, Barbados, May 31, 1758, Alexander Rose, Charleston, August 7, 1762, and James Brown, Kingston, October 13, 1762, Galloway, Maxcy, Markoe Papers, LC.

nearest pound sterling, are given for representative years in war and peace, as follows: [115]

	1740	1745	1750	1755	1761
British commodities	187,877	125,088	266,903	211,813	506,710
Foreign commodities	93,552	72,712	82,517	73,344	38,640

What proportion of these purchases went to Maryland and what to Virginia there is no certain way of knowing, but Governor Sharpe's reports, made with the advice of the provincial council and looking back to 1755 and 1761, estimated, respectively, £150,000 and £160,000 as the annual value of Maryland imports from Great Britain.

These figures alone would make it appear that the purchases of the colony exceeded the value of the staple by at least ten per cent, and that the troubles and complaints common to the tobacco trade were based on an economic unbalance difficult if not impossible to correct. Such a condition is even more strongly indicated by the cost of items which were not included in any of the contemporary estimates. Marylanders made invisible purchases such as transatlantic travel and education, which, while applying to only a few, were charged directly against their accounts in England. More important, the province transferred each year, as will be shown in detail later, £10,000 or more in sterling credit to Lord Baltimore, as his proprietary income.[116] It is not clear, moreover, whether contemporary calculations included either the trade in white servants, of whom about five hundred were purchased each year at from £8 to £20 each,[117] or the slave trade, which

115. Customs House report to the House of Lords, February 25, 1766, House of Lords Manuscripts, LC, Andrews and Davenport, *Guide*, p. 236, item 227.
116. See below, p. 144.
117. Statement of Duncan Campbell to House of Commons, 1779, *Md. Hist. Mag.*, XXVII, 265; Sharpe to Calvert, October 20, 1755, *Archives*, VI, 295.

was dwindling to unimportance.[118] No precise statement is possible, but such figures as there are indicate that the bond and burden of colonial debt must have been quite as heavy as the exasperated commercial correspondence of the period suggests.

Neither the unbalance of the trade with Great Britain nor the development of new business in other directions created an attitude in Maryland unfavorable to the structure and purposes of the old colonial system. Regulation under Parliament and Crown, according to the use and practice of the mercantilist age, was taken for granted; and in its larger aspects it was at no time complained against in letter, newspaper, or assembly. At most the revision of minor statute or regulation was requested in Great Britain. At different times the assembly protested against the trade in convict servants, urging Lord Baltimore to permit restriction by import duties; but it was balked because such regulation would have been contrary to parliamentary statute.[119] Between 1730 and 1760 it also asked the privilege of freely importing salt from Europe, which the northern colonies enjoyed. The assembly argued that a lack of salt prevented the growth of a fishing industry, and the lord proprietor carried the matter to the House of Commons, but without effect.[120] As there was no objection to mercantilist principle, so its practice was also honored. The tobacco trade conformed

118. Slaves were occasionally imported from British dealers, and such merchants as Ringgold and Galloway took part in the trade. But Sharpe said that fees in the treasurer's office proved that the trade was decreasing; and the lower house, in contemplating a slave duty, anticipated collection on only 50 slaves a year. This situation contrasts with the early years of the century, when the slave trade was active. Sharpe to Calvert, October 20, 1755, *Archives*, VI, 296; Lower House Journal, March 11, 1756, *ibid.*, LII, 325; Morriss, *Colonial Trade of Maryland*, p. 79.

119. Baltimore to Governor Charles Calvert and assembly, June 8, 1724, Cecilius Calvert to Sharpe, December 23, 1755, *Archives*, XXXV, 212; VI, 328–330.

120. Many assembly addresses and other documents showing anxiety on the point of salt, in *Archives*, XXXVII, XXXIX, XL. There is also material in Portfolio no. 3, MHRecs.

with the "enumeration" policy, and the iron industry with the Iron Act. Until the last decade of the colonial system smuggling was hardly suspected in the province.[121]

Yet trade, and not conformity with regulation, was the life and purpose of the old colonial system. From such a point of view, the long record of depression in tobacco and the efforts and success of Maryland merchants in establishing new business together represent a situation not well in line with the established principles and values of British mercantilism. The new and growing elements in Maryland trade promised neither to supply the mother country with commodities not produced at home, nor to advance her export trade direct to the province, nor to promote her shipbuilding and carrying business. On the other hand, it did promise to bring Maryland closer to the type of the northern colonies, engaged in shipbuilding and carrying, and at least seeming to compete with British business.

A contemporary version of what was happening and might happen appeared as public discussion in the *Maryland Gazette* in 1762. A writer under the appealing pseudonym of "Philopatris" wrote four long columns to prove, in florid language, that so enchanting a mistress as trade should be wooed, because she provided so bountifully for her favorites. A flourishing commerce, he said, would give employment to the people of Maryland, would increase the number of inhabitants, and would raise the prices of commodities and hence the rent and value of land. The government, he concluded, should do everything possible to advance the trade of Maryland.[122]

No one took direct issue with "Philopatris" in that forum of objection, the newspaper, where he presented his case. Another writer, "A Countryman," criticized his argument, indeed, but did so in such a way as to reënforce

121. Ogle to Board of Trade, December 13, 1749; Sharpe to Cecilius Calvert, January 12, 1755, to William Pitt, February 27, 1761, to Earl of Egremont, October 4, 1763, to Earl of Halifax, October 20, 1764, *Archives*, XXVIII, 468; VI, 164; IX, 490; XIV, 118, 182.

122. "Philopatris," *Maryland Gazette*, March 11, 1762.

the case for trade. "A Countryman" said that it was impossible, with tobacco so low, to identify the interests of the planter and landholder with those of the trader. Maryland's disadvantage flowed from commercial dependence rather than independence. The province needed both manufactures and shipping to relieve it from reliance on other-colony carriers and manufacturers. He cited the greatness of Holland in industry and shipping, and contrasted with it the miserable position of Maryland. He resented that Maryland had no choice but to import the "trifling" wooden ware and the "stinking" rum of the north. They were purchased, he said, at the price of the demoralization of the people.[123]

The two arguments represent a very conscious appreciation of the actual trends of the Maryland economy. All contemporary materials support both writers in their sense of the failure or at least the inadequacy of the staple. "Philopatris," when he urged the benevolent activity of the government in support of trade and when he spoke for the landholders, perfectly represented the great planters' interest which had enacted the tobacco inspection law as a step in economic and political self-determination. "A Countryman" took a wider view, a view in conformity with the trend away from tobacco and toward diversification. He urged steps far in advance of those which were being taken; his mind moved toward economic self-sufficiency and independence. How nicely his patriotism for Maryland expressed the spirit which also dominated politics and sentiment will appear and reappear as we approach the Revolution.

123. "A Countryman," *ibid.*, April 8, 1762.

IV

THE PROPRIETARY ELEMENT IN THE
PROVINCIAL SYSTEM

THREE principal conditions bore on the politics of discontentment which led into the revolutionary movement in Maryland. We have already seen something of two: how a powerful impulse for economic reform sprang from depression in the tobacco trade, and how the liberalism of provincial thought supplied a standard for the criticism of established institutions. The third condition was institutional. The provincial form of government, under a lord proprietor, erected an unavoidable set of divisions and differences in the body politic. While political authority was located in England, in the person of Lord Baltimore, and political function, represented by administration, legislature, judiciary, and voters, was located in Maryland, there was bound to be cross-purpose, jealousy, and conflict.

In the large, such difficulties were common to colonial existence. In the whole British American world of the eighteenth century, only Connecticut and Rhode Island were exceptions to the rule that colonial government should operate directly under the supervision of Crown or proprietor, and no colony was free from debate and issue over jurisdictional questions. In 1715, when Maryland's quarter-century of royal government was ended by return to the proprietary system, the province did not revert to the unique character it had held in the seventeenth century. The authority of the lord proprietor was indeed restored, but the proprietor was now Anglican, not Catholic, and the old Catholic clique was permanently driven from preferment and power. Maryland "is administered in the same manner," wrote Governor Hart to the Board of Trade in 1720, "as when I had formerly the

honor to be governor by commission immediately from
the Crown, save that in the enacting of laws, holding of
courts, issuing of process, and granting commissions, the
lord proprietor's name is solely made use of, as was always
done by his lordship's noble ancestors; the Crown having
made no reservation in the grant of the province, the
faith and allegiance of the people, and sovereign dominion
thereof excepted." [1] In the long perspective of Professor
Andrews, likewise, Maryland after 1715 became, with but
few reminders of the seventeenth-century proprietorship,
"to all intents and purposes a royal province." [2]

Yet, in a narrower focus, many features of the Maryland system were distinctive and not common. Proprietary control brought the land system into close connection with the governmental; patronage was centralized;
and oversight from the mother country, in the nature of
the case, was more personal than with the royal colonies.
In the minds of the discontented members of the lower
house, certainly, those who agitated for the transfer of
control to the Crown, there was a vast difference between
proprietary and royal government. To them the proprietorship was expensive, burdensome, and absolutistic,
whereas royal government held out the expectation of
autonomy and benevolence under the protecting rights of
the British constitution. [3]

As to the externals and forms of government, there is
little question; as Governor Hart said, they were much
like those of crown control. The lord proprietor, like the
king, was represented by a governor, to whom he delegated
the exercise of his power and authority. Lord Baltimore's
commission addressed his governor in the same phrase as
the king addressed crown governors, as "trusty and well
beloved"; it stated that, because of the "special trust and
confidence" reposed in the "loyalty, confidence, and fidel-

1. Letter to Board of Trade, August 25, 1720, *Md. Hist. Mag.*, XXIX,
253.
2. Andrews, *The Colonial Period of American History*, II, 376.
3. See below, chs. VII, X.

ity," of the man designated, he had been "nominated, constituted, and appointed," with the approval of the king, as lieutenant governor[4] and chief governor and commander-in-chief, by sea and by land, of Maryland and Avalon. His powers were broadly stated in the commission. In the name of the proprietor he was to call and summon, and to prorogue and to dissolve, the general assembly. He was to assent to laws which were not repugnant to the laws of Great Britain or to the "prerogative royal" of Lord Baltimore, and to transmit them for the confirmation or disallowance of the proprietor. In general, the governor was to exercise all the "powers, jurisdictions, and authorities whatsoever," which the charter of Maryland conferred. The duration of his tenure of office was to be determined at the pleasure of the lord proprietor.[5]

The wide discretion implied in the general phrases of the commissions was not realized in practice, however, for the governor was controlled by detailed instructions from the proprietor. These instructions, although they bore only the lesser seal and the signature of the proprietor, and, lacking the great seal, were less formal and authoritative documents than the commissions, were nevertheless the most important instruments in the official connection between Lord Baltimore and his province.[6] In long in-

4. In Maryland he was always "lieutenant governor," in place of the lord proprietor, to whom the governorship would revert in the event of residence in the province. There was no second officer precisely comparable to the lieutenant-governors in those crown colonies in which there were also governors. On the colonial governor of Maryland see Mereness, *Maryland*, pp. 159-174; and Charles J. Rohr, *The Governor of Maryland, a Constitutional Study*, JHUS, L (1932), no. 3, ch. II. On the commissioning of the royal governors, see Leonard W. Labaree, *Royal Government in America* (New Haven, 1930), pp. 8-11.

5. Most of the commissions extant are from the seventeenth century. That of Governor Eden, August 1, 1768, is printed in *Archives*, XXXII, 274-276. There is a "form of the patent for the appointment of a new governor in Maryland" in the Calvert Papers, no. 295½, MHS. For a list of the MS. commissions and instructions in the one important collection, see *Calvert Papers*, I (Maryland Historical Society, *Fund-Publications;* no. 28, 1889), 64-71.

6. The following is a salutation typical of the proprietary instructions: "Charles absolute Lord and Proprietary of the Province of

structions, such as were given to a governor at the beginning of his administration, and in short ones, which sometimes dealt with such a minor matter as the appointment of a single official, the lord proprietor expressed his will and interest in the province. Some of the instructions were private, to be seen by the governor alone, but many were entered, either at the governor's wish or according to the proprietor's order, in the journal of the provincial council. Such instructions, which tended to repeat each other, represented the fixed policies of the proprietor for his province, and they were cumulative and made to carry over from administration to administration.[7]

The commissions and instructions of the proprietary governors supply a further insight into the similarities and dissimilarities between provincial government in Maryland and in the crown colonies. Although the forms closely paralleled those used by the king, the forces of colonial control, behind the forms, are revealed as differently aligned. Only one authority, the lord proprietor, exercised real responsibility in determining the choice and policy of the governor. In so doing he enjoyed the freedom guaranteed by the most generous of colonial charters, the one granted in 1632 by Charles I to the second Lord Baltimore.[8] He was advised by only one or two officials,

Maryland and Avalon, Lord Baron of Baltimore & ca., Orders & Instructions, Powers & Authorities to be Observed and pursued by our Dearly Beloved Brother the Honorable Benedict Leonard Calvert, Esqre., our Lieutenant Governor of our Province of Maryland, [lesser seal and signature] Baltimore." The document closes with conventional phrases: "Given under our Hand and Seal at London this 30th day of January in the 15th year of our Dominion, anno Domini 1729. [Initialed] C. B." It was countersigned by the proprietary secretary. Calvert Papers, No. 295½, MHS. For the close similarity to crown instructions see Labaree, *Royal Government in America*, pp. 15–16.

7. Instruction of Arthur Onslow and John Sharpe (as guardians of the sixth Lord Baltimore) to Governor Samuel Ogle, June 25, 1751: "You are to conform to all such orders and instructions as were sent to you by the late lord proprietary or . . . to your predecessors . . . as you shall find them entered in the council books insofar as they have not been altered . . . by subsequent instructions." *Archives*, XXVIII, 521.

8. For the most informed comment on the uniqueness of the charter of 1632, see Andrews, *The Colonial Period of American History*, II, 282.

his secretary or secretaries for the province, and perhaps
in this, as in lesser matters, by English merchants trading
to Maryland. Thus the nomination of the governor, and,
after he had been approved by the Crown,[9] the formulation of his instructions and his policy were the business of
an hereditary viceroy with absolute powers. This contrasts
sharply with the situation in the royal colonies. There the
governors were nominated by a secretary of state and
instructed by the Board of Trade; and both of these
authorities were subject to advice and pressure from many
sources, and acted in behalf of a king who had little personal concern in the matter. Whereas royal government
tended to become stereotyped and traditionalized in its
procedure,[10] the proprietorship encouraged Lord Baltimore's personal control of provincial affairs, and was far
more favorable to administrative revision and innovation.

Insofar as the instructions to the governors remain of
record, their increasing frequency during the half-century
before the Revolution indicates that the fifth and sixth
Lords Baltimore and their secretaries tended to undertake
a more and more active supervision of Maryland affairs.
Although documents which would possibly support another view may have been lost, it seems that, during the
first half of his proprietorship, Charles, Lord Baltimore,
who succeeded as a minor in 1715, delegated most of his
authority to his governors.[11] But during the second half
of his proprietorship, from 1733 to 1751 he sent no fewer
than twenty instructions to the governors.[12] He also sent

9. See below, pp. 186–188.
10. Charles M. Andrews, "The Government of the Empire, 1660–1763,"
Cambridge History of the British Empire, I (New York, 1929), 417–420;
Labaree, *Royal Government in America,* pp. 424–427, 446–448.
11. Mereness, *Maryland,* p. 161.
12. Instructions to Governor Samuel Ogle: June 18, 1733, August 10,
1734, May 26, 1735, August 2, 1735, December 14, 1735, *Archives,*
XXXIX, 501–502, 507, 510–511, 512; October 12, 1736, *ibid.,* XXVIII,
142–143; February 22, 1739, Calvert Papers, no. 295½, MHS; February
2, 1740, John Kilty, *The Land-Holder's Assistant and Land-Office Guide*
(Baltimore, 1808), p. 238; January, 1741, Calvert Papers, no. 295½;
August 12, 1741, *Archives,* XXVIII, 256; December 23, 1741, Calvert
Papers, no. 295½. Instructions to Governor Thomas Bladen: March 24,

instructions to and corresponded with other high officials; he interlined and made marginal comments in their letters; and he checked the loyalty of individuals by the reports of others. When the paper-money law was passed in 1733, moreover, he himself accepted designation under the law as supervisor of the trustees of the stock of the Bank of England, which the province purchased as a reserve for the retirement of the money. As most of the other trustees, if not all, were London merchants trading to Maryland, the proprietor was in this way put in a legal and functional connection with other Englishmen who were interested in the province, and who sometimes addressed and advised him on the passing or rejecting of assembly laws which concerned trade and credit.[13] In such ways the reins of provincial supervision and control were tightened in the hands of the lord proprietor. If, in this respect, the achievement of Charles, Lord Baltimore, was less than that of Frederick, his successor, his proprietorship nevertheless set the pattern of strict oversight which lasted to the Revolution.

The high authority of Lord Baltimore, exercised in England, was represented in the province not by the governor alone, but also by his associates in the "Privy Council of State" of Maryland. This body, which was as old as the colony and which was ordinarily called "the council," consisted of about twelve members who were either named by the proprietor or approved by him after nomination by the governor. Under the chairmanship of the governor it served as an executive body, preparing and approving proclamations, hearing and deciding on complaints against local and minor officials, advising the governor

1742, *Archives,* XXVIII, 304; May 12, 1742 and May 28, 1742, Calvert Papers, no. 295½; March 26, 1743, *Archives,* XXVIII, 502–503; August 9, 1743, Calvert Papers, no. 295½; December 2, 27, 1743, *Archives,* XXVIII, 329–330. Instructions to Ogle (second administration): October 4, 1746, *ibid.,* XXVIII, 385; February 6, 1750, Calvert Papers, no. 295½; June 25, 1751, *Archives,* XXVIII, 520–521.

13. Commissioners of the loan office to Baltimore, August 14, 1746, Black Books, II, MHRecs; ten merchants to Lord Baltimore, n. d., Calvert Papers, no. 295½, MHS.

and lord proprietor on whatever matters they might submit, and acting on Indian affairs, military affairs, and miscellaneous matters. The same body also served both as the provincial court of appeals[14] and, without the governor and under the chairmanship of a president, as the upper house of the legislature.

The superior functions of the council in every department of government comprised only one element in the prestige and power of the members. For the council always included around its board the half-dozen officials whose selection by the proprietor direct, whose duties, and whose income, from fees, commissions, salaries, or fines, made them the very great of the land. Thus the deputy-secretary, who kept the records of the court of chancery and of the provincial court, and who had the appointment of the county clerks, was always a member of the council. He acted in the place of the provincial secretary, resident in England, who appointed him, and whose actual duties were to advise and to act in behalf of the lord proprietor in the general supervision of Maryland affairs. After the governor and the deputy-secretary, the greatest provincial officers were the following: the lord proprietor's agent, or receiver-general, who was in charge of the proprietary revenues; the attorney-general; the commissary-general, or judge of probate; and the two judges of the land office, who had charge of issuing warrants for taking up new grants and who settled disputes about tenure. All of these officials were customarily seated in the council. Also of high administrative rank were the five naval officers; they were the appointees of the governor and were the officials who entered and cleared vessels and collected the provincial customs duties. Often one or two of them were made members of the council. The justices of the provincial court and the court of chancery, too, were ranking officials, although not necessarily men of great influence, and were sometimes appointed to the council. The provincial machinery which these great officers

14. Bond, *The Court of Appeals in Maryland*, p. 1.

supervised had grown out of the governmental and tenurial provisions of the feudally conceived charter of Maryland. With the enlargement of the population and the extension of settlement, the combined system of political control and land administration employed, at midcentury, about seventy lesser officials. These men were administrators in the field, appointed by and responsible to the high officials, and in constant contact with the people of the province. Thus the sheriffs, as the chief executive officers of the counties and as the appointees of the governor, had among their duties the proclaiming of meetings of the assembly and of the various orders of the council. Deputy-surveyors and deputy-commissaries in every county executed the detailed functions of the office of their principals, in the first case locating and designating new land grants, and in the second seeing to the proper recording of inheritances. The collectors of the quit-rents and the stewards of the proprietor's manors collected the annual land revenues, in the first instance, and turned them over to the receiver-general for accounting and transmission to Lord Baltimore. Several of the high officials had the assistance of clerks.

Such minor administrators and employees represent, however, no more than one-fourth of the body of men in the proprietary system as a whole. The justices of the peace, who must have numbered more than two hundred in the several counties, were in a legal and constitutional sense as much a part of the proprietary system as were the administrators of the proprietary revenues. Yet we have already seen that, although the judges were the appointees of the governor, their position represented the prestige and dignity of the established families as much as it represented the delegated authority of the proprietor, and that after appointment, they were free from supervision by the governor.[15] There was much the same independence of control from above in the other areas

15. See above, p. 42.

where the Maryland system served the humanitarian, the commercial, and the local purposes of government, as the eighteenth century understood those purposes. Thus the vestrymen of the parishes, the constables, and the inspectors of tobacco, under the machinery of the law of 1747, were in a position like that of the justices of the peace, more influenced by the community than by the hierarchy of proprietary power.

In spirit and in interest, then, if not in law, the proprietary system in Maryland was a divided thing. The great officials at the top, appointed by the lord proprietor and directly instructed by him,[16] moved in an area defined by their positions: they were the guardians of the land system and of the lord proprietor's revenues; they were the keepers of order in a province where quit-rents, fees, fines, and duties were sacrosanct. Their dominating interest and connection was always and inevitably with Lord Baltimore in England, and they were known in the province as the "court" and the "proprietary family." And in literal truth, the family element was important. Calverts and the relatives of Calverts, such as Governors Bladen and Eden, and their relatives, and the relatives of their

16. Only a few of the proprietor's instructions to other officials than the governor are extant. There are, however, enough instructions to the agents to show that they were sometimes long and detailed, and, like those of the governors, were cumulative: instructions of 1722, Calvert Papers, no. 278, MHS; of 1733, 1735, 1736, *Archives*, XXXIX, 503–504, 508–513; of 1753 and 1756, Portfolio no. 3, MHRecs. There are also instructions to the secretaries, 1717, 1721, 1722, 1724, Kilty, *Land-Holder's Assistant*, pp. 226–229; and 1733, *Archives*, XXXIX, 504–506; to the judge of the land office, 1733 and 1735, Kilty, *Land-Holder's Assistant*, pp. 232–234, 236; *Archives*, XXXIX, 504–506, 509–510; to the surveyors-general, 1733, *ibid.*, XXXIX, 502–503; to the commissary-general, 1733, *ibid.*, XXXIX, 503; and to the receivers of quit-rents, 1733, *ibid.*, XXXIX, 506. The final development of proprietary instructions to the lesser officials came with the establishment of the board of revenue, 1768; see below, pp. 268–269; and *Archives*, XXXII, 420–440. The council as a body did not receive instructions, but the governor's instructions which were entered in its record book, as they determined the policy of the proprietary interest, amounted to instructions to the council as a whole.

relatives, such as the Taskers and the Dulanys, were seated for decades in the council.[17] Such associations and connections made the great of the council a kind of clique or club, to which the outsider was quite foreign.

The character of the "proprietary family," however, was of a sort to put relations within it on a basis which was materialistic enough. There is testimony from a half-century before the Revolution that loyalty in office flourished substantially in proportion to benefits and to expectation of benefits. In 1729 Governor Calvert wrote to his brother, the proprietor, that it was difficult to persuade such men as would be "of much credit and use" to join the council if they were not also appointed to high office;[18] and in 1734 a new councilor wrote a relative that he had been given "several posts of honour but few of profit," as the latter were generally given "to such as can strongly solicit and make large promises."[19] Such cynicism was natural within the circle of the hierarchy, where personal influence and financial interest were the essence of power.

In the local offices, on the other hand, where the connection with the proprietor was merely formal, and where the connection with the people and the conditions of Maryland was continuous, there is no hint of demoralization. The justice of the peace, as a member of the gentry with an aristocratic point of view, might not have quar-

17. Bladen and Eden were the brothers-in-law, respectively, of Charles and Frederick, the fifth and sixth Lords Baltimore. Governor Benedict Leonard Calvert was a brother of Charles, and Benedict Calvert, a councilor in the sixties, was his illegitimate son. Benjamin Tasker, councilor from 1722 to 1768 and president of the council for thirty-two years, was the son of a minor official, the son-in-law of a great official, a brother-in-law of Governor Bladen, and the father-in-law of Governor Ogle and of the younger Daniel Dulany. The provincial secretaries in England all seem to have been relatives of the proprietors. For genealogical information, see *Md. Hist. Mag., passim*, and in this connection, especially the work of J. C. B. Nicklin on the Calvert family (XVI, 50–59, 189–204, 313–318, 389, 394), and of Christopher Johnson on the Bladen and Tasker families (IV, 191–192; V, 297–299).

18. Letter of October 26, 1729, *Archives*, XXV, 609.

19. Richard Tilghman to Abraham Tilghman, July 2, 1734, *Md. Hist. Mag.*, XXXIII, 156.

reled with the phrase of the governor who said that the
purpose of government was "an authoritative influence
for the good order of society." [20] But he would have
thought of the "good order of society" in different terms
from the governor. To him and to his kind, administration
meant the rule of English law, interpreted by Marylanders, and to him it carried no overtones, as to the
hierarchy, of proprietary superiority and power.

The special interests of the high proprietary officials,
mirroring their connection with Lord Baltimore and his
own attitude toward the province, were such as to give
them a place like that of the politically powerful in England. [21] "The Duke of Newcastle is run hard in the political warehouse in Britain," the provincial secretary and
uncle of the sixth Lord Baltimore once wrote, "and in
miniature I with Maryland." [22] The control of revenues
and of patronage made the Maryland system, to those
high in executive power, something more and other than a
mechanism for government and land administration. In
their opportunity the system became more and more a
valued set of financial and social privileges, a thing to be
prized for itself and to be guarded by the ample protection of the authority of the lord proprietor. In modern
terms it was a system of corruption, but in terms of
eighteenth-century England it was the normal thing in
an established aristocratic society. [23]

Incomparably the greatest beneficiaries of the Maryland system were the lords proprietors themselves. Their
long-range policy was well expressed in the instructions of

20. Calvert to Baltimore, October 26, 1729, *Archives*, XXV, 605.

21. The remainder of this chapter closely follows the writer's two
articles, "Property Rights in the Provincial System of Maryland," the
first with the subtitle, "Proprietary Policy," and the second, "Proprietary Revenues," *Journal of Southern History*, II (1936), 43–68, 211–232.
Professor W. H. Stephenson has kindly granted permission to use them.

22. Cecilius Calvert to Governor Sharpe, December 12, 1754, *Archives*,
XXXI, 472.

23. For an admirable analysis of the English situation, see L. B.
Namier, *The Structure of Politics at the Accession of George III*
(London, 1929).

Charles, Lord Baltimore, in 1743, to Governor Bladen. Thus formally the governor was ordered to reject any bill, from the lower house of assembly, which would reduce the "just fees and perquisites of officers" or the permanent appropriation for the support of the government. In 1751 the governor who succeeded Bladen had the same instructions entered in the proceedings of the council as still binding, and two years later, Frederick, the new Lord Baltimore, gave instructions to Governor Sharpe with exactly the same purpose.[24] These instructions, the official acts of the two men whose proprietorships spanned the half-century between the restoration of proprietary government and the very eve of the Revolution,[25] were sufficient to guarantee to the proprietary element its vested interests and incomes, no matter how vigorously or with what economic and political justice they might be attacked by bills passed by the legislature.[26] Another indication of the proprietor's interest is to be found in a letter of 1754 from Frederick, Lord Baltimore, to Governor Sharpe. It contained an order for the annual payment of £100 from the land office to a Mr. John Wogan of Middle. Temple, because "he is a gentleman for whom I have a

24. Instructions to Bladen, March 26, 1743, entered in the Council Proceedings, March 14, 1751, *Archives*, XXVIII, 502–503; instructions to Sharpe, March 30, 1753, MS., Portfolio no. 2, MHRecs. On January 30, 1730, Charles, Lord Baltimore, ordered Governor B. L. Calvert to allow no act to pass reducing the incomes of the clergy of the established church (*Archives*, XXV, 520).

25. The eighteenth-century proprietors were: Benedict Leonard Calvert (1715), Charles Calvert (1715–1751), Frederick Calvert (1751–1771), and Henry Harford (1771–1776). The Calverts were, respectively, the fourth, the fifth, and the sixth and last Lord Baltimore; and Harford was the illegitimate son and heir but not the inheritor of the title of Frederick Calvert. Much information about the lords proprietor is contained in the MS. notes of the late Charles Weathers Bump, editor of the Baltimore *Sun*, now deposited in the vaults of the Maryland Historical Society. Mr. Bump collected many materials in England, but never wrote them into a book. For biographical sketches, see: John G. Morris, *The Lords Baltimore* (Maryland Historical Society, *Fund-Publications;* no. 8, 1874), pp. 44–59; Clayton C. Hall, *The Lords Baltimore and the Maryland Palatinate* (Baltimore, 1902), pp. 142–144, 162–167; *Dictionary of National Biography*, III (New York, 1886), 268.

26. See below, chs. VII, X.

very great regard; 'tis a great happiness to men of power here in England that they can always oblige their personal acquaintances, whereas the great distance of Maryland from this part of the world confines the gift of places to a very few persons." [27] The natural interest of the Lords Baltimore, then, was property-minded and conservative; and they, as individuals, were far from having the industry and the vision, which a Lord Shelburne might have exercised, to study Maryland, to grasp the meaning of assembly opposition, and to make concessions. Administrative arrangements they changed with some freedom, but their attitude was always cast in the proprietary mind and interest.

The translation of attitude and interest into a detailed policy was accomplished by 1733, that is, eighteen years after the restoration of proprietary government and at the time of the visit of Charles, Lord Baltimore, to Maryland. That this was not achieved earlier was due to a number of circumstances. In England, Charles had succeeded to the proprietorship in 1715, while still a minor; his affairs had had to be managed a few years by guardians; and important decisions seem to have awaited his own control and to have depended on his initiative. And in Maryland, the quarter-century of crown government had, by giving the lower house of assembly a new degree of authority and an increased sense of its own importance, injected an element of uncertainty into any plans of the executive which were in the least subject to criticism or interference by the legislature. Further, by about 1725 the increasing need for tobacco laws and for the issue of paper money became so compelling as to give the House of Delegates a powerful leverage in legislative bargaining with the lord proprietor and the governor and the council.[28] With economic distress and political agitation, all things seemed insecure, even the roots and foundations of proprietary government.

27. Letter of December 3, 1754, *Archives*, VI, 127.
28. See below, pp. 215–218.

With a point of view which was determined by the uncertainty of affairs, Governor Benedict Leonard Calvert in 1729 wrote a twenty-three page letter to Lord Baltimore, his brother. In it he described the state of affairs in Maryland; and he was especially careful to explain what the financial stakes of the proprietary element were, and, in view of commercial depression, what their condition.[29] As this letter represents the first systematic consideration of proprietary policy as a whole, and as important decisions were soon to be made with evident reference to its recommendations, it must be considered as a landmark in provincial history.

According to Governor Calvert, the most important question, from the proprietary point of view, was that of securing adequate returns from Lord Baltimore's right to quit-rents from all the land patented in Maryland. Since 1671, no quit-rents had been paid as such, but, under an act of that year, the lord proprietor had been granted an equivalent for quit-rents in the form of a twelve-pence-per-hogshead duty on all tobacco exported from the province; [30] he had been remitted the returns from this duty as fully during the period of crown government as when he himself held political control. With the succession of Charles, Lord Baltimore, the act of 1671 had expired, and in 1717, a new equivalent duty had been passed, this time with a provision of two shillings per hogshead instead of one. But the new law had been made a temporary one, and its continuation depended on assembly action every few years. The case of the quit-rent equivalent in politics—a question which made proprietary revenues in some degree subject to the legislature—seriously troubled the governor, who wanted to have the law perpetuated. As he estimated the quit-rents to be worth a maximum of six

29. Letter of October 26, 1729, *Archives,* XXV, 601–610.
30. In certain cases some few quit-rents continued to be paid while the equivalent law was in operation. The duty compensated the proprietor for alienation fines as well as quit-rents. On quit-rents in this period, see Beverly W. Bond, *The Quit-Rent System in the American Colonies* (New Haven, 1919), pp. 179–181.

thousand pounds sterling, gross, but as likely to yield a good deal less than that, net, he seems to have thought that Lord Baltimore would neither gain nor lose much, financially, whether the equivalent were continued or the payment of quit-rents resumed. He argued, however, that, of the two, the duty was much easier for the proprietor to collect, and that it was also less burdensome for the smaller planters of the province to pay. His discussion carried the thought that, whichever the decision, something different from the prevailing uncertainty in the matter must be achieved.[31]

His second concern, also a grave one, was for the fate of another revenue in the control of the lord proprietor. This too was a tobacco duty, a duty of fifteen pence per hogshead, the income of which was largely assigned to the payment of the governor's salary. Calvert called Lord Baltimore's attention to the fact that the present duty had been incorporated in the same temporary law of 1717 as renewed the quit-rent equivalent, and that it took the place of a long-term twelve-pence-per-hogshead duty passed in 1671, along with the first quit-rent equivalent. The two duties of 1717, considered together, with their rates favorable to the lord proprietor,[32] had represented strong political bargaining power in Lord Baltimore's hands while he had quit-rents to exchange with a lower house which definitely preferred the equivalent duty. But now that the delegates were changing their minds, and were prepared to let the equivalent expire and have the quit-rents resumed, the governor saw his salary in danger.

The people [he complained] are but too sensibly apprized, that [the support of the government] is in their own free choice, to the which you cannot oblige them. And surely it is the greatest advantage that can be had over a government, and things can never go well in the plantations, whilst the planters are so generally proud, petulant, and ignorant,

31. Calvert to Baltimore, October 26, 1729, *Archives,* XXV, 604.
32. The stated reason for the higher duties was the increase in the size of hogsheads, a change which reduced the number exported.

and have the common necessary support of government so much under their thumb. The superiority, as I may term it, of the people over the government, seems unnatural, and is, I am sure, repugnant to the very ends for which government was instituted, viz., an authoritative influence for the good order of society.[33]

After a careful examination of the history of the duty, however, the governor raised the question, hopeful to his interest, whether or not there might not be statutory grounds for continuing to collect twelve pence per hogshead for the support of the government even after the expiration of the present fifteen-pence law. He pointed out that unlike the original quit-rent equivalent, the government duty, although appropriated for an equally long period, had not been assigned to the proprietor during the period of crown government. At first temporarily in 1692 and then permanently in 1704, the assembly had diverted from the proprietor to the queen the shilling per hogshead for the support of the government. Since the duty of 1704 was passed without limitation as to time, and since the act of 1717 was temporary and therefore effective as a repeal of and substitute for the 1704 duty only for the period of its own life, Governor Calvert hopefully pressed the question whether or not, in the event of failure to renew the duty of 1717,

any and what use may be made in your [lordship's] favor of that act of 1704, settling one shilling on the queen, her heirs, and successors, for the support of her government for the time being in this province. Whether by the devolution of government to you, with other rights and adjuncts of government, that one shilling may in any legal sense be deemed to have devolved on you, or be invested in you and for the same purposes.[34]

In view of what followed—namely, that after 1733 the

33. Calvert to Baltimore, October 26, 1729, *Archives,* XXV, 605.
34. Letter to Baltimore, October 26, 1729, *ibid.,* XXV, 607.

lords proprietors always collected the shilling duty on the basis of the act of 1704, that they did so in face of repeated charges of illegality from the lower house,[35] and that their defense lay in elaborate legal argument [36]—the anxiety and the fears of Governor Calvert in 1729 indicate that the proprietary element was not always confident of the sufficiency of the prerogative, and that fresh confidence was bred in the half-century before the Revolution.

The third question affecting the interests of the proprietary element which was open in 1729 was, in the words of the governor, that of "the settlement and rights of the several offices of government." Officials in Maryland were largely paid in fees, and the amount of those fees and the efficacy with which they were collected concerned not only the officials themselves but also and almost equally the lord proprietor. As the giver of offices, he wanted them to attract men of rank and ability and to be of value to his favorites. In 1729 the situation was as confused as possible, for Lord Baltimore had recently disallowed an act reducing fees, and, though by so doing he had prevented the legislature from cutting the value of the offices, he had also denied the officials any statutory basis for collecting what fees they could, since the previous fee law, that of 1719, had expired. Lacking the law, Governor Calvert reported, "the officers are without execution for their fees. . . . Every insolent fellow thinks himself free to refuse payment, and browbeat, as it were, the officers. And it is besides a continual bone of contention, and a specious handle to amuse the ignorant." [37] Without a reduction of the old rates a new law would be almost impossible to obtain, the governor feared; and a reduction, if allowed, would surely lead to others until the officers of the prov-

35. Beginning in 1739. See below, pp. 225–232, and *passim*.
36. For a review of the history of the 1704 duty, see Mereness, *Maryland*, pp. 344–347. The fullest contemporary history is in the principal defense, Daniel Dulany, the younger, *The Right to the Tonnage: the Duty of Twelve Pence per Hogshead on all exported Tobacco, and the Fines and Forfeitures in the Province of Maryland* (Annapolis, 1766).
37. Letter to Baltimore, October 26, 1729, *Archives*, XXV, 607.

ince would ultimately find themselves paid at the level of common writing clerks. But in the matter of the fees, as well as in that of the government duty, Governor Calvert conceived a plan which would release the proprietary element from dependence on the decisions of the assembly. Observing that, in the past, fee laws had been acts for the limitation of preëxisting fees, never for the creation or granting of new fees, he ventured the opinion that fees were due "by original right without an establishment by law," and so could be established anew by mere prerogative action. But such was not the common understanding in Maryland, and Governor Calvert, who had been instructed that fees should be collected according to the rates of the act of 1719, lacked the authority or the courage to act on his idea. In writing to Lord Baltimore he merely asked the question whether or not such power as he suggested could be exercised by proprietary authority alone, and said that for the present he could do little.[38] He made it clear, however, that an arrangement ultimately satsfactory to the proprietary element would depend on independent action.

Altogether then, in 1729, a full decade after Lord Baltimore had taken the control of Maryland from his guardians, his property interests in the province were in an uncertain if not a perilous condition. On what terms would his right to quit-rents be converted into actual money? Would the unquestioned right of the officials to fees be realized in such a way as to promote the dignity and independence of the provincial administration, or would it be demoralized, or made dependent on the legislature? Would the governor continue to receive a salary paid from a permanent duty, or would he have to wait for appropriations by the assembly? All these questions were open, and open at a time when the tobacco trade was seriously depressed, when tobacco legislation, which, because it affected the value of the tobacco currency, gave

38. October 26, 1729, *ibid.,* XXV, 607–608. On the fee issue see Mereness, *Maryland,* pp. 373–400; and Osgood, *American Colonies in the Eighteenth Century,* III, 22–25.

opportunity and reason for new fee legislation, was pending, and when the lower house of assembly, "as hot as possible about the English statutes and judges' oath [controversy]" and well indoctrinated with the Whiggish ideas of Daniel Dulany, the elder, "certainly entertained strange and unreasonable jealousies and prejudices against your lordship's government." [39] The letters from Maryland telling Lord Baltimore of these difficulties were anxious to a degree, and doubtless led him to take the steps he did to put the provincial house in order.

In December, 1732, he came to Maryland for a visit of six months, the only visit in the eighteenth century by a proprietor to the province. He had recently replaced Governor Calvert with Governor Samuel Ogle, who wrote back that Calvert was desperately ill, in considerable measure, probably, because of his difficulties in dealing with the assembly. [40] The situation called for decisive action, and Baltimore's visit became the occasion for establishing the main lines of proprietary policy to last to the Revolution. He came, it is true, at a time when the boundary dispute with the Penns had reached an acute stage, and partly for that reason. But the greater problems to which he attended were internal, the financial ones with which the success and stability of government on a proprietary basis were so closely linked.

As to quit-rents, he made no such effort as Governor Calvert had suggested to secure the passage by the legislature of a new tobacco duty equivalent. Instead, he launched a program for the normal collection of quit-rents from the freeholders, as before 1671. In one proclamation he encouraged western settlement by granting exemption from the payment of purchase money and of the first three years' quit-rents to those who would take up the land,

39. Governor Samuel Ogle to Lord Baltimore, January 10, 1731, *Calvert Papers*, II, 82.

40. *Ibid.* Calvert died at sea in June, 1732, and he was eulogized by two poets. One spoke of his charm and cultivation, especially his classical learning, and the other described him as a martyr exhausted by his duties in office. W. B. Norris, "Some Recently-Found Poems on the Calverts," *Md. Hist. Mag.*, XXXII, 120–128.

where the Germans were just beginning to penetrate. In another proclamation he raised the quit-rent rate from four to ten shillings on new land in the settled area.[41] He also gave a series of instructions to the officials assigned to the renewed tasks of keeping the records and collecting the revenues from land.[42] Thus, beginning in 1733, when the last equivalent duty law expired, the quit-rent system was reëstablished. It became, in the forty years before the Revolution, the most effective of such systems in the American colonies.[43]

In respect of the governor's salary and the officers' fees, Lord Baltimore acted exactly in line with the suggestions of Governor Calvert. At a council meeting held towards the close of the visit, with the lord proprietor himself presiding, it was ordered that the twelve-pence-per-hogshead duty act, passed in 1704 "for settlement of an annual revenue upon her majesty's governor," be recorded in the council proceedings and be separately printed, and that copies be sent to the naval officers, who would collect the duty, to be "affixed" in their offices; and it was further ordered that the law be bound up with the laws of the current session of the legislature, and sent with them to the several counties.[44] Thus easily, by an act of proprietary authority, as far as appears without any question of its fitness and legality, was settled the question so important in provincial history and so alarming to Governor Calvert, whether or not the governor should have a salary from a fixed source outside the control of the legislature.[45] The

41. March 2, June 20, 1733, *Archives*, XXVIII, 25–26, 45–46.
42. June 18, 1733, *ibid.*, XXXIX, 501–506; Bond, *Quit-Rent System*, pp. 188–189.
43. *Ibid.*, pp. 188, 189. The proprietor seems never after 1733 to have been much interested in a renewal of the equivalent. In December, 1735, he instructed Governor Ogle to consider, but not to enact, any equivalent duty bill not too burdensome on his majesty's trade, and to forward it to him (*Archives*, XXXIX, 512). He placed the same restriction on Governor Bladen in 1743 (Calvert Papers, no. 295½, MHS).
44. April 10, 1733, *Archives*, XXVIII, 27–30.
45. To compare with the salary arrangements in the crown colonies, see Labaree, *Royal Government in America*, ch. VIII.

parallel and related question, that of a settlement of the officers' fees, was managed with equal directness, and concluded to the equally complete satisfaction of the proprietary element. When the legislature failed, now in Lord Baltimore's presence as it had earlier, to enact a satisfactory fee law,[46] he issued the famous fee proclamation of 1733.[47] Expressed as though the sole purpose of the proprietor were to protect his people from extortionate charges, the proclamation fixed officers' fees at rates acceptable to the proprietary element. Like the bold revival of the act of 1704, the fee proclamation was an aggressive step in behalf of the security and standing of established authority in Maryland. It removed the matter of fee payment from common dispute, and it postponed any question of the statutory reduction of fees until the lower house should find a *quid pro quo* in terms agreeable to the officials and the proprietor of the province.[48]

The three decisions—that about quit-rents, that about the governor's salary, and that about fees—made of Lord Baltimore's visit a time of orientation in proprietary policy. If, before his coming, questions of right were open and problems of administration were unsolved, after his departure rights were declared and administrative arrangements were provided. The putting into actual execution of the decisions of 1733 was to form the main business of the provincial administration until the death of Lord Baltimore, in 1751. His correspondence shows that he required the execution of his policy substantially as formulated at the time of his visit. Although he allowed some changes in detail during his proprietorship, and there were to be many more during that of his son, at no time before the Revolution were the decisions of 1733 seriously altered, nor was there ever again to be an equally important reconsideration of proprietary policy.

Generally speaking, the administration of proprietary

46. Upper House Journal, March 24, 1733, *Archives,* XXXIX, 13.
47. April 14, 1733, *ibid.,* XXVIII, 31–43.
48. See below, pp. 220–221, 235–236.

finances up to the mid-century seems to have been successful. No new arrangements had to be made to care for either the collection of the 1704 duty or the receiving of the officers' fees. The first naturally fell to the naval officers, who collected all the provincial duties and to whom the new duty was no different from the old; and the second was the duty of the sheriffs, who were accustomed to collect the fees in tobacco as they also collected the parish and county charges assessed in the annual rates. But there was inevitably much work to be done before the collecting of the land revenues could be effectively executed. The administration of quit-rents required clear titles, accurate records, and a capable and loyal personnel; and none of these conditions applied in 1733. Slowly, through a period of years, however, legal snarls as to title were straightened out; a decision was reached to abandon the advanced quit-rent rate and to retain the traditional four shillings per hundred acres; the exact annual payments of individual freeholders were determined; and farmers and receivers of quit-rents were put to work. The essential problem was the' difficult one of adjusting a traditional English land system, which was feudal in derivation and feudal in character, to the actualities of a dynamic and self-conscious colony. The details of this adjustment have been painstakingly worked out by Professors Gould and Bond,[49] and they need not detain us here. The striking thing, as Professor Bond demonstrates, is that a successful system of collecting quit-rents was put into effect at all. Under Lord Baltimore's instructions a body of minor officials— the rent-roll keepers and the receivers and farmers of the quit-rents—was organized, apart from the government proper and independent of any control by the legislature, and to this body were assigned the exclusive duties of perfecting the records and receiving the quit-rents. Responsibility was assured by placing the governor over the of-

49. Gould, *The Land System in Maryland;* and Bond, *The Quit-Rent System,* pp. 188–189. All writers on land questions of this period owe much to Kilty, *The Land-Holder's Assistant.*

ficials, with appointive and supervisory powers. Thus the Maryland system achieved its unique effectiveness. And, as it preserved the features of a medieval form of land tenure, the system stands as a peculiarly appropriate emblem of the conservatism and property-consciousness of the eighteenth-century proprietors.

What was the actual worth of the interest which was so centrally the object of proprietary policy? What sums did the proprietary revenues involve, both those which needed protection from the assembly and those which were beyond attack? Were the financial privileges of the lords proprietors and of the high officials in Maryland great enough to have social and economic significance? In so far as such questions are subject to answer, they will contribute to an understanding of both proprietary purposes and provincial opposition. They will throw whatever light financial fact is capable of throwing on the struggle for constitutional superiority in the colony.

The most important figures in the matter come from a broken series of annual accounts, the so-called "accounts current," rendered by the agent or receiver-general to the lord proprietor. They are almost complete for 1731 and 1733, and, after a hiatus, they may be made so for eighteen of the years, ending at Michaelmas, between 1747 and 1775.[50] The accounts show, first, the main categories of Lord Baltimore's private revenues from Maryland. They were three in number: the income from land, the income from the permanent customs duties, and the

50. The Calvert Papers, nos. 912, 914, 922, 927, 932, 935, 939, 955, 956, 960, 963, 977, 1028, 1030, MHS. The original accounts are for the years 1731, 1733, 1748, 1752, 1753, 1754, 1755, 1757, 1758, 1759, 1760, 1761, 1773, and 1774, and for the periods from November 30, 1769, to September 4, 1771, and from September 4, 1771, to Michaelmas, 1773. Statistics in these accounts are supplemented by others collected by George Chalmers, the contemporary historian who resided for a time in Maryland. Chalmers' figures, which are for the period from October, 1762, to September, 1771, apparently were taken from "accounts current," most of the originals of which are no longer of record. Where they are for the same items as in the remaining originals, the two agree perfectly. They are to be found in manuscript in the Chalmers Papers, Maryland, II, NYPL.

income from minor sources.[51] The accounts also supply substantial information about the actual sums collected in Maryland, and transferred to the proprietor and his subordinates in power.

The largest returns to the proprietor derived, of course, from the land system. As feudal tenant-in-chief of all Maryland, paying the king but two Indian arrowheads each year, Lord Baltimore enjoyed all the revenues from granting and renting land, as fully as the Crown in the royal colonies. These revenues fell into four kinds, namely, in order of amount, the quit-rents, the returns from the land office, which were derived chiefly from caution (purchase) money payments for freeholds newly granted, manor rents, and alienation fines. In 1731 and 1733 the quit-rent equivalent produced, respectively, £5,204 and £6,515 sterling for Lord Baltimore. During the interval between the colonial wars, for which we again have figures, the restored quit-rent system produced about the same amount, for example, £5,752 in 1753. There were variations during the French and Indian War; and they were followed by a fairly steady product of between £7,000 and £7,500 at the close of the colonial period.[52] The returns from the land office to Lord Baltimore varied from a low of £661 in 1733 to a high of £6,114 in 1761; most of the years of record produced from £1,500 to £2,500 from this source. Manor rents were inconsiderable before the mid-century, and from that time produced about £1,000 yearly until the last three or four years of the proprietorship.

51. There is a summary description of the proprietors' revenues in John V. L. McMahon, *An Historical View of the Government of Maryland, from its Colonization to the present day* (Baltimore, 1831), pp. 169–182. For a precise and full statement of the revenues the agent was expected to collect, to disburse, and to remit to Lord Baltimore, see the instructions drawn up by the board of revenue for Bennet Allen, June 30, 1768, *Archives*, XXXII, 400–407. There is a description of the system of collecting revenues in Kilty, *Land-Holder's Assistant*, pp. 258–262.

52. For a full representation of the income from land revenues, as far as they can be determined, see Table II, in the appendix, below, p. 380.

The fines paid on the occasion of the alienation of land ordinarily yielded from £130 to £200 each year.

All types considered, the land revenues represented a very great interest. Certain fluctuations in yield, especially from the land office, reflect the influence of large factors in colonial life. Rises in this category about the mid-century coincided with periods of peace and with the rapid settlement of the outlying areas; declines coincided with the active periods of the French and Indian War; and the final dropping off conformed with the rapid reduction of free land east of the proclamation line of 1763. But behind the fluctuations there is apparent a general upward trend in the land revenues, and particularly in the permanent return from freeholds, the quit-rents—a trend which represents the steady growth of the population and the occupation of more land. Thus, in return for the privilege of being the tenant-in-chief of Maryland, the lord proprietor received, during the years from 1768 to 1774, inclusive, an average annual income of £10,267, net, in sterling exchange payable in London. This was about two-thirds more than in 1733, when the equivalent duty was abandoned in favor of restoring the quit-rents.

The second great category of the lord proprietor's private revenues consisted of the income of two permanent duty laws. The first was the twelve-pence-per-hogshead duty on exported tobacco, which had been enacted in 1704 for the support of the government, then under the Crown, and which had been assumed by the lord proprietor for his own government in 1733; and the second was the so-called port, or tonnage, duty of 1661. As originally passed, the act of 1661 had required a payment of gunpowder, for the defense of the province, from each vessel entering and clearing in a Maryland port, vessels owned in the province alone excepted. By custom the payment had early been commuted to money, at fourteen pence per ton, and it came to be collected by the naval officers for the proprietor's own use. This change the Privy Council itself had confirmed, during the period of royal government; it had assigned the proceeds of the tonnage duty to Lord Baltimore as a part of his private income from Maryland,[53] like the revenue from the quit-rent equivalent. The income from these two duties together amounted to about one-third or two-fifths of the income from the land system. Up to the French and Indian War they produced something near or under £2,500 per year. Between the war and 1775 the tonnage duty, which was transferred direct to Lord Baltimore, yielded never much more or much less than £1,400; the tobacco duty, under the proprietor's control but assigned to the governor, produced about an equal amount, but was subject to greater fluctuations from year to year.[54]

The third general category of the proprietary revenues, namely, the minor revenues, derived from a number of incidental sources. There were the fines, forfeitures, and amercements collected in the law courts, and the fees paid for ferry licenses and rangers' commissions. Such revenues produced from a very few pounds to £200 or more each year. The proprietary accounts do not indicate that any returns ever accrued from fees for pilots' licenses or from such royal perquisites, to which Lord Baltimore had full rights, as waifs, deodands, treasure trove, and the like.[55]

The considerable fluctuations in the minor revenues are not easy to explain; they most probably represent activity and inactivity on the part of the officials who collected them. Fluctuations in the tobacco and tonnage duties, on the other hand, moved in exact proportion with the flow of trade. Like the land revenues the income from the duties

53. *Acts of the Privy Council, Colonial Series* (Hereford and London, 1908–1912) II, 248. For an elaborate account and a justification of this revenue, see Dulany, *The Right to the Tonnage*, pp. 3–9. See also Mereness, *Maryland*, pp. 90–91.

54. For the exact amounts of these revenues see Table III, in the appendix, below, p. 381.

55. For the returns from the minor revenues, see below, *idem*. There is no need to discuss here the politically involved question of the revenue from ordinary licenses; see below, chs. VII, X. On deodands, see C. H. Karraker, "Deodands in Colonial Virginia and Maryland," *American Historical Review*, XXXVII (1931), 712–717.

declined in time of war and increased in time of peace. The underlying influences were the same in both cases: the opportunity for new settlement tended to increase the receipts of the land system, and expansion and population growth increased the flow of trade. As settlement increased before the French and Indian War, and tapered off before the Revolution, so also the product of the duty laws showed a general increase with a levelling off at the end of the provincial period. The duties are another indication of the close connection between the economic condition of the province and the personal fortune of the lord proprietor.

From the several sources—land revenues, duties, and minor perquisites—the gross income of the lords proprietors ran into large figures. In 1731 and 1733 the agent's accounts balanced at £6,620 4s. 9¼d. and at £8,091 9s. 5½d., in 1748 at £11,652 7s. 0d., and in 1754 at £16,440 1s. 1¾d. During the French and Indian War the balance dropped as low as £10,655 16s. 4¼d.; but in 1760 and 1761, when conditions of peace were restored in Maryland, it rose to the high points of £17,422 14s. 0⅛d. and £18,994 17s. 6⅝d. From 1768 to 1774 the annual account averaged £13,171 19s. 2½d. Against these large revenues, few and relatively insignificant charges were made in Maryland. From year to year the only debits for expenses entered in the accounts were the following: for the governor's salary £1000, or, after 1756, the entire amount of the 1704 tobacco duty if it were more than £1000; for the agent's salary, usually £150, but after the establishment of the board of revenue, in 1768, £500; for the rent-roll keepers, a 5 per cent commission on quitrents; and, occasionally, minor charges, such as a gift of a few pounds by Lord Baltimore to a school or an expenditure of a few shillings for stationery, and the like.[56] These debits ordinarily amounted to about £2000, and all the remainder, or about five-sixths of the gross receipts, was

56. See the instructions of the board of revenue to Bennet Allen, June 30, 1768, *Archives*, XXXII, 400–407.

transferred, as his net private revenue, to the lord proprietor. In war and peace, therefore, and whatever the prosperity or the poverty of the colony, he received a munificent income. Under his orders all remittances had to be made in sterling exchange, payable in London, and the amounts were kept secret from the assembly.[57] To compare with the total balances given above, from the 1731 account, Lord Baltimore personally received £5,055 0s 6½d.; from the 1733 account, £5,969 10s. 11d.; from that of 1748, £9,880 17s. 1d.; from that of 1754, £14,960 12s. 8d.; from that of 1760, £14,828 18s. 9⅜d.; and from that of 1761, £15,976 0s. 2⅞ d. In the nine years from 1762 to 1771 his agents transferred to Lord Baltimore a total of £118,952 2s. 3d., or an average of £13,216 18s. 0⅓d. annually.

This transfer of credit was on so large a scale that it must have had a genuine economic as well as a personal and political importance. If the estimate of the yearly value of the export trade of Maryland, calculated above for the final decades of the colonial period, is correct at about £200,000,[58] then Lord Baltimore's revenues, transferred abroad as fluid credit, represent a 6 or 7 per cent tax on that trade. In other terms: for the reason that, in the staple economy, the export trade so largely represented the power of the people of the province to purchase the manufactures, the luxuries, and the education, for which they were dependent on England, the proprietor's personal revenues represented a measurable reduction in that purchasing power. The satisfaction of the privileges of the absentee proprietor, then, through the maintenance of an ancient land law and the administration of a system of revenues, was, in cold statistical fact and in terms of standards of living in the province, an expensive inheritance of the people of Maryland.

57. Cecilius Calvert to Benjamin Tasker, July 9, 1752; Governor Bladen to Lord Baltimore, January 22, 1744, *Calvert Papers*, II, 150–151, 92.
58. See above, pp. 106, 108, 111–112.

From a financial point of view, the proprietary officials in Maryland stand in a position at once like and unlike that of Lord Baltimore. Their share of the financial benefits of the provincial system, like his, was far from inconsiderable. But as their incomes derived from sources different from those tapped by the lord proprietor, or from the same sources before the revenues were handed to the agent, they do not appear in the "accounts current," and information about them is fugitive. The provincial officer was paid in one or more of four ways: first, by allowances for days of service, as in the cases of members of both houses of assembly, the clerks of the houses, and the judges; second, by commissions on monies collected, as with the naval officers and receivers of quit-rents; third, by fees for individual services rendered, as in the cases of the chancellor (the governor), the deputy-secretary, the commissary-general, the surveyor-general, the naval officers, the sheriffs, and the county clerks, commissaries, and surveyors; and fourth, by the receipt of a fixed annual sum from, or a fixed annual proportion of, the income of a lesser official, as in the case of the secretary and deputy-secretary.[59] Income from these sources was nowhere subject to a general accounting, and was always regarded as a very private matter. After an appointment, apparently as a naval officer, in 1744, Edmund Jennings wrote Lord Baltimore that from the best information he could get the net income from his new office should come to about £260 sterling.[60] The idea implied in his statement, that there

59. It was a normal practice for the county clerks to pay one-tenth of their incomes from fees to the deputy-secretary, who appointed them (Lower House Journal, May 14, 1750, *Archives*, XLVI, 389–391). There is also evidence that "gifts" were made by appointees to county clerkships to the secretary, at the time of assuming office ("The Case of Dennis Dulany," an undated MS. of about 1760, Dulany Papers, II, 77, MHS). By an arrangement made while he was still a minor, Frederick, Lord Baltimore, required that the governor contribute £200 annually, the deputy-secretary, £50, the commissary-general, £100, and the judges of the land office, £100, to make up a "salary" of £450 for Secretary Calvert (Baltimore to Governor Ogle, September 17, 1751, *Calvert Papers*, II, 120).

60. The letter is damaged, Jennings to Baltimore, August 29, 1744, Calvert Papers, no. 1121, MHS.

was no way for one not actually holding an office to know its precise value, certainly represented the truth of a quarter-century later, when John Morton Jordan came to Maryland as Lord Baltimore's special financial emissary. Directed to inquire into the value of various provincial offices, Jordan wrote that reports varied greatly and none was to be relied upon, and that he could not possibly make definite statements about the income of the officials unless Lord Baltimore would send special instructions ordering that the "Fee Book of the Office," a record which seems not to have survived, be opened to him.[61]

A few times, however, in the thirty years before the Revolution, a little information about the value of the great offices was obtained and made public by the lower house.[62] More important for the record, three estimates have been preserved, each of which gives a more or less systematic evaluation of most of the proprietary offices. The first, referring to about 1745, was perhaps compiled, as internal evidence suggests, in aid of the effort made by the lower house between 1739 and 1745, to obtain crown government in place of proprietary in Maryland, but this is not certain.[63] The second, dated in 1754, seems to have been a memorandum, possibly by Governor Sharpe, and possibly for his use, as he was then a newcomer in Maryland.[64] The third estimate was prepared in 1761 by Gov-

61. Letter to Baltimore, n.d., Calvert Papers, no. 1300, MHS.

62. The lower house obtained this information when it was considering a bill to restrict tobacco production and to limit fees (in tobacco). Lower House Journal, October 23, 1753, *Archives*, L, 183–187; *Votes and Proceedings of the Lower House of Assembly* (Annapolis, 1771), October 8, 1770; *Maryland Gazette,* October 8, 1770; McMahon, *Historical View*, p. 382 n.

63. "A List of the Several Public Offices, Ecclesiastical Preferments, and other Places of Profit, in the province of Maryland, with their Revenues; in whose Distribution as a Proprietary Government," Massachusetts Historical Society, *Collections* (Boston), ser. I, vol. VII (1801), 202–203. The document as published is undated, but it refers to the proprietorship of Charles, Lord Baltimore, and the conditions of war.

64. List of civil officers in Maryland, 1754, Portfolio no. 3, MHRecs. For a possible suggestion that Col. George Plater of the council was the author of this list, see Sharpe to Calvert, March 12, 1755, *Archives*, VI, 183.

ernor Sharpe, with the help of the council, as part of a report to the British Board of Trade.[65] The three estimates and certain other figures supply more than a suggestion as to the size of the property interest represented by the provincial offices.

The governor, who also had perquisites as chancellor and surveyor-general, of course received the highest income of any of the Maryland officers. The figures differ widely, from £1,000 to £1,861, but there is ample reason to think that the higher figures give the more accurate indication.[66] It is not unlikely that during the years between the French and Indian War and the Revolution Governors Sharpe and Eden often received more than £2,000 annually for their various duties and privileges. The next ranking officers, namely, the deputy-secretary, the commissary-general, the agent, and the judges of the land office received, with all the incidents of office, about £1,000 each, although this estimate may be high for the agent or receiver-general. The naval officers are estimated to have received from £50 to £150; and the sheriffs and the county clerks, with apparent equality, from £80 to £200. The lesser commissioners, registers, and clerks seem to have received less than £100; most often their incomes fell between £50 and £80.

The estimates of the value of the offices do not include the lesser officials of the land system, nor of course those appointive but essentially non-patronage offices of the judges of the provincial and county courts. For this reason, and particularly because the estimates are disparate and incomplete, the total value of the patronage is difficult to calculate. But £8,460, the total of Governor Sharpe's estimate of 1761, must be regarded as too low.

65. Answers to Queries, January 14, 1762, Board of Trade Papers, Proprieties, XXI (1), HSP. See Council Proceedings, December 21, 1761, *Archives,* XXXII, 27.

66. There is as full a statistical statement as the sources will permit in Table IV and the supporting notes in the appendix, below, pp. 382–383. All figures offered in this and the following paragraph are detailed in Table IV.

As Sharpe was reporting to officials of the Crown, and as a comparison of the expenses of Maryland with those of the royal colonies was implied, he may have felt constrained to understate. In any case, he estimated his own income a third lower than the £1,861 he was to report in 1767, when he had to itemize the sources; and his report of the incomes of the deputy-secretary, commissary-general, and the judges of the land office indicated less than a third of what they are known to have received during the far from prosperous years from 1763 to 1769. A calculation made in view of all the contemporary estimates would make it appear that Maryland patronage late in the provincial period was worth from £12,000 to £14,000 sterling, annually. This was an amount roughly equal to the private income of the lord proprietor, from all his rights and privileges, and was a generous allowance for the support, under colonial conditions, of about ten higher officials, counting the naval officers, and of about seventy lesser officials, counting the county clerks.

In the church the distribution of patronage did not have the same connotation, as in the government, of shared political authority. But, as we have seen, it did represent the gift of the best church livings in America, and the rapid growth of population produced, through the operation of the poll tax, a proportionate gain in church revenues.[67] Thus, in the course of the century, Lord Baltimore's prerogative of presenting all clergymen to their benefices came to mean the exercise of a financial privilege comparable if not equal to that of the appointment of officers. In 1766 the forty or more clergymen of the Church of England received 1,920,930 pounds of tobacco, a total which Governor Sharpe valued at £8,163 9s. 0d.[68] This situation makes understandable the appearance of favorites in the church, men more distinguished for their association with the proprietor than for their piety in the Anglican faith.

67. See above, pp. 46–47.
68. "An exact estimate," 1767, Portfolio no. 3, MHRecs.

In coming to conclusions about the proprietary interest and the policy which supported it, two comparisons are
possible which throw some light on the contemporary
meaning of the vested rights entrenched in the provincial
system. The annual cost of those rights may be compared,
first, with the other costs of the provincial establishment,
and especially with the parish and county charges, which
represent the eighteenth-century equivalent of modern
state expenditures for the general welfare. And they may
be compared, second, with what indices exist of the economic productiveness of the province as a whole.[69] The
questions at issue are: how much of the money collected
from the people under the establishment went to the satisfaction of vested rights, and how much was returned in
the form of genuine service by the government? What was
the real or economic cost, as distinguished from the money
cost, of the establishment?

Referring to the year 1766 as representative, Governor
Sharpe said that the ordinary county and parochial
charges—the allowances for the justices of the peace, the
constables, and the jurors, and the payments for maintenance and physicians' charges for the poor, and for re-

69. There is a temptation to offer a third comparison, and with it the
conclusion that *Maryland supported a more expensive establishment
than that of any of the other British colonies,* great or small, in North
America and the West Indies. Such a conclusion would at first glance
seem justified by a report of the Board of Trade in 1766. The report
gives the annual expenses of fourteen colonies, but lacks figures for
Maryland, Virginia, North Carolina, and Georgia. It shows only two
establishments costing more than £10,000 annually, and they are Massachusetts, at £18,000, and Jamaica, at £30,500 exclusive of parish charges.
If it could be assumed that these figures were complete, comparison
with Governor Sharpe's "exact estimate" of the "annual sum paid by
inhabitants of Maryland in taxes, duties, and quit-rents" (Portfolio no.
3, MHRecs) at £37,431 15s. 10d. would suggest the conclusion above.
Several of the Board of Trade's figures, however, are taken from reports as old as 1731 and 1740, and it is impossible to know just what
was included in any of the figures. Perhaps it was the deficiency of
information which led Lord Shelburne to require a statement in 1766,
and to Sharpe's "exact estimate" of 1767. The report is: Board of Trade
to the House of Lords, February 2, 1766, House of Lords Library,
Andrews and Davenport, *Guide,* p. 236, item 228, LC.

pairs to churches, roads, bridges, and the like—came to tobacco worth £14,695 2s. 4d.,[70] which was paid by an annual poll tax levied by the justices of the peace for each county. In the same year three special duties, the only revenues that the province supplied for the support of education in any form, yielded a total of £419 8s. 0d., which was divided between King William's School in Annapolis and the few county schools there were. A fourth special duty yielded £819 3s. 0d. to a reserve maintained as a source from which compensatory payments could be made to the masters of slaves executed under the law. The judges of the provincial court and members of the two houses of assembly were not paid annually, but Governor Sharpe estimated that, on an average, the allowances they were granted cost the province, respectively, £637 10s. 0d. and £1,750 4s. 3d. each year. The entire cost to Maryland of all these items was £18,321 7s. 7d., mostly paid in tobacco.

Governor Sharpe's own figures invite a preliminary comparison. His grand total of the "annual charge of maintaining and supporting the entire establishment of the province of Maryland" was £37,431 15s. 10d. More than half of that total—an amount of £19,109 18s. 3d., the difference between the total and the £18,321 7s. 7d. assigned to government services—he allocated as follows: £9,084 10s. 6d., the income from quit-rents and the tonnage duty, to the lord proprietor's private account; £8,163 19s. 0d., from the proceeds of the tobacco poll tax, to the clergymen of the Church of England; and £1,861 8s. 9d., from various sources, to the governor.[71] According

70. This and other figures not credited to different sources are taken from the "exact estimate," by Governor Sharpe, 1767, Portfolio no. 3, MHRecs.

71. Sharpe's figures, in detail, were as follows:

	£	s.	d.
The 14d. per ton duty, to the proprietor	1100	0	0
Quit-rents, to the proprietor	7984	10	6
The 12d. per hhd. duty, to the governor	1291	9	0
The 3d. per ton duty, to the governor	228	15	9
Marriage licenses, to the governor	341	4	0
The clergy tax	8163	19	0

to Governor Sharpe's own statement, then, three privileged elements in the provincial system, the lord proprietor, the governor, and the clergy of the established church, cost the people of Maryland more than all the public services and the maintenance of the judicial and legislative branches of the government combined.

But Governor Sharpe's figures were not inclusive. Called upon merely to account for the funds collected and disbursed through the government and for the quit-rents,[72] he omitted any statement of the cost of administration and of official prestige, represented by the incomes of officials of the executive branch of the government and of the land system. Likewise, he gave no account of the lord proprietor's income from the land office, from manor rents, and from the minor sources; and his statement that the proprietor's income from the tonnage duty was £1,100, although doubtless accurate for 1766, indicated less than the usual truth. If all these factors be considered according to the estimates in the present chapter, the total cost of the Maryland system, as of the final decade of its history, may be raised more than 25 per cent above the estimate of Governor Sharpe, to about £51,000. In round numbers, this total was distributed as follows: to the use of the people of Maryland, in the form of county and parish charges, the support of the schools, and the local government, £16,000; to the legislative and judicial branches of the provincial government, for essential services, £2,500; to the lord proprietor, for personal use, £12,500; to the patronage officers, for the administration of the province, chiefly the land and revenue systems, £12,000; to the clergy of the Church of England, for administering the established religion, £8,000. The first two items represent little if any vested right in the form of patronage, and may be considered as paying for several of the essentials of government and nothing else. The other items, comprising hardly less than two-thirds of the total, represent incomes entirely within the control of the proprietary element.

---

72. Lord Shelburne to Sharpe, December 11, 1766, *Archives*, XIV, 361.

These incomes paid about 120 men for administration, civil and ecclesiastical, and for the satisfaction of the privileges of the lord proprietor under the royal charter. As more than half of all the income controlled by the proprietary element was concentrated in the hands of the lord proprietor and a half-dozen high officials, the preponderance of privilege is evident.

In considering the entire cost of the provincial system, the value of the export trade, at about £200,000, is not as definite an index as in relation to the lord proprietor's revenues alone. The latter represent an absolute loss to the province, an exportation of capital for which there was no corresponding import, whereas the other costs of the establishment represent credits transferred and services rendered in Maryland. Yet reference to the export trade does have economic significance with respect to those costs, too, for the reason that fees and taxes were nearly always paid in tobacco, that is, in the transferable surplus of the payer, which was also the staple export product of the province. Since the officials and clergymen, who received the tobacco, had no local consumer's market for their tobacco, they had to place it, directly or indirectly, on the export market. They were really paid, therefore, in the form of unstable credit which would ultimately find its value in the British market. It is probably almost as accurate to say that the £20,000 annually received by the patronage officials and clergymen was equal to a 9 to 11 per cent levy on the purchasing power in England of the rest of the inhabitants of Maryland, as to say that Lord Baltimore's income equaled a 6 or 7 per cent levy.

Thus, in the economic view, the rights of the proprietary element involved material values as well as traditional and governmental ones. They involved a large transfer of purchasing power, if not so much of the domestically produced and consumed essentials of life, such as food, then of the manufactures and textiles for which, as well as for the luxuries, the staple colony was largely dependent. In this way the high living traditional in Annapolis and on the great plantations, many of which belonged in families at some time influential in the proprietary element, was related to political preference as well as to the cultivation of broad acres. Even more clearly, the wealth and extravagance of the later lords proprietors would necessarily have been much restricted without their personal revenues from Maryland.

A plainer case of the cultivation of financial and social privileges through the machinery of government than that of provincial Maryland is difficult to conceive. The proprietary policy of advancing and securing every possible privilege, and of doing so by bold prerogative action, seems entirely natural and in accord with the realities of the legal and constitutional frame of things. In a broad view, the observation may be offered that in Maryland the consistent application of British conceptions of land tenure, of office-holding, and of privilege, created a relationship between the governing and the governed for which the tyranny of institutions is a just description.

V

THE REPRESENTATIVE ELEMENT
IN THE PROVINCIAL SYSTEM

"I FOUND but little difference in the manners and character of the people of the different provinces I passed through," wrote Dr. Alexander Hamilton with reference to his journey into New England in 1744, "but as to constitutions and complexions, air and government, I found some variety. Their forms of government in the northern provinces I look upon to be much better and happier than ours, which is a poor sickly convulsed state." [1]

"Convulsed" was the word for Maryland. Dr. Hamilton's comment was written, as it happened, during an acute phase of the struggle between the proprietary element and its natural enemy, the lower house of the assembly. But whether the conflict were acute or dormant, difference of interest and difference of idea was always there, inevitable in the scheme of things which established feudal and viceregal privileges and which also included a representative house in the English parliamentary tradition. "No compromise could be reached," says Professor Andrews, with reference to the conflict of the seventeenth century,

because it was rooted in an irreconcilable difference of claim. When the upper house spoke of its privilege, honor, and dignity, it was referring to a charter the terms of which are traceable to the fourteenth century; when the lower house spoke of its privileges, it had in mind the precedents and practices of the House of Commons in the seventeenth century which it used as guides of its own organization and conduct. [2]

1. Hamilton, *Itinerarium*, pp. 245–246.
2. Andrews, *The Colonial Period of American History*, II, 327.

The narrower terms of political dispute were not just the same in the eighteenth century as in the seventeenth, but the irreconcilability of interest and claim—the "convulsed state" witnessed by Dr. Hamilton—derived from the same basis as earlier, and it persisted to the American Revolution.

To be understood, the institutional vitality of the House of Delegates must be thought of in terms of function and association as well as in terms of inheritance from the House of Commons. As a working part of the assembly it was rooted, beyond question or doubt, in the tradition and in the constitution of the province. The charter of 1632 had anticipated the establishment of an assembly; a first meeting had been called as early as 1635; and, in spite of the host of political, religious, and economic difficulties which beset Maryland, the assembly had developed permanent forms and usages before the Revolution of 1689. The royal period, by eliminating the old proprietary clique, had strengthened the legislature. Although, in the sixty years after 1715, the proprietary governors, each in turn, condemned the policies of the lower house, there was no hint, either from them or from the proprietors, that government might be carried on without it.

Charles, Lord Baltimore, voiced his own complete recognition of the representative element at the time of his visit to the province. "Gentlemen of the lower house," he declared in a formal address, "I cannot take my leave of you without recommending a parliamentary proceeding in your method of doing business, nor can you copy better than after our mother country." [3] This speech, in the context of the proprietor's policies and decisions of 1733, well expresses the situation: the House of Delegates was understood and encouraged to follow the usages and traditions of the British Parliament, as it had long loved to do; but at the same time the spaciousness of that suggestion was offset by those acts of the prerogative through which the proprietor withdrew from the reach of the assembly the

3. April 12, 1733, *Archives,* XXXIX, 54.

financial matters which had in some degree fallen into its grasp. Thus Lord Baltimore spoke like a Hanoverian and acted like a Stuart in 1733, a contradiction which lies in the general tone if not in the literal meaning of his address to the lower house.

To the contemporary, the many duties which the assembly had to perform must have carried the idea that the House of Delegates was a powerful and an enduring body. Year in and year out the sessions added chapter after chapter to the accumulating body of Maryland statutes. Problems of judicial procedure and of administrative arrangement were acted on, private laws were passed, debtors were granted relief, ports and markets were established and regulated, and every sort of matter of provincial business and law was made the object of consideration and legislation. Occasionally, after long delays, a major piece of economic legislation, such, for example, as the paper-money and the tobacco-inspection laws, was passed and approved. In the great majority of cases the business of the legislature was hardly more than a matter of routine and evoked no constitutional claims or controversy. Yet the doing of such business was well worthy of the members of both houses, and, over a long period, it added tradition to the idea of provincial self-government.

Four authorities were brought together in the process of legislation: the House of Delegates, the council—which in legislative session as the upper house was presided over not by the governor but by a president—, the governor, and the lord proprietor. In the seventeenth century the proprietor long denied the right of the Delegates to originate legislation, or to amend the laws which he sent for acceptance; but by the eighteenth century the right to propose laws was admittedly a divided one. Both houses offered bills at will; though the lower house asserted, and the upper house denied, that like the Commons the Delegates had the exclusive right to initiate money bills.[4] In

4. Andrews, *Colonial Period of American History*, II, 300, 302; Mereness, *Maryland as a Proprietary Province*, pp. 222–225.

effect, the proprietor and the governor, too, could offer new legislation, the proprietor by making proposals through instruction and letter to the governor, and the governor by transmitting such orders and presenting his own ideas in messages to the two houses. The four authorities had also about equal power in rejecting proposed legislation. No bill became law without the approval of both houses and the governor, and all laws were subject to disallowance by the proprietor, who himself was careful not to offend the Crown.[5]

Relative equivalence of opportunity to propose and to reject legislation does not, of course, mean that the four authorities were each equally concerned to have new laws enacted, or that they represent four separate interests, checking and balancing each other. In legislative affairs, as in administrative, the proprietor, the governor, and the upper house were bound to each other by the ties of loyalty and interest which were their especial concern and distinction. Only rarely was there difference between the lord proprietor and the Maryland members of the proprietary element.[6] Ordinarily they presented a common political front, a conservative front occupied with defensive more often than with aggressive tactics. The House of Delegates, on the other hand, offered much new legislation. As the members were close to the local interests of the people and were sensitive to provincial opportunity and growth, and as they were elected to their house, it was their natural legislative role to declare and to favor the new and growing interests of Maryland.

From the very beginning of its history the representative element had made a practice of borrowing strength

5. The Crown disallowed no Maryland laws; the laws were not submitted for approval, as the charter of 1632 gave an independence in this respect like that of Connecticut and Rhode Island. But Lord Baltimore was cautious, as he should have been, lest the question of disallowance be raised from the side of the Crown. See below, pp. 190–193.

6. The number of proprietary disallowances was small. On the question of the appropriation of ordinary-license fees, over which the governor and council disagreed with the proprietor, see below, pp. 239–241, 330–331, 335–336.

from the parliamentary tradition of England. In its second recorded meeting, in 1638, the assembly had passed a law declaring that the members should have "power, privileges, authority, and jurisdiction" like that of members of the House of Commons in England.[7] The claim was a pretentious one; power, authority, and jurisdiction like that of the Commons was far from the reach of a tiny colonial assembly. Nor could the House of Delegates legally raise its standing above its constitutional source, the charter granted by King Charles in 1632. The fact that certain clauses of that charter gave Lord Baltimore's authority a special touch of regality added nothing to the power of the Maryland assembly above that exercised by rule-making bodies under other charters, such as the king granted to the boroughs and the commercial companies of England. But, though power in parliamentary terms did not exist to be exercised in Maryland, parliamentary organization, procedure, and privilege had deeply entered the colonial mind. These elements of the parliamentary tradition could be freely assimilated, they could be associated with the actual practice of provincial law making, and they could be openly imitated in a very considerable degree.

In the eighteenth century the process of imitation was far advanced.[8] At the opening of each new assembly, a ceremony was made of presenting the newly-elected speaker to the governor for approval, in much the same way as the speaker of the House of Commons was presented to the king. On that occasion the speaker petitioned the governor for recognition of the fundamental privileges of parliament, and those privileges were granted as mat-

7. *Archives,* I, 75. For this reference, and for an appreciation of the idea of parliamentary privilege in America, I am indebted to the type-written dissertation of Mary P. Clarke, "Parliamentary Privilege in the American Colonies" (Yale University Library). See her article by the same title in *Essays in Colonial History,* pp. 124–144.

8. The following paragraphs about organization, procedure, and privilege are based, where other credit is not given, on the journals of the lower house.

ters of right, as they had been granted in England since the early sixteenth century. After this the standing committees were appointed for the life of the assembly. Although the committees were limited in membership, and in that respect different from the "grand" committees of the House of Commons, the repeated designation of committees on elections and privileges, on laws, and on grievances and the courts of justice, is similar in detail to the establishment of committees under Queen Elizabeth and the early Stuarts.[9] As in England, the committees on elections and privileges, and, often too, the committees on grievances, were made up of leading men. When the committees had been selected, the House of Delegates appointed a clerk, a sergeant-at-arms, and a doorkeeper. It then adopted rules of procedure—this usually meant a readoption without amendment of the rules of the preceding house—and it entered them in the journal, all in good and proper form. When thus provided, and no earlier, the house was ready for business. The session began with a speech from the governor, one which in form and purpose closely paralleled the speech from the throne to Parliament.[10]

During the course of the session, as in the preliminaries of organization, the assembly proceeded in a way which was equally imitative of parliamentary example.[11] In the event of a tie in the lower house, the speaker cast the deciding vote, as was the case in a half-dozen other colonies. The house decided questions of disputed elections, and it

9. J. Franklin Jameson, "The Origin of the Standing-Committee System in American Legislative Bodies," *Political Science Quarterly,* IX (1894), 249–254, 262–264.

10. Readers of the *Maryland Gazette* might have noticed this parallelism perfectly illustrated in their newspaper. The issue of December 23, 1747, carried an address of Governor Ogle to both houses of the assembly which used exactly the same forms as a speech from the throne to both houses of Parliament, printed in the issue of March 23, 1748.

11. For a close analysis of parliamentary procedure in another American colony, see Stanley M. Pargellis, "The Procedure of the Virginia House of Burgesses," *William and Mary College Quarterly Historical Magazine,* series II, VII (1927), 73–86, 143–157.

exercised full jurisdiction over its members, all according to English tradition. No member could be called by
name on the floor, tardiness was prohibited, weapons were
forbidden in the house, and fines were fixed for misdemeanors. The competence of the Delegates for self-regula-
tion had come, by the eighteenth century, to be openly admitted by proprietary authority itself. Even in the heat
of constitutional conflict, Governor Ogle once declared
that when delegates were "guilty of or charged with any
misdemeanor in their duty as members," the house alone
was the proper judge of "how to proceed, and I would not
pretend to interpose." [12] The parliamentary tradition was
sometimes invoked, moreover, by the upper house in its
own behalf. In 1729 it accused the lower house of grossly
unparliamentary procedure because it offered a new bill
on a subject—the season for deer-hunting—concerning
which the upper house had already sent a bill of its own.[13]
The language of legislative procedure, at least, was a common language, though there always remained room for
difference of understanding and interpretation.

Closely bound up with questions of organization and
procedure was the inherited concept of parliamentary
privilege.[14] In Maryland this concept had more value in
certifying and expanding the authority of the House of
Delegates than did any other element in the English legislative tradition. With Parliament, privilege had been a
product of ancient judicial functions, of functions which
had been largely antiquated by the seventeenth century.
But privilege had outlasted the conditions which gave it
rise; it remained a bulwark of security to members of the
House of Commons. This was expressed in the speaker's
petition for the freedom of the Commons from arrest and
molestation, for freedom of speech in debate, for access to

12. March 25, 1734, *Archives*, XXXIX, 149.
13. July 23, 1729, *ibid.*, XXXVI, 330–331.
14. See Carl Wittke, *The History of English Parliamentary Privilege*,
Ohio State University Studies, Contributions in History and Political
Science, no. 6 (Columbus, 1921); and Josef Redlich, *The Procedure of
the House of Commons*, I (London, 1908).

the king, and for the promise that favorable construction would be put on the proceedings of the house. With the Maryland assembly, much as with Parliament: the judicial function had been practiced, in conscious imitation of the English model; and, also in imitation, the judicial function had been accompanied by demand for and the concession of parliamentary privileges. As we have seen, such demand began with the earliest meetings of the assembly; certain concessions, such as that of freedom of speech in 1661, were early granted by the proprietary element.[15] The study of Professor Clarke, whose work in this field is the most thorough, reveals that in 1682 Maryland became the earliest colony, save Jamaica, to have a speaker's petition formally recorded, and with it a full grant of parliamentary privilege made and openly recognized.[16] In her opinion, too, the Maryland assembly was more active than any other in expanding the claims of privilege to its own advantage and power.[17]

How privilege was used in Maryland to justify an expansive view of the authority of the House of Delegates, is illustrated in the following passage from a message to the governor, sent in 1725:

And as the chief end of all parliamentary privilege is to apply properly for the redress of grievances that happen to the people, whether through mistakes in the administration of justice or otherwise, we should but poorly answer the end of our institution and election if we should be wanting in this weighty part; and . . . we desire your honor to consider that all the rights and privileges granted to us by charter, and the benefit of all those acts of our own which we have from time to time at vast expense been making, are rendered useless and unserviceable to us unless you are pleased to appoint such magistrates to administer them to the people as are well inclined, as well as sworn so to do.[18]

15. April 19, 1661, *Archives,* I, 398.
16. October 26, 1682, *Archives,* VII, 335.
17. Clarke, "Parliamentary Privilege in the American Colonies" (Yale University Library).
18. October 28, 1725, *Archives,* XXXV, 360.

In this address the idea of parliamentary privilege was not only joined to the oversight of justice, as was appropriate in the history of privilege, but also to the correction of any public grievances; and such responsibility was joined, in turn, to legislative supervision of judicial appointments. This wide claim, elaborated with reference to historical precedent, was altogether in character both with the aggressive spirit of the house and with the legal-mindedness of the delegates. The address was framed in the midst of proceedings which still retained certain judicial activities, and by a house which called sheriffs to account and brought wrong-doers in administration before its bar. The weighty words of 1725 must have carried a conviction of dignity and power among the members of the House of Delegates.

Beyond privilege and the other borrowings from the practices and precedents of parliamentary history, the lower house had one other intellectual resource which could be made to add to its self-confidence in the struggle for power. This was the natural-rights philosophy. In its political aspects the philosophy of Locke was not, of course, apart from or unassimilated with the parliamentary idea; but the natural-rights idea stood, basically, on metaphysical and moral grounds, and was a weapon of longer intellectual reach than considerations which depended on precedent and admitted usage. Belief in natural law made it possible for the Delegates to declare, when occasion required, that their powers were inherent in the nature of things, and so incapable of reduction or compromise. This type of reasoning did not come frequently from the legalistic minds of the lower house. But when it came, as occasionally it did, through the half-century or more before the Revolution, it came without qualification, as though here, at last, were the essence of the matter.

Thus, in 1725, on the very day when the house made the claim of privilege quoted above, it also took the ground that, "It is we that are the people's representatives for whom all laws are made and human government established." [19] Such an affirmation, in the lower house of Maryland, conforms nicely with the thesis maintained by Professor Corwin, that the thinking of Coke and those students of Coke, the first generation of the American legal profession, held implicit in its legalism the philosophy of natural law.[20] In the seventeen-twenties, at any rate, when Daniel Dulany, the elder, was the leader of both the provincial assembly and the provincial bar, the idea of natural law was invoked hardly less boldly than it was to be during the revolutionary period itself. In 1729, when the proprietor had several times refused to permit a cherished judges-oath bill to pass, the House of Delegates took the high ground that an "ample and full power of legislation is lodged in this province," and that the proprietor's right to veto acts of the assembly was itself subject to question.[21] In saying this the house did not go quite as far as a denial of the right of the proprietor to disallow laws, as Patrick Henry in the Parson's Cause a generation later was to deny the right of the Crown, yet the line of thought was quite as radical. The assumption, that the people had a natural right to make their own laws, might as well have been used to support a denial of the proprietary disallowance, as it was actually used to support an inquiry. It could not have been made to support acquiescence in the disallowance as a just practice of government.

The vigor, the penetration, and the originality of political thought in Maryland is nowhere better illustrated than in the pamphlet of Daniel Dulany, *The Right of the Inhabitants of Maryland to the Benefit of the English*

19. October 28, 1725, *Archives*, XXXV, 357. The upper house would of course admit no such advanced ideas as this. Its own theory it put as follows: "Whilst the powers of the prerogative are exercised with a tender regard to the privileges and conveniences of the people, and the people willingly support those powers of the prerogative, as the only means of preserving them in their privileges, government and obedience become reciprocal acts. . . ." November 5, 1725, *ibid.*, XXXV, 281.

20. Edward S. Corwin, "The 'Higher Law' Background of American Constitutional Law," *Harvard Law Review*, XLII (1928–1929), 175–176, 365–380, 393–398.

21. August 2, 1729, *Archives*, XXXVI, 362–363.

Laws,[22] which he brought out in Annapolis in 1728. When Dulany wrote this treatise he was a young man, already recognized but not yet a preferred member of the inner circle of proprietary office-holders. The pamphlet supported the demand of the lower house, in its decade-long controversy, to pass a statute which would bind the provincial judges to the "laws, statutes, and reasonable customs of England and the acts of assembly and usages of the province of Maryland." [23] This proposal, to have the laws of the mother country applied in the province, was the strongest proposal of the sort in any of the colonies; it has been spoken of by scholars as ill-conceived, because if adopted it would have bound Maryland in too great detail to the laws of England.[24] However unsatisfactorily it might have operated, had it been enacted, Dulany's own words show a plain intention to liberate and not to confine: "What I contend for is that we derive our right to British liberties and privileges as we are British subjects; that as such we have a right to all the laws, whether statute or common, which secure to the subject the right of the subject." [25] As Dulany presented the case, the delegates had no fear of subjection to English statute, but only desired that the great principles embodied in common law and statute law alike should be as thoroughly available in the provincial courts as at home.

Dulany's plea gained force and appeal because it incorporated the two types of political thought which flourished in the assembly. The treatise was, primarily, a lawyer's case, to be established by the citation of precedent and practice; as such it stood precisely in line with the Dele-

22. Reprinted, as Appendix II, in St. George L. Sioussat, *The English Statutes in Maryland*, JHUS, XXI (1903), nos. 11–12, pp. 77–104.
23. This important dispute, which evoked so much political thought and feeling, is fully treated in Sioussat, *The English Statutes in Maryland*. There are substantial accounts in McMahon, *An Historical View*, pp. 112–131; in Mereness, *Maryland*, pp. 257–277; in Osgood, *The American Colonies in the Eighteenth Century*, III, 26–31.
24. Sioussat, *The English Statutes in Maryland*, p. 62; Clarke, "Parliamentary Privilege in the American Colonies" (Yale University Library).
25. Dulany, *The Right of the Inhabitants*, pp. 12–13.

gates' habit of insistence on parliamentary privilege and usage. Thus Dulany cited and quoted such cardinal documents of English constitutional history as Magna Carta, the Petition of Right, and the liberal statutes of the seventeenth century; and he quoted the provincial charter to prove that English law was also Maryland law. But *The Right of the Inhabitants* argued from philosophical as well as from legal grounds, and on this side Dulany quoted some of the more abstract ideas of Sir Edward Coke, portions of Locke's *Second Treatise*, and, in a still longer perspective, the writings of Grotius, Pufendorf, Cato, and Caesar. He used the concept of the original equality of man to indicate that subjects in the colony had rights equal to those of subjects at home, and he followed Locke in the contract theory of the state. Professor Wright, in his study of the natural-law philosophy, expresses the opinion that Dulany's was a more advanced statement of theory than that of John Wise, the minister of Ipswich, and that it was based on wider reading and greater understanding.[26] The argument, from both precedent and principle, was more sweeping than that to be used by the younger Dulany in his successful legalistic pamphlet against the Stamp Tax, *Considerations on the Propriety of Imposing Taxes on the British Colonies.*[27] The plea of 1728 was definitely anticipatory of Thomas Jefferson's *Summary View of the Rights of British America*, where it was again to be urged, on the eve of the Revolution much as a half-century earlier, that colonials had historical and natural rights to the full benefit of English freedom.

Where political thinking was so advanced, and where the study of English precedent, though detailed and imitative, was intended to strengthen rather than to circumscribe, it was natural for the legislature to hit upon usages and habits peculiar to its own needs. The most interesting

26. Benjamin F. Wright, *American Interpretations of Natural Law, a Study in the History of Political Thought* (Cambridge, 1931), pp. 57–59.
27. See below, pp. 305–306.

and suggestive departure from the British model appeared in the determination of the lower house to exclude from membership the holders of appointive office. At the very time when the cabinet system was beginning to place the leaders of both houses of Parliament in high offices of state, and in this way was giving new authority to the legislature, Maryland was moving in an opposite direction. The House of Delegates, to be sure, was thinking rather in terms of seventeenth-century than of contemporary Parliament; it was confronting a lord proprietor who was, as we have seen, a miniature Stuart, a financially independent ruler who controlled, and was not controlled by, the high officials of his appointment. As early as 1722, eleven years before the proprietor fixed upon his permanent financial policies, the house resolved that the members should not hold proprietary office or pension, "according to the practice of the British Parliament." [28] The Delegates thus completely misstated, and equally departed from, the eighteenth-century trend at home. In 1722, the rule of exclusion was not actually applied, however, to the man whose case evoked the question, a naval officer who accepted appointment between the time of election and that of entering the house. Yet in 1734, the Delegates voted, almost unanimously, that four elected members were "disabled" from sitting because they had accepted places of trust and profit from the proprietor. The house proceeded to order a warrant for writs of election to fill the vacant seats; and the governor responded with an address, saying that to deny seats to appointed officers was contrary to the interdependence between the branches of government, so familiar to English usage and desirable to the province. To protect the constitution against such violation, he dissolved the assembly.[29] The following election returned three of the "disabled" four to the house, and they were seated; but during the dozen years to follow the Delegates

28. October 29, 1722, *Archives*, XXXIV, 447.
29. March 25, 1734, *ibid.*, XXXIX, 149, 159.

voted, on widely spaced occasions, to exclude placemen,[30] and ultimately they disappeared from the house. This divergence of legislative growth—the Parliament, where the historic executive was weak, moving towards the domination of the executive; and the provincial legislature, where the historic executive was strong, moving towards a system of checks and balances—marks an early milestone in the history of institutional difference between America and Great Britain.

In the external relations of the assembly there was also differentiation from the mother country. At a time when the House of Commons still hedged its deliberations with a secrecy appropriate to its dignity and position above the mass of men, the Maryland House of Delegates began to publish its affairs. In 1724 and 1725, in the increasing tension of the oath controversy, it had a Philadelphia printer bring out certain proceedings of the assembly for 1722, 1723, and 1724, and with them a printing of the charter of 1632.[31] This was followed by legislation which authorized William Parks, as the public printer in Annapolis, paid by a tobacco tax, to print and distribute the laws and the opening addresses and replies of each session of the assembly.[32] Thus the issue of the sessional laws became a regular thing; and in 1731 there was also launched the *Votes and Proceedings* series, substantially a printed journal of the lower house, which showed the way in which the members voted on each division. This publicity coincided with the beginning of the *Maryland Gazette* and with the pamphleteering on the tobacco problem of the period.[33] With so much done, political affairs

30. The next case, that of a deputy-commissary, came in 1740, and at that time the governor forestalled controversy by a prorogation rather than a dissolution. In 1747 a deputy naval officer was barred from the house and was not reëlected. July 29, 1740, May 18, 1747, *Archives,* XLII, 78–80, 107; XLIV, 507. See Mereness, *Maryland,* p. 213.

31. For bibliographical details, see Wroth, *Printing in Colonial Maryland,* pp. 171–181.

32. Acts, October, 1727, ch. 8, *Archives,* XXXVI, 89–90.

33. See above, pp. 61, 70–71.

became, in an increasing sense, public affairs, far in advance of the usage of the mother country.[34]

The way, and the attitude, in which assembly affairs were submitted to the reading public may be illustrated by another reference to Dulany's famous pamphlet of 1728. In the preface of *The Right of the Inhabitants*, Dulany addressed himself to "all true patriots, and sincere lovers of liberty," and he declared that he printed his case at the wish of the "representatives, of the people of Maryland, whose request bears the weights of a command." As he opened his argument, he advanced to the ground that,

as *laws* are absolutely necessary, for the good government, and welfare, of society, so it is necessary, that people should have some notion of those laws, which are to be the rule of their conduct; and for the transgression of which, they will be liable to be punished, notwithstanding their ignorance.[35]

Dulany's plea, with its legalistic and philosophic language, was hardly written for the common man of the small plantation. And yet, as an instance of the rise of provincial printing, the pamphlet represents a step in broadening the base of politics and in assimilating current theories of popular rights with the practice of the province.

This outward movement of politics, from the assembly toward the people, found a more continuous and in the long run perhaps a more pervasive expression in the newspaper than in pamphlets. The political pamphlet appeared in Maryland at times of crisis, and it spoke with an authority and a thoroughness not matched in other writing. But the *Maryland Gazette*, equally under Parks in the late twenties and the early thirties and under Green in the middle forties and after, always kept political issues

34. In 1747 the lower house even permitted a few visitors to watch proceedings. *Archives*, XLIV, 517. On the secrecy and privacy of Parliament, see A. F. Pollard, *Evolution of Parliament* (London, 1920), pp. 337–340.

35. Dulany, *The Right of the Inhabitants*, p. 1.

and ideas before its readers. Although the *Gazette* was for the most part as indirect and cautious about the expression of opinion as were the English papers, political meaning was ever plain.

One safe and neutral way in which assembly affairs were printed stood directly in line with the public duties of the printer. Both Parks and Green placed in current numbers of the *Gazette* the addresses and replies at the opening of assembly sessions, and they sometimes included similar items from the other colonies. Such material was not lively, but it did publicize the issues of the day. That the House of Delegates attributed use and value to newspaper publicity appears in its occasional practice of ordering its favorite bills printed when they had been defeated by the upper house.[36] Such bills created a kind of political platform for delegates seeking reëlection. Besides the current documents of assembly affairs, Green printed brief notices, reporting the names of members of the lower house, as they were elected, announcing the choice of new speakers, and the like. The present day connotation of "news" hardly applies to these types of political announcement, but in their own time, when the *Gazette* was new, and out-of-colony periodicals were not only infrequent but old upon arrival, they must have carried a great deal of interest.

A second type of political material in the newspaper was the voluntary discussion of public affairs in letters to the printer. Many interested Marylanders wrote open letters discussing all manner of economic and political affairs. The liveliest of such discussion fell in the years around 1730 and 1747, when the tobacco problem, with its cognate questions of crop control, officers' fees, and clergy taxes, was most acute.[37] Contributors to the *Gazette* had the advantage of the guaranty, which was reprinted from time to time, that all varieties of opinion would be printed and that writers so desiring could remain anonymous. In such security they wrote freely and vigorously. They were

36. As in *Maryland Gazette*, July 25, 1750.
37. See above, pp. 82–83, 101–102.

often more savage in attack than the modern editorial writer or columnist, to whose functions they have a real similarity. Written over pseudonyms, which were sometimes local and patriotic in sound, and sometimes classical, or humorous, the letters to the printer indicate both seriousness and pleasure in public affairs, and in every case a vitality which conforms with the aggressiveness of the House of Delegates.

More subtle than either the official document or the open letter to the printer, the philosophical and general essay also had meaning in the politics of Maryland. The fact can hardly be accidental that there is a striking correspondence in time between the appearance of the fullest and keenest critical essays and the occurrence of the most acute controversies in the assembly. Thus "Plain-Dealer," the sceptic, deist, and Whig of 1729, made his plea for English constitutionalism during the judges-oath controversy and at the time of the lower house's most strenuous efforts to secure a tobacco law. Similarly, the essay of "Philo-Eleutherius," in behalf of the study of history, appeared at the time when agitation for a tobacco law was being revived; [38] and a year later, in 1746, the situation had not changed when "Euphranor" declared "that *civil* governments were first instituted for the safety and protection of a people." [39] Again, the satiric mood was never so well expressed in Maryland as in 1773, when the question of a tobacco law and fee regulation once more beset the legislature. At that time a wit, who signed himself "Lexiphanes," wrote his comment on controversy and officeholding in the form of a "glossary" of current "public phrases." "Government," he defined, quoting Cicero, as "Conjuratio contra republicam facta. . . . *A confederacy of the few*, to enslave the many." The provincial council, he said, was composed of "ten fools, and one knave"; and the "patriots" were "the lawyers . . . and their ad-

38. *Maryland Gazette*, February 11, 1728/9, June 7, 1745; see above, pp. 62–64.
39. *Maryland Gazette*, August 20, 1746.

mirers, . . . who like silly sheep, are proud to follow the bell-wethers of the flock." "Lexiphanes" defined government "place" as "the cause of all our disputes. And what would more effectively stop the mouths, and lull to rest our *blustering patriots,*

———— than poppy or mandragora
Or all the drowsy syrups of the East." [40]

The corrosive effect of such satire, written with confidence and in the mood and form of literature popular in Maryland, must have been very great. Very like the writing which in Zenger's paper had so angered the officials of New York, it was of an acid kind which could not have been less damaging to those attacked than the body blows delivered in pamphlet and in assembly speech.

Where, in the social order of Maryland, did the representative element stand? So well equipped with a tradition, both provincial and English, and so aggressive in spirit, did it have real roots in provincial soil? In claiming much, and in becoming, through provincial expression, a part of the liberal way of thought which dominated the thinking of the lower counties, did the House of Delegates have the support of interests which would give it power comparable to that of the proprietary element? Such questions require, if not answers, at least consideration and evaluation, if the problem of revolution is to be held in view.

The principal requirement for voting for candidates for the lower house was the ownership of a fifty-acre freehold or a personal estate worth forty pounds sterling. This was an old requirement, first established by a proprietary writ, in 1670, given a statutory basis under the Crown, and put into permanent form in laws of 1715 and 1716.[41] At the

40. *Maryland Gazette,* July 22, 1773. Compare below, pp. 356–357.
41. Acts, April, 1715, July, 1716, *Archives,* XXX, 270–274, 617–622. This discussion follows the detailed study of Albert E. McKinley, *The Suffrage Franchise in the Thirteen English Colonies in America* (Philadelphia, 1905), pp. 62–78. See also Mereness, *Maryland,* pp. 198–199; Courtlandt F. Bishop, *History of Elections in the American Colonies* (New York, 1893), pp. 33–35, 50, *passim.*

time of the restoration of proprietary government, too, a fine was placed on qualified voters who failed to appear at the polls. In 1718, as part of the extreme anti-Catholic legislation of the period, Catholics were debarred from the vote, lest they make a "party" which "would tend to the discouragement and disturbance of his lordship's Protestant government." [42] Elections were held triennially, or whenever the governor dissolved the house; and four delegates were chosen from each county and two from the incorporated city of Annapolis. A special provision was made for Annapolis, where all householders were allowed to vote, a more liberal provision than the freehold or personal property requirement.

These provincial arrangements follow closely on the model of English law in the matter of voting for members of Parliament. Such had been the exact intention of Lord Baltimore, in his writ of 1670; [43] accordingly, the Maryland franchise laws have in many respects the ring of tradition, and in no respect, unless in the law for compulsory voting, the ring of reform or of democracy. Yet the practice of voting was far from being as exclusive as with English elections to the unreformed House of Commons. Under the letter of the law and the standards of the age, there could be no question, of course, of woman suffrage, or of voting by unfree slaves and servants, or by the propertyless. But the ownership of land was common, not uncommon,[44] and fifty acres was well below the average holding, even among the smaller planters. And even the tenants, who as such could claim no right to vote, are not to be thought of as in a distinct and inferior group, below the smaller freeholders who had the suffrage franchise. Thus no social and economic class, among freemen, was kept from the vote; and, although the exclusion of Catholics and tenants was discriminatory,[45] it does not give the char-

42. Acts, April, 1718, ch. 1, *Archives*, XXXIII, 288.
43. McKinley, *The Suffrage Franchise*, p. 65.
44. See above, pp. 31–32.
45. McKinley, *The Suffrage Franchise*, pp. 74–76.

acter of contemporary exclusiveness in England to the practice of Maryland. A scrap of evidence of a fugitive kind, showing that more than one-third of the number of free white males voted in the "so much talked of Baltimore county election" of 1752,[46] gives a hint, at least, of wide participation in the vote. The idea, once advanced by Professor Jameson in respect of eighteenth-century Virginia, that the social structure of the South did not prevent a substantial element of democracy in the election of burgesses,[47] seems to be true also of proprietary Maryland.

The relations of the assembly with the people, both at election time and between elections, indicate an unstable political balance between the gentry of the lower house and the voters of all classes. The tensions involved in such a balance are not subject to precise estimate; but, even before mid-century, there is reason to believe that the influence of the common voters was a considerable one. In his anxious report of 1729, Governor Calvert told the proprietor that,

things can never go well in the plantations whilst the planters are so generally proud, petulant, and ignorant, and have the common necessary support of government so much under their thumb. The superiority, as I may term it, of the people over the government seems unnatural.[48]

In 1744 and 1745 Daniel Dulany wrote in similar terms to Lord Baltimore. No longer a leader of the lower house but now a favorite of "the court," Dulany said that anticipation of a dissolution made the delegates unreasonable, and that "those who expect to be chosen make a mint among common people of opposing the government at all events." [49] On another occasion he wrote of the dema-

46. The *Maryland Gazette*, March 17, 1752, shows that there were 992 voters. This number may be compared with 2630, the number of free white males of all ages in the county, according to the census of 1755.

47. J. Franklin Jameson, "Virginian Voting in the Colonial Period (1744–1774)," *The Nation*, LVI (1893), 309–310.

48. October 26, 1729, *Archives*, XXV, 605.

49. June 11, 1744, *Calvert Papers*, II, 105.

goguery which he thought to be a serious and a dangerous factor in assembly relations.[50] And again, in 1749, as the first election after the tobacco-inspection law approached, there appeared an extraordinary excitement in the province. When the law had passed there had been popular celebrations in Annapolis and in Talbot county, at least,[51] but now there was doubt and a renewal of tension. According to Governor Ogle many had voted for the law from fear rather than love, others "had kept out of the way," and many had not known which way would please their constituents. Now the common people, who dislike the law, thought that they were gaining strength. Ogle was not sure, but he hoped that they would be disappointed at the polls, and that the reaction against the law would not be too sharp.[52]

Such intimations of the influence of the people on government, written in some alarm by proprietary authorities in Maryland to Lord Baltimore, become the more convincing when viewed in the light of the efforts made to influence the people at election time. The methods were not all savory. Most contemporary references to politics speak of two parties, the "court party" and the "country party," named according to usage familiar in the mother country. As in the England of that time, and different from the modern situation, "party" in Maryland lacked definiteness of association and organization. The phrase "court party" seems to have designated, variously, either the inner group of the proprietary element, or the minority of from ten to twenty delegates, who, in a house of fifty-odd, voted the interests of the proprietary element, or the two together. "Country party" was the designation of those of the majority of the lower house who opposed

50. April 8, 1745, Dulany Papers, II, 33–34, MHS.
51. *Pennsylvania Gazette,* July 30, 1747.
52. Letter to Baltimore, February 12, 1749, *Archives,* XLIV, 699. See also the comments of Sharpe to Calvert, May 20, June 6, 1754, that the Delegates were slow to vote money just before an election. *Ibid.,* VI, 56, 70.

"the court." An occasional bit of evidence tells something of their approach to the voters.

According to a report of the lower-house committee on elections and privileges, in 1749, there had sprung up the practice that candidates, for some considerable time preceding elections, should give "uncommon entertainments, and great quantities of strong and spirituous liquors to the electors." Such a practice the committee feared would destroy the health and peace and quiet of the people, and would foment parties and divisions "hindering a union of interests and councils, the only sure preservative of the common good." [53] The evident though not direct meaning of the delegates was that such corruption was the practice of members of the proprietary element trying to increase their strength in the lower house and to destroy the solidarity of the "country party" there. This investigation in all probability resulted from a recent episode in St. Mary's county, where four delegates who normally voted with the "courtiers" had been elected under suspicious auspices. The charge was that the sheriff, apparently under the influence of a member of the provincial council, had used unfair means to influence the voters and had failed to give a great number of freeholders a proper opportunity to vote. Consequently the House of Delegates voided the election and passed a strong resolution condemning the use of any influence during elections by members of the upper house.[54]

Whatever the literal justice of the complaints and the suggestions of the delegates, Governor Ogle himself has left testimony, also from 1749, of the interest and activity of the great officials in securing spokesmen in the lower house. He wrote to Lord Baltimore that he wanted Dulany to get his two sons elected. "I cannot but flatter myself," he concluded, "that the gentle rubs I gave him may have a good effect. I gave him to understand, that your lord-

53. June 17, 1749, *Archives,* XLVI, 282–283.
54. June 10, 1749, *ibid.,* XLVI, 263–264.

ship had reason to expect from me, that those I gave the most considerable places to, should do your lordship proportional service." [55]

To the delegate and the voter, who must have taken the opposition between the "court" and "country" as something hardly capable of definite issue, the interesting and changing thing must have been the activities and rivalries of different personal factions, within the larger struggle. Around a few men, many an allusion indicates, the delegates formed into cliques. The leaders were such men of property and standing as Dr. Charles Carroll, Philip Hammond, and Stephen Bordley, all of Anne Arundel county.[56] Theirs was the double rôle of speaking for the "country" and acting as political bosses. They dominated the sessions, they introduced and supported candidates for election, and they sought the assistance of relatives, friends, and whoever would help in winning votes. The Scotsman, Dr. Hamilton, wrote an account of an Annapolis election which retains the very flavor of contemporary politics. He had been persuaded, he said, by many of his fellow citizens of Annapolis, to stand as a candidate for the city council. He opposed "a certain creature of the court" whom the proprietary element was trying to force on the city. During the afternoon of election day uproar had been followed by street fighting, the officials had been forced to close the polls, and at the time of writing the matter remained unsettled.[57] The very gusto of the elections—Dr. Hamilton commented that he loved liberty but

55. February 12, 1749, *ibid.*, XLIV, 699.

56. No other source has as many references to factions, leaders, and electioneering, all from the point of view of a participant, as Stephen Bordley's Letterbook, 1740–1747, MHS. Unfortunately initials are often substituted for names, and the meaning is hard to recover. A letter from Michael Earle, a delegate, to "Jemmy" [Hollyday?], December 28, 1754, Corner Collection, MHS, has the same interest and the same fault. See also Bladen to Baltimore, January 22, 1744, *Calvert Papers*, II, 93–94.

57. Letter to Gilbert Hamilton, October 20, 1743, Dr. Hamilton's Letterbook, Dulany Papers, V, 12, MHS. There was worse violence than Dr. Hamilton describes, perhaps killing two men, in the election of 1752, in Baltimore county. *Pennsylvania Gazette*, May 7, 1752.

not such factionalism—bespeaks politics taken seriously by men of standing and participated in by the voters.

A generation and more before the Revolution, then, popular desire and popular vote was an influence admitted by the proprietary element to be powerful and recognized by the delegates to be part of their political life. There were, moreover, occasional indications of political initiative outside assembly walls. Thus about three hundred signers petitioned that Prince George's and Frederick counties be divided and a middle county be set up; [58] and, at another time, a petition from Calvert county led a lower-house committee to report in favor of making the sheriff's office elective rather than appointive by the governor.[59] A writer in the *Gazette*, who signed himself "A Freeman," demonstrated his own belief in the activity and responsibility of the voters; after an invocation, "Oh LIBERTY! Oh SLAVERY! how lovely the one, how despicable the other," he urged the election of good men, not demagogues, to the House of Delegates, and he pleaded for the free vote, cast according to conscience.[60] In Maryland, where the election of delegates was the only election, save that of the vestrymen, and where there was nothing like the New England town meeting to encourage wide participation in government, such a democratic development as the giving of instructions, or a mandate, to the delegates by the constituents was naturally a slow thing. But when such developments did come, in the two decades before the Revolution,[61] they rested on the base of long experience with the vote and at least a generation of the publicizing of legislative affairs.

As an essay in social politics, the writer has sought the testimony of contemporary comment and of the land records, to determine, as far as possible, the standing of the

58. Petitions of May 21, 1751 and later, Black Books, IV, pt. 2, MHRecs.
59. October 14, 1724, *Archives*, XXXV, 105.
60. *Maryland Gazette,* November 13, 1751.
61. See below, pp. 254-255.

House of Delegates in Maryland society. The personal history of most of the members is not to be recovered, but there is a good deal to learn about them as a group. Naturally the most sweeping comment was the most partisan; it was also the least revelatory. Governor Bladen could complain, in a moment of high dispute, that the delegates were "ignorant and illiterate," and could speak of the leaders as "oracles and patriots" and "chief incendiaries." [62] Governor Ogle and Governor Sharpe took the same line, as was natural to their position. Governor Sharpe declared that the house presented "too many instances of the lowest persons, at least men of small fortunes and no soul and very mean capacities, appearing as representatives." [63] On the other hand, William Eddis, who as a placeman had no reason of interest to admire the lower house, paid the following tribute to the standing and equipment of the members:

The delegates returned are generally persons of the greatest consequence in their different counties; and many of them are perfectly acquainted with the political and commercial interests of their constituents. I have frequently heard subjects debated with great powers of eloquence and force of reason; and the utmost regularity and propriety distinguish the whole of their proceedings.[64]

The scrupulous adherence of the delegates to the proper forms, their persistence in their principles, and their knowledge of minutiae, all suggest that Eddis' respect was a fairer judgment of the house than Sharpe's contempt. The two testimonies, however, are not altogether contradictory: the leadership of the house by Bordley and Car-

62. Letter to Baltimore, January 22, 1744, *Calvert Papers,* II, 93–94.
63. Letter to Frederick, Lord Baltimore, June 6, 1754, *Archives,* VI, 68. In a letter to Cecilius Calvert, July 7, 1760, Sharpe adduced the near illiteracy of the members as a reason for not appointing them as deputy-surveyors. *Ibid.,* IX, 427. Ogle's comment is in a letter to Charles, Lord Baltimore, February 12, 1749, *ibid.,* XLIV, 699.
64. Eddis, *Letters from America,* p. 126. The fact that Eddis wrote eighteen years after Sharpe could have little meaning in this connection.

roll supports Eddis, and the contentiousness of the group of provincial Squires Western gives some credibility to Sharpe's opinion.

As to the social and intellectual bias of the delegates, on the point of religion there is only the opinion of Commissary Henderson. It was written early in the century, with evident knowledge: "One third of our assembly are dissenters, and the other two very low." [65] On the point of the influence of the law, there is direct indication, apart from the legal language characteristic of the house, that many of the delegates were lawyers or lay justices administering the law in Maryland. In 1735, for example, a law was passed for the convenience of the members, which fixed the court sessions at times not conflicting with the legislature.[66] And, though other office-holders were kept out of the house, a direct count shows that to the end of the colonial period there were a number of delegates who were also county justices.[67] Very often the members were men who had at some earlier time been justices, or were members of families, such as the Goldsboroughs, the Platers, the Harrisons, or the Barneses, who were regularly represented among the county justices.

A study of the rolls of the assemblies of the eighteenth century shows that the lower house was a remarkably continuous body. In election after election the same delegates, or members of the same families, were returned to the house. For example, St. Mary's county repeatedly elected one member or another of the Key family, and with him was elected a Plater, a Bond, a Greenfield, or a Sothoran, almost as a matter of rule. Anne Arundel county, where politics were very prominent, elected and reëlected Car-

65. Letter to Francis Astry, June 17, 1718, Perry, *Collections*, IV, 112.
66. Acts, 1735, ch. 1, *Archives*, XXXIX, 281.
67. Information on this point is scanty, but the following figures are suggestive. For the counties and years indicated, the figures give the number, among the delegations of four in the house, of those who were also justices of the peace: Somerset, 1751, 3; Kent, 1773, 3; Worcester, 1773, 3; St. Mary's, 1751 and 1773, 2; Cecil, 1773, 2. Goldsborough's List of the Civil Officers of Maryland, 3 MS. volumes, MHS.

rolls, Beales, Hammonds, Worthingtons, and Dulanys; and Calvert county habitually returned a Mackall. From Talbot and Queen Anne's counties, on the Eastern Shore, members of the Goldsborough, Lloyd, Tilghman, and Chamberlaine families were regularly elected. A count of the members of the lower house through the years from 1745 to 1751, years which included three elections and which were marked by struggle and reaction over tobacco inspection and appropriation laws, shows that even under aggravated conditions half or more of the members of the lower house seeking reëlection could win it. Forty-four of the fifty-four members of the 1745 assembly who were available for reëlection in 1746, were reëlected; and, after two more elections, twenty-three, nearly half, of those who had been members of the 1745 assembly were also members in 1751.[68] In less troubled times the stability of the House of Delegates was even more marked, though at no time could it equal that of the upper house, where membership was for an indefinite period.[69] This quality of permanence must have contributed to the traditionalism and the persistence so characteristic of the attitudes and policies of the house.

The economic and social standing of the delegates is well indicated, in tobacco-raising and land-speculating Maryland, by the amount of land they held. Did the gentry dominate the legislature, or did the "men of small fortunes" mentioned by Sharpe? Were the lower house and the upper alike in respect of landholding, or were their interests contrasted at that point as in respect of office-holding? To take historical soundings the writer listed the membership of the two houses for the years 1740, 1758, and 1771, the years of the acutest political difference and conflict between the houses; he then determined, as far as possible, the number of acres held by each individual. With negligible exceptions, this could be

68. These figures are made up from the rolls of the lower house, *Archives*, XLIV, 113, 279–280; XLVI, 250–251, 658–659.
69. See above, pp. 122–126.

done satisfactorily for the full lists of 1758 and 1771, but for 1740 only the records of the Eastern Shore were available.[70]

The striking and important thing indicated about the House of Delegates is that the great number of members were large property-holders.[71] Of 125 estates studied, for the three years, only 16 were smaller than 500 acres; and at least 6 of these belonged to men who can be recognized as members of families wealthy in land. The ordinary member of the lower house was possessed of from several hundred to several thousand acres. A few, but not so few as to be unusual, were, like the "country party" leader, Philip Hammond, with his 17,000 acres, and like Edward Lloyd, the younger, with his 11,000, the holders of some of the largest estates in Maryland. A considerable number entered the house as the owners of from 3,000 to 5,000 acres.

The average holding of members of the upper house was 8,422 acres in 1758, and 7,824 acres in 1771. Such an average associates that house, even more emphatically than the lower house, with the landed wealth of Maryland. The high figure derives, however, from the fact that about half of the membership of the upper house was composed of favorites, such men as Benedict Calvert, the Benjamin Taskers, father and son, Daniel and Walter Dulany, and Edward Lloyd, all of whom represented the greatest landholding families, and who held the high patronage offices. The other half of the upper house was composed of men whose holdings ranged from about 2,500 to 5,000 acres, men whose estates would not have raised them above many in the lower house, or indeed far above the average. The placing of men of moderate fortune on the council was to become, in fact, a policy under Governor Sharpe, who had learned from experience that the

70. The size of the estates was taken from the annual Debt Books, lists compiled for each year and county for the collection of quit-rents. Maryland Land Office, Annapolis.

71. For a fuller picture, by counties, see Table V, in the appendix, below, p. 384.

very wealthiest colonials did not make the most loyal and heedful members of the proprietary element.[72] No poor man, certainly, ever sat in the upper house—William Hayward, who owned some 1,900 acres on the Eastern Shore, was the smallest owner of nineteen members in 1758 and 1771—but many did sit whose estates were not among the greatest. As the protesting members of the seventeenth-century English Commons were often richer and of older family than the lords,[73] so the Maryland delegates were often men of greater estate and members of families of longer standing in the province than the members of the upper house.

Not the difference, then, but the similarity, with respect to their interest in land, emerges from a comparison of the membership of the council and the House of Delegates. The two types of landholders seated in the upper house, the owners of very great and of moderately large estates, were also seated in the lower house, though in different proportions. The many delegates whose holdings were no less than 500 acres and no larger than 2,000 did comprise an element less well-to-do than any in the upper house, but the element was not a poor one. It was not a part of the small planter class, with a low standard of living, nor did it in any distinct way separate itself from the greater owners. Both houses were composed of large planters.

Such a framework of property-holding in the legislature makes the inability of the two houses to agree about proprietary revenues and powers seem not an issue between plebeian and patrician, but a question of the pride and interest of a local squirearchy opposed to the special privileges of an absentee lord and his representatives. Likewise it makes the actual ability to agree, which the houses achieved in the passing of essential economic legislation, such as the paper-money and tobacco-inspection laws, seem not contrary to traditions of disagreement but

72. See the discussion of the case of Edward Lloyd as proprietary agent, below, pp. 262–267.
73. Joseph R. Tanner, *English Constitutional Conflicts*, pp. 6, 90–91.

in accordance with the fundamental similarity which existed between the landed interests of the delegates and the councilors.

Above all, the wealth of the delegates tells us that the representative element in government was as secure and strong as deep entrenchment in the established social order could make it. The traditions and ideas of legislative superiority, so vigorous in the lower house and at once so English and so American, were the voiced convictions of members of the well-established gentry of Maryland. As the gentry were the self-conscious and the unquestioned leaders of every phase of the growing life of the province, whether agricultural, commercial, or cultural, so their chief corporate body, the House of Delegates, achieved a corresponding vitality. Political energy, drawn from such roots, would not fail to challenge whatever opposed the theory and practice of self-government, as Maryland knew it, under the law of England and of the province.

VI

MARYLAND IN THE BRITISH COLONIAL SYSTEM

THE driving impulses toward self-government in Maryland, and ultimately toward revolution, came from within—from the force of domestic need and naturalized liberal ideas and institutions. But the bonds which held the province as a province, in the area of British authority, require as careful an understanding as the impulses to break loose. The proprietary government of Lord Baltimore, which we have already examined, indeed goes further to define those bonds than does the complex of obligations directly imposed by Crown and Parliament. Yet the influence of the home government was far from negligible in Maryland, and, long before the Grenville measures of 1763, 1764, and 1765, it had done its share to evoke the self-conscious will to power of the representative element.

Membership in the old colonial system meant, for Maryland, influences and impacts of a widely various sort —some permanent and almost unconscious, and some intermittent and acutely realized—in the public life of the province. As the ideal of a self-sufficing empire grew in the British mind, parliamentary act and administrative decision piled up an increasing body of regulation and precedent.[1] It affected all the colonies, those with chartered governments equally with those directly under the Crown, for mercantilism loved regularity under the law. The wars of the mid-century, moreover, vastly increased the compulsion toward conformity and coöperation between Britain at home and Britain overseas. Maryland of course felt both types of influences: the long arm of mercantilist law reached into all the ports and plantations of

1. Andrews, *The Colonial Period of American History*, IV; see especially chs. I, III, IX, X.

the province; and military administration made its demands on the assembly and people as it did in all the other colonies. Although there was never real quarrel in Maryland with British mercantilism in its old and recognized aspects, there was nevertheless a great difference in tendency between the increasing economic and political self-sufficiency of the province and the growing demands of the mother country. In time of international war this difference was to produce conflicts as severe as those between the House of Delegates and the lord proprietor.

We have seen in an earlier chapter that the commerce of Maryland centered on the exchange of tobacco for the goods of the mother country, and that in some degree it participated in the rising intercolonial business of the eighteenth century. In such a trade, the province actively conformed with three of the principal provisions of the laws of trade and navigation: it sent a staple commodity regularly to the mother country, as the policy of "enumeration" envisaged; it bought its manufactures principally in the British market, as the Staple Act contemplated; and it gave employment and function to vessels of the British merchant marine, as all mercantilist policy encouraged. While some of Maryland's later commercial activities, such as shipbuilding and sale, were practices beside rather than in behalf of the recognized purposes of the acts of trade, none were in conflict with those laws. Neither were the principles and presumptions of mercantilism ever seriously and openly questioned in those special homes of debate, the assembly and the newspaper of Maryland.

Yet, as we have also seen, conformity in the lines of trade was matched by conscious difficulty if not failure in extracting profit and satisfaction from that trade—in establishing goodwill between Maryland planter and British merchant. And similarly in politics, the institutional irregularities of Lord Baltimore's system were plain to all; the underlying similarity between crown and proprietary government was not apparent or relevant to provincial thought.[2] In the present chapter it will be useful to view these angular features of the Maryland situation in their bearing on the relationship between the province and the mother country. What was the normal functioning connection of the proprietary government with the officers of the Crown? Did the administration of the laws of trade represent a considerable connection between the province and the mother country? Were the military demands of the Crown, during the French and Indian wars, of a sort that Maryland could meet? Were the responses of the colony loyal and just? Did proximity or sentiment or other relationship connect the affairs of Maryland in a very conscious way with the affairs of other colonies? Such considerations will reveal something of the elements of both strength and weakness in the bonds between Maryland and Great Britain during the decades before the intercolonial revolutionary movement matured.

In the relations of the province with the Crown, the position of the governor was hardly less central than in its relations with the lord proprietor. The laws of trade placed the responsibility for the prevention of smuggling squarely on the colonial governors, and the governor of proprietary Maryland stood in this respect on no different ground from that of the governor of a royal province. Under the law, the governor could not assume office until this responsibility had been formally undertaken before, and with the approval of, the Crown. Accordingly, whenever Lord Baltimore appointed a new governor, there was an elaborate procedure to be executed before several authorities of the home government. The process illustrates, in a unique way, the normal connection between the proprietorship and the Crown.

Lord Baltimore had first to make his nominee known to the king in council. He did this in the form of a petition, praying the royal assent. Although on at least one occasion the Privy Council refused for a time to act further than to refer the name to the Board of Trade for investi-

2. See above, pp. 114–115, 118.

gation, it ordinarily issued without delay an order in council which approved the nomination on condition that the requirements of the law as to bonding and giving security for the execution of the acts of trade be entirely fulfilled. The execution of these requirements lay with the Board of Trade. On the receipt of the order in council, and on learning from Lord Baltimore the names of two individuals who would sign the bond (in the amount of two thousand pounds), the board ordered the bond prepared and the governor's trade instructions drafted. After the bond had been drawn up by counsel, and the names of the guarantors, who were likely to be London merchants in the Maryland trade, had been inserted, a copy was sent to the secretary of the Lords Commissioners of the Treasury. It was the duty of the secretary to see that the governor's security was placed in the royal Exchequer; notification that this step had been accomplished came back to the Board of Trade from the king's remembrancer, an official of the Exchequer itself.

Meanwhile the preparation of the trade instructions had been going forward in the Board of Trade. New instructions were based on old, but revisions were made to include new laws, and the drafting sometimes entailed correspondence with such officials as the royal Customs Commissioners, or the counsel, or the secretary of that board. On completion, the instructions were sent with an explanatory representation to the Privy Council. Approval came in the form of an order in council to one of the secretaries of state, requiring him to prepare the instructions for the royal signature. When finally issued, the instructions were formally addressed to the lord proprietor, whose lieutenant the governor was, and not to the governor himself; but the governor's name was repeated in paragraph after paragraph—under the responsibility of the proprietor, he was to know the law, take oath to execute it, and perform the duties which the instructions set forth at length. When the trade instructions were issued and the oath given, the new governor was ready, as far as the Crown was concerned, to take over his duties. The whole procedure of approving, bonding, securing, and issuing the instructions required from two to ten months.[3] Much time seems to have been consumed by formalities, but the governor's duties in enforcing the acts of trade rested on an intricate and growing body of law. The responsibilities defined in the trade instructions gave the governor standing as a high representative of the authority of the Crown, under the laws of Parliament. As these were added to his responsibilities as the representative of the lord proprietor, the governor of Maryland enjoyed a total authority like that of a governor of a royal province such as Virginia or New York.

The trade instructions were the principal instructions which the governor of Maryland ever received from the Crown.[4] They were very bulky documents, largely given to a digest of those commercial laws of Great Britain which had any bearing on the colonies, and to a designation of those provisions which were most subject to abuse, and therefore demanded the most scrupulous attention. The instructions required the governor to see that the naval officers—whom we have already seen as appointees of the governor and collectors of the provincial duties— keep detailed records of all shipping, and that they return naval office lists, noting elaborate data on all vessels entered and cleared. These data were to be prepared in triplicate and sent to the Commissioners of the Treasury, the Board of Trade, and the Commissioners of Customs

3. This discussion is based on Board of Trade papers, HSP. The writer followed the case of Governor B. L. Calvert, November 29, 1726 to September 13, 1727 (Board of Trade Papers, Proprieties, XI, XII, HSP; *Board of Trade Journal, 1722-3-1728*), and compared this with other cases. See Andrews, *Colonial Period of American History*, IV, 116, 401.

4. Governor Sharpe's trade instructions, May 10, 1753, are in Portfolio no. 2, MHRecs; and Governor Eden's, November 30, 1768, are printed, *Archives*, XXXII, 283–301. Except that Eden's lacks a list of the laws to be executed, such as occupies 12 MS. pages of Sharpe's, the two documents are closely similar.

in London.[5] There was also a requirement that the governor should correspond with the Customs Commissioners about any misdemeanors of the customs collectors. Such obligations were detailed and complex, but for the most part they were matters of a routine sort; they presumed no great activity in the governor's relations with the home government. Thus, while the trade instructions set up high responsibilities for the governor and the naval officers, they contained nothing to lead to a very dynamic connection between the Crown and the proprietary system.

Nor were the other instructions and communications, having to do with non-military affairs, such as to establish a very active relationship between Maryland and the home government. Such instructions were very infrequent. In 1727 the Board of Trade sent "orders," as Governor Calvert spoke of them, that he proclaim the accession of George II—a mere matter of form.[6] In 1732, indeed, the king in council sent an imperative warning to Lord Baltimore, in the form of additional instructions. London merchants had complained, the instructions said, that a certain Maryland duty—evidently the port or tonnage duty of 1661—discriminated against them and in favor of the shippers of the province. The proprietor was informed that the law of the realm forbade such duties and that he must assent to no further laws of the sort.[7] But orders

5. The naval officers apparently kept the full records for which the governor made them responsible (see list of the surviving "port of entry books," below, pp. 386, 388). But they were deficient in sending the quarterly lists to England: on this point the writer can support his own impression, from the study of transcribed materials, by the exhaustive searches made in the British records for Dr. John Cox's elaborate statistical analysis of colonial trade, made at the University of California. On the other hand, George Plater, naval officer for the port of Patuxent, once wrote the Board of Trade that he would send it lists, as Governor Sharpe instructed, and that he had previously sent them to the Customs Commissioners (October 10, 1754, BT Proprieties, XIX, HSP). See the discussion of the naval officership in Andrews, *Colonial Period of American History*, IV, 180–191.

6. Calvert to Board of Trade, December 22, 1727, BT Proprieties, XII, HSP.

7. May 5, 1732, *Archives*, XXXVII, 586.

from the Crown were unusual before mid-century, when the French and Indian War increased them; and, for long periods, proprietary Maryland seems to have had an institutional existence almost apart from the British government. The journals of the Board of Trade are indicative: for many years during the period between the restoration of the proprietorship and the French and Indian War—for about one year in four—there were no Maryland entries whatever; where there were entries, they reveal the incidental rather than the important, the reading of occasional Maryland documents, the making of minor recommendations, and the like.[8] Likewise, the very small number of naval-office lists from Maryland still of record in the British archives indicates that the governors were lax in requiring that returns be made as demanded in the trade instructions.[9]

The difference between the relations of Maryland with the Crown and the usual relations of colony and king is indicated at its widest in the matter of the royal disallowance. In the colonies generally the right and practice of the king in council to disallow the laws of the assemblies was an important feature of crown control: it protected the royal prerogative from undue infringement by assembly law; it could be used to safeguard the provisions of the governor's instructions against contrary legislation; it kept colonial law, and especially commercial law, in line with British policy; and in a wide and general way it stood for the constitutional superiority of the Crown in the colonies, and indicated the inferiority of the assemblies.[10] Yet the disallowance did not apply to Maryland, and in this important respect the proprietary province stood in a position of freedom from the Crown which was matched only by the corporate colonies of Connecticut and

8. *Board of Trade Journal, 1714-15-1753.*
9. See above, p. 189, n. 5.
10. Charles M. Andrews, "The Royal Disallowance," *Proceedings of the American Antiquarian Society*, N.S., XXIV (1914), 342-362; Elmer B. Russell, *The Review of American Colonial Legislation by the King in Council* (New York, 1915).

Rhode Island. As with them, this special immunity derived from a seventeenth-century charter which conferred law-making powers without any requirement that the laws be submitted for review. There was in fact no actual disallowance of a Maryland law after the restoration of proprietary government in 1715.

Freedom from the disallowance and from any direct control of legislation was a point of pride with the fifth Lord Baltimore. He had occasion to declare himself in 1749, when there was a bill before the House of Commons to regulate paper money in the colonies, and in the bill a rider which would have made the proprietary colonies as directly subject to royal instruction as the crown colonies. In a petition to the house, the proprietor said that he had no objection to a general paper-money law, although Maryland money was not such as to require limitation, but he did make a strong protest against the rider. Royal instructions as contemplated, he said, would blend all the colonies into a constitutional similarity, particularly because they would forbid and restrict legislation of certain sorts. Lord Baltimore declared that the charter of 1632 reserved the Crown no rights in legislation, and that none were necessary. He said that residence in England made his own interest, and the use of his own veto, conform with the true interest of the Crown, and he added that the Commons would hardly wish to strengthen the Crown over such chartered rights as his own.[11]

Baltimore's essential point, declarative of his legal immunity, was a sound one, as we have seen. His plea to the House of Commons, however, does not signify either that, without the disallowance, the Crown exercised no oversight of Maryland law, or that, without instruction, the proprietor paid no attention to the wishes of the home

11. Petition [1749], *Archives*, XLIV, 700–704. The "additional instructions" of 1732, mentioned above as an unusual instance in Maryland's relation with the Crown, were superficially very like the thing Lord Baltimore denied in 1749. Those instructions were really trade instructions, however, and anyway contemplated no particular laws for disallowance.

government in approving new statutes. Maryland's independence became the object of inquiry and investigation, in behalf of Parliament, in 1732. In that year the Board of Trade reported to the House of Commons that it had little knowledge of Maryland, Connecticut, and Rhode Island, because they did not send their laws for approval or disallowance and did not make returns of their legislative proceedings.[12] The house accordingly directed the board to prepare a full statement about all the colonies; and the board, which had already sent inquiries, informed Governor Ogle of the interest of the Commons, and demanded data about the laws and constitution of Maryland, and about trade.[13] Governor Ogle's "answers to the queries" of the board, accompanied by a copy of the charter, was not the first elaborate report supplied by a proprietary governor, but there had been none for a dozen years; and, although it did not lead to a series of annual reports, as the Board of Trade intended, it did bring information and surveillance to the board—the clearing-house of colonial and commercial information and policy for the British Crown. The report of 1732 was shortly to be supplemented by special data for the board on naval stores, fishing, and provincial duty-laws;[14] and it was to be followed by at least four similar reports: another by Ogle, in his second administration, two by Governor Sharpe, and one by Governor Eden.[15] In the seven-

12. George Chalmers, *Political Annals of the Present United Colonies* . . . (London, 1780), I, 203; David Macpherson, *Annals of Commerce, Manufactures, Fisheries, and Navigation* . . . (London, 1805), III, 187.

13. Alured Popple to Ogle, June 16, 1732, *Archives*, XXXVII, 587–588.

14. Letters to Board of Trade, October 16, 1734, April 7, 1736, BT Proprieties, XIII, HSP.

15. The writer has seen six of the proprietary governors' "answers to queries," as follows: Hart's, August 25, 1720, *Md. Hist. Mag.*, XXIX, 252–255; Ogle's, 1732, *Archives*, XXXVII, 588–589; Ogle's, 1749, *ibid.*, XXVIII, 467–471; Sharpe's, 1756, BT Proprieties, XIX, HSP; Sharpe's, 1762, *ibid.*, XXI (1); Eden's, 1773, *Md. Hist. Mag.*, II, 354–362. Eden's report was merely a revision of Sharpe's second, and did not attempt to bring economic data up to date. For council and legislative proceedings in support of these reports, see *Archives*, XXXVII, 256, 291–

teen-thirties, the Board of Trade also asked for full collections of the laws in effect in Maryland; it made the same request of the corporate colonies of New England. This demand met with much delay, and became a matter of "additional instructions" by the Privy Council in 1752—the Council needed to have the laws for use in judicial session.[16] In 1754 Lord Baltimore instructed the governor to hurry the sending of the laws,[17] but the matter seems to have had to await Bacon's edition of the laws in 1765, the only accurate and official compilation of the pre-revolutionary period.[18]

Beside general oversight, particular issues and interests led to communication and connection between the home government and the proprietary. Concern about paper money raised a query from the Crown years before Parliament took action. In 1740 the lords justices required the Board of Trade to send a circular letter to Maryland, Connecticut, Rhode Island, and Pennsylvania, inquiring what issues of paper had been authorized by law, and what their character. This led to an explanation of the Maryland situation by Governor Ogle, in which he stressed the conservative and self-liquidating provisions of the paper-money act.[19] A few years later the provincial secretary was required to send occasional reports of the natu-

293 (1732); XXVIII, 436–438 (1749); XXXI, 143–147 (1756); XXXII, 19–28 (1762).

16. Baltimore to Lord Fitz-Walter, March 11, 1736, BT Proprieties, XIII; *Board of Trade Journal, 1749-50–1753,* p. 279; Lords Justices to Ogle, April 28, 1752, *Archives,* XXVIII, 561.

17. Instructions to Sharpe, January 5, 1754, Black Books, XI, MHRecs.

18. Thomas Bacon, editor, *Laws of Maryland at Large* . . . (Annapolis, 1765). For a detailed bibliographical account, see Wroth, *Printing in Colonial Maryland,* pp. 95–110, 223. In August, 1720, Governor Hart had sent a book of Maryland laws, 1692–1718. *Board of Trade Journal, 1718–1722,* p. 194.

19. Ogle sent a copy of the law and at least two letters, April 20, December 15, 1740, and John Sharpe made a statement for the proprietor. BT Proprieties, XIV, XV; *Board of Trade Journal, 1734-5–1741,* pp. 345, 347–348, 397; Ogle to Board of Trade, December 20, 1740, *Archives,* XXVIII, 237–238.

ralization of foreign Protestant immigrants, by assembly law, as an act of Parliament provided.[20] In such small ways, the closer supervision and greater influence of the British government, which was to become so crucial in the years before the Revolution, had a good many antecedents in the fourth and fifth decades of the century.

Both the proprietary element and the representative seem to have been sensitive to the interest of the home government in Maryland. If the normal attitude on the proprietary side was defensive, against the Crown, fearing the circumscription of charter rights and of old habits of independence in decision,[21] Lord Baltimore did not fear contact with high officers of state. Maryland never had a colonial agent, properly so called, to represent the province before the Crown and Parliament; but on various occasions Lord Baltimore and his representatives presented their version, at least, of the claims and interests of the province. Thus, the proprietor himself once attended the Board of Trade, and consulted with the London merchants to Maryland and Virginia, on the question of a lighthouse to be erected on Cape Henry; Mr. John Sharpe, variously styled as Lord Baltimore's solicitor and as "Agent for Maryland," appeared in the boundary dispute with the Penns; and Hugh Hamersley, later provincial secretary in England, went before the board as "Agent for the Proprietor of Maryland." [22]

On the side of the House of Delegates, the Crown became the symbol of constitutional and political justice

20. Edmund Jennings to Board of Trade, July 4, 1743, June 12, 1744, July 24, 1746, March 6, 1748, September 5, 1754, BT Proprieties, XVI, HSP.

21. For example, in 1729, before the paper-money law was passed and the Board of Trade had occasion to make inquiries as it did in 1740, Governor Calvert declared he dared not pass such a law without the approval of the Crown, because old instructions of George I forbade laws of "unusual" nature. Letter to Lord Baltimore, October 26, 1729, *Archives*, XXV, 603–604.

22. *Board of Trade Journal, 1722-3–1728*, pp. 441, 443; BT Proprieties, XLVII, April 5, May 17, 1737; XLIX, February 6, 1739; LXI, December 19, 1753, HSP.

as well as of civil justice for the individual. In asserting
the rights of Marylanders, both as men and Englishmen,
against the privileges of Lord Baltimore, the lower house
attempted, in ways which will concern us in the next chapter, to swing provincial controversies into the orbit of the
king in council. There, the assemblymen claimed, a fair
decision could be reached and the true rights of the subject be declared and effected.[23] Lord Baltimore, at first,
naturally opposed letting his authority come to trial, but
he, too, saw political strength to be drawn from the authority of crown office. In 1737 he successfully appealed
to his majesty's attorney-general for a legal opinion
which would support him in an issue with the lower house
over the exercise of the appointing power.[24] Both proprietor and Delegates gravitated toward the home government when they felt that there was gain to be had in the
long warfare of assembly relations.

On a lower plane than high proprietary interest and
the ambitions of the House of Delegates, Maryland's
connection with the Crown was always represented by the
customs officials of the royal establishment, resident in the
province. The daily business of enforcing the laws of
trade lay in the hands of the naval officers, the eyes and
ears of the colonial system,[25] and of the royal officials—
collectors, surveyors, and comptrollers—who collected the

23. On the attitude of the Delegates, see below, chs. VII, X. The
nearest approach to an actual settlement of a Maryland political controversy before the king in council came in 1728–1729, when the clergy
of the province sent a special agent to England to protest the tobacco
law of 1728, on the ground that it unjustly reduced their salaries in
tobacco. The matter was presented to the Privy Council, but did not
come to decision before Lord Baltimore disallowed the law (letter of
C. Calvert, and Baltimore's dissent, January 30, 1729, *Archives,*
XXXVIII, 438–439, 443; *Acts of the Privy Council, Colonial,* III, 252;
see above, pp. 92–93). There were very few individual appeals from the
Maryland courts to the Privy Council (*Acts of the Privy Council,
Colonial, passim;* Bond, *The Court of Appeals of Maryland,* p. 43).
24. Opinion of John Willes, January 22, 1737, *Archives,* XXVIII,
119–120. For a parallel case and a more suggestive one, see below,
pp. 243–245.
25. See above, pp. 188–189.

plantation duty imposed by Parliament in 1673, and who seized vessels for illegal trading. In 1744 there were three collectorships of the customs establishment in Maryland, one of which paid a salary of £80, and the others £60 each. There were also six surveyorships, which paid salaries of £60 in the cases of the larger ports, and £50, £40, and £35 at the smaller and more outlying ones. In that year, however, four of these offices were either unoccupied or held by men whose names were unknown in England —apparently a representative situation. By 1766, just before the American customs establishment was set up in Boston, the Maryland personnel had increased to fourteen in all: four collectors, six surveyors, and four comptrollers.[26] As there was only one instance of a collector and a surveyor being located in the same port, those officers probably performed essentially similar duties in Maryland: collecting the plantation duty and guarding against illicit trade. As the comptrollers, on the other hand, were always located where there was also a collector, their task was probably that of checking the collectors and acting with them in the enforcement of the navigation laws.[27] From fragmentary evidence it seems that the acts of trade were administered at a loss in Maryland; probably there was never a surplus. In 1766 the ports of North Potomac and of Pocomoke produced deficits much greater than gross receipts; and the port of Patuxent produced a net gain, largely from duties on Madeira and British wines and foreign sugar and molasses.[28]

The authority to appoint customs officials lay of course with the Crown and not Lord Baltimore; yet the proprie-

26. Lists, 1744, British Museum, Additional MSS. 8831, f. 123; 1766, Public Record Office, Treasury Papers, 1:452, f. 195, LC.

27. On the duties of the collectors, surveyors, and comptrollers, and of their assistants, see Andrews, *Colonial Period of American History,* IV, 204–213.

28. This of course followed the passage of the Sugar Act (1764) which substituted lower duties on sugar products for the prohibitive ones in the Molasses Act (1733). Account in PRO, Treasury, 1: 442, f. 259, LC.

tary element exercised no little influence in the making of placements. A Calvert and a Tasker held the best-paid offices on the 1744 list, and twenty years later four members or sometime members of the proprietary council were also royal customs officials. Such dovetailing of patronage, provincial and royal, can hardly have made for the best interests of the customs. At one time Benedict Calvert appointed Thomas Chamberlaine, of a prominent Eastern Shore family, to be deputy-collector for the port of Oxford, while Chamberlaine also acted as deputy naval officer in the same port for Edward Lloyd. Thus two different types of duties, which should have checked and balanced each other, were put in the hands of Chamberlaine; and Chamberlaine agreed to act in both offices for only one-third of the fees, and to hand two-thirds to the principal officers.[29] Where proprietary influences did not control, as in the case of Chamberlaine, there were sometimes other influences equally indifferent to the functioning of the service. For example, James Sterling, a Church of England clergyman in the province, went to England, and, with the support, it seems, of Sir George Lyttelton and the future Earl Nugent, secured the creation of a new collectorship on the Eastern Shore and his own appointment in that office. The appointment raised a protest among the London merchants trading into the upper bay, and twenty-two of them petitioned the Lords of the Treasury declaring that the new arrangement was a serious inconvenience to shippers and should be discontinued.[30] There is no sign that any attention was paid to the protest of the merchants or to their suggestion,

---

29. Register of the Collector of the Port of Oxford, Maryland, 1747–1775, MHS.

·30. The documents in this case are printed in full in L. C. Wroth, "James Sterling: Poet, Priest, and Prophet of Empire," *Proceedings of the American Antiquarian Society*, N.S., XLI (1931), 44–45. See also Robert L. Swain, "Chestertown as a Colonial Port, 1706–1775," *Washington College Bulletin* (Chestertown), XIV (1936), no. 6. The influence of the London merchant, John Hanbury, once secured a collectorship for a Maryland associate, Daniel Wolstenholme.

namely, that a riding-surveyor be appointed, instead of a collector, and that he could prevent illegal trade in northeastern Maryland. The Sterling appointment was permitted to stand, a plain matter of social and political influence.

There is very little evidence about the effectiveness of the customs service in Maryland. The many inlets, which could not possibly have been patrolled, and the personnel of the service, would both indicate opportunity for illegal trade. Yet both Governor Ogle and Governor Sharpe denied that there was smuggling, save perhaps some rum brought in by Pennsylvania ·traders.[31] A slender volume of proceedings of the vice-admiralty court of the province for the last two decades of the colonial period shows only nine prosecutions under the acts of trade; in five cases, the vessels were forfeited, and the proceeds ordered divided equally, one-third to the king, one-third to the governor, and one-third to the informant. The libelants who brought the cases before the court ranged from the highest to the lowest enforcing officers: the governor sued once; a naval officer, three times; a collector, twice; a comptroller, twice; and a landwaiter, weigher, gauger, and preventive officer, once. Their successes are enough to show that there was a practical way for British officials to take action, under admiralty law, without a jury, whenever there was illicit trade to be prosecuted. Of the five actions leading to conviction, one was a case of a vessel carrying enumerated commodities without complying with the acts of Parliament, and the other four were cases of failure to register, bond, and enter vessels in the coastal trade.[32] The record

31. Ogle to Board of Trade, December 13, 1749, Sharpe to Cecilius Calvert, January 12, 1755, to William Pitt, February 27, 1761, *Archives,* XXVIII, 469; VI, 164; IX, 490; see above, p. 115.

32. Maryland Vice-Admiralty Court, 1754–1773, MS., LC. Besides these cases under the acts of trade, there were seven cases of maritime law, involving the complaints of mariners against captains, suits for payment by owners and masters, and the like. The vice-admiralty court in Maryland was composed of a judge, commissioned by the governor, and a marshal and a register. The commission was sealed by the great seal of Maryland, and the appointment was proprietary not royal.

is a slender one, not proof of entire regularity in the matter of trade, but clearly not indicative of much smuggling.

The court record tells as much as we can find about law-breaking, but naturally is silent on the inefficiencies in enforcing the mercantilist code. The visit to Maryland, in 1770, of Inspector-General John Williams of the American customs establishment, recently set up in Boston, revealed instances of half-hearted enforcement. In the port of Patuxent, on the lower Western Shore, he discovered not that the traders eluded the deputy-collector, but that they entered and landed goods without real inspection and that when they cleared out they reported quantities of goods and paid duties "at their own elections." A question to the deputy-collector, why things were done so loosely, brought the candid response that he could not take many pains for eighteen or twenty pounds a year, his quarter-share of the collector's fees.[33] At Annapolis, Williams found the service in good shape; but on the upper Eastern Shore, in the office created for Sterling, he found ground for suspicion, at least. There he judged the collector to be an able man, but the collector himself was the owner of a brig in the West India and foreign trade. The management of the vessel, indeed, was in the names of local merchants, not his own, but the whole arrangement was such as to invite smuggling. When Williams admonished him to clear himself of suspicious connections, the collector promised to do so if he were given more money.[34] Williams, like Governor Sharpe, thought that the upper bay was the most likely area for smuggling, but he presented no real evidence.

Laxity within the operation of the law, rather than

33. Williams to Customs Commissioners, Boston, May 12, 1770, *Md. Hist. Mag.*, XXVII, 231–232.

34. Letter to Williams, May 26, 1770, *ibid.*, XXVII, 234. Two years after Williams' investigation, the Boston commissioners advised the Treasury Board in London that the collectorship created for Sterling be redefined, and that Baltimore be made a separate port. September 28, 1772, *ibid.*, XXVII, 235–238.

smuggling in defiance of it, seems to have been the principal abuse of the acts of trade in Maryland. Two years before Williams' inspection of the ports, the commissioners in Boston knew that some of the Maryland customs offices were useless, and that they could be let fall vacant without loss to the service.[35]

A backward view of the normal, peace-time official and administrative connections between Maryland and the home government shows a relationship which touched only a few people in any direct and functional way. From the proprietor and the lieutenant-governor, in their responsibilities and in their contact with the king in council, to the lower officers of the customs service, in their reports and accounts to their superiors, the connection with the British government indeed reveals many signs and symbols of the sovereignty of the king, of the unquestioned authority and rightness of the parliamentary acts of trade and navigation, and of colonial dependency on the mother country. But it also shows, in such matters as the freedom of Maryland legislation from royal disallowance and the infrequency of royal instruction to the governors, that proprietary government made Maryland's relations with the Crown much less intimate than were those of the royal colonies. Only a handful of officials, and the merchants and shippers who dealt with them, could have known much of the reach of the British government to Maryland.

It seems significant, too, that in a community so politically outspoken as Maryland, the principles and practices of British mercantilism never evoked positive expressions of loyalty and approval. Such expression would have been natural in a generation of international rivalry; the silence of the record and the apparent absence of sentiment about British mercantilism stands in complete contrast to the positive feeling of the province about the principles and practices of English constitutionalism and

35. Commissioners to Treasury Board, October 28, 1768, PRO, Treasury, 1: 465, f. 430, LC.

liberalism. It may be, principally, that mercantilist law and administration seemed so entirely matters to be taken for granted, and so far from the common lot and from provincial influence, that praise, blame, or discussion would have had no purpose.[36] Yet this can hardly be the whole truth, for the entire century was one of war and rivalry with the French, and the laws of trade were the common bond of the British colonial world. The besetting difficulties of the tobacco trade may help to explain the silence, and so may the system of patronage in the customs service, so closely associated with the patronage of the proprietary element. Whatever the explanation, the situation reveals a province-and-home-government relationship in which Maryland participated without complaint and without rejoicing. Such a relationship formed a poor basis for the active coöperation and the colonial obedience demanded by the Crown during the third and fourth intercolonial wars.

The beginning of King George's War, in 1739, suddenly expanded the interest of the home government in all of the affairs of the colonies which had any bearing on the military. That interest remained active until the end of the French and Indian War; and the imperial reforms which Grenville and others attempted in 1763 and after were to be half military in purpose. In the two decades of more or less continuous war with Spain and France, the Crown made heavy demands on Maryland only in 1741 and 1746, and from 1754 through 1758. Yet those demands were sufficient to transform Maryland's relationship with the Crown from a passive to an active one. Secretaries of state, whose names would hardly have reached Maryland in time of peace, now sent demands for men and money to the governors; these demands confronted the legislature and the people directly, as appropriations were passed or refused, and as men enlisted or

36. But the assembly was ready to discuss any aspect of mercantilist law which was burdensome to the interests of the province. See above, pp. 114–115.

refused to enlist for service. Military commanders in the field, acting on the authority of royal commissions and instructions, now requisitioned the province for pressing needs. For a brief period, early in the French and Indian War, the common danger of invasion terrorized the western part of Maryland. Frequent correspondence between the governor and crown officials, including the governors of the royal colonies, connected Maryland, for brief periods at least, with the national interests of mother country and sister colonies.

The special fate of Maryland, however, was to be only indirectly and in a general way concerned with the major objective of the wars, the control of the Mississippi river valley. When, as the mid-century approached, France seemed likely to make good her claim to the Ohio and the upper Mississippi, certain Marylanders were interested and concerned for the future growth of the province.[37] But the urgency and the dangers of war were less serious in Maryland than in the neighboring colonies or in the British Empire as a whole. The wide fighting frontiers of Virginia and Pennsylvania enveloped and gave an unearned security to Maryland's narrow frontier and unextended settlements; those provinces had wide transmontane land claims for which to fight, and Maryland had few. The fact that trade focused so largely in the east, and that economic expansion meant the development of grain lands and trade from the Monocacy down to the bay, rather than deep penetration in the west, helps explain Maryland's small part in the wars. In 1758 the two houses of the assembly—which had been in constant controversy about appropriations and the constitutional terms on which they should be granted—united to send formal addresses to the king, the Board of Trade, and the lord proprietor, praying their influence in securing relief from a parliamentary embargo on the provision trade.[38]

37. Dr. Carroll to Governor Ogle, February 17, 1731/2, *Md. Hist. Mag.*, XIX, 291–293.

38. The Board of Trade reported favorably on the request, in so far as Maryland petitioned for freedom to send grain to Madeira or to

Commercial depression, to which the address of the assembly testified, was Maryland's more unanimous concern than victory over the French.

The first military demands, made in 1740, were sent in the form of letters from the secretary of state for the southern department, the Duke of Newcastle, and also in the form of direct war instructions from the king in council. They specified that the proprietary governor should grant commissions to the officers of provincial troops, that the council should act on matters pertaining to the enlistment and the transportation of troops, that the assembly should grant such appropriations as were necessary, and that the people should be called on to volunteer.[39] Thus in making its earliest military demands of the long war period, British authority assumed what it was to continue to assume, namely, that the semi-voluntary system of colonial coöperation would work. In the case of Maryland this involved the further assumption that agreement between the proprietary and the representative elements in the assembly would furnish the working basis for military coöperation between the proprietary province and the Crown.

Such an assumption was of course unjustified. In the next chapter we shall have to examine the political tensions which obstructed Maryland coöperation, under the Crown, in the prosecution of the wars; they will explain much of the growth of lower-house radicalism in the decades before the Revolution. For the present, an external view of what Maryland did and failed to do, in response to the demands of the Crown, will add to our understanding of relations with the home government.

The difficulties of King George's War were not nearly as great as those of the French and Indian War to follow.

friendly European powers, but the Privy Council disagreed. Upper House Journal, December 14, 1757, Liber 35, MHRecs; Board of Trade to Privy Council, July 12, 1758, *Acts of the Privy Council, Colonial*, III, 386-387; William Sharpe to Baltimore, August 23, 1758, Calvert Papers, nos. 1204, 594, MHS.

39. Newcastle to Ogle, January 5, 1740; George II, instructions to Ogle, April 2, 1740, *Archives*, XXVIII, 199-201, 214-216.

The first instance of a specific demand for an appropriation, and for Maryland to participate in military activities outside her own borders, came on the occasion of the Cartagena expedition of 1741. The assembly voted money without difficulty; three hundred-odd Marylanders were mustered, victualed, and transported to the West Indies; and there the royal commander-in-chief took charge, and assumed the financial responsibility for maintaining them.[40] Five years later there was planned another distant expedition; it was to be a great campaign to take Canada from the French. According to Newcastle's orders to Governor Bladen, troops were to be raised and transported to Albany, where they would join others from New York, Pennsylvania, and Virginia, under the command of Governor Gooch of Virginia.[41] Again a supply bill was passed; arms and ammunition were ordered to be taken from the magazines of the province, though with the understanding that the Crown would make compensation; and Marylanders were sent into the royal service. Three companies went to Albany, not a great number of men, but one which compared favorably with the numbers sent by Virginia and Pennsylvania.[42] While Maryland made such contributions to the general cause, the tobacco trade occasionally received the security of a convoy, supplied without cost to the province by the royal navy.[43]

40. Five hundred men were provided in the law, but only 309 were raised and sent. Besides "bounty money," Maryland spent £1,483 12s. 10d. on the expedition. Account of Benjamin Tasker, May 29, 1741, *Archives*, XLII, 162.

41. April 9, 1746, *ibid.*, XXVIII, 360–362.

42. Account, Treasury, 1: 328, f. 122, LC. The settlement of accounts for the expedition was slow. In 1747, Newcastle indicated, through Governor Shirley, that he wished that the colonies would make advances for subsisting their troops at Albany, and that the home government could make repayment later. But Maryland refused advances. Newcastle to Shirley, May 30, 1747, Upper House Journal, December 23, 1747, *Archives*, XLIV, 676–677, 682. Compensation for Maryland's advance of arms and ammunition came slowly, and was perhaps never completed. There was money still due in 1753, and perhaps as late as 1772. Treasury, 1: 351, 483, LC.

43. Petitions of various English merchants to the Lords of the Admiralty, April 10, 1740, September 14, November 9, 1741, House of

The relatively successful coöperation of King George's War was marked, however, by plain signs of Maryland's independence of decision. When Governor Shirley of Massachusetts requested help for his expedition against Louisbourg, the assembly refused to appropriate. More important, from the point of view of relations with the Crown, was the way in which assembly relations prevented Governor Bladen from executing certain orders sent him by the lords justices. In 1743, on the occasion of France's entering the war, they instructed the governor to have the province put in a sound condition of defense.[44] But the passing of a duty for the purchase of arms and ammunition was requisite, and that kind of duty law was one of the most most hotly disputed questions of finance and of prerogative which divided the House of Delegates from the proprietary element. Not even the pressure of royal authority sufficed to bring the two houses to agreement, and the orders of the lords justices were disregarded. This situation demonstrated for the first time what was repeatedly to be the case during the French and Indian War: the balance of power between the Delegates and the proprietor exerted greater influence in Maryland political affairs than any other consideration.

From the time of Governor Sharpe's arrival in Maryland, in 1753, to the fall of Quebec, in the autumn of 1759, the relations of the province with the Crown were particularly intense. Four ministries at home and five military commanders in America[45] plied the governor

Lords Library, Andrews and Davenport, *Guide*, p. 216, item 176, LC. Dr. Carroll spoke of the convoy from Maryland, in a letter to William Black, March 21, 1746, *Md. Hist. Mag.*, XXII, 285. In 1761 Governor Sharpe secured a convoy from Lord Colvill, in Halifax, to protect the tobacco trade. Colvill to Captain Adam of the *Diana*, November 7, 1761, Portfolio no. 3, MHRecs.

44. A. Stone to Bladen, August 15, 1743, *Archives*, XXVIII, 312.

45. Braddock, Shirley, Loudoun, Forbes, and Amherst. The few months in 1754, in which Governor Sharpe himself held the rank of commander-in-chief in America, were fruitless in a military sense. This appointment seems to have been a matter of the influence of Sharpe's brothers and of the merchant, John Hanbury, and it seems to have had

with demands for appropriations and enlistments, and seventeen meetings of the assembly heard those demands and considered them. From the strictly provincial point of view, the French and Indian War divided into three phases: the first lasted from the beginning until the late summer of 1756; the second, the period of the command of the Earl of Loudoun, from 1756 to 1758; and the last, under the command of Amherst and the inspiration of Pitt, from 1758 until the end. Only during the first period was the fighting so dangerously near Maryland as to force her, by sheer military necessity, to take an active part. The second was a period of diminishing risks, but also of increasing pressure from the Crown to coördinate with and assist the other colonies. The final phase of the war was the period of least military activity on the part of Maryland, and one of decreasing official demand. Through all three phases no governor could have had a more difficult task than Sharpe. He was obliged to follow the instructions of both his royal and his proprietary masters, and to try to bring the assembly into harmonious action with them. Real success was impossible, but Sharpe at least kept trying.[46] The remarkable thing, from a modern point of view, is that the system of coöperation survived, that neither proprietorship nor assembly was abolished in the interest of imperial need.

Even before the outbreak of hostilities Sharpe was con-

no political or institutional meaning in bringing proprietary Maryland more closely into the orbit of the home government. Commission and orders, July 5, 1754, *Archives*, XXXI, 52–53.

46. A good deal has been written on Maryland in the French and Indian War: J. William Black, *Maryland's Attitude in the Struggle for Canada*, JHUS, X (1892), no. 7; Eugene I. McCormac, *Colonial Opposition to Imperial Authority During the French and Indian War* (Berkeley, 1911), pp. 63–74; Hayes Baker Crothers, *Virginia and the French and Indian War* (Chicago, 1928); A. M. Schlesinger, "Maryland's Share in the Last Intercolonial War," *Md. Hist. Mag.*, VII, 119–149, 243–267; P. H. Giddens, "The French and Indian War in Maryland, 1753 to 1756," *ibid.*, XXX, 281–310; "Maryland and the Earl of Loudoun," *ibid.*, XXIX, 268–294; "The Coöperation of the Southern Colonies in the Expedition Against Fort Duquesne," *Virginia Magazine of History and Biography*, XXXVI (1928), 1–16, 145–160.

fronted with the problem which Bladen had faced in 1743. Ordered by Secretary of State Holdernesse to have the defenses of the province put in order,[47] Sharpe, too, was unable to get enactment of a proper duty law; again the request of the Crown had to be disregarded. The governor was barely able to secure a small appropriation for sending delegates to the Albany Congress, because the lower house wished to grant no money. At the same time the assembly persisted in refusing a contribution to Governor Dinwiddie's expedition at Wills Creek under Washington, although Sharpe believed and argued that duty to the Crown required an appropriation.

Only twice during the entire course of the war could the assembly be brought to pass tax laws "for his majesty's service." Both were enacted in the early years of the war, and both resulted from fear caused by military defeat so near at hand as to place Maryland in danger. The first followed Washington's surrender of Fort Necessity, in 1754. The assembly at that time passed a bill, raising £6,000 for the defense of the province; the governor signed it, even though the appropriation of certain fees violated his instructions from the lord proprietor.[48] Braddock's defeat impelled the second tax law, passed in 1756; it provided for raising £40,000 currency,[49] and was much the strongest Maryland action in the war. But even under the desperate conditions of 1756, when the people of the back country were driven from their farms—some coming east and a few disguising themselves as Indians to go to the Indian towns to kill and scalp[50]—the assembly almost balked. Governor Shirley, who succeeded Braddock in the American command, had ordered recruiting officers to enlist indentured servants without regard as to

47. August 28, 1753, *Archives*, VI, 3–4.

48. Acts, July, 1754, no. 1, *Archives*, L, 559–566. See below, pp. 238–239.

49. Acts, February, 1756, no. 5, *Archives*, LII, 480–521. See Sharpe to Morris, May 16, 1756, to Board of Trade, June 2, 1756, *Archives*, VI, 415, 435, and below, pp. 240–241.

50. *Pennsylvania Gazette*, May 6, 27, 1756.

whether or not the masters gave their consent. This caused serious resentment in Maryland; though it did not prevent assembly action, it threatened to, and it did lead to the jailing of a recruiting officer and to a minor quarrel of jurisdiction between crown officials and proprietary.[51]

Although the assembly acted more generously in 1756 than at any other time during the war, even then it failed to do its full duty, as set forth by crown authority in America. A council of war had met in Albany late in 1755, under the leadership of Shirley; Governor Sharpe had attended. On his return, the governor specified that the items needed were money for concerted colonial campaigns against Crown Point and Fort DuQuesne, an appropriation for gifts to the southern Indians, and the fixing of an embargo on the export of military provisions. He also asked for an appropriation for provincial defenses and for a more complete militia law.[52] The law of 1756, when enacted, fully provided for only three of the five requests: Indian money, local defense, and the embargo. The militia law was entirely refused and money was appropriated for the movement on Fort DuQuesne only, not for Crown Point—and this at a time when the DuQuesne expedition appeared certain not to be executed as planned. The DuQuesne appropriation, amounting to £25,000 and the larger part of the £40,000 to be raised, was later to be re-appropriated, and assigned to the western defenses of the province. Thus £4,000, the amount assigned to the southern Indians, was the only money

51. Sharpe to Shirley, February 2, 1756, and to Morris, August 25, 1756, *Archives*, VI, 342–343, 472. The recruiting officer was thrown in the Kent county jail, and, when he appealed to Sharpe, he received cold comfort. On request, the attorney-general wrote an opinion that a servant had no right to enlist without his master's consent, and that legal action could be taken against a recruiting officer who took a servant without such consent. The officer was released, but Maryland officials did not see fit to support his recruiting. R. Sterling to Sharpe, March 21, 1756, Attorney-General Dorsey to Sharpe, March 22, 1756, Sharpe to Shirley, March 23, 1756, *ibid.*, VI, 378–380.

52. February 23, 1756, *ibid.*, LII, 219–221.

directly provided for expenditure out of Maryland during the French and Indian War.

Yet the full independence and intransigence of Maryland in the question of his majesty's service came into view only in 1757, the year of the command of the Earl of Loudoun. Loudoun brought to America a commission, briefly worded and in very general terms, which represented, according to Professor Pargellis, "the greatest extent of authority which the British government ever tried to exercise over the colonies as a unit." He came to the colonies a unique commander-in-chief: in military affairs his authority was as absolute and as complete as the Crown could make it; he always kept in close contact with the Duke of Cumberland, the captain-general and the ranking officer of the realm; and he also exercised a certain civil authority, though it was an ambiguous one. "He was empowered to ask the colonies for recruits, money, quarters, and transport, and to request the aid of provincial troops; but he could not compel them to grant his requests." [53] All that he said and did bore the prestige of high authority and of his own noble rank. He notified Governor Sharpe of his appointment in the summer of 1756, well in advance of arrival, and promised to communicate with him later. Lord Baltimore sent special instructions that the governor should work with Loudoun in every way.[54]

In a minor respect, reminiscent of the command of Shirley, Loudoun incurred the resentment of Marylanders very early in his command. In the winter of 1756 and 1757, he sent men to be billeted on the inhabitants of a none too flourishing section on the upper Eastern Shore. There was no particular objection in the first instance; but when, the next year, he sent five more companies, this time to Annapolis, the governor himself complained. The

53. Stanley M. Pargellis, *Lord Loudoun in North America* (New Haven, 1933), pp. 58, 80, and *passim*.
54. Letter of March 9, 1756, *Archives*, XXXI, 152–153.

city council made what provision it could, but the burden was a heavy one and seemed quite arbitrary, and the assembly made serious protest.[55] The affair was an ostentatious and aggravating display of royal authority.

But the greater clash with Loudoun, and a significant one in view of his high position as military and civil representative of the king, arose over the question of the control of the troops of Maryland. When Loudoun and the southern governors planned the defense of the southern colonies, Maryland's quota was fixed at five hundred men. The House of Delegates passed a supply bill for that number, but it insisted on having them stationed at Fort Frederick, which Sharpe had had erected on North Mountain, on the western edge of Maryland settlement. The house refused money for men at Fort Cumberland, where Loudoun wanted them, and declared the fort to be beyond the boundaries of the province.[56] Under the circumstances the supply bill could not be passed, and Loudoun was forced to pay Maryland troops at Cumberland from his own funds.[57]

The action of the House of Delegates was no less than a challenge to the military and civil authority of Lord Loudoun, and he became very angry about it. He wrote to Governor Sharpe that the independence of Maryland tended "to subvert all government, and at once to throw

55. Sharpe to Calvert, November 30, 1756, February 4, December 26, 1757; to Loudoun, December 22, 1757; Lower House Proceedings, April 13, 1757, *Archives,* VI, 513, 522, 523; IX, 114, 121; LV, 52; Pargellis, *Loudoun,* pp. 204–205.

56. In the quota arrangement, Maryland and South Carolina were not required to send men out of the province, although the other provinces were expected to do so (Pargellis, *Loudoun,* pp. 218–220). Such a higgling procedure as declaring Fort Cumberland out of the province must have been especially irritating to Loudoun.

57. Sharpe to Stanwix, December 17, 1757, *Archives,* IX, 109–110; Stanwix to David Ross, October 28, 1757, Loudoun to Sharpe, January 2, 1758, report of Loudoun and Abercromby, March 11, 1761, showing advances made to Captain Dagworthy, the Maryland commander of provincial troops, to Ross, for supplies, and to Sharpe, for travel, Loudoun Papers, Huntington Library (copies kindly supplied by Dr. Pargellis).

off all submission to the government of the mother country." [58] He expressed no less strong opinions to the Duke of Cumberland, to whom he declared that, "if there is not an effectual stop put to that precedent now begun in Maryland, the king will at once lose the command of all troops raised by the provinces. This seems to be a very bold attack on the prerogative, and as the disposition every where is to levelling [encreases], it will be followed universally." [59] Loudoun thought, in fact, of going to Annapolis and settling the matter of Maryland independence; he regarded Maryland's as the extremest colonial defiance with which he met. Indeed, with the advantage of the long view, the situation is not to be judged differently from his own opinion: Maryland's was a denial of the power of the Crown which, should it achieve the value of a precedent, could only be subversive of the authority of the mother country.

During the final and victorious phase of the war, the attitude of the province did not change. Many further requests to assist, even when they were the appeals of Pitt himself, brought no grants of men and money. Nothing more than written demands was ever made; no Lord Loudoun marched into the assembly to settle the matter. In modern language, the House of Delegates was never coordinated, and the lord proprietor was never liquidated.[60]

58. Loudoun to Sharpe, November 3, 1757, *Archives*, IX, 98–99. This letter shows that the governor kept Loudoun in close touch with assembly affairs.

59. Letter of June 22, 1757, Stanley Pargellis, editor, *Military Affairs in North America, 1748–1765* (New York, 1936), pp. 376–377.

60. Sharpe himself believed that only the action of the British Parliament could "remove all occasion of dispute," and he favored a colonial tax imposed by Parliament. Letter to Baltimore, January 12, 1755; to Dinwiddie, July 10, 1755, *Archives*, VI, 161, 244–245. When he could not get military appropriation, Sharpe led volunteers and encouraged subscription-giving by the gentlemen of the province. He was not satisfied with the method, of course, and Daniel Dulany said that the subscription-money, which was raised principally by merchants and in one area, was insufficient and unfair in incidence. Sharpe to Calvert, July 23, August 11, 1755; to Forbes, September, 1758, *ibid.*, VI, 261–263; IX, 270; Dulany, "The Middle Colonies in 1755," *Pennsylvania Magazine of History and Biography*, III (1879), 26.

Maryland entered the last fifteen years of colonial history with recent memories of institutional stresses and strains, but without essential institutional or political change. In war as in peace, the influence of the home government had been less strong than local conditions, and no consideration had been as influential as the determination of the lower house to have its own way.

Non-coöperation in the wars defines independence of action from the other colonies as much as from the home government. Maryland's contributions to intercolonial military action had been of the slightest in King George's War; and, as we have just seen, there were almost none in the French and Indian War. Governor Sharpe could speak, many times indeed, of a sort of negative coöperation with Pennsylvania: as Governor Calvert had once blamed the radicalism of New England for the extreme ideas of the House of Delegates,[61] so Sharpe blamed the "pusillanimity" of the Pennsylvania assembly, in voting war measures, for the refusals of the lower house.[62] Assembly independence was probably in some degree communicable,[63] but Sharpe almost certainly exaggerated the influence of Pennsylvania politics in Maryland. Maryland's attitude was too rigid and too traditional to be imitative. It is unlikely, moreover, that members of the lower house knew much about what Pennsylvania did; the *Maryland Gazette*, it is true, carried more Pennsylvania and Virginia news than the newspapers of those colonies carried Maryland news, but there was not much. The public and private papers of the period bear such manifest indication that Marylanders were deeply concerned with their own politics, and so little that they were concerned with the politics of the other colonies, that Sharpe's blam-

61. Letter to Baltimore, October 26, 1729, *Archives*, XXV, 605.
62. For occasions when Sharpe spoke of the influence of Pennsylvania, see letters to T. Robinson, January 12, 1755, to Calvert, August 11, 1755, to Baltimore, November 3, 1758, *ibid.*, VI, 165, 262–263; IX, 296.
63. After Braddock's defeat, the council advised calling an assembly only if Pennsylvania should pass a military appropriation. August 15, 1755, *ibid.*, XXXI, 71–72.

ing Pennsylvania for Maryland's deficiencies has the sound of the apologist.[64]

A summary view of Maryland as a member of the old colonial system shows a minimum of administrative connection with the mother country, and a minimum of conscious interest in the military and other affairs common to the British colonial world. The wars throw a strong light on the House of Delegates, and show in a crucial way how decisive an influence the house—with its power to appropriate—actually exercised in the external affairs of the province. We must now look more closely at internal affairs, if we are to understand the drift of Maryland into the positions and attitudes which were soon to lead to revolutionary action.

64. The present writer began with a presumption different from the opinion offered here. In an effort to visualize and establish a close connection between the obstructionism of the Maryland, the Pennsylvania, and other assemblies, he searched the newspapers carefully. The *Maryland Gazette* of the forties had no news of Pennsylvania politics, and in the critical war years, 1754–1758, it had much in 1757 only. But the *Gazette* printed many local criticisms of Governor Sharpe for ordering militiamen from their homes. The *Pennsylvania Gazette* had more of Maryland weather and crime than of politics; the *Virginia Gazette* carried almost no Maryland items.

VII

THE ANTI-PROPRIETARY MOVEMENT 1733–1764

AT no time in the eighteenth century, from the restoration of proprietary government to the Revolution, was there even an interval of real political peace in Maryland. Occasional urgency forced the upper and lower houses to agree, to be sure, on a new and important law; and there was nothing to prevent a yearly product of routine legislation. But there was little real understanding and faith within a common constitution. The situation was the opposite of the healthy one in a system of representative government: instead of there being underlying agreement at the constitutional center, and disagreement and compromise at the political periphery, Maryland suffered division and disagreement at the center, although that division was somewhat masked by the practical necessities of law-making.

Constitutional differences in Maryland were of the same order, as we have seen, as the historic differences between the absolutist ideas of the Stuarts, one of whom signed the charter of 1632, and the Whiggish liberalism of John Locke, the colonists' own philosopher. The great question of Maryland politics in the eighteenth century was how far the Delegates could make their Whiggish ideas good in the balance of legislative power. The seventeenth-century revolutions had made archaic the exercise of crown prerogative in British domestic affairs; but in the provinces the prerogative was nowhere obsolete. The "prerogative royal" was never exercised more decisively in Maryland than by the lord proprietor in the reforms of 1733. What could the House of Delegates do to implement its opposite ideas of government? If the citadel of proprietary power was impossible of capture, what political gain could the lower house achieve to match the endless invocation of parliamentary tradition and of natural-rights philosophy? Did the house have any real resources for bargaining with the governor and council?

The gist of the matter lies in the refusal of the House of Delegates to make war appropriations; the representative element had always the constitutional power to act on new expenditures of the public money. If it could not secure the enactment of its own proposals, it could at least refuse and frustrate the proposals of the proprietary element; it could be bold in criticism even while it was strait-jacketed in action. This was a negative, minimum power. The right to deny and the opportunity to object, however, had many applications, and in time of crisis could give the Delegates great leverage. After 1739 the exercise of the power to deny and criticize supplies the central theme of assembly relations. Before 1739, the story is somewhat more varied.

No period in the century, indeed, was more crowded with controversy than the decade following 1722. The depression accounts for some of it; the enactment of the tobacco laws of 1727, 1728, and 1730, and of the paper-money law of 1733, came only after long argument and bargaining between the houses.[1] The expiration of the legislation of 1671, regarding the lord proprietor's revenues accounts for still more: bills to provide the governor's salary and to renew the equivalent duty for quit-rents urgently demanded consideration. Both were passed, but the Delegates insisted that they be made temporary rather than permanent or long-period laws.[2]

This was the time, above all other decades in the eighteenth century, when the House of Delegates was most aggressive in claiming and extending parliamentary privilege and right. Its questioning, in 1729, of the right of the

1. See above, pp. 92–94.
2. See above, pp. 130–132. The law of 1671 had been enacted for the life of the third Lord Baltimore. Such security as it gave, to 1715, did not extend to Charles, the fifth Lord Baltimore. Act, March, 1671, *Archives*, II, 284–286.

proprietor to exercise the veto power, represented political thought, as we have seen, which was hardly less than republican in direction.[3] In this decade, the lower house succeeded, moreover, in winning the passing of a journal of accounts—the periodic appropriation to cover the expenses of government for a number of years—which omitted any allowance to members of the council for their meetings in executive session. The upper house reserved "all rights to claim" the money in future journals;[4] but even a temporary concession of a proprietary privilege marked a legislative clipping of the prerogative power. While the lower house was attacking the greater it also attacked the lesser beneficiaries of the proprietary interest. It proposed that the sheriff be made an elective, not an appointive, official, and that his authority, which was found to be greater than that of the sheriff in England, be made responsible to the people rather than the governor.[5] The house subjected the established clergy, too, to extensive criticism. It proposed having the immoral among them brought into a proper court, their claimed immunity under provincial law to the contrary notwithstanding; and it also threatened repeal of the clergy tax.[6] The whole decade of controversy was overarched by the long dispute about the judges-oath bill, whether or not the laws and liberties of England should be applied in the courts of the province.

The variety of proposals and advances made by the House of Delegates indicates not only the principles but at least something of the confidence of English Whiggism—the very confidence and, as he saw it, the wrongheadedness which alarmed Governor Calvert in 1729 and perhaps hastened his death. But even in this period of

3. See above, p. 163.
4. October 26, 1723, *Archives,* XXXIV, 588.
5. October 30, 1724, *ibid.,* XXXV, 59–60; see pp. 162, 175, 177, 363. Somewhat similarly, a newspaper writer proposed, nearly a quarter-century later, that the county judges, who, as fixers of the local rates, exercised the power to tax, should be made elective. "Freeholder," *Maryland Gazette,* February 10, March 16, April 20, 1748.
6. October 27, 31, 1724, *Archives,* XXXV, 139, 163–165.

aggressive claims, the house came nowhere near establishing the sovereign claims which lay implicit in talk of
parliamentary power and in the ideas of the natural rights
of the people and the legislature. The judges-oath law,
the product of the greatest controversy of the period, indicates the situation. As finally passed, the law provided
that the acts and customs of the province should be the
"primary guide" of the judges, and that where they were
silent, English laws "as used and practiced" in Maryland,
should serve.[7] This phrasing, as it admitted some application of the English statutes, marked a concession from
Lord Baltimore; and the lawyer-historian, McMahon,
tells us that under the law the judges introduced such
English laws "as were accommodated to the condition of
the province without regard to the inquiry, whether they
had been practiced upon or enacted previously to the act
of 1732." [8] But if the oath law represented a victory for
the lower house, it was a moderate one—it was not clear-
cut or of obvious political advantage. Nor did the tobacco
laws of 1728 and 1730, embodying the house's own policy
of crop control, bring much gain; the first was disallowed,
and the second was permitted to lapse without renewal.
None of the more extreme proposals of the Delegates was
adopted: the proprietor's veto went unrestricted; the
clergy were not brought into court; and the sheriffs remained appointive officers. Only the paper-money law,
which was not strictly a lower-house proposal, stood as a
clear and positive achievement of the decade of controversy.

One proposal, made in 1725, particularly reveals that

7. Acts, July, 1732, ch. 5, *Archives,* XXXVII, 519. See above, pp.
164–165.
8. McMahon, *Historical View,* p. 128. Baltimore's instructions to
Governor Calvert, January 29, 1731, forbade the passage of a law
introducing the English statutes "in the gross" (*Archives,* XXV, 538).
The law did not literally contravene that instruction, but it permitted
contravention. Besides McMahon, see William Kilty, *A report of all
such English Statutes as existed at the time of the first emigration of
the people of Maryland, and . . . have been found applicable . . . and
of such others as have since been made in England . . . and have been
introduced, by the courts . . .* (Annapolis, 1811).

the House of Delegates itself was dissatisfied with the weakness of its political leverage against the proprietary element. The proposal took the form of a bill to support a colonial agent in London, an agent to be named and instructed by the House of Delegates alone. The purpose of the bill was declared to be "the representing and soliciting such [of the province's] grievances in Great Britain as are not redressed here, and generally to negotiate any affairs there that may be found necessary by this house for the interest and safety of freemen of this province." In rejecting the bill, the upper house pointed out that it could not approve appropriations for an agent who would be nominated by the Delegates alone. Four years later, when the lower house renewed the question, the council expressed its refusal in general terms, saying that no agent was at present desirable, but that it might concur when the public need demanded.[9]

An agency bill as the lower house framed it—an appeal to the Crown for the redress of grievances which the governor and council would not admit to be grievances— was in the nature of the case a political tactic of last resort. The upper house and governor were invited to approve and appropriate money for a spokesman to go over their heads in protest against the prerogative power of the lord proprietor; naturally they did not pass the bills of 1725 and 1730, or those of later decades. Yet the lower house could couch its plea in terms of the desirability of a regular colonial agent,[10] as Maryland had had a commercial agent during the period of crown control. While jealousy of the lord proprietor had force, the agency bill would have relevance; one of the lasting features of the struggle for power was thus established.

Altogether then, the aggressions of the House of Delegates in the twenties did not carry far, in a constitutional

9. November 5, 1725, August 1–2, 1729, *Archives,* XXXV, 404; XXXVI, 354, 361. See B. W. Bond, "The Colonial Agent as a Popular Representative," *Political Science Quarterly,* XXXV (1920), 373–374.
10. August 26, 1731, *Archives,* XXXVII, 267–268.

sense; and the alarmism of Governors Calvert and Ogle over the "strange and unreasonable prejudices" of the province seems exaggerated. In this perspective, Lord Baltimore's decisive prerogative acts of 1733 appear rather to have settled administrative problems than to have changed the balance of constitutional power. He required the collection of quit-rents, but no one had questioned his right to quit-rents; he made the governor's salary independent of lower-house influence, but the Delegates had never tried to withhold the salary or to bargain with it; he established fee rates by proclamation, without a statute, but the power of the assembly to limit them remained unquestioned.[11] The decisions of 1733 did not reduce the powers of the lower house, nor enlarge those of the upper. Rather they demonstrated the fact that the lord proprietor's prerogative still represented power, as his privileges represented wealth—a fact which the large claims of the lower house, in the preceding decade, had done a good deal to obscure from view.

After 1733, the struggle between the houses naturally quieted; there was little to bargain about. As if to be doubly sure of prerogative and privileges, Lord Baltimore took into the proprietary circle the able pamphleteer and leader of the Delegates, Daniel Dulany, the elder. Dulany had received appointment as attorney-general at the time when the lower house was beginning its objection to the presence of office-holders in the house. This office was not a lucrative one, however; and, as Governor Benedict Leonard Calvert displayed open antagonism for Dulany,[12] it is not strange that no early attempt was made to expel him from the lower house. But in 1733 he was made receiver-general, and shortly afterward, commissary-general; he held two of the best paid offices in the province. In his changed character, the House of Delegates voted to expel him, together with three other ap-

11. See above, pp. 135–137.
12. Ogle to Baltimore, January 10, 1732, Calvert Papers, no. 1088, MHS.

pointees to proprietary office. This was the important case of 1734;[13] and the strong reaction of the governor, in dissolving the assembly, seems to have been influenced by a desire to seal Dulany's loyalty on the proprietary side. Dulany was one of the three "disabled" members reelected, and on his return to the lower house he was not only seated but also elected speaker. The upper house might indeed rejoice that "those party prejudices and passionate heats" against the proprietary seemed actually diminished.[14] During the next year, moreover, the Delegates enacted a journal of accounts granting the same allowances to councilors which it had stoutly refused ten years before—the vote was even, and was decided by the speaker, now Mr. James Harris.[15] At no other time between 1715 and the Revolution was there such a reversing in the House of Delegates as is represented by these votes of 1735 and 1736.

The old ideas and the old habits of resistance to the "government," however, were never truly abandoned. The lower house soon began to sense that Lord Baltimore had gained, and the people of Maryland had lost, by the substitution of quit-rents for the equivalent duty. In 1735 the Delegates proposed a new duty, and they found the governor and council ready to listen, although very critical and defensive. During the next year negotiations between the houses advanced, but it appeared that the proprietor would accept no less than a three-shilling duty, or half again as much as before 1733, and that the lower house would offer no more than two shillings sixpence. Dulany, still a delegate, wrote Lord Baltimore that if a new equivalent law were approved the lower house would regain bargaining power, and might soon ask permission to pay in paper money. The next year Lord Baltimore took the position that the method of collecting quit-rents

13. See above, p. 166.
14. Upper House Journal, April 22, 1735; Lower House Journal, March 20, 1735, *Archives*, XXXIX, 210, 221. See Sioussat, *Economics and Politics in Maryland*, pp. 47–56.
15. May 4, 1736, *Archives*, XXXIX, 461.

seemed more "natural" than an equivalent, and that the offers of new equivalents had been altogether insufficient.[16] This declaration all but closed the matter, and it was little discussed at any later time.

During the same period, beginning in 1735, the lower house returned to the question of the officers' fees. In an address to the upper house it declared that fees ought to be settled by statute and made payable in current money, and it asked for a conference on the subject. The upper house replied that the proprietor in council had established the fee rates by proclamation, and that as this was perfectly legal there was no necessity for the houses to confer.[17] Thus repulsed, the lower house began to speak of the fee proclamation of 1733 in terms of its Whiggish theories. In 1738 the committee of grievances reported that the tobacco fees paid to the "ministers, servants, and officers" were excessive in amount, and unjust in their incidence on the "tradesmen, artificers, laborers, and others throughout this province making no tobacco." It further declared that, because the common and statute law of England—"which of undoubted right the subjects here . . . enjoy"—placed the regulation of fees under Parliament and the courts of justice, the fees collected by virtue of the proclamation of 1733 were illegal. According to the reasoning of the committee, "Proclamations or orders of council binding or determining the right of property are invasions on the fundamental constitution of this province under the royal charter and against the lawful rights and liberties of his majesty's liege subjects." [18]

Perhaps a recognition of its circumscribed influence and bargaining power impelled the lower house, in the thirties, to be particularly touchy about its rights. Reviving an old dispute about procedure, the house dead-

16. Upper House Journal, April 15, 23, 1735, April 20, May 1, 4, 1736, April 26, 1737; Lower House Journal, April 29, 1736, *Archives,* XXXIX, 189, 215–216, 406, 427, 428–429, 454–455; XL, 3; Bond, *The Quit-Rent System,* pp. 190–193; Gould, *The Land System in Maryland,* pp. 45–47.

17. April 10–11, 1735, *Archives,* XXXIX, 180, 183.

18. May 16, 1738, *ibid.,* XL, 196.

locked with the council in 1736 over the question whether
or not the council had a right to retain engrossed bills, as
it claimed, from the time of approval by the houses to
the completion of the enactment, by the governor. The
issue was small enough, but the deadlock could be broken
only by the governor's proroguing the assembly.[19] Two
years later the houses again came to an impasse over procedure. This time the dispute arose over misunderstand-
ings as to whether or not the council had insulted the
lower house when the clerk of the council interrupted the
speaker, and as to whether messages between the houses
could permissibly be sent by a clerk, and not by members
themselves.[20] This conflict was as trivial as that of 1736,
and as little subject to compromise; again the obstruction
had to be ended by a prorogation. Thus two assembly
meetings became "conventions," not "sessions" properly
so called, because no laws were passed. The charges of
meetings had been incurred, the members' time taken, and
the assembly shown futile and of no practical purpose.

At only one point, between 1733 and 1739, did the
House of Delegates exercise real bargaining power against
the proprietary element. Provincial need required money
for the purchase of arms and ammunition for local defense—this was prior to the war demands of the Crown.
A duty of three-pence per hogshead on exported tobacco
was traditional in Maryland; it had been provided since
1671 by the various laws which had fixed tobacco duties
for the support of government and for the commutation of
quit-rents. Defense money had thus been connected with
some of the most troublesome problems of assembly relations, and the last arms duty had expired when all the
temporary laws were allowed to expire, in 1733; at that
time the lower house had rejected a proposal to enact a

19. Upper House Journal, April 9–10, 1736, *ibid.*, XXXIX, 363–366.
20. Upper House Journal, May 18, 22, 1738, *ibid.*, XL, 163–165, 167–
168. In this same session the lower house called the justices of Talbot
county before the bar and severely reprimanded one for abuse of the
house. May 15–23, 1738, *ibid.*, XL, 193–207.

separate duty. The question of a supply of arms arose again in 1735, when the Delegates proposed a different kind of tax, and added the proviso that they should select representatives to share with the governor and council the function and responsibility of spending the proceeds. This the upper house refused, and the lower agreed to pass a three-pence duty, like the old one, though only on a temporary basis.[21] There the matter rested until 1738, when at the close of the assembly session, the duty would normally have expired. But this was the meeting which the governor prorogued on the occasion of the dispute about the right procedure in sending messages between the two houses. Under the terms of the militia law —"to continue for three years, and to the end of the next session . . . after the expiration of the said three years" —the duty continued. A convention was not a session; and the lower house was cheated of its expected control of the duty bill.

When Governor Ogle again met the assembly, in 1739, political lines were drawn more tightly than at any time since 1733. The imminence of war with Spain added force, indeed, to his plea for a renewal of the arms and ammunition duty. On the other hand, the prorogation of the year before had angered the lower house; the Delegates had naturally taken Ogle's tactics as a serious affront to their dignity. The election of 1738, moreover, had placed a new leader in the lower house: Dr. Charles Carroll—the physician, landholder, merchant, ironmaster, and intellectual— had won a seat, and had been appointed at once to the committee of laws. His character, as a man of mind and means, and his knowledge of parliamentary procedure combined to give him a rank in the "country party" very like that of the lost leader, Daniel Dulany. In 1739 the political situation promised a return to the explosive conditions of the twenties.

The address of the governor in opening the session

21. Lower House Journal, April 9, 1733; Upper House Journal, April 16, 1735; Acts, March, 1735, ch. 9, *ibid.*, XXXIX, 85, 190, 298–299.

asked for further paper-money legislation, for laws to encourage settlement in the back country, and for the arms and ammunition duty. Each of these proposals was put in such a way as to carry some advantage to the proprietary element. The governor's message was so phrased, moreover, as to be patronizing, and irritating to the lower house: he had much to say of the "ill effects of heats and animosities" between the two houses, of the liability of "the wisest of assemblies . . . to be misled by the too great warmth even of honest and well meaning men," and of the recalcitrancy of "the most malicious enemies of the government." [22]

In reply the House of Delegates gave little time to the proposals for legislation, but devoted the great part of its message to a broad attack—the first of its kind—on the privileges and powers inherent in the proprietary system of government. Among many declarations of the good will of the house, the message charged that,

From many consequences we find that this government hath for some time past pursued its own profit and benefit, but how far that turns to the public good those who are sensible thereof will best judge. . . . This house have so many recent instances of the people of this province being made a property to his lordship's officers and the many evils that proceed therefrom, that they are under the greatest apprehension of every act that may put them into their power or mercy, the effects of which hath too often and daily doth demonstrate itself in the ruin and oppression of many.[23]

In speaking of western settlement, the lower house declared that the occupation and protection of the land was not the business of the assembly as much as that of the proprietary element, because "excessiveness of fees and offices and the high terms of rent at present preserved (far exceeding anything of the kind in any other part of his majesty's American dominions that we know of)" power-

22. May 1, 1739, ibid., XL, 210.
23. May 4, 1739, ibid., XL, 290.

fully discouraged settlers from coming to Maryland. In so speaking the lower house approached the sweeping denial of proprietary rights and policies which, once made and declared, it was never to abandon.

During the month that followed, the committee of grievances surveyed the whole financial side of the Maryland system, and it found many faults. It reported to the house that the fourteen-pence tonnage duty, taken for the lord proprietor's personal revenues, had lapsed; that the 1704 hogshead duty had been intended for the royal government, and that it could not legally be inherited by the proprietary, the decision of 1733 to the contrary notwithstanding; that the collection of court fines and forfeitures for the proprietor was illegal; that the fixing of fees by proclamation and not by statute was wrong in principle; and that there was abuse in the administration of the quit-rent system. To this indictment, the committee added offense to the proprietary element: it summoned five members of the council, all naval officers, to give testimony concerning the proprietor's revenues. The council resolved that its dignity would allow no such procedure.[24]

On the basis of the findings of the committee, the lower house addressed the governor. It begged leave, first of all, to present grievances, and declared its belief that once conditions were truly known, the governor would be glad to assist in determining on remedies. "The right [that British subjects] have of not being subject to any payments, whether they be taxes, duties, imposts, fees, or under any other denomination whatsoever; but what shall be raised, settled, and appointed by laws to which by themselves or their substitutes they give their assent is a matter we conceive can admit of no contradiction."[25] From this Lockeian assumption, the house questioned the legal right of the proprietary element to most of its financial

24. Lower House Journal, May 10, 21, 26, 29, 1739; Upper House Journal, May 15, 1739, *ibid.*, XL, 303–304, 320–337, 353–358, 359–360, 364–365, 222.

25. June 5, 1739, *ibid.*, XL, 392.

privileges. Closely following the committee of grievances, the House of Delegates charged, first, that the tonnage duty of 1661 had expired in 1704, and, second, that the "power of late assumed by his lordship of settling and ascertaining fees . . . by proclamation" was opposed both to the terms of the charter and to British usage, certainly since the Glorious Revolution. The house went on to criticize the practice of selling county clerkships, and even the operation of the land system. The taking of alienation fines was, it declared, "contrary to the tenor and conditions of our grants, a project introduced to drain money from the people within these three or four years last past." Finally, the house criticized the naval officers. It found them guilty of violating the paper-money law, as they insisted on collecting their fees for entry in and out in sterling, not the paper of the province. "Strange!" the house declared, "that the holding an office (the fees and perquisites whereof arise from the labor and industry of a people) should set persons above the law and invest them with a power to oppress that people." The exemption the naval officers claimed, as councilors, from appearing before the lower house or its committee, seemed to the Delegates certain to justify the idea that officials, who were keepers of public money, might "with impunity commit what frauds, extortions, or embezzlements they shall think fit by being adopted into his lordship's council." [26]

This address was followed by another the next day which advanced a step further the protest already lodged against the collection of the shilling per hogshead under the act of 1704. The fact that the lower house had made

26. June 5, 1739, *ibid.*, XL, 392–395. The grievance against the naval officer and his fees was of course particularly felt by the merchant-exporter. Dr. Charles Carroll illustrated this nicely in a letter to Daniel Dulany of December, 1742, in which he asked for an opinion about fees charged by a certain naval officer. When I have your opinion, he said, "I shall know what of right I ought to pay or whether our laws are old ballards or of any consequence to protect the weak against the mighty." *Md. Hist. Mag.*, XX, 180.

no complaint between 1733 and the present, while many had objected "out of doors," did not, the house declared, now deprive it of a right to demand redress. The house could see nothing in the law of 1704 to show that the duty was ever intended for the proprietor, but it declared itself willing to submit the question to the Crown for decision. It rejected as impossible the proposal of the governor, that a perpetual confirmatory law be passed for the support of the government.[27]

Not only the ideas but also the tone of the House of Delegates was radical, and Governor Ogle became very much excited. In an address early in the session, he said: "I must confess myself truly sorry to hear from the lower house of assembly that my good resolutions, so often published, have been frustrated and rendered void, by the malevolent influence of evil councils. . . . May I not ask what malevolent councils threw out the revenue bill, hindered our paper money to pay the clergy and officers, . . . or what other mischief it is that these same evil councils have done?"[28] When the governor was forced to defend his own salary, as collected under the act of 1704, he asked the Delegates whether the duty had not "been universally looked upon by every part of the legislature since that time as a law in force and being till some gentlemen of the new light (for I find we have a new light in politics as well as in religion) lately undertook to deceive in this particular."[29] Comparison of their politics with the religion of the Great Awakening irritated the Delegates, and Governor Ogle offered a kind of apology. He said that he had not really thought that any members had the new light, "but as to politics, which you say you conceive the undoubted right of every British freeborn subject, you have certainly advanced many things you yourselves must allow to be altogether new, however just and reasonable you may think them to be."[30] There was some

27. June 6, 1739, *Archives,* XL, 395–396.
28. May 10, 1739, *ibid.,* XL, 300–301.
29. June 5, 1739, *ibid.,* XL, 385.   30. June 9, 1739, *ibid.,* XL, 411.

justice in this comment, for so general an indictment of proprietary privilege as that of 1739 was new to assembly relations. But the indictment itself argued from old premises, long familiar in the lower house.

In a way which was also familiar in the assembly, Governor Ogle answered the constitutional arguments of the lower house about the laws and practices he had to defend. He stood on sound grounds, historically, when he denied the contention of the lower house, that subjects could not be required to make any payments, whether taxes, duties, imposts, or fees, without their own consent or that of their representatives. He illustrated from the fact that the people of Maryland were at that very time paying duties under the Molasses Act of 1733 and other acts of Parliament, which were passed without the consent of the people of Maryland. He cited also the charges for postage, the levy on sailors' wages for the support of Greenwich hospital, and "the many fees levied and paid in the several colonies of America and the West Indies by the sole prerogatives of the Crown." [31] Governor Ogle could make a good historical and legal case; and the Delegates could make a good theoretical one, from the Whiggish point of view.

There was no possibility of agreement or compromise in the assembly. Appeal to the king in council was the only way suggested as a possible avenue to a settlement, and here the lower house had a political advantage. By merely reverting to its policy, begun in 1725 and continued in 1729, 1730, and 1731, but since then discontinued, of asking for a colonial agent in England, the house could add an attractive argument to its case against the proprietary element. Referring to Lord Baltimore's disputed right to the duty of 1704, for the support of government, the house declared that "this matter must be determined by a judge indifferent both to his lordship and us, and . . . we expect your honors' concurrence to the bill . . . for taxing ourselves for that purpose, lest

31. June 8, 1739, *ibid.*, XL, 402–406.

if that should be refused, the world might say that we are attacked unarmed, and denied the necessary means of doing ourselves justice, . . . and of that great advantage due to his majesty's American subjects, of applying to his person for redress and protection." [32] When the upper house rejected the agency bill, as expected, it argued, much as in 1725, that the proposed agent would represent the lower house alone, not the province as a whole.[33]

Utterly unable to resolve their differences, the two houses had exchanged messages for five weeks when the upper house informed the lower that unless an arms and ammunition duty were passed, the house, in executive session as the council, would advise the governor to prorogue the assembly. As the Delegates failed to act, the meeting of 1739 like that of 1738 became a "convention," and the old duty legally held over. Also as the year before, prorogation meant futility: no laws had been passed and the meeting stood a memory of political difference and constitutional controversy, but of no legislative achievement.

In this respect, however, the Delegates had acted with evident foresight. After they had received the council's rejection of the agency bill, they sent, on June 6, a message which was intended as a kind of manifesto for the public, and as such requires quotation:

We are . . . little surprised at your negative to the bill for payment of an agent. . . . However, as you desire your reason for not assenting to be made public, we hope you'll not take it amiss, if we set it in its proper light, and so the meanest capacity may be capable to judge of it.

The people of Maryland thinks the proprietary takes money from them unlawfully.

The proprietary says he has a right to take that money.

The matter must be determined by his majesty who is indifferent to both.

32. June 4, 1739, *ibid.*, XL, 254.
33. June 5, 1739, *ibid.*, XL, 255–258.

The proprietary is at home and has this same money to enable him to negotiate the affair on his part.

The people have no way of negotiating it on their part but by employing fit persons in London to act for them, and those persons must be paid for their trouble. . . .

The upper house tells us, you shall not have that bill, unless you let the governor and us, or rather the proprietary (with whom we contest) have as well the nomination of the persons to be made use of on this occasion, as to determine what, or if anything, shall be paid them for their trouble.[34]

There the matter stood, in very fact. The lower house spread the defeated bill, like the messages, on its proceedings.[35] In this way it was made certain of publication in the printed *Votes and Proceedings*.

Before the meeting ended, moreover, the House of Delegates recorded, in the most formal way at its command, its full indictment of the proprietary system. In an elaborate set of resolutions it once more declared the tonnage duty for the proprietor and the hogshead duty for the governor to be illegal; it declared the fee proclamation to violate the charter, the buying and selling of clerkships to tend to the ruin of the province, the collection of alienation fines to be contrary to the terms of the land grants, and the collection of the naval officers' fees in gold and silver to be a violation of the paper-money law. This indictment and these resolutions were to become, by repetition, a permanent part of the policy and attitude of the lower house.[36]

To conclude the matter the house prepared two addresses, one to Lord Baltimore and one to the king. The first was temperate in tone; it reviewed the grievances of

34. June 6, 1739, *ibid.*, XL, 259.
35. June 5, 1739, *ibid.*, XL, 390–391.
36. June 8, 1739, *ibid.*, XL, 414–417. See similar and repetitive resolutions: December 13, 1754, September 30, 1757, *ibid.*, L, 598; LV, 208. Such resolutions were also passed with the opening of new assemblies in October, 1758, March, 1762, November, 1765, May, 1768, November, 1771, June, 1773, *Votes and Proceedings*.

the people and it entreated relief.[37] The second was ordered to be held for three months, and if at the end of that period the proprietor had not acted favorably it was to be sent to the king. This plea was not an elaborate one, for it merely intimated the complaints of the province, but it strongly requested the Crown to instruct Lord Baltimore to permit the appointment of an agent. The lower house alone could not spend public money for handling this appeal; but it did place in charge a committee of nine delegates, including Dr. Carroll and his associate in leadership, Philip Hammond, and it empowered the committee to support the plea by sending to England "several copies of records from this province and other necessary papers," and even to employ any person or persons necessary to present the case to the Crown.[38] Thus the "convention" of 1739 ended with appeals in every direction, to the people of "meanest capacity," to the proprietor, and to the Crown. As in the twenties, lower-house radicalism moved toward extramural politics, but in this case—in the lack of a newspaper, and perhaps because of the recent reverses suffered by the house—greater confidence was placed in appeal to the authority of the king than to the sentiment of the people of Maryland themselves.

In the long view, the line-by-line story of assembly relations in 1739 has a unique and special importance. A grand attack on proprietary privileges was the natural answer of the House of Delegates to the grand act of the prerogative, in 1733. The difference of claim and assumption, which had always underlain the thinking of the two elements, here and for the first time came to mean ultimate conflict and irreconcilability. The manifesto of June 6 named the lord proprietor as enemy; and the reports and resolutions of the lower house attacked not only his prerogative in government but also his financial privileges, excepting, of course, his income as landlord. And even the land revenues were not an entire exception, because quit-

37. June 12, 1739, *Archives*, XL, 420–421.
38. June 11–12, 1739, *ibid.*, XL, 416, 419–420.

rents were criticized as to administration, and at least remembered as having been within the orbit of assembly bargaining. From this time through the thirty-five years to the Revolution, the central question in provincial politics, plainly, was to be neither the formulation of principle nor the laying down of challenge to the proprietorship, for the formulas were made and the bill of protest registered. It was rather to be the development of political methods and tactics. How could the sweeping protests of 1739 be made to count? Could the vitality of the politics of discontent be sustained at the level of a great and inclusive denial? The vigor of protest in the twenties had been nourished by large ideas and small victories in the assembly. What now, as politics became more extramural, outside the walls of the assembly, and reached towards the Crown, and as the liberal goal became not compromise but a radical revision of the proprietary system?

One year of the new tactics demonstrated the difficulties: the "court" in Maryland remained obstructive, the lord proprietor proved unresponsive to petition, and the Crown difficult of approach. After the prorogation the council refused the lower-house committee permission to transcribe the records it wanted; the council acted on the ground that the committee had no authority when the legislature was not sitting, and thus earned the censure of a lower-house resolution in 1740.[39] Time would be needed for the new politics.

The lower house persisted, however, in its determination to put the matter before the king in council. In the 1740 session, the house received word that the messages of 1739 had been put in the hands of Ferdinand John Paris, the agent for Pennsylvania. It drew up a new and longer address to the Crown, and this time, instead of merely alluding to its difficulties, it recited all the financial

---

39. Dulany gave an opinion, July 31, 1739, in support of the action of the council (*ibid.,* XXVIII, 165–166). The protests of the lower house occupied two weeks in the 1740 session (April 26–May 12, 1740, *ibid.,* XL, 522–548).

grievances in full.[40] The transcripts ordered in 1739 were now sent on, and the house succeeded at last in transmitting its full plea to England. An attempt, at least, was made to raise money by popular subscription in Maryland. But all this, even, was not enough; to win a hearing before the Privy Council proved beyond the reach of the House of Delegates. Whether due to financial failure, or for some other reason, the silence of the record indicates that neither Paris nor any other representative brought the grievances of the House of Delegates in any full and formal way to the attention of the Crown.[41]

Meanwhile the actual outbreak of war did create a need, as we have seen, which gave political leverage to the lower house. The house passed the supply bill for the Cartagena expedition only on condition of appropriating the income from ordinary-license fees, money which was by custom a perquisite of the provincial secretary's office.[42] Here was a small victory over the prerogative. In respect of the question of the arms and ammunition duty, the opposition between the houses continued. The Delegates would pass no duty for longer than a year, because they wished to assure themselves of annual sessions,[43] as the British Commons had done by passing mutiny acts for one year only. This condition the council would not meet, the duty lapsed, and the defenses of the province went unprovided. The fact that the old duty could no longer be

40. May 9, 1740, *ibid.*, XL, 575–579. A letter of Stephen Bordley, July 14, 1739, indicates that he thought the appeal to the Crown a feasible procedure. Stephen Bordley's Letterbook, 1738–1740, MHS.

41. The records of the Privy Council show nothing of Paris' activity in behalf of Maryland, nor do the Paris letters in the Historical Society of Pennsylvania. The provincial council did, however, once address the king with an explanation of Maryland's poor military part, in terms of lower-house politics. Such a move may betray some anxiety about the Delegates' appeal. June 5, 1744, *Archives*, XXVIII, 315–318. See Bond, "The Colonial Agent as a Popular Representative," *Political Science Quarterly*, XXXV, 373–374, and Edwin P. Tanner, "Colonial Agencies in England in the Eighteenth Century," *ibid.*, XVI (1901), 28.

42. This right was acknowledged by law in 1717. Lower House Journal, June 6–8, 1717, *Archives*, XXXIII, 84, 85, 88, 105.

43. Address to upper house, May 17, 1740, *ibid.*, XL, 466–470.

continued by prorogation, to the satisfaction of the council, may also be called a small victory for the lower house.

For a period of years after 1740 there were no real changes in the political balance in Maryland. The sessions of 1741 and 1742, indeed, were less strident than those just preceding, but there was no alteration of declared attitudes and policies. Only in 1743, four years after the address of the lower house, did Lord Baltimore respond openly to the plea for amelioration. Then his reply was merely a cool acknowledgment of the petition of the house, and a promise of a fair hearing for any grievances.[44] Lord Baltimore's more particular, but undeclared, answer had been framed in 1742, when he selected Thomas Bladen, a native of Maryland, to succeed Governor Ogle, who had become thoroughly unpopular. In his instructions the lord proprietor ordered Bladen to yield nothing to the lower house; he was to take no step which might in any way abate proprietary claims to the income from either the tonnage duty of 1661 or the hogshead duty of 1704; he was not to permit the reduction of officers' fees; and he was to obstruct the movement for a colonial agency.[45] Behind the public scene, the proprietor's reply was a complete negative; and under Bladen, accordingly, the balance of political power was not subject to change from the deadlock of 1739 and 1740.

The actual rigidity of the situation is revealed by the continued deadlock over old issues. In 1744, the new governor presented to the assembly the order of the Crown to put the province in the best condition of defense. The House of Delegates, in turn, offered an arms and ammunition bill which would have taken the control of the funds from the provincial treasurers, appointed by the governor, and placed it in the hands of the speaker of the lower house.[46] In the proprietary view, this proposal represented an effort to discredit the government, and

44. August 12, 1743, *ibid.*, XLII, 505–506.
45. May 28, 1742, *ibid.*, XLII, 649–651.
46. Lower House Journal, May 10, 1744, *Archives*, XLII, 525–528.

even a possible means of securing funds which could be diverted to pay an agent;[47] inevitably no action was permitted. In the same session, the lower house continued to challenge the tonnage and hogshead duties, and to communicate with Mr. Paris, with whom the house still maintained some kind of a connection. During the next year, it "tacked" onto a money bill for the Louisbourg expedition a provision that part of the funds be assigned to the payment of an agent; and, after Louisbourg had been captured—without Maryland aid—the house made occasion to congratulate the king and to restate its wish to submit the grievances of Maryland through an agent.[48]

Meanwhile the Delegates did not cease to make fresh statements of liberal theory and parliamentary rights. Apropos of an inquiry into the amount of the proprietary income from fines, forfeitures, and amercements, the lower house told the governor that he was wrong when he said that the proprietary officials were accountable to Lord Baltimore alone for the casual revenues. Such monies could be taken only in trust, it declared, for the benefit of the people among whom they were levied, and the lord proprietor received them in a public and not in a private capacity.[49] In 1746, during the final session of Bladen's administration, the house passed a series of ten resolutions. It stated essentially the same grievances as in 1739, and made the same demands,[50] in a renewed effort to win justice from the king in council.

The year 1747, however, marked a real tapering off of the politics of simple frustration. The sessions of the assembly lacked any of the old wrangling about procedure and privilege, and Governor Ogle, who had been restored to office, complimented the lower house on new harmony. Now, with the war nearly ended, an arms and ammunition

47. "Observations of the Bill . . . for Arms," MS., 1744, Calvert Papers, no. 396, MHS.
48. August 23, 1745, *Archives*, XLIV, 92–93.
49. September 2, 1745, *ibid.*, XLIV, 130–132.
50. June 27, 1746, *ibid.*, XLIV, 333–334.

duty was enacted; the funds were placed, in the traditional way, in the hands of the treasurers, not the speaker
of the lower house; but the duty was provided for one
year only.[51] The greatest achievement of 1747 was of
course the enactment of the tobacco-inspection law—the
omnibus act which, in establishing an inspection system
like that of Virginia, also reduced the tobacco dues of the
clergymen of the establishment from forty to thirty
pounds per poll, and reduced proprietary fees to lower
rates than those of the proclamation of 1733. Viewed as
the work of the assembly as a whole, this was a decisive
act of self-government, as we have seen. Yet, because the
law was favored by the council as much as by the lower
house, and because reductions in income-rate were made
in expectation of economic gain, and involved no sacrifice
of constitutional principle, the inspection act was not a
partisan victory for either "court" or "country party."
A journal of accounts was passed with the inspection law,
and the session ended with the members of the two houses
drinking healths together.[52]

From 1747 until the preliminaries of the French and
Indian War, there was but one recrudescence of the harsh-
est feeling between the two branches of the government.
During the brief session of 1750, the House of Delegates
again passed its old resolution condemning the twelve-
pence hogshead duty as invalid and unconstitutional, and
it sent a new address to the lord proprietor in which it
compared the position of Maryland unfavorably with
that of the royal colonies.[53] Aside from this, political tension slackened. The years were proving that the politics
of grand remonstrance could not be sustained without
victories; and the anti-proprietary movement had few
victories to show. After a decade only one of the grievances
of 1739, the fixing of fee rates by proclamation, could be

51. Acts, May, 1747, ch. 19, *ibid.*, XLIV, 652–653.
52. See above, pp. 100–103, 182–183; *Pennsylvania Gazette*, July 30,
1747.
53. Lower House Journal, May 31, June 2, 1750, *Archives*, XLIV,
440–444, 450–451.

considered as corrected; and that, we have just seen, was the result of willing concession by the proprietary element without sacrifice of principle. The period of lower-house complaint seems, indeed, to have induced a new solidarity in the proprietary element: this is plain in the correspondence between the proprietor and members of the council,[54] and it contrasts with the divided state of the "court" before 1733. At mid-century, the lord proprietor might have congratulated himself; neither the movement for a hearing before the king in council nor the new habit of the House of Delegates, of making sweeping denials of proprietary rights and powers, had in any practical way affected the balance of power in the assembly.

During the interval between the wars, changes occurred in the three highest places in the Maryland system. In 1751, Frederick, the sixth and last Lord Baltimore, succeeded to the proprietorship; he was a minor, but very soon reached his majority and made appointments to the provincial secretaryship in England and to the governorship of Maryland. As secretary he selected his uncle, Cecilius Calvert, who had earlier served Charles, Lord Baltimore, as private secretary, and had been one of his advisers on Maryland affairs. Calvert was to have an unprecedented opportunity to make the secretaryship an influential office. To succeed Governor Ogle, who had died, the new Lord Baltimore sent Horatio Sharpe, a man of administrative ability and good family, and the brother of one of his guardians and advisers.

These changes in the personnel of power were to introduce some new arrangements in administration,[55] but they brought no alteration in the attitude of the proprietor

---

54. Now and then Benjamin Tasker, Daniel Dulany, and Edmund Jennings wrote to Lord Baltimore. At various times they urged an inspection law, reported on lower house politics, discussed the appeal to the Crown, and even requested the recall of Governor Ogle. Letters of 1743–1745, Calvert Papers, nos. 1105, 1108, 1109; Gilmor Papers; Dulany Papers, MHS. Some of the proprietary letters have been printed (*Archives*, XLII, 664–667; *Calvert Papers*, II, *passim*).

55. See below, pp. 256–262.

towards the prerogative and the rightful limits of assembly power. In his general instructions, the proprietor ordered Governor Sharpe to pass no law which would affect the prerogative, unless he himself had approved a draft of the bill, or it contained a suspending clause delaying its enforcement until his approval had been received from England.[56] The accompanying secret instructions were more specific: the assembly was to be permitted no repeal or "enervating" of the tonnage duty or the hogshead duty of 1704;[57] no agency bill was to pass unless it named Secretary Calvert as the agent; no act was to affect the proprietor's private rights in land without his own consent; and particularly, Governor Sharpe was told to reserve to the proprietor the income from ordinary licenses, which Governor Ogle had allowed to be appropriated for military use. Above all things, a "due weight and authority" was to be preserved in Maryland.[58]

Thus Governor Sharpe was bound to the same constitutional policy as his predecessors, Ogle and Bladen, and that at the time when the French and Indian War was about to make heavy demands for provincial coöperation. His position was to be far more difficult than theirs: the assembly conflict over finance had by now become a tradition, and was recognized as irreconcilable; Lord Baltimore's demand for the income from ordinary licenses put the "court" in a politically aggressive rather than a merely defensive position; and this war was to be much harder, both politically and militarily, than the last. Even before hostilities had properly begun, and before the home government had made serious demands for war service, Sharpe had sensed that he was "reduced to great streights, by the people's determined resolution to make

56. March 17, 1753, *Archives,* XXXI, 11.
57. In a long letter to the governor, January 5, 1754, the secretary rehearsed the history of the duty of 1704, and argued that it was legal. *Archives,* VI, 24–30.
58. Additional instructions, March 17, 1753, Calvert Papers, no. 1147, MHS; March 30, 1753, Portfolio no. 2, MHRecs.

his majesty's service and his lordship's interest clash." [59] During Braddock's year he was to say much the same thing, finding that his most pessimistic anticipations were true: "His majesty's and the proprietary's interest and instructions must be made to clash; and no money is to be raised unless his lordship's private claim be made to submit to the demands and caprice of an infatuated assembly." [60] Every stage of the war, in fact, was to demonstrate the ability of the House of Delegates to use the war demands of the Crown as a fulcrum from which to pry the lord proprietor from his revenues.

The first step in military preparedness requested by the Crown was the enacting of an arms and ammunition duty. The lower house refused to move; it took the somewhat contradictory position that, if, as the house would not admit, the collection of the 1704 duty were constitutional, money for arms should be taken from that source.[61] More directly stated, the Delegates meant that they would make the appropriation which the Crown desired only on condition that the lower house be given legislative control of the governor's salary. When the first and smaller of Maryland's two war-tax laws was passed, in 1754, the house agreed only on the condition that the income from ordinary licenses be appropriated, as it had been during King George's War. The governor violated his instructions in consenting to this, but he did so with the support of Dulany and others of the council, and in the end secured the acquiescence of the proprietor.[62]

59. Letter to Calvert, May 3, 1754, *Archives,* VI, 62.

60. Letter to William Sharpe (?), 1755, *ibid.,* VI, 174.

61. November 16, 1753, *Archives,* L, 254; see above, p. 207.

62. Not only Sharpe's earliest instructions, but new ones, which came to hand while the bill was in the making, forbade this appropriation (April 17, 1754, Black Books, XI, MHRecs). The governor believed, moreover, that another appropriation in the bill, that of peddlers' and hawkers' licenses, was a covert attack on Baltimore's claim to court fines and forfeitures; but his reasoning in the matter is not clear (letter to Baltimore, June 6, 1754, to Calvert, August 8, 1754, *Archives,* VI, 68, 88–89). Dulany's opinion, that the "whole province" was so firmly convinced by the case of the lower house that it would hardly

The enactment of the £40,000 law of 1756 was also accomplished only by disregarding some of the governor's instructions—it was passed in a period of the severest conflict between the houses. Through a session which lasted twelve weeks, or nearly twice as long as any earlier one, according to Sharpe, the House of Delegates did all it could to increase its own power and to tap the lord proprietor's revenues. It projected its authority into new fields of financial and military control; it stipulated how the appropriations should be spent, it named commissioners to divide with the governor the administration of provincial defense and of Indian relations, and it even specified how and where forts were to be built, with little discretion left to the governor. The taxes and assessments which the law imposed were unique and complex. Duties were placed on imported wine and spirits; there were taxes on billiard tables, on pitch and turpentine imported, and on a great variety of legal documents. From the point of view of assembly relations, the most significant provisions were two: first, a land tax of twelve pence per hundred acres, which violated the instruction forbidding any impairment of the proprietor's rights in land, because his manors were subject to taxation; and, second, a double tax on Roman Catholic landholders, which violated the instruction in behalf of religious equality.[63] Only the mili-

surrender the issue if the enemy invaded the heart of the colony, indicates that the council itself was largely convinced (Daniel Dulany, "The Middle Colonies in 1755," *Pennsylvania Magazine of History and Biography,* III, 25). Sharpe wrote his brother William, May 2, 1756, that the instruction of Lord Baltimore (September 9, 1755, Black Books, XI, MHRecs) which permitted the appropriation was not generous, and not so regarded in Maryland (*Archives,* VI, 399). On the other hand, Secretary Calvert, in an account of the law of 1754 presented to the Board of Trade, January 9, 1756, declared that the ordinary-license fees were worth double an estimated £640 yearly, and that Baltimore's conceding them, and the hawkers' and peddlers' licenses as well, should bring assembly conflict to an end (BT Proprieties, XIX, HSP).

63. Acts, February, 1756, no. 5, *Archives,* LII, 507–508; see above, pp. 207–208.

tary hazards of the months following Braddock's defeat can account for the enactment of such a law.

Neither the proprietary nor the representative element could be well satisfied with the measure. Governor Sharpe explained that in five futile sessions the assembly had fallen out over the old question of ordinary licenses, and that now the council realized no new act could be had without a concession.[64] He regretted the double tax on Catholics, but said that to withhold approval on that account would have been to identify the proprietary interest with the Catholic element. The land tax, which applied to the leased and productive lands of the proprietor, but not to his unproductive reserves, the governor estimated as likely to cost about £400 per year for five years, or from 50 to 65 per cent of the normal income from the manors. But this loss, the governor thought, was to be compared with the proprietor's loss of £1600 in western rents during Braddock's year.[65] Due to such considerations, the law of 1756 was permitted to cut into the proprietary revenues and to convey certain powers to the lower house. But the law was enacted for five years only, and in no way compromised the proprietor's permanent claims.

On the side of the lower house, too, the law of 1756 brought explanations and half-apologies. Because the upper house had persuaded the lower to go into conference, which the latter thought improper in the case of a money bill, the house resolved,

That being urged by the dangerous situation of affairs, and the miserable distress of the back inhabitants of this province . . . , [the Delegates] had been put under the necessity of

64. The council considered the matter in executive session, with the governor present, May 12, 1756. *Archives*, XXXI, 120–121.
65. Sharpe to Calvert, to John Sharpe, May 27, 1756, to Board of Trade, June 2, 1756, *ibid.*, VI, 418–421, 425–428, 435. Calvert reported to the Treasury Board, June 19, 1759, on the sums granted the Crown since 1754, PRO, Treasury, 1: 397, LC.

going into many irregularities in their mode of proceeding, and even departing from their ancient and undoubted rights and privileges, and that therefore no irregularity of proceeding, concession, or condescension whatsoever, had or made in respect of that bill . . . ought hereafter, by any branch of the legislature, to be drawn into or insisted upon as precedent.[66]

Such a feeling, about so necessary an act, goes far to explain the failure of the assembly to pass other laws, when the military risk was diminishing.

Within assembly walls, the war controversies evoked fresh declarations of old ideas about the rights and the authority of the House of Delegates. Thus in 1757 a question of disciplining a justice of the peace led to a nice statement of natural-law philosophy. The Delegates declared that, like the historic Commons, they would insist upon their "inherent right" to investigate the acts of those who had been "by original compact" vested with executive power.[67] Again, in 1762, the lower house argued that it had the exclusive right to propose money laws, "unless it be shown (which we cannot conceive) that our dependent state, upon our mother country (of which we are duly sensible, and in whose wise determination we shall always cheerfully acquiesce) necessarily deprives us of any of them." [68]

The period of the French and Indian War inevitably revived the frontal attack on the proprietary system begun during the last war. The earlier criticisms, and the proposals for making them effective, were frequently renewed in the lower house. In 1755 the house proposed a duty law to support a provincial agent; and, as earlier,

66. May 22, 1756, *Archives,* LII, 440.
67. May 6, 1757, *ibid.,* LV, 104–105. For an appreciation of the proprietary and anti-proprietary cases, as argued in 1758, see Professor Andrews' review of *Archives,* LV (referring especially to addresses by the upper house, April 17, May 4, and an address and resolutions of the lower house, April 27, May 9, *ibid.,* pp. 480–491, 499–519, 621–630, 674–677) in *Md. Hist. Mag.,* XXXIV, 292.
68. *Votes and Proceedings,* April 15, 1762.

an effort was made to raise money by subscription, when the duty bill failed.[69] The colonial agency became a repeated feature of the proposals of the lower house, but one which was so certain of failure as to have rather the character of a political cliché than of a practical proposal for action. The evidence is not plain, but only in 1762 does the record give the name of one who might, even for a moment, be called the Delegates' agent; and then it was only as the lower house requested Benjamin Franklin to present its loyal addresses to King George III on his accession. The house could not do this through Lord Baltimore, because it included in its address a plea for the correction of abuses in the proprietary system.[70]

When two years of assembly disagreement had schooled Governor Sharpe in Maryland politics, he came to realize that the extremism of the lower house could be traced to 1739. He then had his secretary compile the two revenue laws, the legality of which was questioned, and all the proceedings of both houses concerning them. He became convinced not only that legal right lay on the side of the proprietary element, but also that the proprietor's unwillingness to allow an appeal to the king in council was short-sighted, because it encouraged the thought, in the province, that the proprietor feared the judgment of the Privy Council.[71] Sharpe took a common-sense view: why not reverse the direction of the appeal to authority—let it come from the proprietary rather than the representative side—and direct it to the attorney-general of the Crown, rather than to the Crown itself? The governor perhaps knew that in 1737 Attorney-General Willes had given an opinion favoring the lord proprietor in a dispute with the

69. Lower House Journal, July 4, 7, 1755; Sharpe to Calvert, May 27, 1756, *Archives,* LII, 161, 169; VI, 421; Dulany, "The Middle Colonies in 1755," *Pennsylvania Magazine of History and Biography,* III, 26.

70. *Votes and Proceedings,* May 28, 1761, April 24, 1762. Messages concerned with the agency were printed in the *Maryland Gazette,* April 29, May 6, 1762.

71. Letter to William Sharpe, May 2, to Calvert, May 27, to John Sharpe, June 1, 1756, *Archives,* VI, 401, 421–422, 434.

lower house about his right, under the charter, to appoint the provincial treasurer.[72]

The governor's idea was well justified, and the matter was shrewdly managed. Attorney-General Pratt was asked for an opinion, not on the bill of complaint of 1739 and after, but on the current most controversial issue between the upper and lower houses. This was the military supply bill offered by the lower house in 1757, in response to Lord Loudoun's demand; after rejection by the upper house it was repassed in session after session, in substance the same; and it was as consistently refused, because it was injurious to the lord proprietor's interest. An opinion on the bill would also be an opinion on the most extreme principles and policies of the lower house.

As Sharpe had anticipated, the thought of the attorney-general moved in just the same channel as proprietary policy. In his opinion, Pratt objected to clause after clause: the bill should not locate in the lower house the entire control of new offices proposed in the bill; such offices were to be paid by a general tax and should be controlled by the houses jointly; the bill should not compel proprietary officers, such as the receiver-general, to come under statutory control and to perform public services; there should be no double tax on Catholics, such a tax amounted to a breach of faith subverting "the very foundations of the Maryland constitution"; the lord proprietor should resist a tax on uncultivated land, because it was aimed principally at his estates; and the upper house should oppose a tax on the governor—it was "uncivil" if not "unjust." In two instances in the opinion, first in opposing the demand of the lower house to examine the proprietary records and second in a kind of *obiter dictum*, the attorney-general denounced the claim of the

72. Opinion of January 22, 1737, *Archives*, XXVIII, 119–120; see above p. 195, n. 24. On April 8, 1745, the elder Dulany had written Baltimore that opinions by the attorney-general and solicitor-general would prove the case against the proprietor to be worthless. Dulany Papers, II, 33–34, MHS.

House of Delegates to powers like those of the House of Commons:

> The constitutions of the two assemblies differ fundamentally in many respects. Our House of Commons stands upon its own laws, the *Lex Parliamenti;* whereas assemblies in the colonies are regulated by their respective charters, usages, and the common law of England, and will never be allowed to assume all those privileges which the House of Commons are entitled to justly here, upon principles that neither can nor must be applied to the assemblies in the colonies. . . .
>
> I shall only add here a general piece of advice to Lord Baltimore: That in this disposition of the lower house to assume to themselves any privilege which the English House of Commons enjoy here, his lordship should resist all such attempts, where they are unreasonable . . . ; for I am satisfied neither the Crown nor the Parliament will ever suffer these assemblies to erect themselves into the power and authority of the British House of Commons.[73]

Governor Sharpe could not have hoped for a stronger opinion, on the proprietary side, than Pratt returned.

The governor presented the opinion to the House of Delegates in 1760. The assumptions and premises of the attorney-general were so different from those of the lower house that there was hardly cause or opportunity for argument. The house merely acknowledged receipt of the document, and observed, in reply, that Pratt must have given it, "as we presume, only as a private counsel of the lord proprietary."[74] The opinion did not change the direction of assembly history; it led neither to the enactment of a supply bill nor to the abandonment of the demand for a colonial agent. It could no more persuade the lower house to abandon its parliamentary claims than the resolutions of 1739 could persuade the lord proprietor

73. Opinion of Charles Pratt, *Votes and Proceedings,* March 22, 1760.
74. *Ibid.,* March 25, 1760.

to abandon his privileges. Like those resolutions, Pratt's opinions clarified the irreconcilable differences between the proprietary and the representative elements in Maryland, and it added to the tensions and conflicts in the relations between the houses.

While both sides in the assembly struggle were seeking the support of high authority in England, war politics in Maryland were becoming more and more extramural. Jonas Green, the printer, had a central part in this democratizing process: the new *Maryland Gazette*, launched in 1745, again made possible the publicizing of provincial affairs, as they had been publicized by Parks in the late twenties. Whereas little political publicity had been possible during the radical assembly thrusts of 1739 and 1740, because Green was just establishing himself and doing no more than official printing, during the later years of King George's War, he brought out in the *Gazette* many of the opening addresses and the messages of the sessions. During the French and Indian War he continued and enlarged the practice.

Many factors combined in this enlargement. Apart from the constitutional issues, everyone in the province was concerned with the decisions about war appropriations and campaigns; and the number and length of the sessions gave the provincial printer, in publishing the *Votes and Proceedings* and the *Acts of the Province*, much more to do than ever before. The *Gazette*, too, carried an unprecedented amount of political material. From 1752 to 1756 it printed the current journals of the House of Delegates; they usually began on the first page, and covered from two to five columns. Thus the Maryland reader knew not only the opposite positions of the council and the lower house, but also the votes of the individual delegates, and the tactics of the assembly struggle. After the journals were discontinued, he still had the addresses of the governor and the messages of the houses, in great number. The futile assembly meetings of Loudoun's year, 1757, and the bill, which was to receive Pratt's condemnation, were represented by many columns in the *Gazette*.[75] The Delegates ordered the bill itself printed separately, along with the proceedings related to it; and copies were sent to the members of the house and to the county clerks, who were to keep them for the reading of the people. The printed bill showed that the lower-house leaders, Carroll, Hammond, and the Tilghmans, had participated in preparing it; that it would have effected a 5 per-cent tax on quit-rents and on the incomes of the office-holders; and that it passed the lower house by a vote of 40 to 10.[76]

This printing of the most controversial bill of five critical years of assembly controversy was matched, in England, by open newspaper debate about the rights and wrongs of Maryland's poor part in the war. A writer in the *London Chronicle* took the side of the lower house. Referring to adverse comment in the London *Public Advertiser*, he said that he would write in the form of queries, presenting the case as he knew it from Maryland correspondents; the friend of the proprietor could answer if he wanted. He proceeded to ask twenty-nine questions in all. He wished to know whether the land tax of 1756 really cost Lord Baltimore much, and whether the proprietor paid any other Maryland tax. Aside from manor-rents— the income subject to tax—did the proprietor not receive in "other ways very large incomes or revenues from the province?" Did he pay "a penny, a farthing, or even half a farthing per pound, more or less, per annum, on those revenues?" Did not the new supply bill of 1757 propose to tax the proprietor on equal, but no more than equal, grounds with other property-holders in the province? Had not so just a bill received all the opposition the gov-

75. Is there accident, or a design of the proprietary element, that during 1757 there was a marked decrease in assembly materials in the *Gazette?* Was Loudoun's presence intimidating? And why was the printing of the lower-house journal not continued in the *Gazette* after 1756?

76. *An Act for Granting a Supply of Twenty Thousand Pounds for his Majesty's Service* (Annapolis, 1758). Printing a rejected bill was not a new device of the lower house; it had had its militia bill of 1756 distributed, and in 1760 it was to order three bills printed. See Wroth, *Printing in Colonial Maryland*, pp. 207, 209–210, 213–214.

ernment could muster, "both within and without doors," and, in spite of it, had not the bill passed the lower house 40 to 10? Had not the militia been forced from their homes needlessly, and did not many Marylanders think this a method of distressing the people into urging the Delegates to pass appropriations? Did the people of Maryland have an agent to present their complaints, and did they not deserve one? Finally, did not the internal conflicts of the proprietary colonies make necessary an investigation, and make desirable a move to "put them on a better footing?" [77]

These queries, written by one who styled himself as a Maryland trader, were barbed enough, but they did not precipitate controversy in England to parallel that in the province. Some friend of the proprietor, perhaps Governor Sharpe, did compose an answer; it was replete with facts, figures, and references to Pratt's opinion.[78] It is uncertain, however, that the answer was written at once, and it seems never to have been printed, until just recently for its historical interest.

This silence did not, however, end the transoceanic discussion of Maryland affairs. In 1762, the Delegates again ordered that a rejected supply bill be printed, as the flyleaf put it, "for the perusal of the inhabitants." The bill offered an appropriation requested by Pitt; and, like the bill of 1757, it was intended to carry further than 1756 the taxation of the lord proprietor and his appointees. As printed, the supply bill was accompanied by selected passages from the lower-house journals relating to it; and a vote was recorded which showed that it had passed the Delegates, 26 to 21. The messages of the lower house pleaded the old case for rights and powers like those of the House of Commons; they went so far as to declare that only an "inadvertency," which was "little short of infat-

77. *London Chronicle,* September 16–19, 1758, reprinted in *Md. Hist. Mag.,* XXXIII, 229–233. Was Franklin the writer?
78. "Answers to Queries in the *London Chronicle,*" *ibid.,* XXXIII, 233–247.

uation," had ever permitted the council to become a constitutional part of the legislature; they said the council, as upper house, brought "upon us all the evils naturally flowing from the introduction of a dependent branch of legislature into our constitution. Evils, which the people of this province most sensibly feel, and which we fear their latest posterity will have cause to lament." On the money side, the language of the house was equally extreme. It doubted not that a scheme of taxation which "would leave the proprietary estate, and the great officers, either totally untouched, or very complaisantly handled, would be very agreeable to your honors." The house declared that the bill satisfied its duty to sovereign and to constituents, and that responsibility for military failure lay on the proprietary side.[79]

This printed booklet, of bill and messages, included full statements of the argument of the upper house. There were printed both a message to the Delegates, and an address to Governor Sharpe.[80] To the lower house, the council spoke in terms like those of Pratt:

We cannot think ourselves justifiable either to his majesty, our consciences, or your constituents, in giving up his prerogatives and by subverting our present constitution, introduce numberless evils. . . . The true general question in debate is . . . [not a] dispute between the lord proprietary and the great officers of this government of one part, and yourselves on the other, on the point of taxing, or not taxing, his estate

79. *A Bill for Raising a Supply for His Majesty's Service* . . . (Annapolis, 1762), pp. 5–6.

80. The inclusion of the council's address to the governor seems unnatural in a *Bill* ordered published by the lower house. There are plain indications, moreover, that the inclusion was not intended by the Delegates: the title-page speaks of "All the Messages between the Two Houses," and of no others; and the pagination is irregular—the messages are paged regularly (pp. 1–10), the address follows, without page numbers, and then the bill is paged as though it were intended to follow the messages (pp. 11–59). The author of *Remarks upon a Message* (see below p. 250, n. 83) implies that the address was inserted later (see also Sharpe to Calvert, May 11, 1762, *Archives*, XIV, 51–54). Did the governor or council compel the printer to do this irregular thing?

and their offices, . . . [but] whether the lord proprietor, the upper house, and people, shall be subjected to a new and unconstitutional power of oppression, without any remedy, or not? The parties are the two houses, the lower house has been contending for the affirmative, and this house for the negative, in nine successive struggles upon this important question.[81]

The council accused the Delegates of "extraordinary" constitutional doctrines, and found them guilty of "declamatory" language, of the sort to inflame an assembly of constituents, but not worthy of answer in kind. In addressing the governor, the council relied principally on Pratt's opinion in justifying its own stand. It also quoted the Board of Trade in the opinion that "it is vain to negotiate away his majesty's prerogative, every new concession becomes the foundation of some new demand." [82]

The printed argument was taken up again in 1764, when a brilliant and sarcastic writer addressed himself to the superior claims of the Maryland council. His pamphlet, entitled *Remarks upon a Message, sent by the Upper to the Lower House of Assembly of Maryland*,[83] concentrated on the message of April 15, 1762, quoted above, as it was printed with the supply bill. The author may have been Benjamin Franklin, and the pamphlet was perhaps printed at his press; [84] whoever the author, the writ-

81. *A Bill for Raising a Supply*, p. 9.
82. *Ibid.*, address of April 24, 1762.
83. *Remarks upon a Message, sent by the Upper to the Lower House of Assembly of Maryland, 1762. Containing a Vindication of the latter, in their Conduct relative to a Supply Bill for His Majesty's Service; and occasionally interspersed with some curious and interesting Particulars respecting the Constitution of the said Province*. By a Friend to Maryland. 1764.
84. L. C. Wroth says that there are typographical reasons for believing the *Remarks* to have been printed by Franklin and Hall, Philadelphia. Sharpe once thought James Tilghman the writer; but Dulany thought Franklin, and Wroth seems to agree (for a full discussion see Wroth, *Printing in Colonial Maryland*, pp. 221–222). The committee of the lower house, which in 1762 sent Franklin the address of congratulation to the king, was the same as that which framed the message to the

ing was that of one entirely familiar with provincial politics and conditions. The attack opened with a consideration of the political tactics, rather than the constitutional law, of the upper house. It accused the councilors of sharp practice in timing their important messages too near to prorogation for proper consideration. The writer next moved to theory: provincial dispute must now be put in a "new channel . . . before the impartial tribunal of the public, without being perplexed with the forms of parliamentary proceedings, or obstructed by the machinery and influence of government." The "new channel" of thought, invited by the writer, was the natural-rights philosophy. He would not argue, he said, with the council's contention that the House of Commons and the House of Delegates stood on different constitutional foundations, and that for that reason the Delegates could not achieve the rights and powers of the Commons. The lower house actually and rightly exercised parliamentary powers not from usage and history, but from principle. In his own words, the true assumption was

that the free born subjects of England, and consequently their representatives, have a right to grant their own money in their own way. . . . If the lower house have no right to the *Lex Parliamenti* of the House of Commons, because they are a distinct body, I apprehend it will just as well follow, that the courts in this province ought not to judge according to the laws of England, because they are distinct bodies from the courts at home.[85]

Here the writer enlisted on his side one of the most keenly felt convictions in provincial history.

upper house, printed with the bill of 1762; Tilghman was one of the committeemen. The contact between Franklin and the assemblymen may have encouraged one or the other to write the *Remarks*. Franklin's knowledge of Maryland here, if it actually was his, corresponds with that exhibited in the queries in the *Public Ledger* (see below, p. 253, n. 90) and elsewhere. See Smyth (ed.), *Writings of Benjamin Franklin*, IV, 227, 426–427; V, 12.

85. *Remarks*, pp. 12, 14.

His assumption of principle gave him easy grounds from which to denounce Pratt's opinion. Should a community, he inquired, be dissuaded from its cherished rights and interests by the mere word of a lawyer in behalf of an "intriguing, oppressive proprietor?" This led to the agency question, and to the declaration that a bill for the support of an agent had been urged by the lower house at almost every war meeting of the assembly. Why should not the real reasons, which made Maryland "a poor contemptible figure" in military performance, actually have a judicial hearing before the Crown? Why should not the council permit a colonial agency, instead of heaping it with all the "billingsgate of the bar?" The pamphlet closed with an appeal two ways: let the people judge the intentions of the Delegates, and cast their votes accordingly; and let the king judge the sufferings of the colony, and palliate them with justice. Even this might not be enough: "Time, and a more happy concurrence of circumstances may be requisite to effectuate the complete and radical cure every friend of Maryland so fervently and devoutly prays for." [86]

There was no answer to the *Remarks* printed in America. But in London, where a new series of queries, drawn to embarrass Lord Baltimore, had been printed in the *Public Ledger*,[87] and where Secretary Calvert was very much disturbed by so much publicity, there was an answer. It came in a sort of double pamphlet, *An Answer to the Queries . . . Also an Answer to the Remarks*,[88] which aimed to set in a favorable light the governmental system of Maryland. The answers to the queries were a matter-of-fact reply to questions about appointment and power

86. The short quotations are from *ibid.*, pp. 6, 23, 28, 30, 70–71.

87. November 17, 1763.

88. *An Answer to the Queries on Proprietary Government, inserted in the Public Ledger, Also an Answer to Remarks upon a Message . . .* (1764). Wroth expresses doubt about the place of publication, but thinks London. It is clearly addressed to English readers. For Wroth's discussion, and full citation of the evidence, see *Printing in Colonial Maryland*, pp. 220–221.

in the province. The writer—who may have been the secretary, assisted by the Reverend Thomas Bacon[89]—stressed points of similarity between Maryland and the royal colonies, and he minimized the questions most barbed with objection and irony. He said, for example, that the querist overestimated in thinking that any of the provincial offices were worth £4,000 a year; he declared that Mr. Cecilius Calvert's name on the court calendar as agent for Maryland was a misprint. The longer part of the pamphlet, in answer to the *Remarks*, was phrased in language as far as possible from the bite and brilliance of the original. It quoted messages of the assembly from 1739 and 1762, principally, and gave Attorney-General Pratt's opinion in full. *An Answer* gave the legal sort of case which the proprietary element could always make, but which, compared to the argument in the *Remarks*, lacked philosophical and literary interest. It evoked no further discussion.

In the long view, this little war of printed bills, pamphlets, and newspaper queries, which followed on Maryland's poor part against the French, has a significance as great for what it took for granted as for the constitutional principles it presented. Although we know little about the writing of the *Queries*, the *Remarks*, and the *Answers*, and still less about the extent to which they were read, they all testify, as do the published bills and messages, to the thought of political constituencies and to the importance of opinion, both in the province and in London.[90] So much publicity, with its implication of a public

89. Calvert to Baltimore, January 10, 1764; D. Dulany to Calvert, September 10, 1764, *Calvert Papers,* II, 214, 233.

90. Dulany said that copies of the *Remarks* were delivered to every councilor by the doorkeeper of the lower house. He also said that Franklin was known to be the author of the Queries in the *Public Ledger.* Secretary Calvert's comments show that the London papers disturbed him. Dulany to Calvert, September 10, 1764; Calvert to Baltimore, March 28, 1764, Calvert Papers, nos. 1288, 1280, MHS. Sharpe did not take the pamphlets seriously, but spoke of the "scribbling itch," to Calvert. May 8, 1764, July 10, 1765, *Archives,* XIV, 157–160, 200–201. Sharpe made a good deal, at this time, of the influence of anti-proprietary poli-

interest, seems quite as discordant with proprietary assumptions as does the high parliamentary tone of the lower house.

On the side of Maryland, moreover, there is a good deal of evidence that the conditions of war vastly excited the people, especially in the direction of anti-Catholicism, and that there was a wider popular participation in politics than at any earlier period. In 1754 a "great number of the freemen" of Prince George's county signed "instructions" to their delegates, and asked to have them published in the *Maryland Gazette*. On November 19, the paper said, a "remarkable and almost unanimous" meeting had conceived it "to be the undoubted right of *British subjects* to instruct their representatives in such material points as may be the subject of their deliberations." The delegates, accordingly, were desired and expected to support a bill to dispossess the Jesuits of their estates, to exclude Catholics from public office, and to prevent them from sending their children to foreign seminaries.[91] In another instance, this time on the Eastern Shore, one hundred fifty freeholders of Somerset county instructed their members, with a fine flourish of patriotic phrase, to appropriate money for the campaign of 1755.[92] Again, but in the more conventional style of a petition to the lower house, the "freemen of Anne Arundel county" declared that the lord proprietor's taking the twelve-pence hogshead duty under the order of 1733 was a grievance; and they urged the lower house to act on it as such.[93] Such democratic or near-democratic forms of political action as the instruction of representatives did not come as readily in pro-

tics in Pennsylvania. The connection, whatever it was, with Franklin, lends reason to his fear. Also, the *Maryland Gazette*, April 5, 1764, printed the unanimous resolutions of the Pennsylvania assembly against the Penns; and the issues of November 8 and 15, 1764, give accounts of Franklin's going to England in behalf of the house.

91. *Maryland Gazette*, November 28, 1754; *Pennsylvania Gazette*, December 19, 1754.
92. *Maryland Gazette*, March 6, 1755.
93. Petition, 1756, Black Books, IV, pt. 2, MHRecs.

prietary and plantation Maryland as they did in Congregational and town-settled New England.[94] But coming, a little and at last, in the context of anti-proprietary politics, they had the same ring of popular government as in the Puritan north.

Thus as the great pre-revolutionary crisis of the Stamp Act period drew on, the anti-proprietary movement in Maryland approached the maturity which would make it a matter of many people and of mass feeling. By 1764 the sixth Lord Baltimore had been deprived of no revenues and of no claim of prerogative which his father had had in 1733. Institutionally and economically considered, the movement had gained nothing. But provincial affairs had been altered by it. The clash and conflict which had always been latent in claim and counter-claim, and which had been diffused in many issues during the twenties, had come into focus and great issue in 1739. And what had been intramural, then, had been heard by many in the period of the wars. The conservative social character of the House of Delegates was indeed such as to make talk of decision by the king, according to the perfect constitutional justice of England, much more natural than appeal to democratic action. But the location of the house was in Maryland. As talk of the people's rights actually reached the people, time and the newspaper and the pamphlet inevitably broadened the anti-proprietary movement. When, within a decade after 1764, the proprietary system was actually to disintegrate, it would be at the hands of the gentlemen and people of Maryland, and not at the behest of an all-just sovereign.

94. See Kenneth Colgrove, "New England Town Mandates, Instructions to the Deputies in Colonial Legislatures," *Publications of the Colonial Society of Massachusetts* (Boston), XXI (1920), 411–449. To make comparison with England, see William E. H. Lecky, *A History of England in the Eighteenth Century,* III (New York, 1882), 188–196.

VIII

PROPRIETARY AFFAIRS UNDER
GOVERNOR SHARPE 1753–1769

WHEN Governor Sharpe came to Maryland in 1753, he bore instructions not merely to defend the prerogative against infringement by the legislature, but also to develop and extend its administration. The land system was to be made to produce a maximum of income. All the proprietary revenues were to be administered more strictly, under the supervision and responsibility of the governor.

Such a development of the proprietary policies of 1733 and after bears the stamp of the personalities newly in control in England. Frederick, Lord Baltimore, the proprietor, and Cecilius Calvert, the secretary—who were to be so reluctant to waive their doubtful claim to the income from ordinary-license fees—were not the sort to curb the naturally expansive tendencies of colonial wealth and power. The last Lord Baltimore was a dissolute young man, a traveling and horse-racing spendthrift, and a dilettante who sometimes pleased himself with the writing of little essays. His Maryland letters show that he never thought of the province in other terms than those of property and power—it was merely and simply his own. He leased and deeded the province in a marriage contract;[1] he never spoke of a community of people with needs and ideas deserving his study and consideration.

His suitable counselor in managing Maryland affairs was his uncle, the secretary, to whom he first offered the

1. February 3, 1761, *Archives*, XXXII, 62–82. For what slender biographical materials there are, see above, p. 128, n. 25. Not all of Lord Baltimore's income derived from Maryland. He held about £35,000 in stocks—East India, Old South Sea, New South Sea, and Bank annuities —and they returned him about £1,000 annually. Calvert Papers, nos. 959, 1012, MHS.

governorship. The minutiae and the tone of demand in Calvert's letters give the caricature, rather than the picture, of an administrator of the mercantilist age. None could have been more anxious and assertive than the secretary as to details of administration and appointment. In view of the youth and character of the proprietor, and of Calvert's long connection with Maryland through his brother, the fifth Lord Baltimore,[2] it is altogether likely that after 1753 proprietary policy lay largely in his hands, that even the proprietor's acts represented his own suggestions.

Proprietary affairs are better known for the period of Sharpe's administration than for any other period, because of the governor's enormous official correspondence, now printed in more than three thick volumes of the *Archives of Maryland*.[3] That correspondence itself was a matter of policy; in accordance with early instructions from Lord Baltimore, Calvert and Sharpe exchanged many detailed letters about every sort of provincial matter. Lord Baltimore wrote, too, and received letters from the governor, though with what personal interest and initiative it is impossible to say. Until Calvert's death in 1765, it was his five letters or so a year, rather than Lord Baltimore's one, which transmitted the great bulk of particular orders and inquiries to the governor; and it was Sharpe's ten or a dozen letters to him, more than his eight to Lord Baltimore, which brought about a new elaboration of report and connection between administration in the province and proprietary authority at home. Sharpe's correspondence as a whole, considered together with the frequency and the fullness of the formal instructions which he received,[4] marks a new tightening of the reins of

---

2. From 1729 Calvert served as private secretary to Baltimore. Calvert Papers, no. 295½, MHS.
3. *Correspondence of Governor Horatio Sharpe, 1753–1771, Archives*, VI, IX, XIV, supplemented by *Letters to Governor Horatio Sharpe, 1754–1765, ibid.*, XXXI, 471–572. See biography by Lady Matilda Edgar, *A Colonial Governor in Maryland, Horatio Sharpe and His Times* (London, 1912).
4. Whereas Charles, Lord Baltimore, sent about twenty instructions to

proprietary control beyond anything earlier in the century. Charles, Lord Baltimore's visit in 1732 and 1733 had been more decisive than any step to be taken by his son and successor, but it did not lead directly to such elaborate oversight from England as was now undertaken. Early instructions to Governor Sharpe and to Edward Lloyd, the new receiver-general, reveal twin tendencies in proprietary policy after 1751.[5] The first was a tendency toward conservatism, requiring the continuation of the financial security achieved by Charles, Lord Baltimore; it was indicated, in the large, by the instructions of 1753, which, as we have seen, ordered the governor to permit no act to touch the proprietary revenues unless with the consent of Lord Baltimore. The governor was likewise required to prevent the reduction of officers' fees by law, unless it were by permanent legislation approved by the council.[6]

The other tendency was toward efficiency. The governor and agent were ordered collectively to see that the management of the land office was put in better condition. They were also instructed, individually, to assume certain

his governors, during three administrations, from 1733 to 1751 (see above, p. 121, n. 12), his son sent about twenty-five, perhaps more, in addition to all the letters, to Sharpe, 1753–1769. Those known to the writer are the following: March 17, 1753, *Archives*, XXXI, 8–14; March 17, 1753 (additional), Calvert Papers, no. 1147, MHS; March 30, 1753, Portfolio no. 2, MHRecs (see *Archives*, XXXI, 15, 17–19); January 5, 28, April 17, July 6, 1754, August 2, September 9, October 27, 1755, December 16, 1756, October 23, 1757, Black Books, XI, MHRecs; undated instruction of 1758 (?), Portfolio no. 3, MHRecs; March 17, 1759, July 8, 1760, Black Books, XI; October 30, 1760, *Archives*, XXXI, 424–426; December 20, 1760, Black Books, XI; December 20, 1760 (additional), Portfolio no. 3; January 14, 1765, *Archives*, XIV, 189–193; January 16, 1765, *ibid.*, XIV, 188–189; January 20, 1765, Portfolio no. 3; February 7, 1765, *Archives*, XXXII, 143–144; February 21, 1766, *ibid.*, XXXII, 395–396; March 22, 1766, *ibid.*, XXXII, 396–397, also in Kilty, *Land-Holder's Assistant*, pp. 242–243; August 6, November 8, 1766 (printed in *ibid.*, XXXII, 243–245), July 15, 1768, Black Books, XI.

5. The treatment of financial policy here closely follows the writer's article, "Property Rights in the Provincial System of Maryland, Proprietary Policy," *Journal of Southern History*, II, 55–68. Permission granted by Professor Stephenson.

6. The governor's instructions here referred to are those of March 17 and 30, 1753. See above, n. 4.

responsibilities relevant to collecting and transmitting the proprietor's revenues. The governor, who appointed the naval officers, was required to name only "fit" persons, such as would occupy the office themselves, though they might, under special circumstances, be permitted to name deputies. The agent was to give the naval officers strict directions about the performance of their chief obligation, the collection of the hogshead and tonnage duties, the returns from which they transferred to him; he was also to be rigid about taking their security for the exact and full performance of duty. The agent was further required to submit to Lord Baltimore, along with and in addition to the summary "accounts current," full statements about each source of proprietary income. For example, he was to send accounts detailing the revenues from the quit-rents, the manors, and the land office, and the product of the provincial duties paid at every port. All remittances to Lord Baltimore were to be made in bills of exchange payable in London and not elsewhere, or in foreign gold at its exchange value.[7]

With respect to the land system, the source of his principal revenues, Lord Baltimore's early instructions to the governor and agent were especially full. Two of his orders contemplated the collection of revenues which were not being collected at the time of his succession. He first required, as his father had done for the years between 1733 and 1737, that the rate of quit-rents be advanced from four to ten shillings per hundred acres. Under the conditions of the French and Indian War, however, he moderated the order, and later did not try to effect it.[8]

7. This last was an old requirement, but one the breach of which had inconvenienced the proprietor (Calvert to Benjamin Tasker, July 9, 1752, *Calvert Papers*, II, 150–151). The agent's instructions here referred to are Baltimore to Lloyd, March 30, 1753, copy given Daniel of St. Thomas Jenifer as his own, October 14, 1766, Portfolio no. 3, MHRecs.

8. The order to raise quit-rents was inserted in the instructions of March 17 and 30, 1753, but was countermanded within nine months by an instruction (January 5, 1754, Black Books, XI, MHRecs) which ordered the governor and agent and their advisers to fix whatever rate, not lower than four shillings and as much higher as possible, could be

He also ordered that alienation fines, which had been largely disregarded, must be paid in full; but this plan, too, proved economically and administratively impossible, as high officials in Maryland advised.[9] Other instructions relating to land simply tightened the administration of unquestioned revenues. There were several orders of this kind: that arrears of rents, fines, and penalties be paid; that exact methods of accounting be used; that the rent-rolls, which had been ordered years before, be at last perfected; that each surveyor make a plat of the proprietor's manors in his county, keep a copy, and send duplicates to the agent and the proprietor; and that squatters who had settled without right be reported. With an apparent purpose to deprive private speculators of great gain, and to reserve for Lord Baltimore the profits of Maryland growth and settlement, the instructions forbade the granting of more than one thousand acres in any settled area to the members of a single family, and required the creation of new manors in the name of the lord proprietor.

The most important instructions affecting the administration of land revenues carried forward the old principle of centralizing and elevating the control of the quit-rent system. Lord Baltimore assigned a number of mutual duties to the governor, the agent, the deputy-secretary, and the judges of the land office; he gave them the func-

collected. The officials in Maryland successfully opposed raising the rents (see letters, Sharpe to Calvert, February 10, 1754, *Archives*, VI, 37; Daniel Dulany to Calvert, September 10, 1764, *Calvert Papers*, II, 241–242; and a memorandum, of about March 15, 1762, by Governor Sharpe, Receiver-General Lloyd, and Judges of the Land Office Benedict Calvert and George Steuart, Calvert Papers, no. 1162, MHS); but, despite the listing of good economic reasons, they seem never fully to have convinced those in England that the step would be a wrong one (Sharpe to Secretary H. Hamersley, March, 1767, Hamersley to Sharpe, July 20, 1767, *Archives*, XIV, 381, 405). See Bond, *The Quit-Rent System*, pp. 198–199; Gould, *The Land System in Maryland*, pp. 10–12; and Paul H. Giddens, "Land Policies and Administration in Colonial Maryland, 1753–1769," *Md. Hist. Mag.*, XXVIII, 148–150.

9. Sharpe to Calvert, April 19, 1761, *Archives*, IX, 503–506; Dulany to Calvert, September 10, 1764, *Calvert Papers*, II, 234–239; Gould, *The Land System in Maryland*, p. 32.

tion and authority, although not the name, of a special board, within the provincial council, to supervise the revenues from land. Their particular tasks were four: to determine what could be done to reduce the cost of collecting quit-rents, to direct the survey of sites for new proprietary manors, to decide on proper and easy terms for granting western lands to new settlers, and to exercise a limited discretion in determining quit-rent and purchase-money rates. Such an assignment, under the proprietor's order, gave the greatest emphasis to the policy of making the land system as profitable as might be. The arrangement which brought together the highest officials of Maryland anticipated, at the very outset of the proprietorship, the future board of revenue, which fifteen years later was to represent the climax of Lord Baltimore's administrative reforms.

Yet when the officials came to consider the problems put before them, there was little that they could do. Quit-rents could not be raised; new manor sites were lacking, for the reason that all the very good tracts had been occupied; and in time of war the western part of the province was so upset that no attractive terms could be offered to newcomers. Only toward the end of the war could Sharpe report that he had ordered a new manor erected. It lay on the very western frontier of Maryland, beyond Fort Cumberland, and was the only desirable place where there was a large area unbroken by earlier grants.[10] The proprietor had tried too late to reserve to himself the whole increment of Maryland settlement; the disposal of new lands had already passed from his hands into those of settlers and speculators.

As to reducing the cost of collecting quit-rents, Governor Sharpe made a vigorous effort to follow instructions, and met with some success. His first plan, put into

10. Sharpe to Calvert, May 4, July 7, 1760, *Archives*, IX, 402, 434. The site probably lay west of the proclamation line of 1763. About this manor, and the impossibility of erecting others, see Sharpe to Hamersley, March, 1767, April 1, 1768; to Baltimore, March 31, 1768, *ibid.*, XIV, 380, 478–479, 485.

effect shortly after his arrival in Maryland, was simply to reduce the commissions of the farmers from 20 to 15 per cent. He had to abandon it, however, under pressure from above, because Lord Baltimore asked for a further economy, namely, that of requiring the sheriffs to act as collectors, at 10 per cent. This proposal failed, also, because some of the sheriffs, who belonged to the class of large landholders and assemblymen, preferred to resign rather than to collect, especially on so low a commission. Finally, at the governor's suggestion, most of the collecting was assigned at 10 per cent to collectors not connected with the government, who were each made responsible for several counties, and so could afford the decreased rate.[11]

Governor Sharpe's administration was not three years old when it appeared, especially to Secretary Calvert in England, that an initial error had been made in the appointment of Edward Lloyd as receiver-general. Secretary Calvert himself had arranged the appointment at the time when Sharpe had been sent to the province, and had done so in the belief that his lordship's revenues would be placed in safer and more efficient hands that those of President of the Council Tasker, who had been receiver-general.[12] But Lloyd was the possessor of more than thirty-five thousand acres on the Eastern Shore and one

11. Many letters in the Sharpe correspondence refer to the collection of quit-rents, but the following are especially important: Sharpe to Calvert, May 3, 1754, October 20, 1755, May 5, 1756, Sharpe to Baltimore, October 22, 1755, August 15, 1765, March, 1767, *ibid.*, VI, 60, 295, 299, 409; XIV, 214–215, 375–376. See Bond, *The Quit-Rent System*, pp. 200–201; and Giddens, "Land Policies and Administration in Colonial Maryland," *Md. Hist. Mag.*, XXVIII, 150–151. On questions of financial administration there was a natural division of opinion between the lord proprietor in England and his officials in Maryland. Lord Baltimore and his secretary, away from the scene of action, always counseled perfection: complete and exact accounts, resurveys, the collection of every penny due. Governor Sharpe and his associates pointed out in reply that there was a point of diminishing returns where demanding the most from the landholder, especially in cases of uncertain boundaries, did not pay. For the difficulties in administration, see Sharpe to Calvert, July 30, 1757; to Baltimore, August 15, 1765, *Archives*, IX, 61–63; XIV, 214; Bond, *The Quit-Rent System*, pp. 203–207.

12. Calvert to Lloyd, July 9, 1752, Calvert Papers, no. 1147, MHS.

of the greatest landholders in Maryland,[13] was a member of an established family which had for three-quarters of a century had members in both houses of assembly, and was a resident at Wye House across Chesapeake Bay from the seat of government at Annapolis. Hence he was neither dependent enough on the favor of the "court" nor convenient enough to the other officials to render the heedful service which Calvert wanted. By 1756 Calvert knew that Lloyd's office was in confusion, and wrote him, as he had Tasker, asking him to set his accounts straight and to collect as effectively as he could;[14] but the warning failed to bring an improvement.

Serious reform in this instance waited until war conditions had passed. In 1761, after receiving a great deal of advice about Lloyd from Governor Sharpe, Lord Baltimore took firm steps to put life and order into the work of the receiver-general. In new instructions, which closely followed the recommendations of Sharpe, he ordered the agent to have a permanent office built in Annapolis, and to have it equipped for the housing and proper filing of leases, rent-rolls, debt books, naval officers' accounts, and the bonds given by the collectors and farmers of quit-rents. He ordered especial care in the administration of the manors, which had fallen into serious confusion; and he demanded that the plats, which had been ordered in 1753, be made, and kept with the manorial rent-rolls. Most important of all, the receiver-general was required for the future to present his annual account of Lord Baltimore's revenues to a group of the great provincial officials for auditing. These officials, namely, the governor, the deputy-secretary, the commissary-general, the land-office judges, and the attorney-general, were the same, with the addition of the attorney-general, as those designated in the instructions of 1753 for the oversight of land revenues. The new instructions, then, were a step in a

13. Debt Books, Maryland Land Office, Annapolis; Gould, *The Land System in Maryland*, p. 82.
14. Calvert to Lloyd, March 9, 1756, Calvert Papers, no. 1181, MHS.

maturing policy; they called for a wider application of the practice of concentrating the attention of the highest and most responsible officials on the revenues of the lord proprietor.[15] But even these orders were to prove insufficient to make Lloyd a satisfactory receiver-general. Although he remained in office, he continued delinquent and slow in the performance of duty, much to the dissatisfaction of Sharpe, who reported in full to Lord Baltimore and Secretary Calvert.[16]

Impatience with the receiver-general probably influenced the lord proprietor in reaching the decision to sell his manor lands. There were also strong financial reasons for such a step. In September, 1764, Deputy-Secretary Daniel Dulany advised Calvert in a long and convincing letter that lessors in Maryland had trouble enough finding tenants for their manors, and that when they did they suffered from the destruction of timber. His conclusion was that it was impossible "to get an annual rent equal to half the interest which would arise from the money for which the land would sell," and that the difficulties were doubly great for Lord Baltimore, because he "suffers more from the abuses of waste . . . than other gentlemen upon the spot generally do." [17] Shortly after the receipt of this

15. Instructions to Lloyd, October 8, 1761, *Archives*, XXXII, 391–395. For Sharpe's ideas and suggestions, see, especially, his letters to Baltimore, May 23, 1760, April 20, June 23, 1761, *ibid.*, IX, 403–415, 508–509, 524–525. An instruction to Sharpe, December 20, 1760 (Portfolio no. 3, MHRecs), shows that a year before the orders to Lloyd the proprietor had adopted Sharpe's main ideas. See Giddens, "Land Policies and Administration in Colonial Maryland," *Md. Hist. Mag.*, XXVIII, 167–169; Bond, *The Quit-Rent System*, pp. 202–203; Mereness, *Maryland*, pp. 66–67.

16. Mereness (*Maryland*, p. 66) thinks that fear of offending so influential a man as Lloyd explains Lord Baltimore's retaining him in office. This is a natural interpretation, and one to which the antiproprietary thrust in politics adds strength. As to Lloyd's delinquencies, see Sharpe's letters, to Calvert, September 27, 1763 (about housing the records), to Baltimore, August 15, 1765 (about the rent-rolls), and to Hamersley, March, 1767 (about leases), *Archives*, XIV, 117–118, 213–216, 382–383.

17. September 10, 1764, *Calvert Papers*, II, 242–243. Dulany, as inheritor of large landed interests in the west, was hardly a disinterested

letter, Lord Baltimore sent joint instructions to the governor, the deputy-secretary, the agent, the judges of the land office, and the attorney-general—the same officials as those nominated to audit the agent's accounts, except that the commissary-general was excluded and the agent included—ordering them to sell about 28,500 acres of manor lands. He fixed the selling price at £50 per hundred acres, or ten times the rate of caution money for lands in unsettled areas; and he specified that alienation of the land should carry a fine equal to the quit-rent for one year, and that as the land was disposed of and became freehold every care should be taken to perfect the records and to collect the charges.[18] The event proved that the commissioners could not carry out these instructions, which had been written with too little knowledge of the actual conditions of tenure to be applicable. But the policy of selling was not abandoned. A year later Baltimore issued a special joint commission to the governor, Dulany, and John Morton Jordan, a merchant and newcomer to Maryland who may be considered as a sort of special financial emissary from Lord Baltimore. The new commission and accompanying instructions authorized the sale of all the reserved lands and manors, totaling about 115,000 acres, which belonged to the proprietor; they changed the rates somewhat, fixing the sale price at £100 per hundred acres of tenanted and cultivated land and at £30 per hundred acres of untenanted land; and they established other conditions of sale.[19]

adviser, and his argument omitted reference to possible gains through the increase in land values. But it had force, and under the circumstances of the receiver-general's office, strongly appealed to the spendthrift lord proprietor. See Calvert to Sharpe, January 16, 1765, Hamersley to Sharpe, February 20, 1766, *Archives*, XXXI, 555; XIV, 267; Gould, *The Land System in Maryland*, pp. 99–100.

18. January 16, 1765, *Archives*, XIV, 189–193.

19. February 21, 1766, *ibid.*, XXXII, 134–140. See also, Hamersley to Sharpe, February 20, 1766, *ibid.*, XIV, 267; Kilty, *The Land-Holder's Assistant*, pp. 242–245; Gould, *The Land System in Maryland*, pp. 100–101; Giddens, "Land Policies and Administration in Colonial Maryland," *Md. Hist. Mag.*, XXVIII, 163–166.

The process of selling proved to be slow business, and, although continued throughout the lifetime of the proprietor, did not, in terms of his large income, bring great returns. Legal complications which needed to be straightened out before clear titles could be given were sometimes troublesome, but the chief difficulty was economic. The manorial tenants on the soil could not afford to purchase their own tenancies, and, although the sales were regularly advertised, there were few bidders. Even after sales had been negotiated, remittances came in slowly.[20] In the spring of 1768, after two years of effort, out of 86,000 acres offered only about 17,000 had been disposed of. The total value of the sales to that date came to £18,431 14s. 5d., but only a third of the money had been received. Four years later, at the time of Lord Baltimore's death, only £12,360 13s. 7d. worth of manorial lands had been sold in addition.[21] Through the six years from 1766 to 1772, not only did the sales not clear Lord Baltimore's books of his doubtful asset, the manorial lands, but rather they complicated the situation by dividing the previously contiguous manors with freeholds. They brought Lord Baltimore considerable credit, but the money payments were not great and his income from rents was diminished.

In April, 1768, a new institution was launched, the provincial board of revenue. Like the sale of the manors, it was partly a result of the proprietor's dissatisfaction with Lloyd. The authority of the board seems to have derived from a special commission of February 21, 1766, issued by Lord Baltimore to the governor, deputy-secretary, commissary-general, attorney-general, and the judges of the land office. This commission, accompanied by supporting instructions,[22] ordered in the most formal

20. Sharpe to Baltimore, July 19, October 22, 1766, October 29, 1767; Hamersley to Sharpe, November 8, 1766, *Archives*, XIV, 319–320, 335–336, 343–344, 424.

21. The figures for 1768 appear in a statement of sales, Portfolio no. 3, MHRecs; and those for 1772 (January 14) in an account, Calvert Papers, no. 1028, MHS.

22. The commission seems to be lacking, but it is referred to in the instructions. See instructions, Baltimore to Sharpe, February 21, 1766,

way the auditing of the agent's accounts and the prosecution of reforms in the administration of the revenues. Whereas in 1761 Lord Baltimore had tried to secure improved administration by sending detailed instructions to the agent, and by auditing his accounts—enlarging rather than decreasing the functions of the office—he now shifted the responsibility. In creating the board of revenue, he transferred from Lloyd to Governor Sharpe and his associates the responsibility for such reforms as the proper housing of the records (which was now promptly provided) and the more rigid supervision of the manor lands. Further, Lord Baltimore made the desired reforms more specific and far-reaching: he gave the governor "access to every office and control over every officer," he ordered the reduction to a minimum of all commissions for the collecting of revenues, and he required the auditing not only of the agent's general account but also of the accounts of the individual receivers of quit-rents. Under the new arrangement the agent became less an executive and more an accountant, and an inner circle of the provincial council far more than earlier became the active guardian of the lord proprietor's financial interests in Maryland.

Through the seven years of its history, from 1768 until the Revolution, the board was harassed by the negotiations required by a series of changes—there were four in four years—in the office of receiver-general. Colonel Lloyd, who had been found in arrears to Lord Baltimore at the first auditing of his books and who resented the censure implied in the creation of the board, now resigned;[23] but the resignation solved no problems, for the board was compelled by instructions from Lord Baltimore to appoint

to Sharpe, Dulany, and Morton, March 22, 1766, *Archives*, XXXII, 395–397. The judges of the land office were not actually named in the commission, or the first instructions, but this seems to have been an oversight, for the instructions of March 22 explicitly provided for their inclusion in the board.

23. Sharpe to Baltimore, July 14, 1766, March 31, 1768; to Hamersley, March, 1767; Hamersley to Sharpe, March 28, 1768, *Archives*, XIV, 316, 478–479, 382–383, 474.

an irresponsible favorite, the Reverend Bennet Allen. We shall have to review Allen's scandalous career in connection with church affairs; for the present it is sufficient to note that he had incurred the particular enmity of the Dulany family, two of whom sat on the board. Doubtless as a result of the representations of members of the board, Baltimore soon ordered the appointment of a new agent, and the board selected Daniel of St. Thomas Jenifer, who proved to be a conscientious and competent official. But he had held office only a year when John Morton Jordan, he who had been named in the commission to sell the manors, returned to Maryland from a visit to England bearing a commission from Lord Baltimore as agent. During his stay in England, which had coincided with the launching of the board, Jordan had been authorized in "a short kind of commission" to be "supervisor of accounts, lands, and revenues in and from the province of Maryland," a new and unprecedented office which gave him the duty of receiving and reviewing duplicates of all the accounts sent from Maryland and of corresponding "with such persons as he may think properly qualified to give either information or assistance toward the improvement or collection of my revenues." [24] Apparently this appointment had been intended to supply Lord Baltimore with a special financial counsel in England; and Jordan's return to Maryland involved a decision, wholly consistent with Lord Baltimore's general policy, to place in the office of agent a man well known to be closely attached to the proprietorship. But Jordan's tenure, although it seems to have been successful, was short, for he died after about two years; and he was succeeded by Major Jenifer, the last to hold the office. These changes in office meant work and trouble for the board of revenue, because an exact accounting, a transfer of the books, and an issue of instructions was involved in every case. [25]

24. Commission of John Morton Jordan, August 16, 1768, *ibid.*, XXXII, 410–411. See also Kilty, *The Land-Holder's Assistant*, p. 262.
25. The description of the work of the board in this and the next two paragraphs is based on the Minutes of the Board of Revenue, *Archives*, XXXII, 397–489.

In the performance of its normal supervisory duties, the board, in the short period of its history, proved a successful institution. It met regularly, according to rule, three times a year and for such special sessions as occasion demanded.[26] It provided itself with a clerk, who was a good accountant, at a salary of £80 a year. Ordinary meetings were devoted to advising with the agent, the surveyors-general, the rent-roll keepers, or lesser officials, about disputed questions of procedure and jurisdiction. Probably the most thorough and important piece of work done by the board was the drafting, in 1768, of forms of instructions for all the financial officers, namely, the agent, the rent-roll keepers, the receivers of quit-rents, the judges of the land office, the county surveyors, the commissary-general, the deputy-commissaries, the clerks of the courts, the attorney-general, the sheriffs, the examiner-general, and the naval officers. In no other place were the duties of the provincial officers so carefully set forth as in this series of instructions.

The board of revenue at last combined the elements which, for the best financial interests of Lord Baltimore, needed combining. The governor and his associates in the board—in its first year, Governor Sharpe, the able Daniel Dulany, his brother Walter, and one other official frequently made the quorum—brought together at a single responsible center the requisite prestige, authority, knowledge of local conditions, and loyalty to the proprietor. The board of revenue is to be regarded as the culmination, on the eve of the Revolution, of that process begun in 1733, of introducing system and energy into the property interests of Lord Baltimore.

Yet the lord proprietor and the secretary who so prized the reform of the revenue system also prized the patronage which sometimes contradicted system and energy. The secretary, who thought and spoke of his power in Maryland as that of a lesser Newcastle, and the lord proprietor,

26. An exception must be made for the years 1772 and 1773, when there were few and irregular meetings.

who would appoint a Bennet Allen to the office of agent, while he was trying to reform it, were plainly the sort to put as high a value on what patronage would buy, for themselves and for their favorites, as on what order and regularity would save of the proprietary income.[27] Calvert's own appointment mirrored their notion of office as private property. At the time of his accession, Lord Baltimore settled a "salary" of £450 on the secretary; he required that the amount be contributed, under a sort of levy on the incomes of the governor, the deputy-secretary, the commissary-general, and the judge of the land office.[28]

Almost from the beginning of his administration, Sharpe noted an officiousness in Calvert in the handling of patronage affairs. An early letter of the secretary had invited the governor to correspond privately about placements, and to destroy the letters received; and the secretary had promised, in respect of appointments, "to render your administration as easy to you as possible."[29] But Sharpe's earliest instructions had named four men to be appointed to naval offices, places which he himself, in his responsibility for enforcing the laws of trade, was supposed to control. He soon discovered that Calvert included in almost every letter some request to put a friend in office, and he came to feel that he had no real chance to appoint the men he wanted as advisors and administrators.[30]

27. Even before he achieved his majority, Baltimore wrote Calvert, February 29, 1752, "to write over to Maryland my desire, that all livings which are to be given away henceforth, may be for me, by which means I shall have an opportunity of obliging those I think fit" (*Calvert Papers*, II, 129). The importance of favoritism over other considerations, even in the revenue system, appears in the case of Jordan, as well as of Allen. Charles Carroll of Carrollton knew a rumor, at least, that Jordan achieved preferment not for his own merits but on account of his pretty wife, of whom Lord Baltimore was fond. Letters to Daniel Barrington, March 17, May 29, 1766, *Unpublished Letters*, pp. 111, 122.

28. The proprietor made the following assessments for annual payment to the secretary: the governor, £200; the deputy-secretary, £50; the others, each, £100. Letter to Ogle, September 17, 1751, *Calvert Papers*, II, 120.

29. December 12, 1754, *Archives*, XXXI, 471–472.

30. Letter to William Sharpe, May 2, 1756, *ibid.*, VI, 400–401. Sharpe did not completely control even the appointment of sheriffs. See letters

The governor was greatly irritated, moreover, by Calvert's practice of corresponding, sometimes secretly, with other officers, especially the councilors, about public and private affairs. By so doing Calvert lessened their regard for himself, and at the same time, Sharpe felt, reduced their dependence on and respect for the authority of the governor.[31] When he was relieved of office, he wrote in retrospect: "'Tis true indeed, I have had the mortification to see some of those I thought deserved well of your lordship and myself disgraced or slighted, while others who for fifteen years and more have been in opposition to your government are . . . distinguished with peculiar marks of favor." [32] Sharpe never knew quite where he stood in favor and power.[33]

The most lavish use ever proposed for proprietary patronage was the purchase of the votes of the delegates. This was Secretary Calvert's idea, and in 1760 he wrote a very long and secret letter, which he headed as follows:

General Review of the Constitution and Government of Maryland and of Proper Regulations to pervent Turbulent and Malevolent Spirits . . .; And so to Knit and unite the several Branches of Power there, as to form one Grand and Regular Movement, all tending to the Honour and Prosperity of his Lordship and the Happiness and Welfare of the whole Province.[34]

to Sharpe from Calvert, May 29, 1756, from Hamersley, November 8, 1766; Sharpe to Baltimore, July 19, 1766, *ibid.,* VI, 213; XIV, 347, 321–322.

31. That Sharpe was just in thinking that the secretary wrote prying letters to lesser officials is illustrated by a letter to D. Gresham, July 9, 1752, Calvert Papers, no. 1147, MHS. See Sharpe to William Sharpe, July 13, 1759, July 8, 1760, *Archives,* IX, 352, 438.

32. Letter to Baltimore, October 31, 1768, *Archives,* XIV, 551.

33. At the moment he retired he thought that misunderstanding and jealousy about patronage was the reason for losing office (letter to Hamersley, October 30, 1768, *ibid.,* XIV, 537). More probably the reason was Baltimore's wish to give the governorship to his brother-in-law, Robert Eden. See Paul H. Giddens, "Governor Horatio Sharpe Retires," and "Governor Horatio Sharpe and His Maryland Government," *Md. Hist. Mag.,* XXXI, 215–225; XXXII, 156–174.

34. Letter to Sharpe, March 17, 1760, *Archives,* IX, 375.

Calvert said that the Maryland system was inherently the best in America, but for the time being answered none of the purposes of government. With due respect for Sharpe's good intentions, which were such "as every governor ought to have," he feared that the governor was "overscrupulous" in politics. The way to bring a "Grand and Regular Movement" out of assembly conflicts, he said, was to create the same sort of loyalty to the proprietor in the lower house as existed in the council; he reckoned that about two dozen delegates could swing the house into conformity with proprietary policies. As inducements to loyalty he listed the offices of the sheriffs, the quit-rent farmers, the deputy-commissaries, and the deputy-surveyors. These were mostly county offices; there were about fourteen holders of each; and tenure was for three years or could be made so—that is, it corresponded with the periods between assembly elections. Why not insinuate to certain delegates, Calvert asked, that there would be vacant offices to be filled when the assembly dissolved? If promises made were always kept, but no rewards given till earned, the secretary was sure that a new harmony could be brought into Maryland politics.

As a matter of fact, Sharpe had not always been as "overscrupulous" as Calvert implied, for he favored the occasional secret use of patronage to buy a delegate's vote.[35] But his good sense rebelled at the secretary's plan for wholesale corruption, and he succeeded in preventing an attempt. In protest, Sharpe pointed out that there was not enough patronage available for Calvert's scheme. Members of the house would not be tempted to abandon hope and chance of reëlection in return for a three-year tenure of any of the offices named except the shrievalties, and there were too few of them. Because patronage controlled the House of Commons was no reason, the governor said, that it would bring regularity into a colonial assembly. Instead of buying members, he suggested that the proprietor strengthen his side by taking a course which

35. Sharpe to Calvert, March 8, 1756, *Archives*, VI, 356.

would attract the loyalty of the substantial people and voters. He did not say just what concessions or proposals such a policy would require. But he was convinced that his predecessors had already experimented too much with political corruption, and that the assembly conflicts he had to face were in part a result of it.[36] Sharpe was more forceful and more successful in this instance than generally in dealing with Secretary Calvert about a matter on which they disagreed.

The governor's principal reason for thinking that he was not master of his house came from the rapid increase of the power of the Dulany family. Sharpe had arrived in Maryland after the death of the elder Daniel Dulany, but he knew of his eminence as a lawyer and of his usefulness as a proprietary office-holder. He soon sensed, too, that the younger Daniel, a member of the House of Delegates, inherited his father's abilities; and he proposed him to succeed his father in the council and to share the commissary-general's office with his father-in-law, Benjamin Tasker. Secretary Calvert, however, objected, and appointment to the council was not given until 1757. The governor misjudged the situation; he thought that Calvert stood in the way of Dulany in order to seat a worthless favorite in the council, and he was very angry about it.[37] Actually the secretary was playing a deeper game, but one no more flattering to Sharpe. While the governor was recommending Dulany, Calvert was writing him directly to remain awhile in the lower house, to be a conservative influence there, but that he would soon be advanced to high position.[38]

When advancement came to Dulany, it came too rap-

36. Letters to Calvert, July 7, 1760, April 19, 1761, *ibid.*, IX, 423–425, 502.

37. Sharpe to Baltimore, May 2, 1754, July 13, 1756; to William Sharpe, May 2, 1756; Council Proceedings, June 12, 1757, *ibid.*, VI, 55, 450, 400–401; XXXI, 221. John Grove, of Leceistersfields, England, favored the Dulanys before the proprietor. Letter of April 10, 1751, Dulany Papers, I, 41, MHS.

38. April 17, 1754, Dulany Papers, I, 17, MHS.

idly, and too far from the governor's control, for Sharpe to like it. On Dulany's becoming a member of the council, Calvert at once made him deputy-secretary, and one of his brothers, Dennis, was appointed a county clerk. Sharpe had hoped that the deputy-secretaryship would fall to his personal secretary and favorite, John Ridout, and he was resentful about it.[39] He feared that the closely related Dulanys and Taskers would be able to dominate the council, for they now had three votes, and the quorum was often small. Under the circumstances, the relations between Sharpe and Daniel Dulany became strained; and in 1763 the governor opposed Calvert's suggestion that a third brother, Walter, be made receiver-general in place of Lloyd.[40] In consequence Walter Dulany was temporarily assigned to minor offices. But four years later, when his advance was urged by the mercantile house of Hanbury, he received the commissary-generalship and was seated in the council. This time Sharpe did not object, and when the board of revenue was formed, he and Daniel and Walter Dulany served on it together. Sharpe had been needlessly afraid of the power of the family, and had been wrong, as he seems to have come to understand,[41] in think-

39. Letters to Calvert, March 27, May 4, 1760, April 19, 1761; Calvert to Sharpe, December 29, 1760, *Archives*, IX, 389, 401, 497–501, 479. Soreness about Ridout continued. Sharpe succeeded in having him made naval officer and councilor; but his rise was publicly satirized in 1764, in the *Remarks upon a Message* (pp. 49–52). Perhaps it was this which made Sharpe suspect Dulany of association with the writing of the *Remarks* (see Wroth, *Printing in Colonial Maryland*, p. 221).

40. Letter to Calvert, August 21, 1764; Calvert to Sharpe, February 29, 1764, *Archives*, XIV, 111–112, 131.

41. Sharpe to Hamersley, October 30, 1768, *ibid.*, XIV, 537. A letter of Daniel Dulany from England, September 10, 1764, speaks mildly of Sharpe as a good-natured effective governor, perhaps too much influenced by his "Jack Daw [Ridout], strutting in a borrowed plumage." It also indicates that Dulany made no effort to do Sharpe or Ridout harm with the proprietor or with the secretary (*Calvert Papers*, II, 227–230). It is doubtful that there was any close understanding between the English Calverts and the Dulanys. When the proprietor needed an apologist in the colony, he would appoint a Dulany, as in the case of the two Daniels; he could also be influenced by them, as in the case of Walter (Walter Dulany to Hamersley, September 29, 1768, Dulany

ing that they came between him and Lord Baltimore. But no case indicates so plainly the inroad on good faith and understanding which patronage cut in the highest places in the provincial system.

In church rather than in state, however, the evils of proprietary appointment became most flagrant, and apparent to the people of the province. Whereas patronage in civil office was everywhere regarded as a private matter —office was property—and was seldom publicized, in the established church the appointment of ministers was the common concern of all Anglicans. The church was no more liberal than earlier; the parishes were gaining no authority in the selection of clergymen, and Sharpe's instructions required him to permit no change in Lord Baltimore's single-handed control.[42] Proprietary control meant, as we have seen, the enjoyment of patronage but no supervision of the clergy as pastors; there had been no commissary in the province for twenty years before Sharpe. Even so, the church was an institution for all men. In its sins it always offered a chance for reform from within, and always proclaimed ideals not written in the governor's instructions.

Less than a fortnight after Sharpe's arrival, fifteen ministers gathered in a "self-moved" meeting, the first of its kind and the only meeting of clergymen since Henderson's commissaryship.[43] Their principal formal business was to address the new governor, and to assure the new proprietor of their loyalty and their determination "to cultivate a firm and lasting harmony between the numerous inhabitants of this flourishing colony, and those to whom your lordship shall think fit to commit the administration of the government." Beyond their formal business, however, they approached the matter of church

Papers, II, 51, MHS). But even a Dulany sometimes quarreled over his deal ("The Case of Dennis Dulany," undated MS., Dulany Papers, II, 77), and the favor the family received suggests Baltimore's opportunism rather than the power of the Dulanys.

42. March 30, 1753, Portfolio no. 2, MHRecs.

43. Allen, Synodalia, LC.

reform. They sent the governor a remonstrance urging him not to induct a certain clergyman of evil character, and they planned a meeting to discuss church affairs in the fall. At the same time two of the ministers, one a relative of the Dulanys, sent a letter to the Bishop of London. They reminded him that the late Lord Baltimore had inducted scandalous and ignorant men, and they begged that he see and urge the young proprietor to make a provision for the discipline of the clergy.[44]

The fall meeting of the ministers was also a small one. It was addressed, however, by Thomas Cradock, of a Baltimore county parish, in what may well have been the most courageous Anglican sermon of the pre-revolutionary period. Cradock began by saying that he had long hoped that someone else would speak, but that none had, and he could remain silent no longer. He described two "monsters of wickedness" in the Maryland church: one minister had fallen into a fire while drunk and burned to death; and another had almost certainly been guilty, though unpunished, of murdering his wife. Many of the worthless clergymen were now dead, Cradock went on, and he prayed that that kind would never again be given parishes. The only safeguard lay in some form of clerical discipline, and while he did not feel competent to specify a method, he spoke at some length of the movement to establish a colonial bishop. From this point he turned to the condition of religion among the people. He admitted that the Catholics were gaining, but placed the principal blame on the corruption of the established church. The number of dissenters did not trouble him; he preferred to note with pleasure that their position was "every day drawing nearer to us." Cradock envisaged the growth of an essential Christianity, enriched by the vision of Bacon, Boyle, Newton, and Addison. The one great enemy was the irreligion of those who "make a jest of the Christian scheme

44. "Proceedings of the Parochial Clergy," August 22–23, 1753, *Md. Hist. Mag.*, III, 257–273; Henry Addison and Hugh Jones to Bishop of London, August 27, 1753, Perry, *Collections*, IV, 331–332.

. . . [and] *laugh* at the *Bible* as fit only for the amusement of old women and children." But here the difficulty was moral, not intellectual, and could be remedied better by men than by books. "I dare say there are but *few* in this audience but must have observed, that the people, especially the lower classes of them, have been better or worse, more or less religious, according to the conduct of the pastor they have had." [45] Thus one minister, at least, put the responsibility for irreligion on the careless clerical appointments made by the lord proprietor.

The fall meeting as a whole was not so bold. Half the clergymen, prompted by Dr. Charles Carroll, addressed the lower-house committee on grievances about Catholicism in Maryland. The others, led by the Reverend Thomas Bacon, made a moderate address to the governor. Neither group seems to have cared or dared to condemn the evils of the establishment as Cradock had condemned in his sermon to the clergymen and people.[46]

On the proprietary side the reform movement made no gain. Governor Sharpe was sufficiently impressed with the need for clerical discipline to propose a system of bonding the rectors on the occasion of their induction, but the idea won no approval in England. Calvert wrote that such a scheme would almost certainly lead to conflict with the Bishop of London. He said also that Lord Baltimore contemplated a different kind of discipline, which he would elaborate at another time.[47] Actually proprietary authority did nothing; it did not like the voluntary and unofficial meetings of the clergy, and it had no intention of circumscribing its own entire authority.[48] There were no more

45. Allen, Synodalia, LC.
46. "An Account of what passed at a Meeting of the Clergy at Annapolis in October, 1753," *Md. Hist. Mag.*, III, 364–384; Lower House Journal, October 29, 1753, *Archives*, L, 198.
47. Sharpe to Calvert, May 3, 1754, Calvert to Sharpe, December 10, 1754, *ibid.*, VI, 60–61, 129.
48. The lack of entire sympathy between the administration and the established church of Maryland became plain as early as 1728, when the council agreed to a tobacco law opposed by the clergy as a group. See above, pp. 92–93.

meetings of the clergy until a formal one in 1769, to address Governor Sharpe on his retirement. Conscientious clergymen, such as Henry Addison, who sincerely desired reform, had little to do except to wait and hope for an American bishopric. The policy of letting the church alone meant inevitable scandal in the parishes. The first case to come to Sharpe's attention was that of Coventry parish, located in that old home of church discontent and Presbyterian dissent, Somerset county on the lower Eastern Shore. The parish suffered from the ministry of Nathaniel Whitaker, a clergyman notorious in the province. The governor learned of scandal and difficulties as early as 1754, and would have liked to see the man removed, but there was no way to force him out.[49] The grievance hung fire until 1766, when Whitaker died, and when the parish, with real initiative, invited Dr. Thomas Chandler to come and preach for a trial period. Dr. Chandler, who was soon to become a distinguished writer in behalf of an American episcopate, preached sermons which pleased everyone; the vestry and a number of others of the parish sent Sharpe a petition, accompanied by testimonials of character, urging his permanent induction.[50] This the governor refused to give, but instead inducted the rector of a neighboring church, a man whose character was very like that of Whitaker. The governor's action, with a single eye for his instructions and with none for the merits of the case, precipitated a miniature reformation movement in Coventry.

The vestry took the lead in the protest which followed. It replied to the governor with an argument which cut just as far beneath the ecclesiastical authority of the lord proprietor as did the most radical declarations of the House of Delegates beneath his political authority. The people, the vestry said, were the true founders of the church of Maryland, all powers of church government

49. Sharpe to Baltimore, June 6, 1754, *Archives*, VI, 69.
50. Petition of May 16, 1767, Gilmor Papers, I, 2, MHS; J. Riggin and others to Sharpe, November 25, 1766, *Archives*, XIV, 349–350.

originally derived from them, and the powers they had delegated they could reclaim. Such a radical application of the natural-rights theory could have no meaning or force, in the nature of the case, to dissuade the governor from the exercise of the prerogative. But the vigor of the protest, very likely aided by the example of nearby parishes in Virginia, where the vestries selected their own ministers, did alarm the rector Sharpe had named, and he decided to remain in his present living.[51]

The governor at once gave a new induction to the Reverend Thomas Hughes, a man of reputation as unsavory as those of the other two. Hughes went to Coventry prepared. He took with him a legal opinion written by Daniel Dulany, who at the time enjoyed great popularity because of his pamphlet against the Stamp Act. Designed both to quiet the opposition and to support authority, the opinion blamed all past troubles on the character of Whitaker, and at the same time it entirely unheld Hughes' position as the legally inducted minister.[52] The great Dulany's words, however, no more moved the vestrymen than the opinion of Attorney-General Pratt changed the convictions of the delegates. The vestry declared that it would never give up "freedom to monarchy, but only desire that an equilibrium may ever be the motto of every Englishman." It insisted, moreover, that it would act, even by force if necessary, "as we presume by the laws of God, nature, and man." [53] A few days before Christmas, 1767, the vestry lived up to the principle of the congregational church polity it had announced; it gathered a number of parishioners in the churchyard at Rehoboth, and asked them whether, as the possessors of ultimate sovereignty, they would grant an induction to the minister the governor had named.[54] They voted that they would not, and declaration led to violence.

First they bolted and nailed the church against him, so

51. The early history of the affair is reviewed in a letter from the vestry of Coventry to Sharpe, [1767], ibid., XIV, 363-369.
52. Council Proceedings, April 29, 1768, Archives, XXXII, 224-227.
53. Vestry to Hughes, [1768], ibid., XXXII, 228-229, 231.
54. In a meeting of December 21, 1767, the vestry informed Hughes

that he could not perform a service and read the document of induction, which he was required to do to make the induction legally complete. But he managed somehow to enter the church; he celebrated the Nativity, and read the induction. After that, according to Hughes, he was prevented from entering the different chapels of the parish. His legal possession was opposed, he said, by "all the vestry men and church wardens in arms, (to the terror of some honest men and families,) with swamp men and shingle makers and the rest of their banditti, which they had been collecting for two days and nights." [55] Hughes thereupon appealed to the provincial council, and easily persuaded it to have the attorney-general proceed in the courts against the violators of the public peace.[56] Yet it was inertia, rather than either legal action or mob violence, which concluded the matter. There were a few recurrent outbreaks in the fall and early winter of 1768 and 1769, but Hughes held some quiet services at his church at Rehoboth. The Coventry parish affair drops from the record with a letter from Hughes to Sharpe in June, 1769, in which the rector declared himself determined to stay until the disputes should finally die away.[57]

Thus, on the surface of church affairs, the resistance

that if he were to be given a popular induction he would have to resign the governor's. Then he would be given his full tobacco income, lacking one pound. This proposal may have been copied from an irregular arrangement at St. John's parish. St. John's paid its clergyman his full due except for one hundredweight of tobacco. When Sheriff J. Nicholls informed the vestry, July 10, 1759, that the practice had been questioned, it replied that the minister was not fully and technically inducted, and that the church wished to keep him on just such terms as the payment implied. Such an evasion, it felt, was "well winked at," for it kept the minister in doubt whether he was in or out of a living "in this irreligious old province." Gilmor Papers, II, 2, MHS.

55. Hughes, "Remonstrance" to Sharpe, April 29, 1768, *Archives,* XXXII, 223.

56. Council Proceedings, April 29, 1768, *ibid.,* XXXII, 231. Sharpe ordered the justices of Somerset county to "prevent irregularities," but what the court did is unknown. Baltimore and Secretary Hamersley were pleased with Dulany's opinion. Hamersley to Sharpe, July 18, 1768; Sharpe to Hamersley, October 30, 1768, *ibid.,* XIV, 514, 548; Sharpe to justices of Somerset county, October 21, 1768, Gilmor Papers, I, 2, MHS.

57. June 13, 1769, *Archives,* XIV, 562–563.

of the men of Coventry parish won no concession from the governor's right to control inductions. But the affair demonstrates a vulnerable rigidity in proprietary practice. The decision of Sharpe to reject Chandler for the parish rested on no consideration of local needs, but simply on Lord Baltimore's instruction that only proprietary nominees be presented to livings. The governor's action was entirely single-minded. The resistance of the parish, moreover, signifies not so much violence quelled and defeated as a conviction spread and spontaneously declared. The unusual and important thing was the aggressive use of the social-compact idea in behalf of local freedom; it was the transformation of the Church of England, in the minds of the members of one parish, from terms of traditional to terms of radical church theory, and all of this by men far from Annapolis and from the educated inner circle of the governing class.

The most public and the most disgraceful of all church and patronage affairs occurred contemporaneously with the outbreak in Coventry. It centered on the personal history of Bennet Allen, a friend of Lord Baltimore, it was said, "through a similitude of studies." Like the proprietor, the favorite had a penchant for scribbling worthless stuff, which he thought had literary value.[58] One of his first offenses in Maryland was to boast about literary honors at home, his position as a fellow of Wadham College, and the wealth and high position of his family in England. There was little truth in what he said, but his boasts helped make him enemies in the province.[59]

58. His writing had demonstrable financial value. He once began a letter to Lord Baltimore with observations on his romantic turn of mind. He salted what he said with quotations from Rousseau, and spoke of dreaming of life with "the free and happy tenants of the shades"—the Indians. He said, though, that constitution and education prevented his living with them, and he therefore asked for the receiver-generalship of Maryland. It was given to him. Allen to Baltimore, August 27, 1767, Calvert Papers, no. 1307, MHS. Boucher says that Allen's pen had defended Lord Baltimore, when on trial for the rape of Miss Woodcock, and that this accounts for his coming to Maryland (*Reminiscences*, p. 55).

59. Jonathan Boucher to Rev. Mr. James, Whitehaven, March 9, 1767, November 26, 1768, *Md. Hist. Mag.*, VII, 340–341; VIII, 35.

Allen came preceded by letters from Lord Baltimore and Secretary Hamersley; they simply said that he was an Oxonian in holy orders, and that he should have the best church living available in Maryland. When he arrived, late in 1766, however, he preferred St. Anne's parish in Annapolis to a vacancy on the Eastern Shore, even though that church paid the larger salary. His idea was to establish himself in the capital, and to have the advantage of nearness to the seat of power. To the embarrassment of Governor Sharpe, he made every effort to associate with the proprietary family, he attempted to ingratiate himself with Daniel Dulany, and he made a habit of asking favors. From the governor's point of view, there was no restraint or decency in the man.[60]

Serious difficulty first arose over the question of giving Allen two benefices. He had brought with him a letter from Lord Baltimore recommending that he have two livings if necessary to provide an income of £300. The governor was very reluctant, however, because he knew that objection and conflict would certainly follow on such an arrangement. The act of establishment, he said, forbade pluralism except in special circumstances, and then the consent of both vestries was required. He told Allen that he would rather allow him £50 annually from his own pocket than grant his request, and he wrote the proprietor for further advice. Allen replied with a long letter, in which he argued, with elaborate reference to the laws of England and Maryland, that the proprietor had a perfect right to grant plural holdings, and even that the consent of the vestries was not required. For whatever reason, Sharpe yielded. Pending a formal induction, he licensed Allen to preach at St. James, a parish at Herring Bay and not far from Annapolis, which produced an income of £300 a year. He did so with a warning that there would be much opposition, and again inquired from Hamersley just how

60. Sharpe discussed the whole Allen affair in retrospect, with reference to former letters, in a letter to Hamersley, October 30, 1768, *Archives*, XIV, 538–544.

far to favor Allen, with pluralism the question at issue.[61]

From the beginning it became clear that the vestries would not consent, and that Allen had engaged the enmity rather than the friendship of the powerful of the province. Walter Dulany was one of the vestrymen of St. Anne's, and he had wanted Jonathan Boucher, then in Virginia, to have the parish. With him in the vestry were two distinguished lawyers and radical assemblymen, Brice Worthington and Thomas Johnson. All three violently opposed pluralism. A conflict was certain between the authority of the vestry of St. Anne's and that of Sharpe and Allen, when a fresh quarrel, involving prominent men in St. James parish, focused the matter at Herring Bay, rather than in Annapolis.

The affair had had its beginning at a meeting of Allen and Samuel Chew at the home of William Paca in Annapolis. In the course of the evening's conversation they had spoken of their common personal acquaintanceship with Lord Baltimore. This was at about the time when Allen was licensed at St. James, and he had seized the opportunity to show the letters from the proprietor which favored him for a second benefice. He had begged and received Chew's promise to vote for him in the St. James vestry. Chew later explained that he had made the promise because Allen had assured him that if inducted he would simply supply the church with a curate whom the vestry might retain or remove at will. But Chew's acquiescence had not been a considered one; and, when the vestry voted to consent to Allen's induction only if St. Anne's would first approve the pluralism, Chew voted with the others. Embarrassed by his incautious promise, and no doubt incensed by reports of Allen's licentious living,[62]

<hr>

61. Sharpe to Baltimore, October 29, 1767; Allen to Sharpe, [1767]; Sharpe to Allen, November 27, 1767, *ibid.,* XIV, 424–425, 437–456, 459–461.

62. Chew reports an interview between J. Chew and Allen, as follows: Allen said that the £300 from St. James would scarcely keep him in liquor. Chew replied that he himself spent about £50. "But, says Mr. Allen, you have many advantages that I do not, as for instance, *you*

he determined to let Allen know his actual opposition. An occasion presented itself on January 6, 1768, just before a vestry meeting. Allen came to his house, and was overheard to say that he planned to rent the St. James glebe at Pig Point. Chew turned on Allen and warned him that he should not do that until he was sure of the parish. Chew declared that he desperately wished he had never given Allen any encouragement, and he justified the reversal of his vote by saying that he had recently discovered that the act of establishment forbade pluralism. Recriminations followed: Allen shouted that "a Dulany" had influenced Chew, not the law of Maryland. Chew swore on the Bible that he had had nothing to do with the Dulanys. When Allen refused to leave, Chew called him a "damned scoundrel," dragged him to the door, missed hitting his bald head with a cane, and hoped he was through with the man. Allen sent back a challenge, however, and a duel was arranged. Chew went to the field of honor with a blunderbuss, and Allen, who said later that he had heard of Chew's unfair weapon, did not appear at all.[63]

Allen's next and rashest move was to carry his affairs into the columns of the *Maryland Gazette*. His quarrels had cost him nothing, for Sharpe actually gave him the full induction into St. James. His idea in public writing was to square himself with Walter Dulany, whom he believed to be more responsible than anyone else for the opposition to pluralism. He was probably piqued, too, at failure to remove Dulany from the vestry of St. Anne's,[64] and because he had earlier tried to cultivate the friendship of the family. He seems never to have thought twice about

have a wife; now it will cost me *something considerable to enjoy the pleasures* you are possessed of; *and* concluded by saying *I wish I had never taken the gown."* MS. statement in Dulany Papers, I, 24, MHS. Substantially the whole document was printed in the *Maryland Gazette*, June 2, 1768.

63. *Ibid.* Allen's statement of the case, January 17, 1768, is in Gilmor Papers, I, 2, MHS. See Sharpe to Baltimore, February 9, 1768, *Archives*, XIV, 465–467.

64. Sharpe to Hamersley, February 11, 1768, *ibid.*, XIV, 467.

challenging so powerful an enemy, nor to have considered the fatuity of taking a case like his own into a newspaper so full of the language of self-government.

He wrote over the pseudonym of "Bystander," but the replies in the *Gazette* show that his authorship was perfectly recognized. His first contribution consisted of long citations from the law and precedent of England to show that no councilor could legally serve as a vestryman.[65] Walter Dulany, writing as "C. D.," at first answered him in his own legalistic language; but many other writers wrote satirical pieces about "Bystander." "Crambo" printed scurrilous rhymes about him; "Rusticus" followed in kind; and "Omicron" called "Bystander" names which he compounded from Greek syllables and analyzed for their hidden meaning.[66] After about two months the controversy, which had begun on legalistic grounds, had dropped to its proper level of personal conceit and animus. Finally, at the end of May, after more than four months of "Bystander" and those who wrote about him, Jonas Green, the printer, closed his columns to the controversy. "Bystander," he said, unlike all other writers under pseudonyms, refused to give him his real name, according to rule; and, in any case, subscriptions were dropping off from the printing of so much invective, and there could be no gain from continuing. In a special supplement of the next issue, however, Samuel Chew was given space to review the whole story of his quarrels with Allen, and to identify him publicly as the "Bystander." [67] With this, Allen's affairs dropped from the *Gazette* for a period of three months, but no longer.

In reply to Sharpe's anxious questions, Hamersley had written that Lord Baltimore wanted Allen to have a high office in the financial system, but that there was no need

65. *Maryland Gazette*, January 28, 1768.
66. *Ibid.*, March 10, 24, 31, 1768. Some of the replies were written by Boucher, whose account of the Allen affair is in *Reminiscences*, pp. 53–57.
67. Green, handbill "To The Public," May 28, 1768, Gilmor Papers, I, 2, MHS; *Maryland Gazette*, June 2, 1768.

to push the case for pluralism. The governor and the board of revenue, accordingly, placed Allen in the receiver-generalship. At the same time Allen retained St. James parish but gave up St. Anne's, which went to his curate and friend, Mr. Edmiston. But even with as much preference as this Allen was not satisfied. He saw one other place which he badly wanted, and he hounded the governor for it.

Since arrival in the colony Allen had envied Thomas Bacon the parish of All Saints', in Frederick county, the richest parish in Maryland.[68] In May, 1768, Bacon lay dying, and Allen's hopes rose. But at the same time it appeared that as soon as Bacon died the people would petition the assembly to pass an act dividing the parish, as they had long desired. Under the law, no parish could be divided during the incumbency of a rector, unless with his consent. Bacon had known of the people's wish, and had thought it justified by the too great size of the parish, but had hoped that it would not be urged in his lifetime.[69] If the division were to be made now, the income would be cut in half, and Allen's hopes would be defeated. Under the circumstances Sharpe once more did what Allen desired: he anticipated Bacon's death by giving him the induction. On the day of Bacon's funeral, therefore, a Tuesday, Allen appeared in Frederick town. He arrived a few hours after a petition for dividing the parish had been sent off to Annapolis.[70]

Allen planned to wait for the Sunday service to take possession of the parish. On Saturday, however, he heard that letters had arrived from Annapolis, with a bag full of the "last curious performances" of "C. D." in the

68. Referred to in Sharpe's correspondence as worth £800 a year, but as £452 in a Fulham Palace document (Perry, *Collections*, IV, 336–337). On May 8, 1768, Allen wrote Sharpe that All Saints' was the parish Baltimore intended for him (*Archives*, XIV, 494).

69. Bacon to Walter Dulany, September 24, 1760, Dulany Papers, I, 7, MHS.

70. Sharpe to Baltimore, May 15, 1768; to Hamersley, May 27, 1768; Allen to Sharpe, June 6, 1768, *Archives*, XIV, 498, 499–500, 501.

Gazette. He convinced himself that his enemies were instigating violence against him in Frederick, and to make doubly sure of his living he went to the church at once. Before a congregation of two, a "tippling old barrister" and one other person, he read prayers, the Thirty-Nine Articles, and his induction, and so completed legal possession.

On Sunday morning, when he went for service, the vestry approached and said that he had offended their privileges by failing to show them the induction. By way of reply, Allen snapped back that he knew not their custom, but was familiar with the letter of the law, namely that his induction perfected his possession of the parish. He then leaped into the pulpit and began the service. In his own words:

The congregation was called out. I proceeded as if nothing had happened till the second lesson. I heard some commotions from without which gave me a little alarm, and I provided luckily against it or I must have been maimed if not murdered. They called a number of their bravest that is to say their largest men to pull me out of the desk. I let the captain come within two paces of me and clapped my pistol to his head. What consternation! They accuse me of swearing by God I would shoot him, and I believe I did swear, which was better than praying just then. They retired and I proceeded, but the door and windows lying open and stones beginning to rattle, my aid-de-camp Mr. Dakein advised me to retreat, the fort being no longer tenable. We walked through the midst of them facing about from time to time till we got some distance when stones began to fly; I luckily escaped any hurt and Dakein got but one blow.[71]

Victorious in All Saints', Allen put a curate in charge of the parish, and himself went to Philadelphia, where he

71. Allen to Sharpe, June 6, 1768, *ibid.,* XIV, 501–502. There are other accounts of this episode in *Maryland Gazette,* September 1, 1768; and in Walter Dulany to Hamersley, September 29, 1768, Dulany Papers, II, 51, MHS.

shortly printed a petulent but clever defense of his actions and an apology to the parish.[72] On return, however, he continued in the bad graces of the people, and seems to have let the routine business of the parish fall into the hands of the vestry.[73]

After this Bennet Allen's career in proprietary affairs consisted only of continuing in All Saints' and being removed from the receiver-generalship. His feud with the Dulany family was never made up. The episode in Frederick county was followed by a brief renewal of controversy with Walter Dulany, without pseudonyms, in the *Maryland Gazette* and the *Pennsylvania Chronicle.* As political rivalry disappeared, ill will boiled down to hatred. After the Revolution, in London, Allen forced a challenge from Lloyd Dulany; the two duelled in Hyde Park, and Dulany was killed.[74]

There is no possible way to know how far the "Bystander" controversy, and the other newspaper, pamphlet, and handbill literature of the Allen case actually went in making a public grievance out of this flagrant scandal in church and civil patronage. A few newspaper items reflected on Governor Sharpe's compliance with Allen's demands, on his failure to oppose Lord Baltimore's worst use of the patronage. But comment was mostly particular and not general, and if the discussion led readers to think

72. Allen, *An Address to The Vestrymen, Church Wardens and Parishioners of The Parish of All-Saints'* (Philadelphia, 1768), Gilmor Papers, MHS. The pamphlet makes an odious comparison of Walter Dulany and the writer. Allen also defended himself in the *Pennsylvania Chronicle,* September 12, October 24, November 14, 1768.

73. In the *Maryland Gazette,* January 19, 1769, two vestrymen, not Allen, advertised for curates for the parish. The register of the parish advertised for three curates, *Pennsylvania Chronicle,* May 8, 1769.

74. On Sunday, November 6, 1768, Walter Dulany met Allen while walking in Annapolis. They engaged in a street fight before they could be parted (handbill, by Daniel Wolstenholme, November 9, 1768, Gilmor Papers, I, 2, MHS). Two years later Allen tried to induce a servant to assassinate Dulany, offering him freedom and money ("Memorandum about Parson Allen," September 18, 1770, Dulany Papers, II, 53, MHS; deposition in *Maryland Gazette,* September 27, 1770). There is information about the London duel in the Dulany Papers, II, 80 and in PRO, Home Office, 42.

that the proprietor must be wholly indifferent to any value of the church save favoritism, that sort of idea had little place in public discussion. Yet the newspaper space given to Allen's controversy and affairs was greater in amount than that given to resistance to the Townshend duties, which were contemporary. The mood of challenge was abroad, and Coventry parish, if not All Saints', was ready to apply the formulas of self-government to the ecclesiastical branch of the prerogative.[75] Both parishes were ready to apply violence.

This final stage of proprietary policy and relations shows that in a century and more of experience the Calverts had learned little of colonial government. They could improve the technique of exploitation, as the board of revenue amply illustrates. But they had neither eyes nor ears for needs and ideas not immediately their own.

It is not merely that they disregarded the more extreme pleas of the House of Delegates. The sway of the prerogative was generally regarded in the mother country as fit and right for the colonies; and Frederick, Lord Baltimore, only mirrored his class and type, in his Toryism and in his love of power and property. Had he been moderate in that respect, his government would have evoked no more than traditional opposition. The special significance of his proprietorship is that he added something, visual and dramatic, to the old difference of premise between government by authority and government by consent. Here was the prerogative not merely in its essentials but with new excesses in the exercise of power. The quality which insisted on the last penny of proprietary revenue, and which added caprice and irresponsibility to independence in making church appointments, was a quality of blindness for which the mother country provided no cure.

75. Samuel Chew achieved recognition in Boston as a champion of religious liberty. "Opposition to the most dangerous of all tyranny hath sprung up in [Maryland] in the person of Col. Saml Chew. The last hero is idolized at Boston. . . . Mr. Otis is determined to enter into a correspondence with him." Lloyd Dulany (Philadelphia) to Walter Dulany, March 20, 1768, Dulany Papers, II, 45, MHS.

IX

PROVINCIAL RESISTANCE TO IMPERIAL REFORM
1763–1770

FOLLOWING the peace of 1763, the common necessity of the British government and the American
colonies alike was to find a way out of the contradictions of the war period. Could the home government, recently so unsuccessful in reconciling the war leadership of
the mother country with the decentralization of the colonies, now do better with the new administrative problems
of the peace? Could the untried obligations of territorial
empire, north and west, which financially and administratively were not so different from the obligations of war,
find a better solution than the requisition system which
had handicapped Braddock and Loudoun and Pitt?
Where would proprietary Maryland stand in the new
imperial situation? Would the House of Delegates once
more reject all else than that which conformed to its own
advanced ideas of provincial self-government?

The first great question which British statesmanship
decided was that of the government of the new transmontane territories. The famous proclamation of the king in
council, of October 7, 1763, provided that for the time
being the Ohio valley should be maintained as an Indian
preserve, closed to settlers. This offended many interests
in the larger seaboard colonies, especially the speculators
and the land-hungry poor, but it had little significance
in Maryland. Some hunters, indeed, passed beyond the
"proclamation line," and Governor Sharpe reported that
he could not prevent them; but apparently there was no
great need to do so, for they caused no trouble.[1] Sharpe

1. Sharpe to the Earl of Shelburne, December 23, 1766; to Baltimore,
March 31, 1768, *Archives*, XIV, 361–362, 478–479; Gage to Shelburne,
January 22, 1768, Clarence E. Carter, editor, *The Correspondence of*

stopped the granting of land west of the line, though not for long. Five years after his retirement, in 1774, certain wealthy speculators of Annapolis applied for warrants for new western lands, and the land office made concessions. The judges justified doing this by saying that the line had long been disregarded in Maryland.[2] The proclamation of 1763 was printed in the *Maryland Gazette*, but it provoked no newspaper discussion, nor was it criticized in the lower house. When, in the summer of 1763, the western settlements were thrown into confusion by Pontiac's Conspiracy, the governor thought that a much worse situation had been prevented by the presence of Colonel Bouquet with a detachment of troops at Fort Pitt. The proclamation of October 7, as it stood for peace in the west, favored rather than injured Maryland.[3] Lax enforcement eased whatever restrictions it might have imposed on the few expansionists of the province with interests so far afield.

The colony was likewise little affected when Parliament developed the acts of trade in a way intended to correct the faults shown up during the war. Minor revisions, which were included in the laws sponsored by George Grenville in 1764, placed a number of new commodities on the list of colonial goods "enumerated" for exportation to the mother country only, and established new bounties to encourage certain colonial raw materials. Maryland received something from the new bounty on hemp,[4] but pro-

General Thomas Gage with the Secretaries of State, 1763–1775 (New Haven, 1931–33), I, 156. Thomas P. Abernethy, in his *Western Lands and the American Revolution* (New York, 1937), finds little Maryland activity in the west prior to 1775.

2. The receiver-general, Daniel of St. Thomas Jenifer, clashed with the judges of the land office, George Stewart and Benedict Calvert, over granting lands beyond Fort Cumberland, west of the line. See Minutes of the Board of Revenue, *Archives*, XXXII, *passim*, especially p. 485, and Kilty, *Land-Holder's Assistant*, pp. 264–266.

3. The same was true, in Sharpe's opinion, of the establishment of the new imperial commissioners for Indian affairs, because they would help maintain stable conditions across the mountains. Sharpe to Board of Trade, October 18, 1764, *Archives*, XIV, 179–180.

4. See George L. Beer, *British Colonial Policy, 1754–1765* (New York, 1922), pp. 217–218n.

duction and exportation was little influenced by these regulations. Further enactments of the same series provided for tightening up the enforcement of all the acts of trade. But they were designed principally to prevent illicit trade in the northern colonies, and had little bearing on Maryland or any of the southern colonies. Smuggling was not considered serious enough there to concern the home government greatly,[5] and British remedies for northern smuggling did not offend the people of Maryland.

One of the mercantilist reforms of 1764, the act forbidding the issue of legal-tender paper money, was aimed at conditions in the southern colonies. Virginia, especially, by juggling the purchasing power of her currency and injuring the credit of British merchants, had abused the colonial control of legal tender. In 1751 Parliament had taken this power from the northern colonies, and now did so from the southern.[6] Maryland came within the scope of this remedial and disciplinary law, but at a time when her own money was ready for retirement. Outstanding bills of credit were promptly and fully paid; and, when the accounts had been closed, the province found itself possessed of a surplus of £25,000, in the stock of the Bank of England, left from the sinking fund. Although Governor Sharpe was at first doubtful on the point, the act of 1764 placed no restriction on the issue of such colonial paper as was not made legal tender for sterling debts. Thus the surplus gave the assembly a favorable basis on

5. On October 20, 1764, Sharpe assured Lord Halifax that there was little illicit trade in Maryland. Apparently in reply to a question, he said that even a great increase in the customs establishment could not supervise the many inlets of Maryland. He thought a few cutters in the bay would be more effective than many officials. Letter in PRO, Treasury, 1: 442, f. 343, LC. See Beer, *British Colonial Policy*, p. 237 and *passim*.

6. The trustees of the Maryland sinking fund, merchants in London, tried to influence Parliament, first, without success, to exempt Maryland, and second, successfully, to make textual amendments favorable to the province. Later they tried to secure repeal. Letters to the Maryland commissioners, April 12, 1764, May 6, 21, 1767, Black Books, V, 1, MHRecs.

which to act, and three more emissions were authorized before the end of the colonial period. The new money kept its value, and even under parliamentary restrictions was useful to the province.[7] Unlike that of Virginia, Maryland paper money never earned the censure of the home government.

Both a mercantilist and a financial measure, the Sugar Act, also of 1764, was the first of the Grenville acts to cause a great protest in America. Here for the first time Parliament imposed a tax for revenue on the colonies: the old prohibitive duty on the importation of molasses from the foreign West Indies was scaled down; the machinery of collection was improved; and the principal purpose, the raising of money, was plain to be seen.[8] Secretary Calvert feared that the act would lead to remonstrance in Maryland, and he told Sharpe to guard against the sending of protests to England. But the governor was not apprehensive, and responded that little popular feeling was likely to arise, for the reason that the duty did not touch the pockets of the people. Sharpe's judgment proved correct. While the northern colonies complained, Maryland, with a very small molasses trade, did not stir.[9] At most the law produced a certain uneasiness and a topic for anxious conversation among those who were especially sensitive and informed. Men were saying, according to

7. Behrens, *Paper Money in Maryland*, pp. 51, 55–56; Gould, *Money and Transportation in Maryland*, pp. 108–109. "A.B." in the *Maryland Gazette*, November 16, 1769, and Sharpe, in letters to Baltimore, Calvert, and Hamersley, expressed opinions that Maryland money was sound (*Archives*, XIV, 174, 213, 251–252, 318, 352, 391). The new money, issued after the act of 1764 and in compliance with it, was not really different from the old. Daniel Dulany explained to Secretary Calvert, September 10, 1764, that the old law had required no creditor to accept the bills if the debt had been contracted in other money—this in favor of Lord Baltimore and the British merchants (*Calvert Papers*, II, 245–246).

8. See Beer, *British Colonial Policy*, pp. 276–281.

9. In 1764 and 1765 the amounts of £40 0s. 0d. and £15 8s. 9d., respectively, were the collections from the molasses duty. In 1765 Maryland imported 3,400 gallons, out of an American total of 928,852½. PRO, Treasury, 1: 434, ff. 53, 164, 447, LC. Sharpe's prophecy is in a letter to Calvert, August 22, 1764, *Archives*, XIV, 175–176.

Sharpe, that if a tax should be placed on Maryland, the provincial judges would not sustain any officers who tried to collect, because the charter of 1632 guaranteed the people against any tax not enacted by the authority of the province.[10]

The Stamp Tax was not to affect Maryland so lightly. As early as September, 1764, when the tax was only a plan, months before enactment and more than a year before going into effect, Daniel Dulany seriously concerned himself with the economic aspects of the matter. There was every reason, he told Secretary Calvert, to fear that a general tax would affect bad ·trade conditions to worsen them, and would subject the commercial bond, the most important bond between the mother country and the colonies, to an oversevere strain. "Every shilling," said Dulany jealously, "gained by the American commerce hath entered in Britain, and fallen into the pockets of the British merchants, traders, manufacturers, and land holders, and it may therefore be justly called the British commerce." [11] A new tax in America, he reasoned, would reduce colonial purchasing power, and diminish the business and profits of the merchants at home. A reduced importation of British manufactures, moreover, would force colonial prices to rise and in turn encourage native industries. Any parliamentary tax would operate as a bounty on American manufactures, and so be destructive of the recognized aims of mercantilism. Dulany hoped that such considerations would be duly weighed by the great in England before a new tax was definitely imposed.

10. Letter to Calvert, August 22, 1764, *ibid.,* XIV, 175–176. The relevant clause in the charter was the twentieth, in which Charles I did "covenant and grant . . . that We, our heirs and successors, at no time hereafter, will impose, or make, or cause to be imposed, any impositions, customs, or other taxations, quotas, or contributions whatsoever, in or upon the residents or inhabitants of the province. . . ." The charter is printed in Francis N. Thorpe, *Federal and State Constitutions and Colonial Charters* . . . , III (Washington, 1909), 1669–1686; in J. Thomas Scharf, *History of Maryland* . . . (Baltimore, 1879), I, 53–60, and in Mereness, *Maryland,* pp. 507–520.

11. Letter of September 10, 1764, *Calvert Papers,* II, 244.

Dulany's economic reflections truly represented a discouraging state of affairs. The tobacco trade had rallied, after the adversities of war, in a brief advance of 1763, but in 1764 it dropped into a severe decline which was marked by both falling prices and diminishing exportations.[12] Tobacco was hardly to improve before the end of the decade. Nor were conditions in the provision trade much better, or in any position to offset depression in the staple. Samuel Galloway, the merchant of West River, heard in letters, all dated in June, 1764, that Thomas Philpot, his London correspondent, "never knew things to go so heavy," that his correspondents in Antigua and Madeira found poor grain markets, and that Thomas Ringgold, his associate on the Eastern Shore, thought the West India trade very bad.[13] Galloway, for one, tried new devices to improve his credit,[14] but the period was a hard

12. English Tobacco Importations from the Colonies, and the Average Annual Wholesale Price of Tobacco in Philadelphia, 1761–1770

Year	Pounds of Tobacco	Price, Shillings per Cwt
1761	47,065,787	21.52
1762	44,102,491	21.42
1763	65,173,752	19.48
1764	54,433,318	17.71
1765	48,306,593	18.13
1766	43,307,453	20.42
1767	39,140,639	21.89
1768	35,545,708	21.83
1769	33,784,208	25.12
1770	39,188,037	28.73

The importations are from PRO, Treasury, 1: 64, f. 276, LC; and the Philadelphia prices from Bezanson, *Prices in Colonial Pennsylvania*, p. 422.

Maryland correspondence indicates the same trends as these figures: a good market was reported in London in 1763, but a bad one in Glasgow, which remained bad. Sylvanus Grove, after years in the Maryland trade, felt compelled to withdraw. Letters in Galloway, Maxcy, Markoe Papers, LC; and Hamilton Papers, MHS. See P. H. Giddens, "Trade and Industry in Colonial Maryland," *Journal of Economic and Business History*, IV, 519–521.

13. Letters from Ringgold, June 1, 1764; from Philpot, June 12, 1764, Galloway Papers, I, NYPL; from Benjamin Binney (Madeira), June 10, 1764; from J. Searle (Antigua), June 20, 1764, Galloway, Maxcy, Markoe Papers, LC.

14. Late in 1763 Galloway tried the following venture, a unique one, as far as the writer knows: he sent a vessel with a cargo of provisions to Hispaniola, with orders to sell both; if the captain could not find

one for him, and for all the merchants and people of the province.

From the great and the lowly alike, there was but one report, that of depression, in 1764 and 1765. The councilor, Benedict Calvert, wrote to his uncle, the secretary, that

Our trade is ruined, we are immensely in debt, and not the least probability of our getting clear. Our gaols are not half large enough to hold the debtors, upon every road you ride you meet people going from different parts of the province to get out of the way of their creditors. I can venture to say that the people of America were never in such a distrest situation as they are at present.[15]

From the other side of the bay, on the Eastern Shore, and from the other end of the social scale, just above the unfree, Henry Callister, now almost a bankrupt, wrote in terms very like Calvert's own:

All ranks of people here, the people in general, seem to be in a state of bankruptcy, and not a little of fraudulent kind. It is madness now to sue for debts. If people are not able to pay, you must let them walk off or stay to defy you. The laws are for them in both theory and practice. We have no currency in Maryland but that is imaginary. The real value of land, slaves, and all manner of property is sunk within these 2 or 3 years about 100 per cent or more in some parts. The nominal value remains as before. The agents of my creditors in England through compassion valued my estate low, hoping I might during the term of the mortgage sell off sufficient to pay and reserve a moderate farm to myself.[16]

a buyer for the vessel he was to take a new cargo and sail for Bordeaux. At Bordeaux the deal was completed, and the credit transferred to London. Letters from Captain Kell, January–August, 1764, Galloway, Maxcy, Markoe Papers, LC.

15. Letter of June 24, 1765, *Calvert Papers*, II, 261–262.

16. Letter to Sir Ellis Cunliffe, September 8, 1765. Callister describes conditions similarly in letters to H. White (New York), to Sharpe, and to Thomas Bacon, Callister Papers, Md. Dioc. Lib.

At no other time in the century, not even in 1729, have we had reports quite so distressing as these.

Credit was the nub of the matter, as Callister said, and the period of the Grenville acts was also a period of demand for relief from the legislature. Writers who styled themselves as "Philalethes" and "Zedekiah Homony" urged new emissions of paper money in the columns of the *Gazette*, and Daniel Dulany wrote Secretary Calvert that paper was essential to the welfare of the province.[17] New issues were actually enacted, as we have seen, but only after a delay; the first new paper, after the retirement of the old, did not come until 1766. Meanwhile the people of western Maryland were suffering not only from general conditions but from the losses of the war period and of Pontiac's Conspiracy. The assembly had not voted a journal of accounts to pay off the public debt since 1756, and the deficiency held up the payment of western militiamen, who now felt the need. Accordingly four hundred fifty "subscribing inhabitants of Frederick county" addressed Governor Sharpe in a plea for action, and for the release of long overdue public money.[18] But this matter, too, did not reach the stage of action until 1766.

The Stamp Act came upon Maryland, then, after a year and more of sharp depression, and before the legislature had taken the mildly inflationary steps of which it was capable. As a contributor wrote in the *Gazette*, "The great scarcity of money, low markets abroad for the produce of the plantation, the heavy restraints and impositions the colonies are already laid under (exclusive of the *intolerable ones* we have reason to surmize impending) are sufficient to strike a damp into the most serene minds." [19] No time would have been a good time, but this

---

17. *Maryland Gazette,* May 13, 1762, September 15, 1763; Dulany to Calvert, September 10, 1764, *Calvert Papers,* II, 245–246. Governor Sharpe wrote Baltimore, December 7, 1766, that provincial credit was in a desperate condition, and he believed it due to exportation of money to England. A nice point to the recipient of the proprietary revenues from his representative! *Archives,* XIV, 352.

18. March 5, 1766, *ibid.,* XXXII, 124–125.

19. *Maryland Gazette,* May 23, 1765.

was a particularly bad and restless time for a new tax to be imposed by Parliament.

Announcement of the Stamp Act came to Maryland in a way which displayed at the outset the propagandist rôle to be assumed by the *Maryland Gazette*.[20] In the issue of April 18, 1765, Jonas Green declared, between heavy mourning bars, that the newspaper, "Alas! must soon droop and expire, at least for some time, if the melancholy and alarming accounts, we have just heard from the northward, prove true, that an act of Parliament is shortly to take place, laying a heavy and insupportable *Stamp Duty* on all American gazettes, &c, &c." From April 18 until October 10 there was almost weekly news or discussion of the tax. Much of it came in the form of items from outside the colony: a report of the final enactment, from Rhode Island; the fifty-five resolutions of the House of Commons, printed in full; Isaac Barré's "Sons of Liberty" speech in the House of Commons, quoted in the issue of June 6; the radical resolutions of the Virginia House of Burgesses, offered by Patrick Henry; and, in the middle of the summer, the invitation of the Massachusetts House of Representatives to attend the congress to be held in New York, in October.[21] There was also much from within the colony. Contributors filled Green's columns with arguments against the tax, and they iterated and reiterated the ideas and phrases common to the Whiggism of the lower house. They used such favorite names as Cato and Lycurgus as pseudonyms, they spoke of the contractual nature of the state, they stressed the responsibility of those who rule to be guided by reason, and they unanimously denounced the tax as unconstitutional and wrong.[22] Not a single contributor under-

20. To compare with the northern papers, see A. M. Schlesinger, "The Colonial Newspapers and the Stamp Act," *New England Quarterly,* VIII (1935), 63–83. The present materials are considered, from a somewhat different angle from the writer's, in P. H. Giddens, "Maryland and the Stamp Act Controversy," *Md. Hist. Mag.,* XXVII, 79–98.

21. *Maryland Gazette*, April 25, May 2, June 6, July 4, July 25, 1765.

22. A letter of "Y.Z." shows that unanimity against the Stamp Tax

took to defend the Stamp Act or to apologize for it. After three months and much space devoted to the hearing of principles, the *Maryland Gazette* carried an item which brought the tax home to the province. Zachariah Hood, a merchant of Annapolis who had gone to England on business, was now returning, in the new capacity of stamp distributor for Maryland. In the issue of August 22, the *Gazette* had a letter from a "Gentleman in London," who said that Hood had been heard to say that, if his country must be stamped, it might better be done by a native. "It gives too many here pleasure," said the "Gentleman," "to find, that, let them make what laws they please, to cramp your trade, and destroy your freedom, there are not wanting sycophants enough in your own country to sue for commissions to put those very laws in execution among their nearest relations and friends. Oh! degeneracy of ancient Britons! America! how thou art fallen!" The letter was incendiary, and was immediately followed by the first popular meetings and outbreaks against the tax.

On August 26, a "considerable number of people, assertors of British American privileges," gathered in Annapolis. Their leader was Samuel Chase, the future Supreme Court justice, then twenty-four years old, a rising lawyer and a recently elected member of the House of Delegates. They made an effigy of Hood, put papers in its hand, placed it in a cart, and drew it over the rough streets of the city. According to the description in the *Gazette*, it nodded penitently on the way to the gallows, where it was burned. This performance was followed in a few days by violence. Three or four hundred rowdies in Annapolis pulled down Hood's warehouse. Also within days, there followed several demonstrations and burnings in effigy,

did not mean forgetfulness of old jealousies. The factors of great British merchants, he said, had formed a committee to send home a statement of their objections to the act. Why should not the planters turn their arguments for liberty against the factors, their real enemies? *Ibid.*, July 4, 1765. Scharf quotes many newspaper items in his *History of Maryland*, I, 524–556.

one in Baltimore and about a dozen in the smaller communities of the colony.[23]

These events thoroughly upset Hood, and warned the governor, who was the only other official in any direct way connected with the execution of the law.[24] Hood asked Sharpe whether or not he had better resign, but Sharpe had no authority to accept or advise resignation, or to do anything except to support and protect him. The governor offered a refuge in his own home, although he held the opinion that only a military force could execute the law;[25] Hood wisely decided to flee to New York. There he found security for only a little while. The New York Sons of Liberty forced him, on November 28, to resign his office. He returned later to Maryland, but found that he could not reënter business. He went on to the West Indies, and to destitution; and in 1771 petitioned the Crown for relief.[26]

The expulsion of Hood, the earliest case of violence in the southern colonies, was immediately followed by another outbreak. The "mob," as Sharpe put it, was still in a ferment from the destruction of the warehouse, when a tender from his majesty's sloop *Hornet* put in at Annapolis. The vessel had barely anchored when a number of men boarded and demanded of the commander, Mewbray, whether or not he brought stamped paper. Actually he had not, he had come up the bay in pursuit of a smuggler. But the question angered him, he refused to answer, and he put the intruders off his vessel. That evening, accord-

23. *Maryland Gazette,* August 29, September 5, 1765.

24. The Lords of the Treasury asked Sharpe to help Hood in any way he could, and he was ordered to see that Hood had enough assistants and gave security for dutiful performance. Charles Lowndes to Sharpe, September 14, 1765, *Archives,* XIV, 227–228; XXXII, 116–117. Sharpe had given Halifax a list of taxable documents, October 26, 1764, *Md. Hist. Mag.,* XII, 372.

25. Sharpe to Halifax, September 5, 1765; to Gage, September 6, 1765, *Archives,* XIV, 221, 222. Gage sent Sharpe an order for 100 troops from Fort Pitt to protect the stamps. Gage to Conway, September 23, 1765, *Gage Correspondence,* I, 68.

26. *Maryland Gazette,* January 30, 1766; Hood to Lords of Treasury, February 19, 1771, *Md. Hist. Mag.,* IV, 138–139.

ingly, when he went to town to dine in a public house, he went under popular observation and suspicion. During the meal a man entered the room with a paper marked, "No Stamp Act," attached to his hat. Mewbray took this as an affront, ordered the man out, and posted sailors to see that he did not return. A little later, one of Mewbray's dinner guests, who was drunk, fell into argument with Mr. John Hammond, a popular member of the lower house from Anne Arundel county. Words led to a brawl, and blows excited someone to shout through the streets that Hammond was being murdered. A crowd gathered, some were armed, and Mewbray and his party were forced to flee. Just what followed is not clear, but the officer and those with him had to swim for their lives, and Mewbray may have been wounded. This riot was the last such affair in Annapolis in the Stamp Act period, and was thoroughly disapproved of by the gentlemen of the city. They all abhorred it, Sharpe said, few would admit having seen it, and none would say that he had participated.[27]

Yet as the summer advanced, and November first, the date of incidence, approached, Maryland achieved more and more solidarity in opposition to the act. Shortly after the Mewbray affair, the "freeholders and freemen" of Anne Arundel county sent a "Remonstrance with some Instructions" to their delegates in assembly, all of whom were prominent in the "country party." In familiar phrases but with force, the people declared that the Stamp Act compelled them to be careful to preserve the rights of freemen which "an unalterable law of nature" gave them. They cited the charter guaranty against royal levy, and did so in such a way as to make it appear that Maryland had a special freedom from parliamentary taxation. The freeholders and freemen gave their delegates a general charge: they must carefully protect the rights of the people. They further asked specifically that a lower-house committee be sent to the Stamp Act Congress, and

27. Sharpe to Calvert, September 10, 1765; to Gage, September 23, 1765, *Archives,* XIV, 225–227, 229.

that addresses be made to Barré and Conway, out of gratitude for their services to liberty.[28]

While the freemen of Anne Arundel were using the new method of political instruction to urge resistance, the lawyers of the colony, too, began to stir. They petitioned Sharpe to advance the date for the assembly session, from October to September, so that there might be time and opportunity to send delegates to the congress. The council was in a position to resent, as Benedict Calvert particularly did,[29] the injury which the Stamp Act did to the prerogative, represented by the immunity Charles II had granted Lord Baltimore. It supported the lawyers in their request to convene the assembly. Governor Sharpe, who had been glad that the time fixed for the session would have come too late for sending delegates, now felt obliged to do as he was advised. If he had not done so, the delegates would have met extra-legally, on their own initiative, and a new grievance would have been added to the accumulation of differences within the assembly. Thus under pressure from politics outside assembly walls, the province achieved a moment of agreement, and the assembly convened on September 23, 1765.[30]

Nearly all the members of the House of Delegates were present. Governor Sharpe made a very brief address, saying simply that he had called the session out of deference to the wishes of the members, that he wished to gratify them, and that he asked only that the upper and lower houses harmonize. The speaker at once read the lower house the unanimous invitation of the Massachusetts House of Representatives to send delegates to meet in congress in New York during the first week in October. The house then resolved to consider no other business during the present session; and, as if to school itself for

28. *Maryland Gazette,* October 10, 1765, second supplement, issued October 24.

29. Letter to Sharpe, February 26; to Cecilius Calvert, June 24, 1765, *Calvert Papers,* II, 259–262.

30. Sharpe to Calvert, August 2, October 2, 1765; to Baltimore, October 3, 1765, *Archives,* XIV, 212, 230–232.

doing a great deed, it had read the Petition of Right and the Bill of Rights before it proceeded to business.[31]

Three men, Colonel Tilghman, William Murdock, and Thomas Ringgold, were elected to go to New York for the congress. They were instructed to join with the committees from the other colonies in dutiful, loyal, and humble representations to his majesty and Parliament, praying for relief from the Stamp Act and from the recent restrictions placed on trade. They were ordered to assert the principle that all the colonists had a right to be free from taxation to which neither they nor their representatives had consented.[32]

After making the instructions, the house passed a series of eight unanimous resolutions declarative of the constitutional rights of Maryland. This province enjoyed, the house declared, the full rights of Englishmen, brought over by the earliest "adventurers and settlers." It therefore enjoyed the full protection of Magna Carta, the Petition of Right, the Bill of Rights, "and other good laws and statutes of *England*," against "tax, tallage, aid, or other like charge, not set by common consent of Parliament." One of the resolutions quoted two long paragraphs from the charter of 1632, the first guaranteeing to the settlers "all privileges, franchises, and liberties of this our kingdom of England," and the other promising immunity "from taxations, quotas, or contributions whatsoever" imposed by the king. The other resolutions favored jury courts against non-jury, with evident reference to the vice-admiralty; declared that Maryland was unrepresented in Parliament; that the people of Maryland had "always enjoyed the right of being governed by laws, to which they themselves have consented, in the articles of taxes, and internal polity"; that the Maryland assembly alone had the "sole right to levy taxes and impositions on the inhabitants of this province, or their property and

31. Sharpe to Baltimore, October 3, 1765, *ibid.*, XIV, 231–232; *Votes and Proceedings*, September 23–24, 1765.
32. *Ibid.*, September 25, 1765.

effects"; and, finally, that for any other authority than the assembly to pass taxes was "unconstitutional and a direct violation of the rights of the freemen of the province." [33] With both instructions and resolutions, the lower house had made a powerful case: the first had declared, in essence, that right reason and sound philosophy protected all Americans against the Stamp Act; the second, that Maryland had perfect guarantees in the charter of the province and the law of England and Maryland.

With declarations made, the lower house sent the council the nominations of delegates to go to New York, their instructions, and an ordinance granting £500 for the expenses of the trip. Although the upper house had no part in naming the men or planning their instructions, it approved what the lower house offered, without objection. Governor Sharpe agreed to sign the ordinance at once, so that there need be no delay. Before proroguing the Delegates, however, the governor asked their advice about the course to be taken when the stamps should arrive. The house refused to accept any responsibility in the matter, putting Sharpe off with the statement that the voters had given no instructions about what they wanted done.[34] The session closed with the House of Delegates in strong position; it had had its own way, under the pressure of general feeling, and it was about to make political connections with the like-minded outside of Maryland.

Not only did Maryland, through its lower house, participate in the Stamp Act Congress, but it also succeeded at last in making connection with an agent in England. The committee of delegates, Ringgold, Murdock, and Tilghman, sent three petitions to Charles Garth, agent for South Carolina, for transmission, one each to the king, the House of Lords, and the House of Commons. Garth thought them impolitic, in that they challenged Parliament's right to tax the colonies, and were not en-

33. *Ibid.*, September 27, 1765, quoted in Mereness, *Maryland*, pp. 479–482.
34. *Votes and Proceedings*, September 28, 1765.

tirely correct in form; so he withheld them, in the interest of repeal.[35] But in their correspondence with Garth the Delegates had, at last and in one respect, achieved the overseas reach in political struggle which they had so long wanted.

With the action of the assembly, every political element in Maryland had declared itself: the *Gazette* had publicized the Stamp Tax; the people had protested and acted; the lower house had called the tax illegal; the upper house had agreed; and the governor had permitted the opposition. If anything were still needed to add volume to the voice of the province, it was the pamphlet of Daniel Dulany, which carried the force of Maryland opposition into the other colonies and to England. *The Considerations on the Propriety of Imposing Taxes in the British Colonies for the Purpose of Raising a Revenue, by Act of Parliament* came from the press of Jonas Green on October 14, while the Stamp Act Congress was in session in New York.[36] Anonymity on the title-page did not disguise the writer; the younger Dulany was widely known and his authorship generally recognized.

Brought out after the province had spoken, the pamphlet pleaded the case against the Stamp Tax in terms which, while general, mirrored the special features of political thought and expression in Maryland. It took for granted, without accent, the natural-rights philosophy. Dulany quoted Coke at the outset in support of the presumption that "all men have natural, and freemen have legal rights" of which no legislature can deprive them; such a right was that of self-taxation. From this premise forward the plea was legal and historical rather than philosophical: "virtual representation" was a just doc-

35. Garth to Ringgold, Murdock, Tilghman, February 26, March 5, 1766, *Md. Hist. Mag.*, VI, 282–305. Garth speaks of the receipt of money, but it is not clear whether this was part of the £500 appropriation for the congress or something else.

36. The first edition is reprinted in *Md. Hist. Mag.*, VI, 376–406; VII, 26–59. There was a London edition in 1766. See *ibid.*, VI, 374–375; and Wroth, *Printing in Colonial Maryland*, pp. 223–226.

trine in England, where the early history of Parliament proved that representation had never been direct or complete; it was unjust in America, where interests were so different, and colonial charters and colonial history had provided representation in the assemblies. On the economic side, Dulany elaborated his thinking of the year before; he discussed the heavy burden of taxes and of charges on the tobacco trade, and the added strain the Stamp Tax would impose, to the encouragement of colonial manufactures. The writing was directed to the informed, for there were long quotations of English precedent in legal Latin, and there were flashes of wit and satire. The argument was focused on parliamentary taxation. There were also larger implications favorable to self-government in its wider aspects, but Dulany's *Considerations* was not, as we have seen, as sweeping a liberal plea as his father's *Right of the Inhabitants*, a generation before. The conservatism of the *Considerations* was probably its strength in England, where it was to catch the eye of Pitt and to become an influence towards repeal.[37]

As November first drew near, it appeared that Marylanders would certainly refuse in practice to comply with the tax which they had for six months repudiated in words. The excitement of the time becomes unusually plain in a letter of young Charles Carroll of Carrollton, only ten months home from his studies in England: "Should the Stamp Act be enforced by tyrannical soldiery, our property, our liberty, our very existence, is at an end. And you may be persuaded that nothing but an armed force can execute the worst of laws." [38] Carroll anticipated that the people would burn the stamps and that business would suffer.

Jonas Green must have contributed to the sense of im-

37. For discussions of the pamphlet in general American history and literature, see Moses C. Tyler, *The Literary History of the American Revolution* (New York, 1897), I, 101–111; Randolph G. Adams, *Political Ideas of the American Revolution* (Durham, 1922) pp. 70–78.

38. Letter to E. Jennings (?), London, September 28, 1765, Rowland, *Life of Charles Carroll of Carrollton*, I, 73-74.

pending crisis by the way in which he retired the *Maryland Gazette* from circulation. The last of the many resolutions he printed about the Stamp Act were the eight passed by the House of Delegates. This was on October third. On the tenth he announced that, although three weeks remained before "Dooms-Day," the present would be the last regular issue, as it came at the end of the fiscal year of the *Gazette*. In the place of the usual heading he printed, between wide mourning bars, "THE MARYLAND GAZETTE *Expiring:* In uncertain Hopes of a Resurrection to *Life* again"; and in the lower right hand corner, in the place of a stamp, he printed a death's head. He massed the news in this issue, and in the three weekly supplements which followed, in such a way as to magnify the impression of great events and great uncertainties. From Boston there were accounts of the activities of James Otis, Samuel Adams, Harrison Gray, and Samuel Wells; and notes from Connecticut and other colonies told of the forced resignation of Jared Ingersoll as stamp distributor, and of the excitement of the people along the seaboard. "A.A.," in a series of queries, asked whether business must stop, if no stamps could be sold, and whether or not contracts made on unstamped documents would be invalid.[39] No public answer was made, but Green, by virtue of the fact that he closed his own newspaper business, showed that he thought the answer was the desperate one, in the affirmative. In half a column he bade "Farewell to the Reader!" and discontinued the *Gazette*.

The question of "A.A." was the most serious one Maryland had to face. The situation stood at an impasse. The law of Great Britain required stamped paper to validate business documents; the stamp distributor was in New York; and all sorts and classes had repudiated the law. The first consignment of stamps reached Maryland just before November first. Governor Sharpe consulted first with the council and then with the Delegates, who were in

39. *Maryland Gazette,* October 10, 1765, second supplement, October 24.

the second session of 1765. The lower house once more, as in the last session, refused to take any responsibility for advising the governor what to do. He therefore asked the commander of the naval vessel bringing the stamps to keep them aboard; and he did the same in December, when the second lot arrived.[40] Meanwhile the port officers felt the pressure of events in a very practical way. Six collectors and comptrollers of the royal establishment and three naval officers wrote to the Customs Commissioners asking whether or not they should enter and clear vessels without stamped documents, and what they should do in the "delicate dilemma" they faced.[41] As the year 1765 ended, the ports were closed, and so likewise were the provincial courts and offices in Annapolis. But the northern colonies were doing business as usual, and Governor Sharpe feared that their example, which he regarded as treasonable, would be too suggestive for Marylanders to resist.[42]

The first sign that the colony would disregard the tax came from Frederick county, in November. The county judges decided that, since they had never received official notice of the Stamp Act, they would proceed with the regular business of the court, as if they had no reason to believe that special circumstances existed. The decision was celebrated in a fitting manner. Self-styled "Sons of Liberty" of Frederick town honored the judges with a ball and many patriotic toasts. They buried the Stamp Act in a mock funeral, where the only mourner was an effigy of Zachariah Hood.[43] In the same month a group of "freemen" gathered in Talbot county, on the Eastern Shore, and resolved that they would risk their lives and

40. Council Proceedings, October 26, 1765, *Archives*, XXXII, 108–109; *Votes and Proceedings*, November 4, 1765; Sharpe to Calvert, November 11, 1765; to Baltimore, December 24, 1765, *Archives*, XIV, 239–240, 256.

41. Letter of November 2, 1765, House of Lords Library, Andrews and Davenport, *Guide*, p. 235, item 221, LC.

42. Letter to Calvert, November 11, December 24, 1765, *Archives*, XIV, 239–240, 253–254.

43. *Maryland Gazette*, December 10, 1765.

fortunes, if they must, to preserve the rights which the Stamp Act threatened to destroy. Although their county judges had adjourned for four months, not wishing to do business in contradiction to the act, these "freemen" seem to have meant that they were ready for active defiance. They erected a gibbet, twenty feet high, before the courthouse door, and hung the effigy of a stamp informer there, to remain *in terrorem* until repeal.[44]

By December such defiance had won approval and imitation even among the rich and influential in the colony. Speaking of Frederick county, Charles Carroll of Carrollton said: "This conduct, in my apprehension, is but rational and a necessary consequence, if the people would act consequentially, of what they have already done: since a suspense from business implies a tacit acquaintance of the law, or at least the right of the power of imposing such laws upon us." [45]

Very shortly Jonas Green was thinking, and acting, in the same way. After suspending his paper no more than five weeks, he published, on December 10, "AN APPARITION OF THE late MARYLAND GAZETTE." This shadow of the real thing appeared, he said, in consequence of the urging of many, and would be continued if enough cared to subscribe. Green evidently received plenty of encouragement, but had trouble in getting paper. Another issue did not appear until January 30, 1766, nor the next until February 20 and March 6, but thereafter the *Gazette* was published weekly. Before the end of the year, moreover, there was some sign that trade might reopen in the ports. An applicant for clearance papers for a cargo of wheat was refused by one officer, at Oxford; but, when he inquired at Choptank down the bay, another officer reasoned that his majesty would require no such impossibility as the use of stamps when there were none, and made the clearance. By the end of January both the port of Oxford and the port of Annapolis were open.[46]

44. *Idem.;* Tilghman, *History of Talbot County,* II, 44–45.
45. *Unpublished Letters,* p. 104.
46. *Maryland Gazette,* January 30, 1766.

The next two months, February and March, saw Maryland go the full way in defiance of the law. On February 24 several of the "principal gentlemen" of Baltimore county met in the market place of Baltimore and formed a "Society for the Maintenance of Order and the Protection of American Liberty." The members called themselves "Sons of Liberty," in imitation of the "Sons" in New York, who had proposed the organization in Baltimore.[47] They determined to go to Annapolis at once in order to force the proprietary officers to open the courts and offices, and to do business without stamps. They communicated with Samuel Chase and his fellow-lawyer, William Paca, in Annapolis, and asked for help from the Sons of Liberty in the other counties. There followed a meeting of the people of Annapolis, at which letters from New York were read, and the question of opening the offices was discussed. There was some "unguarded" talk, Carroll said, but "most of the thinking men of the town," who hoped for an early repeal, preferred waiting to forcing the opening of the offices.[48] Two days later, however, a considerable number of Sons of Liberty from Baltimore and Anne Arundel county came to Annapolis. They made written demands on the chief justice of the provincial court, the secretary, the commissary-general, and the judges of the land office. Their proposal, that the offices open no later than March 31, and earlier if more than half the northern colonies did likewise, brought ambiguous answers from the officers. None acceded, and none flatly refused, but all made their future actions depend on each other. The Sons took the answers, however, and distributed copies in all the counties. They invited the Sons of Liberty in every county to pass resolutions conforming with the demands made on the officials, and to send delegates, not fewer than twelve from each county, to a meeting to be held in Annapolis on March 31.[49]

47. Carroll of Carrollton to D. Barrington, March 17, 1766, *Unpublished Letters*, p. 112.

48. *Idem.*

49. *Maryland Gazette,* March 6, 1766.

On April first, four days before the news of repeal reached Annapolis, the Sons of Liberty won their case. At a meeting they first presented a petition like the earlier one, and were refused. But when they insisted, as the *Gazette* put it, with "united hearts and voices," the provincial court ordered the clerk to issue processes and to transact business without stamped paper. The court gave an attested copy of its order to the Sons of Liberty, and agreed to do judicial business again within a week. The Sons of Liberty were equally successful with the judges of the land office and the registrar of the prerogative court. With so much gained at Annapolis, and with six county courts, five besides that of Frederick, already open, the victory of the radical out-of-door element in politics was almost complete. Jonas Green reports that an "utmost decency" was maintained in all the proceedings, and that acts were done "from the impulse of the heart" and without violence.[50] Carroll's private comment on the "clamour of the people" proceeding "from their ignorance, prejudice, and passion"[51] is not so democratic. But in the eyes of both, the politics of popular action had risen to a new level.

The news of the repeal brought great rejoicing and a cooling of animosities to Maryland. The citizens of Annapolis celebrated twice: when they first heard of the repeal they gathered for the drinking of "all patriotic toasts"; and in June, when official notification had been received, they had a city commemoration directed by the "worshipful mayor."[52] There were festivities and illuminations in all the outlying towns. None was more appropriate to what had preceded than the celebration at the home of Thomas Baker, in Queen Anne town, not far from Annapolis. Many gentlemen and freeholders gathered,

50. *Maryland Gazette,* April 3, 1766.
51. Letter to D. Barrington, March 17, 1766, *Unpublished Letters,* pp. 110–111.
52. The *Maryland Gazette* printed news that repeal was certain, April 10, 1766. Official word from Secretary Conway and congratulation from Lord Baltimore came later.

according to the *Gazette*, dug a hole, buried the emblems of "Discord," and raised a column to "Concord"—the party drank twenty-three toasts in the process.[53] Governor Sharpe and Charles Carroll of Carrollton both thought that the repeal would satisfy Maryland. "It will not hurt us much," said Carroll, "to resolve or pass an act that the Parliament has a right to tax America, if they never put it into practice."[54]

Within the assembly, as out of doors, the repeal was taken to be altogether satisfactory. Although Charles Garth made entirely plain the meaning of the Declaratory Act, and the House of Delegates was as sensitive as possible on questions of constitutional right in its quarrel with the proprietary element, there was no protest about either that act or the Sugar Act. Sharpe had no trouble in obtaining from the lower house an appropriation of one hundred pounds to recompense Hood for his warehouse, as Secretary Conway had asked.[55] The house also voted money for a marble statue of Pitt, and for a portrait of Lord Camden, to be hung in the provincial courtroom. The house voted a resolution to thank the Earl of Chesterfield, Lord Shelburne, Secretary Conway, General Howard, Sir George Saville, and Alderman Beckford, because they had proved their friendship to American liberty by supporting the repeal of the Stamp Act.[56] The appropriation for statue and portrait was so proposed, however, as to be rejected by the council as unconstitutional in form. This incident, considered in view of the uncharacteristic complacence, even dullness, of the lower house on the point of the Declaratory Act, suggests that the house was deliberately magnifying the victory of self-government against Parliament, and turning the momentum of ad-

53. Accounts of the celebrations are in *Maryland Gazette*, April 10, May 29, June 12, 1766; and in Sharpe to Hamersley, June 15, 1766, *Archives*, XIV, 313.
54. Letter to D. Barrington, May 29, 1766, *Unpublished Letters*, p. 121.
55. *Votes and Proceedings*, December 6, 1766; Sharpe to Hamersley, December 8, 1766, *Archives*, XIV, 358.
56. *Votes and Proceedings*, November 26, 1766.

vance against the proprietary element. Certainly the attack on Lord Baltimore's privileges lost nothing of spirit
or vigor, now, as the House of Delegates renewed the
offensive.[57]

When, in 1767, the mother country again acted to reform administration and to raise a revenue in America, the
politically sensitive Charles Carroll of Carrollton anticipated trouble. The determination of the House of Commons, to provide duties which would support the colonial
governors and other officers of state independent of the
"people," would certainly, he predicted, produce a powerful reaction. Carroll further predicted that the Townshend duties on American imports of certain British goods
would reduce the amounts purchased; and, with conscious
exaggeration, he declared that, as parliamentary statute
already prohibited slitting mills (he had an interest in the
Baltimore iron works), he would now expect to hear that
all colonial manufacturing was to be prohibited, and that
Americans would have to choose between English goods
and nakedness. "If England forces her colonies to rebellion, she must take the proper steps to make that rebellion
ineffectual by reducing their strength, and the most effectual way of doing this is by putting a stop to the increase
of our people; but whether this will answer the end of
colonization, I submit to the wisdom of higher powers." [58]
The young thinker, who considered Pitt's constitutional
hair-splitting about Parliament's sovereignty in America
to be a little absurd, was not one to be patient with the
taxes and reforms undertaken under the leadership of
Charles Townshend.

Carroll's voice was prophetic, but considerably ahead
of his time in Maryland. The most important change in
administration was the establishment in Boston of an
American Board of Customs Commissioners. Under act of
Parliament, the new board was to supplant the authority
of the Customs Commissioners in England, in respect of

57. See below, pp. 336–337.
58. *Unpublished Letters*, pp. 148–149.

the continental colonies. This reform led to an investigation of the customs establishment in Maryland,[59] and to the issue of instructions to the officers there that they were to use general writs of assistance in prosecuting smugglers. But investigation produced little change, and the attorney-general and the provincial court delayed and prevented the issue of the writs.[60] Thus the spot which had been so sore in law enforcement in Boston never became irritated in Maryland. Carroll probably spoke for all well informed Marylanders when he said, late in 1768, that the American board was a sign and symbol of the increasing tendency of Parliament to exert authority in America.[61] Yet the point did not become a matter of general grievance; and the reorganization of the vice-admiralty courts, also accomplished by one of the Townshend acts, seems to have made no difference and to have attracted little attention in the province.

A different kind of change did have some bearing on Maryland affairs. In 1768, parallel with the incidence of the Townshend laws, the Earl of Hillsborough became the first royal secretary of state for the colonies. This altered somewhat the official relations of the proprietary government with the Crown. Hillsborough and his successor, the Earl of Dartmouth, kept a much closer surveillance over Maryland affairs than had the secretaries of state for the southern department, their predecessors in colonial control. Their efforts had the more meaning because the new secretaryship carried with it senior membership in the Board of Trade. When Hillsborough asked Governor

59. Letters of John Williams to Customs Commissioners, Boston, May 12, 26, 1770; Commissioners to Lords of Treasury, September 28, 1772; list of customs officers, Maryland, July 5, 1776, *Md. Hist. Mag.*, XXVII, 231–239. See above, pp. 198–200.

60. Richard Reeve, Boston, to Lords of Treasury, August 25, 1769; Robert Heron and Andrew Ragg, Maryland, to Commissioners, Boston, [July 1, 1773?], PRO, Treasury, 1: 492, LC. The courts of New York, Pennsylvania, Virginia, Georgia, and East Florida likewise refused the writs (*ibid.*, 1: 501).

61. Letter to William Grave, December 23, 1768, *Md. Hist. Mag.*, XII, 179–180.

Sharpe to supply him with copies of the provincial laws as they were passed, and with the proceedings of the assembly and the council minutes, he was asking only a little more than the Board of Trade had asked, thirty-five years earlier. But the old request, for Maryland laws, had never been regularly honored; and, though Sharpe now complied, he thought the request exceptionable under the charter.[62] Governor Eden, who succeeded Sharpe, maintained an elaborate correspondence, however, with the secretaries; he sent detailed accounts of provincial politics, and forwarded copies of the assembly documents and of the *Maryland Gazette*. These letters, as they found their way to the Board of Trade, meant not only colonial supervision, but also, for the first time, that new Maryland laws came up for regular review by counsel for the Crown. The presumption of the royal disallowance was there, although it never came to execution.[63] Thus at the very close of the colonial period, the prerogative of the Crown was enveloping that of the lord proprietor. The matter did not, in so short a time, come to issue between the two, or to public issue in Maryland. It was one more aspect, however, of the current towards authoritarianism in England, at the moment when the opposite current was running wide and strong in Maryland and the other colonies.

The big change of the Townshend period, the laying of a parliamentary tax on colonial importations of tea, paper, glass, and painters' colors, found Maryland in somewhat better economic position than in 1765. The public debt had been paid by the assembly and an issue of paper money distributed. The whole quantity of tobacco

62. Sharpe to Baltimore, May 15, 1768, *Archives*, XIV, 497–498. On the colonial secretaryship and the Board of Trade, see A. H. Basye, "The Secretary of State for the Colonies," *American Historical Review*, XXVIII (1922), 15–16.

63. "The Correspondence of Governor Eden," 1769–1777, principally with the secretaries, is published in *Md. Hist. Mag.*, II, 1–13, 97–110, 227–244, 293–309. With Eden's letters in the Board of Trade papers are opinions of Maryland laws by Richard Jackson, June 9, 1771, February 9, 1773, BT Properties, XXIII, HSP; *Board of Trade Journal, 1768–1775*, p. 340.

trade was still declining, but prices in London and in America now tended to rise a little.[64] At the same time, the trade of Maryland was favored with improved grain markets in Ireland, Portugal, and Spain.[65] Such conditions were much less productive of apprehension than those of the Stamp Act period, and excitement was much slower to rise.

The *Maryland Gazette* did not have quite such dramatic opportunities as before; there was no chance in 1767 to speak of the paper's expiring or to print death's heads in place of stamps.[66] The paper nevertheless assumed essentially the same rôle as it had against the Stamp Tax; for months it printed communications representing the rising tide of protest in the commercial colonies in the north. But there was little sign of local response. Even when a report reached Maryland that Boston had retaliated against the mother country by encouraging domestic manufactures at the expense of imports,[67] no local patriot praised or publicly suggested following this example of protest. In December, John Dickinson's *Letters of a Pennsylvania Farmer* began to appear serially in the *Maryland Gazette*, but they struck little fire in Maryland. Controversialists were at this time concerning themselves with the argument between "Bystander" and "C.D.," and never once discussed the tea, lead, paper, and glass duties. Governor Sharpe wrote complacently, and apparently with truth, that the infection of discontent in the north was failing to spread in Maryland.[68]

64. See above, p. 295, n. 12. The improvement in London prices is noted in letters to Clement Hill and Samuel Galloway, 1766–1769, Hill Papers, MHS, Galloway, Maxcy, Markoe Papers, LC.

65. Letters to Galloway from correspondents in Cork, Lisbon, and Barcelona, December, 1765–July, 1769, Galloway, Maxcy, Markoe Papers, LC.

66. For comparison, see Schlesinger, "Propaganda and the Boston Newspaper Press," *Publications of the Colonial Society of Massachusetts*, XXXII (1937), 396–416.

67. *Maryland Gazette*, November 19, 1767.

68. Letter to Hamersley, February 11, 1768, *Archives*, XIV, 468. In the *Pennsylvania Chronicle*, September 12, 1768, a contributor explained

Only when the famous circular letter from the Massachusetts House of Representatives, dated February 11, 1768, came before the lower house, did any Maryland group move in opposition. And then the action of the Delegates was affected by their relations with the governor as well as by desire for a united protest against the duties. Secretary of State Hillsborough had sent a copy of the letter to Sharpe, as he did to all the governors, saying that in the eyes of the Crown the appeal was "factious" and likely to encourage a denial of the authority of Parliament and a subversion of the constitution. He therefore ordered the governor to dissuade the assembly from action if he could, and otherwise to prorogue or dissolve it. Governor Sharpe, who could have no official knowledge of the business of the lower house save as it was formally communicated to him, felt obliged by Hillsborough's instructions to address the house, displaying Hillsborough's letter, and to request that no notice be taken of the Massachusetts circular, if it had been received.[69] The governor disliked the duty; Hillsborough had required him to challenge the freedom of the house, and he knew that such procedure would only complicate matters. The Delegates, in turn, sent the kind of reply he had anticipated. They were angry that a responsible official should describe as "factious" and "subversive" the words of loyal subjects who merely sought to petition the Crown for a redress of grievances. They told the governor that they would "not be intimidated by a few sounding expressions, from doing what we think is right." [70] The action of Hillsborough and Sharpe had practically forced the lower house to declare itself.

that Marylanders were slow to protest the Townshend duties because they were asleep and because they had a provincial controversy (Allen or the agency issue in the lower house?) to concern them. The writer nevertheless knew of a Cecil county jury's appreciation of Dickinson, and versified it, concluding with, "To worth so exalted, what mortal is blind? *America's* Saviour, and light of mankind!"

69. Hillsborough to Sharpe, April 21, 1768, *Archives*, XIV, 491; *Votes and Proceedings*, June 20, 1768.

70. *Votes and Proceedings*, June 22, 1768.

Under difficult circumstances, the Delegates maneuvered nicely. Anticipating the prorogation, which they knew would follow the defiance of Sharpe, they prepared a reply to the speaker of the House of Representatives and a petition to the king. The letter to Massachusetts, which Speaker Lloyd sent in the name of the house two days after the session closed, declared that the Maryland house agreed with the circular letter, and that it was always ready and glad to have proposals from a sister colony about common difficulties. There went enclosed Sharpe's speech against considering the circular letter, and the address of the house in reply.[71] Lloyd forwarded the petition to the Crown through Mr. Garth. It was not an extreme document, but followed the line of reasoning made familiar in 1765: no Englishman can be deprived of his property without his consent or that of his representative; Marylanders have the rights of Englishmen; and their charter gives them a special guaranty of immunity. Emphasizing the argument from the charter, the House of Delegates begged relief from the Townshend duties.[72] Conservative phrasing, however, did not make the petition acceptable to the Crown; Hillsborough said that it set up claims tending "to draw into question the supreme authority of Parliament, . . . which authority his majesty is determined to preserve." The king also disliked the unwillingness of the Delegates to approach him, as would have been proper, by sending their petition by way of the proprietor, or the governor, rather than independently.[73] The petition had simply registered the fact that the Maryland Delegates understood the principles at stake, in their own terms, and were sensitive to the request of another colony.

Yet assembly action had come only after six months of the enforcement of the Townshend duties, and a year more,

71. *Maryland Gazette,* July 28, 1768.

72. *Ibid.,* March 23, 1769. Petition, and letter to Garth, June 24, 1768, *Md. Hist. Mag.,* XII, 377–381.

73. Hillsborough to Sharpe, November 15, 1768, *Archives,* XIV, 552–553.

to a day, was to pass before the signing of a Maryland non-importation agreement. Meanwhile the *Gazette* continued in its rôle of propagandist. A few weeks after the Delegates had petitioned the Crown, the paper printed Hillsborough's letter ordering the governors to prevent action on the Massachusetts circular.[74] Most of the news came from the north, and so gave frequent examples of more radical opposition to the duties than Maryland's own. Early in July, Maryland readers learned of mob action, when customs officials seized John Hancock's sloop, the *Liberty;*[75] and in the late summer and early autumn, the texts and accounts of the non-importation agreements made in Boston and New York were printed at length.[76] Then Marylanders could read of the actual working-out of the prophecies of Dulany and Carroll, namely, that parliamentary taxation would inevitably lead to a reduction of the purchases of manufactures from the mother country, and to the encouragement of colonial manufacturing. Such news was accompanied by stirring accounts of the arrival of soldiers in Boston, and of the insults which passed between them and the people. With such events, the Townshend duties came at last to appear alarming, as the Stamp Tax had, in the columns of the *Maryland Gazette*. They evoked a new warmth of feeling in the province, and an occasional statement that the grievance was common to all America.[77]

Retaliatory boycotts, like those in the north, were, however, very difficult to arrange in the plantation colonies. Non-importation could be put into practice only by well-organized machinery for observation and enforcement,

74. *Maryland Gazette,* July 14, 1768.
75. *Ibid.,* July 7, 1768.
76. *Maryland Gazette,* September 22, October 6, 13, 1768. My debt to the works by Charles M. Andrews, "The Boston Merchants and the Non-Importation Movement," *Publications of the Colonial Society of Massachusetts,* XIX (1919), 159–259; and by Arthur M. Schlesinger, *The Colonial Merchants and the American Revolution* (New York, 1918), is of course apparent here and in what follows.
77. As in the Poet's Corner, *Maryland Gazette,* July 14, 1768, when the verse "Come, join Hand in Hand, brave Americans all" was printed.

and such machinery was not easily constructed where trade was decentralized and not a matter of town life. It was natural, therefore, for the non-importation movement in Maryland to begin in Baltimore, where commercial conditions and industrial beginnings essentially like those of the northern cities applied. On March 20, 1769, under pressure from Philadelphia merchants, who themselves had arranged an association only ten days before, Baltimoreans signed an agreement. They bound themselves not to purchase British manufactures until after the Townshend duties had been repealed.[78] This was the first Maryland action, outside the assembly, to strike for repeal of the duties.

The non-importation movement carried further only after the passage of some weeks. Considerable discussion arose at Annapolis. The first strong argument from a local pen was that of "Atticus," which appeared in the *Gazette* in the first issues in May. The writer declared that all news from the mother country illustrated the prevalence of venality and corruption, that she suffered the same ills as Rome in the late empire, and that, under the circumstances, "Well may the ministry apprehend a civil war in America." Let us not trade with such a country, urged "Atticus," while she tyrannizes over us with unjust taxes.[79] Just at the time when this moralistic plea reached the public, an invitation was given to the "merchants, traders, and gentlemen" of Anne Arundel county, to meet at the courthouse in Annapolis on May 19. The meeting was accordingly held, and Anne Arundel county undertook to boycott British imports.[80] County action

78. *Maryland Gazette,* April 27, 1769; Schlesinger, *Colonial Merchants,* p. 138.

79. The plea has the sound of Charles Carroll of Carrollton. *Maryland Gazette,* May 4, 11, 1769.

80. *The Proceedings of the Committee appointed to examine into the Importation of Goods by the Brigantine Good Intent Capt. Errington, from London in February, 1770* (Annapolis, 1770). This pamphlet not only reviews the case of the *Good Intent,* but discusses the origin of the non-importation movement. Reprinted in *Md. Hist. Mag.,* III, 141–157, 240–256, 342–363.

rather than town action, this agreement, rather than that of Baltimore, set the pattern for the province as a whole. Within a month most of the counties had done as Anne Arundel had done, and, on June 20, the movement was launched to establish a general association to include all of Maryland.

On that date a general meeting for forty-three "merchants, traders, freeholders, mechanics, and other inhabitants" was held at Annapolis. The invitation had been issued on behalf of the Anne Arundel associators by Brice Worthington, of the House of Delegates, James Dick, of the mercantile house of Dick and Stewart, and John Dorsey and Charles Carroll, Barrister.[81] In the course of a few days of heated discussion, they drafted an elaborate non-importation agreement. According to the preamble, the tea, lead, paper, and glass duties were "contrary to the spirit of our constitution"; they tended to deprive the people of political freedom; and they made necessary the practice of frugality, because they were so expensive to colonial purchasers. The signers accordingly pledged themselves not to import any of the taxed articles, nor, during the continuance of the duties, any of a list of about 125 other commodities, including many such imports as textiles, India goods, spirits, metalware, jewelry, leather goods, and hardware. The signers agreed to conserve the local supply of wool by refusing to sell or kill ewe lambs. To provide for enforcement, the associators pledged themselves to refuse to do business with anyone who imported the forbidden commodities, and declared that they would not house or purchase such goods brought from neighboring colonies unless a committee of merchants of the vicinity certified that they had been imported before the agreement. Maryland "tradesmen and manufacturers" agreed not to raise prices, but to sell for the prevailing prices of the past three years. Anyone, signer or non-signer, who contravened the agreement was to be con-

81. Broadside, Annapolis, May 23, 1769, MHS; Eden to Hillsborough, June 23, 1769, *Md. Hist. Mag.*, II, 228.

sidered and treated as an enemy of the liberties of America; public sentiment was to support boycott in the matter of enforcement. The association was to hold until the repeal of the duties or until a general meeting at Annapolis, made up of not more than four representatives from each county, should determine otherwise.[82]

The launching of the association was thus accomplished in the name of all the inhabitants of Maryland. But the names of the signers show that it was not the work of an equal association of "merchants, traders, freeholders, mechanics" and others. Of the forty-three signers, twenty-two were members of the House of Delegates elected in 1768,[83] and five others were to be elected in 1771. Provision was made for a meeting of county representatives with power to amend or revoke the association; this was little more or less than an extra-legal session of the lower house. Its first meeting, moreover, was held, not by accident, on the morning after the prorogation of the 1769 assembly, and it reaffirmed the association.[84] The list of associators includes some, not delegates, who are recognizable as merchants, such as James Dick and Charles Carroll, Barrister. But more of the names are recognizable as lawyers, some members and some non-members of the house. Clearly the "traders, freeholders, and mechanics," of the lower order, were neither many nor influential. The Maryland association was, then, principally the work, not of upstart traders, as in Baltimore, but of the "country party" of the lower house, working together with some of the important provincial merchants. If it was not as plainly a matter of lower-house action as in Virginia, where the House of Burgesses drew up the non-importation agreement, it was substantially the same.[85] The Brit-

82. The agreement was printed as a handbill for distribution (copy in Gilmor Papers, III, 2, MHS). It also appeared in the *Maryland Gazette*, June 29, 1769; and is reprinted in Scharf, *History of Maryland*, II, 111–114; and in *Md. Hist. Mag.*, III, 144–149.
83. Names checked, as delegates, in BT Proprieties, XXII, HSP.
84. *Maryland Gazette*, December 21, 1769.
85. Governor Eden avoided mention of the association in addressing

ish factors as a group, especially the representatives of the Glasgow firms, opposed the movement.[86]

The enforcement of non-importation was carried out with vigor and devotion of the principle of freedom from parliamentary taxation. In every part of the colony, with the possible exception of the lower Eastern Shore, self-chosen committees confronted the hesitant with the choice between compliance and the loss of trade and standing in the community. The first case of enforcement occurred at Frederick, when wagonloads of non-importable commodities arrived from Philadelphia and Baltimore without the proper certificates. They were taken over by a committee and put in storage at the risk of the consignees.[87] Importations from Great Britain were returned when they came to Baltimore, to a Patuxent river landing in Charles county, to St. Mary's county, and to Talbot county. The offenders were most often factors, and those who enforced the association appear in the newspaper as "inhabitants" working in large committees.[88]

Most active in enforcement were two adjoining counties in the best tobacco-raising section of the western shore, Anne Arundel and Prince George's. The committee system there, under the immediate influence of Annapolis, became both very elaborate and very effective. In April, 1770, when several British merchant vessels were momentarily expected in the Patuxent, the inhabitants of Prince George's county met and selected four committees of enforcement, one each from Upper Marlborough, Nottingham, Queen Anne, and Magruder's Landing. Minutes were kept of the meeting, an account was printed in the *Gazette*, and notices were sent to the gentlemen of Bladensburg, Broad Creek, and Piscattaway, that they

the assembly, to prevent its becoming an added political issue. Probably this was just as the lower house itself wished. Eden to Hillsborough, June 23, November 23, 1769, *Md. Hist. Mag.*, II, 229, 232.

86. *Maryland Gazette*, May 24, 1770.

87. *Ibid.*, October 19, 1769.

88. *Ibid.*, November 30, 1769 (Patuxent), May 24, 1770 (St. Mary's), May 31, 1770 (Baltimore), July 12, 1770 (Talbot).

would be expected to do likewise. The names of the committeemen reveal the participation of members of the county families: two Spriggs, two Bowies, two Gantts, a Hall, a Magruder, and a Wootton appear on the published lists.[89] No crisis of enforcement followed the establishment of such a substantial organization.

The most dramatic case of action, that of the brigantine *Good Intent*, involved the Annapolis firm of Dick and Stewart. The members of the firm had been among the originators of the association; and in September, 1769, they had been open and scrupulous about receiving goods which might or might not come under the association, and which they agreed to store.[90] Now, in the spring of 1770, they had a consignment on the *Good Intent*, sent by their London correspondent, Buchanan. They made no attempt to conceal their interest; they claimed that extenuating circumstances explained the case; and they advertised in the newspaper for a meeting of the committees of Anne Arundel, Prince George's, and Baltimore counties, the counties which would be affected if the goods were landed and sold as they wished. But after extended hearings, the argument of Dick and Stewart won the support of only the Baltimore members of the joint committee.[91] The majority voted that the goods must be returned. The consignees expressed perfect willingness to store the goods, as they had done before, and Governor Eden intervened to the extent of showing a letter from Hillsborough, which promised that all the Townshend duties, save the one on tea, were to be repealed. But the committeemen would not yield.[92] Against the law of the ports, according to which an entered vessel was required to be unloaded, the *Good Intent* was sent back to England, to the great loss of her owners.

The case of the *Good Intent* seemed to the committees

89. *Ibid.*, April 12, 1770; *Pennsylvania Gazette,* April 19, 1770.
90. *Ibid.*, October 12, 1769.
91. *Maryland Gazette,* April 19, 26, 1770.
92. Eden to Hillsborough, February 21, August 19, 1770, Hillsborough to Eden, June 12, 1770, *Md. Hist. Mag.,* III, 234–236, 238–239.

to be a test, and they gave it much publicity. Accounts of the proceedings were published in the *Gazette*, currently, and later in a long pamphlet, which considered the history and purposes of the association. The issues at stake, the writer said, were the great ones of the British Empire. The future of parliamentary taxation of the colonies, and the continuance of such grievances as the Board of Customs Commissioners in Boston, the extension of the vice-admiralty courts, the suspension of the New York legislature, and the quartering of troops in Boston, all would depend on the temper of the colonies.[93] The writer was borrowing trouble perhaps, and speaking of grievances little felt in Maryland. But in so doing he represented a great advance in sentiment in opposition to the policy of the home government. A few months of experience with the non-importation movement had led from indifference to affirmation of the singleness of the cause of Maryland with that of the other colonies.

When Governor Eden had learned, in the middle of the summer of 1769, that the ministry had decided to remove the Townshend duties, except the one on tea, he had the news published in the *Gazette*.[94] He had hoped to discourage the work of the association at an early stage. But even the definite news, a year later, that the duties had been actually removed, had no immediate effect.[95] The issue of political and constitutional principle, represented by the tea tax, continued; to those sensitive to political theory, partial repeal was no answer. To the tobacco counties, moreover, the economic advantages of arresting the flow of British imports, and of stimulating the newer branches of trade were considerable. The planters and committeemen were thus saved from increasing their debts to correspondents overseas. Whatever the reason, the

93. *The Proceedings of the Committee, passim.* See above, p. 320, n. 80.
94. *Maryland Gazette,* August 10, 1769; Eden to Hillsborough, August 14, 1769, *Md. Hist. Mag.,* II, 229–230.
95. Eden to Hillsborough, August 19, 1770, *ibid.,* II, 240. The repeal was announced by a six-page leaflet, containing the act of Parliament, printed at the Annapolis press. Copy in Black Books, I, MHRecs.

breakdown of non-importation came when disagreement and distrust cracked the fragile structure of the association. Depending on public opinion for strength, it could not long outlive the enthusiasm of the community. In the course of the summer and early autumn of 1770, differences and difficulties outside the colony began to demonstrate the instability of the non-importation system. Maryland had been united in the spring. At that time, when Newport, Rhode Island, temporarily abandoned the movement, the inhabitants of Baltimore and Annapolis and the committee of Talbot county resolved on a boycott, and two Rhode Island vessels in the Patuxent were refused permission to unload.[96] But at mid-summer, at the time when Maryland learned that New York had abandoned the association, there was trouble in enforcement at Annapolis. The local committee tried to discipline Williams and Company, and only stirred up a controversy; Williams insisted that there had been laxity and favoritism in enforcement.[97] This sign of bad faith in the province was followed by more news of breakdown to the north; such commercial towns as Marblehead, Salem, and Newburyport were reported to have abandoned the movement.[98]

For Maryland, the decisive external event was the action of Philadelphia, which dropped the association in September. Baltimore merchants felt at once that they could afford only to do likewise, and they therefore advertised in the *Gazette* for a general association meeting at Annapolis.[99] The meeting tried, but failed, to prevent the breakdown of non-importation. Besides the Baltimore merchants, there were present committeemen from the Eastern Shore, where a recent resolution had favored continuing the association until the repeal of the tea tax;[100] there were also present more than half the mem-

96. *Maryland Gazette*, June 7, 14, July 12, 1770.
97. *Ibid.*, August 2, 9, 16, 1770.
98. *Ibid.*, August 30, 1770.
99. *Ibid.*, October 11, 1770.
100. In Talbot county. *Ibid.*, August 23, 1770.

bers of the House of Delegates, and a number of merchants and others resident in Annapolis. The Baltimoreans declared that they were determined to trade freely, except in the dutied tea, which they would continue to boycott. A vociferous majority condemned them for taking a step toward the destruction of liberty and union in America, and passed resolutions restating belief in the association as a means of coercing Great Britain and promoting frugality. The meeting voted to continue non-importation, to print its resolutions in the *Gazette,* and to send copies to each of the other colonies.[101] But the vote of assemblymen, who were versed in the politics of protest, did not change the minds of the Baltimore merchants, or turn back the flow of trade already renewed in the north and now penetrating Maryland. The association had outlived its economic if not its political purposes; and when any one community in the province had had enough, the others could not stand alone.

With the breakdown of non-importation, the province reverted to old commercial habits. The committees evaporated, and no boycott was retained, even on tea. This dutied article was extensively imported, sold, and drunk, without public objection, even in southern Maryland. As the system of resistance fell apart, the intercolonial play of news, attitudes, and policies almost dropped from sight in Maryland. Except for the single notice—"Everything here peaceable; the opposition is dead, and our corporation patriots and our aldermanic incendiaries sunk into contempt" [102]—Boston was hardly mentioned in the *Maryland Gazette* during the three-year period from the breakdown of the association to the Tea Party.

Yet these years of close concern with imperial policies and intercolonial affairs had marked new levels in Mary-

101. *Ibid.,* November 1, 1770. A merchant writer in the *Pennsylvania Chronicle,* December 17, 1770, scorned the "fortuitous collection, not merchants, but of counsellors, representatives, lawyers, and others," who "out of their mere motion" attempted to tell the merchants what to do.
102. *Maryland Gazette,* July 9, 1772.

land's political consciousness, and opened wide areas for thought and protest. Probably never before 1765 had any Marylander written, as Delegate Matthew Tilghman did, that he constantly revolved in his mind the question of freedom or slavery for America. I revere, he said, "the spirit of the northern people, and am clearly of opinion they are right in their warm and unrelaxing opposition, and am ashamed to think that the southern colonies do not keep pace with 'em. . . . I cannot write on this subject without warmth." [103] Before the sixties Marylanders rarely considered provincial affairs as a part of continental affairs; during the sixties they became dramatically involved in American events.

Out-of-door politics had been important, at election time, before 1750, and they had increased during the French and Indian War. Now, in the decade of the sixties, as they achieved the stage of intercounty and intercolonial action, and the psychology of group victory, they prepared the way for future protest against the Intolerable Acts, and for the accelerating movement into the Revolution. But the momentum of highly organized politics was first to have great significance in Maryland's own provincial affairs. The decay, almost dissolution, of proprietary government in the early seventies was to flow not only from inherent weakness and old dispute, but from the new strength of the opposition, recently schooled in voluntary and extra-legal association.

103. Damaged letter, Portfolio no. 3, MHRecs.

X

THE FINAL CRISIS IN PROVINCIAL AFFAIRS
1769-1774

THE anti-proprietary movement, so vigorous during the French and Indian War, and so well publicized at the end, lost something of its force during the next few years. The situation in the assembly may be compared with that of the period between 1733 and 1739. Although there was now no interval of hesitancy and loss of leadership, as then, the lower house did lose political bargaining power, the power which demand for war appropriations had given it.

In the final decade of colonial history, the House of Delegates had to stand on its own provincial feet. No outside factor was to take the place of the war requisitions of the Crown, giving the house a sort of unearned strength in combat with the governor and council. Success against the Stamp Act and Townshend duty might increase political experience and heighten confidence, in a general sort of way; but it gave no legal pry against the proprietor, nor were its lessons in organization and intimidation readily applicable to the established strategy of the anti-proprietary movement. Conditions were none too favorable for lower-house advance, especially in the decade of the sixties.

The current changes in administrative policy and in the personnel of proprietary power did not directly affect politics; the coming of Governor Eden, in 1769, placed a more personable figure than Sharpe at the head of state, but his instructions were the same.[1] And the succession of Henry Harford to the proprietorship, in 1771, meant

1. August 29, 1768, March 2, 1773, *Archives,* XXXII, 302–305, 501–503. See Bernard C. Steiner, *Life and Administration of Sir Robert Eden,* JHUS, XVI (1898), nos. 7–9, pp. 15–16.

only that the last and least worthy of the noble Calverts had left his Maryland estate to his infant illegitimate son. The framework of assembly struggle was set, rather, by certain peripheral aspects of the prerogative, which were open to bargaining, and by new developments of the old needs of Maryland for economic legislation. The real and final crisis was to come in the seventies, when the expiration of the tobacco-inspection law opened fresh conflicts over the rates of officers' fees and clergy dues. But during the sixties, at the close of Sharpe's administration, there was a kind of preliminary crisis, which took the form of a revival of old issues and old proposals.

The lines were drawn in the fall assembly session, 1763. At that time the income from ordinary licenses, which had been appropriated in the war tax of 1756, became unencumbered, and the House of Delegates made a fresh demand for the money. It made the cause as popular as possible by proposing that the funds be devoted to establishing a college at Annapolis; the house wished to accomplish by public means what the cities of New York and Philadelphia had recently accomplished by private.

The need for a college had been felt for a decade at least, and now the Delegates did some nice maneuvering. A committee found that the continuation of a few war taxes, principally the levy on ordinary keepers, would suffice to maintain a college, and that "Bladen's Folly," a mansion intended for the governors but never completed for lack of appropriations, would do nicely for a building. On the basis of these findings, the lower house passed a bill to establish the college. Action was stalled, in the upper house; the councilors, evidently in disagreement among themselves, gave the absence of certain of their numbers as excuse for delay.[2] Actually the lower house had once more opposed itself to the governor's instructions;

2. *Votes and Proceedings,* October 13, November 22, 1763. On May 21, 1754, a lower-house committee reported on education, including the possibilities of a college. *Archives,* L, 490–492. See Sharpe to Calvert, June 23, 1761, *ibid.,* IX, 525.

the proprietor had forbidden the appropriation of the license money for purposes other than defense, and had ordered that "Bladen's Folly" be completed for the governor's residence. As in war time when license money was the issue, the council disagreed with the proprietor; to oppose the lower house on the college bill, it well knew, would have been to open a controversy on the wrong side of a popular issue. Sharpe prorogued the house, which had also offered the usual agency bill.[3] Both sides had reverted to the old strategy of irreconcilable differences. For the first time since King George's War, ordinary-license money went unappropriated.

The governor's letters to Secretary Calvert show that he was worried and that the "court party" was not united. He said that Daniel Dulany and others wished to pass the college bill, and that all agreed that the license money could not be better appropriated. He himself did not believe that the assembly could ever be induced to grant money to put the governor's house in repair for its original purpose, especially since the proprietors themselves made such a provision in Pennsylvania. He wished to know what course to follow in the matter.[4] Calvert replied that he should yield none of the proprietary revenues, but at the same time reported to Lord Baltimore, who was in Warsaw. In 1765, the proprietor sent his decision direct to Sharpe. He said that "the priviledge of granting and regulating ordinary licenses is the very essence of my prerogative, and such as every lawyer in the kingdom agrees I can never be divested of without my consent, which I shall most certainly never give."[5] No harm, he concluded, could come from letting the bill wait.

On the side of the lower house, as on that of the proprietor, the interval between the 1763 session and the next sessions, those of 1765, produced increasing signs of

3. One vote opposed. *Votes and Proceedings,* October 18, 1763.
4. Sharpe to Calvert, December 28, 1763, March 13, May 8, 1764, *Archives,* XIV, 125-126, 152-153, 156.
5. February 5, 1765, *ibid.,* XIV, 194.

extremism, rather than of compromise. In the election of 1764 Samuel Chase was chosen delegate from Annapolis, with parties "running higher," Dulany said, than ever before in Maryland. Chase stood, with the support of Charles Carroll, Barrister, against Dr. Steuart of the "court party," who had cast the one vote against the agency bill of 1763. "At this hard-contested election," said Charles Willson Peale, "every engine was employed that each party could supply. The court dependents of office were threatened to be put out if they voted for Chase. On the other hand, banners were displayed to designate the freedom of tradesmen, and parades of this nature were made through all the streets with the friends of Chase at the head of them." [6] Before Sharpe convened the assembly, in the atmosphere of the Stamp Act, the unpaid journal of accounts had become, as we have seen, a matter of public grievance among the militiamen of the west. When the lower house at last met for provincial business, then, in November, 1765, political tension had risen to high pitch.

The most compelling business was the journal of accounts, for Frederick county was known to be seething with unrest. But there was a fresh quarrel with the proprietary element to inhibit action; trouble arose from a variation on the old question of voting public money to the members of the council for allowances for their days of meeting in executive, as distinguished from legislative, session. The contention of the lower house had been that the councilors, as such, were servants of the proprietor not of the public. In 1756, after thirty years and more of disagreement, the lower house had won the concession from

6. Peale's autobiography, quoted by H. W. Sellers, in "Charles Willson Peale, Artist-Soldier," *Pennsylvania Magazine of History and Biography,* XXXVIII (1914), 262. Walter Dulany and Samuel Chase, both of whom were returned from the city, received, respectively, 132 and 88 votes; Steuart received 59. In the 1764 election, 42 delegates were reëlected to their seats; 4 were elected who had been members before, but not in the last assembly; and 12 were elected for the first time. *Maryland Gazette,* November 29, December 20, 1764.

the upper that it would not insist on daily allowances for executive session.[7] Now in 1765 the lower house held up the journal because the council insisted on an allowance for the salary of its clerk. The Delegates applied the old argument: the clerk was as much a servant of the prerogative as the councilors themselves, and he should have no public money.[8] As the controversy developed, word came to Annapolis that Thomas Cresap, old Indian trader and fighter and now a Frederick county delegate, had rounded up three or four hundred Sons of Liberty armed with guns and tomahawks. They intended to march from Frederick to Annapolis, to compel Secretary Ross to waive his claim, and to bring the upper house to pass the journal without his salary. Ross became thoroughly frightened; and the lower house—which Cresap had saluted as certain, like the Roman senate, to espouse liberty—was itself embarrassed. Not many, but some men did come to Annapolis from the "upper parts"; there was a petition rather than intimidation; no action was forced upon the assembly.[9] Failing to win its point, the lower house turned once more to the procedure of protest familiar since 1739.

Early in the session it launched a new effort to investigate the proprietary revenues and the income from the great offices. Two special committees were set up, one of eight and one of ten members, to report by what right his lordship collected the proceeds of court fines and forfeitures, to discover the amounts of the annual duties, imposts, and other sums received in his private account by "or under colour of laws or customs of his government

7. May 4, 1756, *Archives*, LII, 409; see Mereness, *Maryland*, p. 367; and above, pp. 216, 220.

8. In 1763, when there was an attempt to pass the journal, the lower house proposed to vote money to the clerk for whatever itemized services he could show to have been public services. *Votes and Proceedings*, November 25, 1763.

9. Depositions on occurrences in the west, *Votes and Proceedings*, December 10, 11, 14, 1765; Council Proceedings, December 10, 1765, *Archives*, XXXII, 110–111; Sharpe to Calvert, December 21, 1765, *ibid.*, XIV, 253; Carroll of Carrollton to D. Barrington, December 22, 1765, *Unpublished Letters*, p. 105.

here," and to determine the profits of each of the great offices of state.[10] The House of Delegates also protested the two-year period since the last assembly. The representatives of the people should meet often, in crucial times, it declared, because they were the best qualified to speak and act for the common good.[11] In this vein, and with a new urgency, the house turned again to the question of a colonial agent. Just such questions of constitutional right as that of the payment of the clerk of the council, it argued, proved the necessity of an appeal to the king in council.

In political tactics, at least, the upper house now made a concession. For the first time in a half-century of struggle, it chose to admit that an agency might be possible. It proposed alternatives: either that each house send an agent of its own, or that both houses send one agent not altogether in the control of either.[12] But neither proposal could be considered seriously by the lower house. It would not grant funds for an agent of the council, for it had long said that the lord proprietor amply represented that interest. It also refused to compromise its generation-old endeavor to have an agent of its own. The 1765 session, accordingly, ended in a deadlock, as so many had since 1738. When Governor Sharpe prorogued it, the journal was still unpaid, the investigations were hanging fire, and an agency law was as far as ever from achievement.

During the next spring, while Daniel Dulany was very popular by reason of his pamphlet against the Stamp Act, the American members of the proprietary element took steps to strengthen their position by reason and moderation. Just as the assembly was convening Dulany brought out a new pamphlet, *The Right to the Tonnage, the Duty of Twelve Pence per Hogshead on all Exported Tobacco, and the Fines and Forfeitures in the Province of Mary-*

10. *Votes and Proceedings,* November 15, 1765.
11. *Ibid.,* December 13, 1765.
12. *Ibid.,* December 16, 1765.

land.[13] In this forty-page essay, Dulany pleaded the strong legal case the proprietor had for collecting the revenues called in question by the old investigations of the forties, and now again by the committees of the lower house. There was little that was not familiar in his justifications, but these justifications were now made public with a new and convincing fullness. The tonnage duty was traced to its origins in 1661 and shown always to have been the proprietor's own; the tobacco-hogshead duty of 1704 was justified for the proprietary government, because the lord proprietor was the representative of the king, for the support of whose government the law had been passed; and the proprietor's taking of the fines and forfeitures in the common-law courts was demonstrated to be entirely in line with English common law and practice. It may have been the timeliness and strength of Dulany's case, or it may have been that he omitted a defense either of the proprietor's claim to ordinary-license money or of the clerk of the council's claim to public payment, but whatever the reason, the assembly session of May, 1766, was a quiet one. The lower house passed resolutions ordering the proceedings of the Stamp Act Congress published, and directed its committee to keep in touch with Garth about British policy.[14] There was no controversy or public demonstration when adjournment came without a journal of accounts, and when the upper house again refused to appropriate the license money.

In the very month of this session, the council, meeting in executive capacity, recommended, as it had during the war, that the claim to the license fees be waived. Dulany urged the council that Lord Baltimore's claim, so forcefully expressed in his instruction of 1765, had no real historical or constitutional validity, and that to follow it

13. Issued anonymously, as the *Considerations* had been, from the press of Jonas Green, late in April or early in May, 1766. *Maryland Gazette,* April 17, May 8, 1766. On September 10, 1764, Dulany had written privately and at length to Secretary Calvert about the revenues, *Calvert Papers,* II, 237–248.

14. *Votes and Proceedings,* May 27, 1766.

would endanger the public interest. The council voted in agreement, and Sharpe transmitted their action to Lord Baltimore.[15] Unlike the governor's questioning letter of two years before, this led the proprietor to reverse his position, and to issue formal instructions to that effect. Secretary Hamersley explained that his lordship had never really understood the issue before, and was very glad to yield.[16] As a result, when the assembly reconvened in November it had but one negotiable dispute still open, that of the salary of the clerk of the council.

This narrowing and focusing of differences made possible the passing of the journal, but it did not reduce the ultimate disagreement between the houses. After devoting the entire month of November, 1766, to the arrangement of terms, a law was enacted which provided that the claim of the clerk of the council should be levied as a tax, but then impounded, not paid, until final decision could be reached about the validity of the claim. If the king in council should uphold the clerk, he was to have the money; otherwise it was to revert to the public credit. Thus at long last the presumption of appeal to the Crown for constitutional justice was written into a Maryland statute; and at the same time public credit to the value of some £30,000 sterling was released in the province.[17]

Governor Sharpe and the council had now twice admitted that the lower house might appeal to the king in council.[18] Although this admission was far from equal

15. Council Proceedings, May 23, 26, 27, 1766, *Archives*, XXXII, 143–147; Sharpe to Hamersley, May 28; to Baltimore, May 29, 1766, *ibid.*, XIV, 308–311.

16. Instructions, August 6, 1766, Black Books, XI, MHRecs; Baltimore to Sharpe, August 2, 1766; Hamersley to Sharpe, August 7, 1766, *Archives*, XIV, 323, 327–328.

17. *Sessions Laws,* 1766, ch. 34; financial estimate, Chalmers Papers, Maryland, I, NYPL.

18. On March 22, 1766, Hamersley had written Sharpe that Lord Baltimore did not object. *Archives*, XIV, 283. Bennet Allen, who was a political realist, while telling Lord Baltimore that "Every attack on your government is an attack upon your revenues, and vice versa," also said that the appeal was not dangerous. Letter of February, 1767, Calvert Papers, no. 1303, MHS.

to real coöperation in approaching a judicial settlement of constitutional differences, the lower house moved ahead. Its committees of investigation made it entirely plain that the new plea to the Crown would not be confined to the question of the clerk's allowance, but would be cast in the same general terms as the appeal of the seventeen-forties. The committees now declared that Lord Baltimore had no right to the hogshead duty of 1704, and that in taking the proceeds of the court fines and forfeitures he was exercising even greater authority than the king of England with respect to similar funds. The House of Delegates voted unanimous approval of the committees' findings, recommended that their work be carried farther, and passed a series of resolutions to provide for a final settlement of provincial disputes. In formal language it rehearsed once more the injustices that Maryland suffered from the lack of an agent; it presented the current issue of the secretary's salary; and it urged the long-felt wish of the people to have their permanent grievances against the proprietor brought to hearing and justice before the king.[19] The house named Charles Garth, M.P., who had represented it in the matter of the Stamp Act, to be its advocate. As the council was as unwilling as ever to vote an appropriation for an agent instructed by the Delegates alone, the house provided that Garth should be retained with funds raised by popular subscription and by a lottery. Charles Carroll of Carrollton spoke of this as a face-saving procedure; but a letter from a leading delegate indicates that it was taken seriously and with some hope of success.[20]

The members of the lower house contributed about £150 from their own pockets, and a committee undertook to raise £1,000 more, through what it named the "Liberty Lottery." It put 5,000 tickets on sale at 30 shillings each; there were to be 2,500 prizes worth £6,500 in all, and

19. *Votes and Proceedings,* November 15, 29, December 6, 1766.
20. Carroll to E. Jennings, March 9, 1767, *Unpublished Letters,* p. 142; Thomas Ringgold to S. Galloway, November 21, 1766, Galloway Papers, II, NYPL.

2,500 blanks. The lottery was advertised over a long period in the *Maryland Gazette*,[21] the *Virginia Gazette*, and the *Pennsylvania Chronicle*. The advertisement used the slogan, "Life without Liberty is worse than Death," and displayed the anti-proprietary resolutions of the House of Delegates.

Yet this effort at propaganda and money-raising was doomed to failure. The one favorable report of progress appeared in the *Maryland Gazette* of February 27, 1767; it said that the draw would probably take place sooner than intended, the last of May, because tickets were selling so rapidly. All other evidence shows that the public was apathetic, as well it might be, with tickets priced so high. In the middle of March, Governor Sharpe expressed the opinion that only Pennsylvania buyers kept the lottery going; and the time for the draw had passed by more than a month when the *Gazette* announced that there were still 800 tickets to be sold, and that the draw would be postponed until October.[22] But October came and went and the advertisement was printed intermittently until May, 1768. At that time the managing committee announced that the delegates had taken 500 tickets among themselves, and a few remained.[23] Beyond this point, the Liberty Lottery drops from sight, a new kind of procedure in out-of-door politics but one that was unsuccessful in its intended purpose.

Failure to raise much money in Maryland paralleled and perhaps contributed to the failure of Garth to bring the protest of the house to the conclusive hearing it desired.[24] When Secretary Hamersley heard of the lot-

21. The first advertisement in the *Maryland Gazette* appeared December 11, 1766, and fifteen followed until May 28, 1767. There were no more until July 9, and after that there were twenty-six, the last on May 12, 1768.

22. Sharpe to Hamersley, March 11, 1767, *Archives*, XIV, 384; *Maryland Gazette*, July 9, 1767.

23. *Ibid.*, June 2, 1768. There is a Liberty Lottery ticket in Galloway Papers, II, NYPL.

24. In a letter of February 14, 1767, Garth replied to the Delegates' inquiry about what he would think "handsome for a year's salary"; he

tery, he was cautious enough to retain two special counselors for all disputes with the lower house. But the political idealism of the provincial assembly, which anticipated that British authority would listen to, understand, and favor the plea against the proprietorship, was not tuned to Hamersley's ear. He asked for copies of the *Maryland Gazette* with the lottery advertisements, because they seemed "so extraordinary as scarce to gain credit." Even as he engaged counsel, he thought that the resolutions of the Delegates were "calculated as by a kind of fatality to counteract" their own purposes, by reason of their radicalism. The idea that delegates should seek and take subscription money seemed to him grossly unparliamentary and even a matter for prosecution in the courts.[25]

It is quite probable that Garth was held back by a feeling not unlike that of Calvert, that the plea of the House of Delegates was so extreme as to be futile. The evidence is scanty. We know simply that when he was approached about acting as agent he asked for "power of discretion" in executing the instructions of the house; he wished to choose the time and opportunity of acting, and to be free to act or not, according to his own best judgment.[26] If he did hold back, he was consistent with his course in 1766, when he had thought that the Delegates' pleas against the Stamp Act would lose rather than gain support in the

said that South Carolina paid £200 and costs, amounting to about £160 a year, and that Virginia paid £500 for all except the charges for which vouchers could be returned. Rather than state an amount himself, he preferred to leave the matter to the discretion of the Maryland house (L. B. Namier, "Charles Garth, Agent for South Carolina," *English Historical Review*, LIV [1939], 636). It is not certain whether the Delegates ever sent money beyond their payment for Garth's handling of the Stamp Act business. Some "Garth Correspondence," edited by J. W. Barnwell, is printed in the *South Carolina Historical and Genealogical Magazine*, XXVIII–XXXI (1927–1930).

25. Letters to Sharpe, February 20, July 20, 1767, Maryland MSS., Miscellaneous, Box I, NYPL.

26. Namier, "Charles Garth, Agent for South Carolina," p. 639. We know that Garth did not break his connection with Maryland. Letter to "My Lord" [Hillsborough?], October 1, 1768, *Md. Hist. Mag.*, XII, 381–382.

House of Commons. In any case, Secretary Hamersley wrote to Governor Sharpe, in the spring of 1768, that no actual move had been made toward the appeal and that there was no more talk of it.[27] Thus, after three decades of trying, the lower house was still unable to overcome the obstacles to a hearing in England—to put actual force into its long stroke for a sweeping settlement under English law.

For a brief interlude, the anti-proprietary movement was stopped; there was no political leverage immediately available to the Delegates. In 1769, when Governor Eden arrived in Maryland, he met a very moderate session of the assembly; it was largely given to formalities. But in 1770, the situation changed. In that year the tobacco-inspection law, first passed in 1747, came up for a third renewal. The second renewal, in 1763, had been the occasion of much difference between the houses; there had been especial disagreement because the Delegates had tried to place a rider in the bill, to make the quit-rents payable in currency, not in British sterling.[28] Since then the investigations of the special committees of the lower house had revealed something of the high incomes from fees of the great officers of state, and the case of Bennet Allen had displayed church patronage at its most scandalous. Now the House of Delegates saw an opportunity to clip fees and clergy incomes. The easier condition of imperial affairs favored the consideration of local affairs, and recent successes in the intercolonial politics of propaganda and organization were well remembered. Because tobacco inspection, official fees, and clergy dues had been bound together in the law of 1747, and were connected in the thinking of the province, the stage was set for a major conflict between the houses of assembly.

Conditions of overproduction of the staple and of competition with Virginia for the market still required a tobacco law, much as earlier. Tobacco had not lost its first

27. March 28, 1768, *Archives*, XIV, 475.
28. *Votes and Proceedings*, October 25, November 4, 1763.

place in the economy of Maryland; and the members of
both houses of assembly, now as before, were of the large
landholding class which preferred inspection as a method
of crop control. Yet, for all the continuity of need for
maintaining an inspection system, there were also new
conditions which encouraged a certain freedom of reconsideration and action. In the early seventies the tobacco
trade was greater in amount than ever before, and prices
were rising to the high point of the pre-revolutionary
period.[29] "Our planters' hopes," said Ringgold, from
the Eastern Shore, "are unbounded with respect to
tobacco."[30]

Hopes may well have outrun the advantages of the situation. As Charles Carroll, senior, pointed out, financial
distress had been so acute in the sixties, and the habit of
the colonists to import British goods—more than they
could afford, he said, for their "imaginary wants"—had

29. For the period September 4, 1771 to September 29, 1773, the shill-
ing-per-hogshead duty amounted to £3,394 11s. 5¾d., or more than for
any other two consecutive years for which there are figures. The amount
for the year ending September 29, 1774 was £1,564 15s. 4¾d. (Calvert
Papers, nos. 1028, 1030, MHS). At the same time the tonnage duty, representing all trade in out-of-colony vessels, achieved a new high, both
in absolute amount and in proportion to the tobacco duty. This indicates that, while tobacco was gaining, other products were gaining more
(see Table III, in the appendix, below, p. 381).

The following figures, continuing the table above, p. 295, n. 12, show
that Maryland's tobacco gains were part of a general gain.

Year	Pounds of Colonial Tobacco sold in Great Britain	Price in Philadelphia, Shillings per Cwt
1770	39,188,037	28.73
1771	58,079,183	32.50
1772	51,493,522	32.29
1773	55,928,957	——

From PRO, Treasury, 64: 276, LC; Bezanson, Prices in Colonial Pennsylvania, p. 422.

There is information about Maryland prices in Eden to Hillsborough,
August 21, 1772, Md. Hist. Mag., II, 297; and in many letters in the
Galloway, Maxcy, Markoe Papers, LC; in the Wallace, Davidson, and
Johnson Letterbook, 1771–1774, MHRecs; in the Hill Papers; and the
Corner Collection, MHS.

30. Letter to Galloway, May 17, 1772, Galloway, Maxcy, Markoe
Papers, LC.

become so fixed, that a long time would be necessary to achieve real solvency and stability.[31] And even at the time when the price of tobacco was favorable in England, credit conditions were adverse. A number of important firms went bankrupt in 1772 and 1773, and forced the commercial houses to retrench; this in turn led to more than usual strictness in calling loans, and to embarrassment and complaint among Maryland traders.[32] In the trade balance with the mother country, therefore, the years immediately after the repeal of the Townshend duties were years of economic hope and doubt, when tobacco was better but many things were uncertain. In 1770 the plain and agreeable thing was the improvement of conditions over the depression of 1764 and 1765.

The closest view of the dynamics of Maryland commerce for these years, or for any years, is to be found in the letters of Joshua Johnson to his partners, Charles Wallace and John Davidson, in business in Annapolis.[33] In 1771 Johnson was sent to London to represent the firm: to investigate and make purchases for export to Maryland, to arrange for freight, to make payments, and in general to secure for the firm the advantages of independence from British correspondents. For a while he ran into difficulties in getting credit, because many of the London merchants were cool to a newcomer who was in some degree their competitor. But after a period of having to live too "Zac. Hoodlike" to suit him, Johnson found that he was able to afford good quarters, and was obliged to hire help in his office. With a degree of success, his sense of opportunity increased, and his activities became legion. He visited the north of England with a plan to buy

31. Letters to Carrollton, April 20, 1770, June 30, 1772, *Md. Hist. Mag.*, XII, 348; XIV, 275.
32. The scarcity of money in England is frequently mentioned as a factor disturbing colonial trade, in letters in the Galloway, Maxcy, Markoe Papers, LC; and in the Wallace, Davidson, and Johnson Letterbook, 1771–1774, MHRecs.
33. *Idem.* This little-known and very valuable MS. volume has only recently been made available to students.

metal goods for export; he did not find the purchasing advantages he had expected, and he was distressed by the conditions of life under the putting-out system; but he did order nails for shipment to Maryland. He had intended to manage an export business exclusively, trading with the credit supplied by his partners. But he soon urged them to send him tobacco, in full competition with the British merchants; when they complied he succeeded in marketing it. "The great mystery made of the management and sale of tobacco," he declared, in 1774, "has only been held up as a scarecrow to our countrymen to deter them from entering into the business." [34] He wrote from London, during the period of the bankruptcies, that the Scottish firms were expected to fail; [35] and he expressed confidence that in such times small companies, like their own, had the advantage. His sense of advantage led to thought of expansion, and Johnson urged his partners to deal with the planters of Calvert county and even to set up a store in Frederick, where he thought that an Annapolis firm might win some of the profits which otherwise flowed north. The firm actually did spread its activities from Annapolis to Queen Anne and Nottingham, a moderate expansion which won only critical approval from Johnson.

The whole enterprise of a Maryland firm with a representative in London is a suggestive reversal of the traditional arrangement, by which British firms sent factors to the provinces. It marks a step in commercial independence far beyond that of either the great planters, who, though managing the sale of their own tobacco, were obliged to accept the terms of their British correspondents; or of the provincial merchants, who were swinging from the staple to trade in foodstuffs or other secondary

34. Letter to Charles Carroll, Barrister, February 25, 1774, *ibid.*

35. This anticipation was groundless, but the Scottish firms seem to have had a hard time. Hamilton, the factor at James Brown's store at Piscattaway, did a diminishing import business in the seventies. Maryland and Virginia Firm Accounts, Inventories and Invoices, LC.

products. For his own firm, Johnson's work in London was the equivalent of the reform proposed by Henry Darnall, in 1729, that Maryland exporters maintain a commercial agent to guard their interests at the "head of trade." [36]

Wallace, Davidson, and Johnson had connections, moreover, which suggest that commercial aggressiveness against the London merchants offers an accurate and significant parallelism with lower-house aggressiveness against the proprietary element. Joshua Johnson was a brother of Thomas Johnson, the prominent lawyer and Anne Arundel county delegate who was now emerging to political leadership, and was in time to become the first revolutionary governor of Maryland. The firm handled the tobacco business of Charles Carroll of Carrollton; and it carried on friendly correspondence with Charles Carroll, Barrister, the supporter of Chase, and with Delegates John Hammond of Anne Arundel and Richard Tilghman Earle of Queen Anne's county. Its connections were all on the side of the "country party." Commercial and political aggression could hardly have been unrelated in the minds of the members of the firm and their associates; the two activities were parallel in a common advance against established British interests.

When the inspection law expired, Walter Dulany wrote to Secretary Hamersley that political momentum, alone, would cause a great deal of controversy. "The patriots," he said, "must distinguish their zeal for popular regulations, to recommend themselves to the suffrage of the people. Great reductions are talk'd of both with respect to the fees of the officers and the revenues of the clergy, which they say must take place or the inspecting act fall to the ground, which indeed, wou'd be attended with terrible consequences to the whole province." [37] Dulany might have added to his prophecy that the administration of tobacco control—whether to be in the interest of great

36. See above, p. 92.
37. September 15, 1770, Dulany Papers, II, 52, MHS.

planters or small—would evoke no such debate as it did before 1747. The form of regulation was now secondary. The principal issue of assembly politics during the years from 1770 to 1773 has been correctly known as the "fee struggle," [38] for it was officers' fees and not tobacco inspection which held the stage.

The familiar questions of constitutional right rose at the very outset. The old law expired on October 20, while the two houses were discussing and disagreeing about a new one. So the question was raised at once, what should be done about the collection of fees, if there were no inspection and fee law? The lower house made a test case: its committee of grievances reported that William Stewart, the clerk of the land office, had collected fees and administered oaths after the expiration of the old law, that is, without any statutory right whatsoever. The committee took from the journal of 1739 a resolution, passed while the proclamation of 1733 regulated fees, which declared that the assembly, as entitled to the "customs, common law, and securitative statutes of the rights and liberties of subjects of Great Britain," ought to settle the amounts of official fees. The committee found, and the House of Delegates resolved, that Stewart had overstepped the limits of the British constitution. The lower house further resolved that the right to enact taxes and fees, which it regarded as much alike, lay entirely with the assembly, and that for the prerogative to fix them, as in the instance of Stewart, was an oppressive act. The sergeant-at-arms was directed to lodge the offender in the county jail, until discharged by future order.[39]

This act was a deliberate political aggression. The lower house had moved to an advanced position and struck a body blow. Governor Eden at once accepted the challenge. With the advice of the council, he prorogued the assembly, simply to release Stewart; and then reconvened

38. There are good accounts in McMahon, *Historical View*, pp. 380–396; and in Steiner, *Eden*, ch. IV.
39. *Votes and Proceedings*, November 1, 1770.

it to carry on with legislative business. The Delegates complained that the interruption was extravagant of time and the public money, and Eden retorted that they had made it necessary by jailing an innocent man.[40] Discussion now moved to the amount of income fitting for the officers of state. The upper house made what a wealthy planter called a "foolish and insolent" proposal, namely, to abolish all fees for the most lucrative offices —those of the secretary, the commissary-general, and the judges of the land office—and to substitute salaries of £600 sterling annually for each.[41] The lower house rejected this; it investigated the offices through a committee, and ordered printed a table of fees such as it would allow. It also passed a series of resolutions declaring that the upper house was too thoroughly attached to the interest of wealth and power to pass a just inspection and fee bill, and that being dominated by selfish considerations, it endangered the liberties of the people of Maryland.[42] The session closed with as much ill feeling between the representative and proprietary elements as at any time during Sharpe's administration, and with controversy on the basis of a more specific discussion of proprietary incomes than ever before.

At the end of the session, the controversy had reached a stage which made it certain to become a great affair, just as the House of Delegates wanted. All men and classes had a stake in the enactment of a tobacco law. The lower house had taken a high stand in terms of self-government; its language was equally that of the old anti-proprietary movement and of the recent successes against parliamentary taxation. The governor and council would now have

40. *Ibid.*, November 5, 8, 20, 1770.
41. *Ibid.*, November 10, 1770. Charles Carroll wrote to his son, Carrollton, November 2, that the council was foolish in publishing that they thought the offices worth £600, and insolent in presuming that the "representatives of the people" would demean themselves so much as to enter into a treaty with them. He thought that there was not an aspirer for office who would not accept £300. *Md. Hist. Mag.*, XIII, 69–70.
42. *Votes and Proceedings*, November 21, 1770.

to make some provision for fees, if administration were to survive: they would have either to make concessions, to be written into a statute, or use the prerogative in such a way as was sure to lead to popular reaction.

Immediately after he had dissolved the legislature, Governor Eden issued the famous fee proclamation of November 26, 1770. A brief document, the proclamation simply ordered that all officers who took fees must not ask more than the old inspection law provided. It was written, as the proclamation of 1733 had been written, in the language of a defense of the people against exorbitant charges.[43] It had the same constitutional standing as earlier proclamations. That of 1733 had been guaranteed in advance by expert legal opinion in England; and now this was to have the confirmation of distinguished counselors, including Edward Thurlow, the future lord chancellor.[44] Yet legal certification in England had no power to persuade the lawyer-delegates of the lower house. In the Stewart case, the house had taken its unalterable stand against fees fixed by prerogative power; it had committed itself to oppose the fee proclamation weeks before Eden issued it. If such an attitude had the character of Coke's stand against the prerogative of James I,[45] so much the better for the Delegates, who loved the memory of Coke, and were as little likely as he to yield to the prerogative.

An election before the session of 1771 gave the members of the lower house special cause and opportunity to put their case before the public. Before the old house had been dissolved, it had ordered to be printed that part of the report of the committee to inspect public offices which showed that the provincial secretary received tobacco fees worth from £1,000 to £1,500 a year, and the clerk of the land office upward of £1,800. Such huge incomes gave point and purpose to the resolutions of the lower house,

43. Text printed in Steiner, *Eden,* p. 44, n. 6.
44. Opinions of E. Thurlow, A. Wedderburn, and J. Dunning, [1773], *Archives,* XXXII, 493–501.
45. Tanner, *English Constitutional Conflicts,* pp. 37–38.

which were also printed.[46] The elder Carroll commented that this printing of its stand was a spirited thing for the Delegates to do. Yet it did not stir up a public controversy;[47] no writer yet cared to defend the proprietary side of the issue.

Without much expression of out-of-door sentiment in the newspaper, however, it is clear that the province as a whole stood with the lower house. Within days after the close of the session, people at the shipping centers, so recently experienced in voluntary organization in restraint of trade, set up an extra-legal inspection system to compensate for the official one which was lost. Twenty-five "buyers of tobacco" at Port Tobacco, on the Potomac, agreed to keep the quality of the exported staple high by purchasing only at stated times and then only such tobacco as one of their number had inspected and passed, according to the standards of the old act. A number of gentlemen of Queen Anne, on the Patuxent, made a similar agreement, because, they said, there was no chance that the upper house would pass the kind of inspection law they wanted. The nearby towns of Upper Marlborough, in Prince George's, and Indian Landing, in Anne Arundel county, also provided for voluntary inspections; and so, apparently, did other shipping centers on both shores of the bay.[48]

Here was popular participation in public affairs on a new basis: these associations were designed not merely to coerce, but also to administer. One who opposed them in the *Gazette* admitted that most people favored them and that he himself could see that they might do real service to Maryland trade, but he feared that they were a step toward the control of the masses. He quoted with approval a saying of Voltaire, that "frequent associations of indi-

46. *Maryland Gazette,* November 8, 15, 22, 29, December 6, 1770.
47. Letter to Carrollton, November 30, 1770, *Md. Hist. Mag.,* XIII, 71.
48. *Maryland Gazette,* December 6, 13, 1770, February 21, March 28, June 20, 1771, June 18, 1772; Carroll to Carrollton, April 12, 1771, *Md. Hist. Mag.,* XIII, 175.

viduals are critical symbols of a sick commonweal"; and
he concluded that the extra-legal tobacco inspection was
leading to government by a faction—"force of club law,"
another said—and would produce "a monster." [49] There
was truth in this writer's estimate of the situation. A voluntary inspection stood in line with voluntary militia
service in 1755 and with a voluntary subscription to support an agent. The politics of Maryland were too "sick,"
in very fact, for government to provide normal and
expected services.

The election introduced no new line in assembly relations; and the two-month session, which began in October,
1771, was devoted almost entirely to the fee controversy.
The lower house resolved unanimously in condemnation
of Governor Eden's proclamation. On the old ground that
the "representatives of the freemen" had the sole right to
establish "taxes or fees," the house declared that the proclamation was illegal, unconstitutional, arbitrary, and oppressive, and that those who advised taking such a step
—the councilors, whom the Delegates would rather blame
than the new governor—were enemies to the peace, welfare, and happiness of the province, and to its law and
constitution.[50] The Delegates said that their great constitutional victory of 1747, that of inserting a fee schedule
in the tobacco law, would be lost altogether if the prerogative power were to make good its claim to authority
to control fees by proclamation. Here the lower house
took a position more anxious than accurate; the law of
1747 had limited fees, but no more than limited them, as
we have seen; the law had involved no constitutional
victory for the house. But the present aim of the house,
necessarily, was a popular statement of its history and

49. *Maryland Gazette,* March 7, June 20, 1771. The writer sounds like
Carroll of Carrollton, who had recently heard from his father that there
was a committee forming at East River, but that there was little to be
expected from it. Letter of April 12, 1771, *Md. Hist. Mag.,* XIII, 175.

50. All except one of these resolutions were passed unanimously. In
the one instance three members voted in the negative. *Votes and Proceedings,* October 18, 1771.

attitude; its appeal now was to the people of the province, not the Privy Council. It accused Governor Eden of playing the rôle of "tyrannical king," and of having covered his true motive, to bring the legislative power under the executive, with a false pretense of saving the people from extortion.[51] The Delegates said that English history furnished no precedent for such arbitrary procedure; they cited the works of Coke and the resounding title of *De Tallagio non Concedendo*, which the English parliamentarians of the seventeenth century had also cited, from the reign of Edward I.[52]

All of this the governor parried. He reminded the house that the fee proclamation of 1733 had actually determined rates for fourteen years, and that Lord Camden, himself, whom Americans now honored for opposition to the Stamp Act, had, as Attorney-General Pratt, been the author of the opinion of 1758.[53] Irreconcilable views made any legislation impossible, and Eden prorogued the assembly.

The formalities consequent upon the death of Lord Baltimore and the succession of Harford prevented another assembly before 1773. During the interlude the question of tobacco law and fee regulation lay open before the colony. How effectively the extra-legal associations carried on the functions of an inspection system, there is little evidence from which to judge. But it is clear that public issues occupied and agitated the minds of the people. Jonathan Boucher, clerical friend of the Dulanys, declares that, "The times were grown beyond measure troublesome: men's minds were restless and dissatisfied, for ever discontented and grumbling at the present state of things, and for ever projecting reformations. . . . This had long been the constant state of things; but it was now much worse. There was a fierceness in opposition

51. *Ibid.*, November 20, 1771.
52. *Ibid.*, November 22, 1771.
53. *Ibid.*, November 30, 1771; Eden to Dartmouth, January 29, 1773, *Md. Hist. Mag.*, II, 301.

that was unusual." [54] Discontent produced a flood of newspaper writing, controversial and satirical. "Who," questioned young Daniel Dulany, a nephew of his eminent namesake, when someone sent him copies of the *Maryland Gazette* in London, "are all of these poets and writers that have started up among you all at once? As to some of the party disputes, I cannot help saying that I think they flavour very considerably of toddy." [55]

By far the most distinguished and important of the newspaper controversies was fought during the early months of 1773, between Charles Carroll of Carrollton, who attacked the fee proclamation, and Daniel Dulany, who defended it. Not the least significant part of the controversy is that it brought young Carroll into the public life, from which his Catholicism would ordinarily have excluded him. He had returned to Maryland from his continental and English studies in the Stamp Act period, and had early directed his thinking to political ideas and conditions. While still abroad, he had said that, "America is a growing country: in time must and will be independent." [56] He was impressed and influenced by Dulany's *Considerations* in 1765; but his mind was more imaginative and moralistic than legalistic, his training at the Inns of Court to the contrary. Refinement of constitutional distinction did not please him, and in 1766 he predicted that British acts in restraint of American trade and manufacturing would in "a few years" seem as oppressive as

54. Boucher, *Reminiscences,* pp. 68–69.
55. Dulany Papers, II, 58, MHS.
56. Letter to his father, November 12, 1763, *Md. Hist. Mag.,* XII, 21. In 1773 Carroll repeated this idea. He spoke of the "astonishing emigrations" to America, and said they bade "fair to render British America in a century or two the most populous and of course the most potent part of the world." Letter to William Graves, September 5, 1773, *ibid.,* XXXII, 219. Beside the biography of Carroll, by Rowland, and the *Unpublished Letters,* already cited, the following materials are useful: "Extracts from the Carroll Papers," 1750–1774, *Md. Hist. Mag.,* X–XVI; J. G. D. Paul, editor, "A Lost Copy Book of Charles Carroll of Carrollton," 1770–1774, *ibid.,* XXXII, 193–225; Joseph Gurn, *Charles Carroll of Carrollton, 1737–1832* (New York, 1932); Lewis A. Leonard, *Life of Charles Carroll of Carrollton* (New York, 1918).

tax laws.[57] His father, with whom he was in close intellectual sympathy, once wrote a London merchant that "Trade in its nature is free";[58] and the father and son came closer to the free-trade convictions of Franklin and Dean Tucker than any other Marylanders known to the writer. There was a recurrent feeling for aristocracy in Carroll's thinking, which sprang from a tendency to "despise" and "laugh at" the "clamors of a mob";[59] but in the early seventies his mind was burning with the liberal principles of the Enlightenment. The flame was fed by a sincere intellectual life of reading and writing, and by a great pride, as we have seen, in his native Maryland.

In 1771 he wrote a friend in London:

The vast influence of the Crown, the luxury of the great and the depravity of the common people are unsurmountable obstacles to parliamentary independence. The liberty of the press yet remains a check upon the ministerial or royal power: a few years will destroy or greatly weaken that bulwark of liberty.

The English seem to be arrived to that degree of liberty and of servitude which Galba ascribes to the Roman people in his speech to Piso: *imperaturus es hominibus, qui nec totam servitatem pati possunt, nec totam libertatem.* Those same Romans a few years after that period deified the horse of Caligula. . . . [The Senate] lent its name to the worst of tyrannies—Will the British dominions long admit of the present form of government?

An aristocratic government is the least fitted of all others to extensive empire: and I think the English government approaches nearer this day to an aristocracy than to any other kind of government. The House of Commons, which ought to be the representative of the people, is become the instrument of the ministry to raise money from the subjects:

57. Letter to Edmund Jennings, May 29, 1766, *Unpublished Letters,* p. 117.
58. Letter to William Graves, December 23, 1768, *Md. Hist. Mag.,* XII, 180.
59. Letter to his father, September 16, 1760, *ibid.,* X, 328.

the ministry is commonly composed of rich noblemen and some rich commoners connected together by the ties of kindred or of interest.[60]

There is temptation to quote still more of this long letter, because it reveals the mind of Charles Carroll of Carrollton. He was a Catholic who could repulse an inquiry about his faith in the language of liberalism,[61] a man of the Enlightenment who conceived destiny in historical rather than theological terms, and a gentleman who was heir to all the assurance that classical education, wide reading, and the associations of cultivated living could give him. This was the equipment with which he engaged the great and experienced Daniel Dulany in public controversy.[62]

The real opening of the debate, although not so intended, came with a contribution by Dulany to the first issue of the *Maryland Gazette* in 1773.[63] Apparently in the thought that he could help remove the most troublesome issue in Maryland politics—possibly he was thinking back to 1766—he composed a clever satirical dialogue.

60. Letter to Edmund Jennings, August 9, 1771, *Md. Hist. Mag.*, XXXII, 197–198.
61. Letter to William Graves, August 15, 1774, *ibid.*, XXXII, 222–223.
62. Josiah Quincy, Junior, leaves a suggestive sketch of Dulany, with whom he once visited for about three hours. "Dulany is a diamond of the first water, a gem that may grace the cap of a patriot or the turban of a sultan." Quincy speaks of the fee dispute as "conducted with good sense and spirit, but with great acrimony, by Daniel Dulany of the council, and the speaker, Tillingham [Tilghman] of the lower house." Rowland, *Life of Charles Carroll of Carrollton*, I, 102.
There is just a scrap of evidence to suggest that a private matter may have added impulse to the public controversy. In 1771 the elder Carroll had litigation against Walter Dulany, whose behavior he thought to be scandalous and deserving no tender treatment. Is this a Maryland parallel to the Otis-Hutchinson complication in Massachusetts? See letter to Carrollton, May 30, 1771, *Md. Hist. Mag.*, XIII, 260.
63. *Maryland Gazette*, January 7, 1773. The whole controversy is reprinted in full in Elihu S. Riley, *Correspondence of "First Citizen"—Charles Carroll of Carrollton—and "Antilon"—Daniel Dulany, Jr., 1773, With a History of Governor Eden's Administration in Maryland, 1769-1776* (Baltimore, 1902). It is reviewed in Steiner, *Eden*, chs. VII–VIII; and briefly discussed in Charles F. Mullett, *Fundamental Law and the American Revolution* (New York, 1933), pp. 106–107.

The speakers were named, "First Citizen," who opposed the proclamation, and "Second Citizen," who successfully defended it. A month later, Carroll entered the argument. In his first letter, he also used the form of the dialogue and named the same speakers; but he gave the better part to "First Citizen." Three long letters from each writer followed.[64] Both abandoned the dialogue and entered into direct debate; Carroll retained the pseudonym of "First Citizen," and Dulany assumed the name of "Antilon."

Their discussion, though long, could hardly have been intended to contribute new ideas to the fee struggle. But it did make the ideas of the two houses the property of all Maryland, in a way which the mere printing of resolutions could not do. In true provincial fashion, the question of fees was run back to the beginnings of the colony, and English precedents were cited as being as relevant as provincial; Carroll compared the executive control of fees to King Charles's taking ship money. Historical and legalistic argument was accompanied, here as so frequently, by the application of the natural-rights philosophy, by literary quotation, and by personal invective. Six months of such discussion gave real drama to the issue. The true names and characters of the writers were widely known, and their vigor and cleverness in debate excited the readers of the *Gazette*. A member of the lower house wished, he said, that the "scribblers" could have "avoided personal abuse; but good often springs from evil and I think it likely that many points will be explained that may tend to public advantage." [65]

The best indication of feeling about the controversy is

64. Letters from Dulany, *Maryland Gazette,* January 7, February 11, April 8, July 1, 1773; letters from Carroll, February 4, 27, May 6, June 3, 1773. Carroll had been thinking about the fee question for at least a year and a half. On December 3, 1771, he wrote Charles Carroll, Barrister, that Maryland politics were "as contemptible, and more pernicious, than those of England. Could you imagine that the right of fixing officers' fees by proclamation would be claimed at this time of day?" *Md. Hist. Mag.,* XXXII, 209.

65. Ringgold to Galloway, March 15, 1773, Galloway, Maxcy, Markoe Papers, LC.

the sudden achievement of popularity by Charles Carroll of Carrollton. Hitherto almost unknown, he now became the associate of the leaders of the lower house. He dined with William Paca, Samuel Chase, and Thomas Johnson, the three who were destined, as state governors and signers of the Declaration of Independence, to become Carroll's associates in revolutionary leadership. "First Citizen" was widely acknowledged as "a most flaming patriot." His writings were especially liked in the neighborhood of Baltimore and in Marlborough;[66] and open letters in the *Gazette*, from several county delegations to the lower house, show that the radical element acclaimed him as its intellectual leader. "It is the *public voice*, Sir," said one of these letters, "that the establishment of fees, by the *sole authority* of prerogative, is an act of *usurpation*—an act of tyranny, which, in a land of *freedom*, cannot—must not—be endured." With a pointed reference to Dulany's education, a group of writers, who signed themselves as "Independent Whigs," bade, "Blush Cambridge! blush!—If such be the fruits of thy famed nursery, our boys shall never cross the Atlantic." [67]

In May, while Carroll and Dulany were bringing their controversy to a close, there was held the election made necessary by the succession of Harford to the proprietorship. This was to be the last election under the proprietary régime; and it was different from all that had preceded it. Electioneering and election celebrations were carried on after the manner of Stamp Act protests; and election politics for the first time became a matter of public demonstrations, not only in Annapolis, but in many parts of the province. When the people of the capital

66. Carroll to Carrollton, March 17, 28, April 1, June 24, 1773; Carrollton to Carroll, April 3, 1773, *Md. Hist. Mag.*, XIV, 368; XV, 58, 59, 62–63, 276.

67. *Maryland Gazette*, February 11, 1773. Letters approving Carroll are quoted in Riley, *Correspondence, passim;* and there are others in *Maryland Gazette*, May 20, 27, June 3, 10, 1773. One hundred five signers from Baltimore county, however, protested when the delegates from that county approved Carroll. *Ibid.*, June 17, 1773.

elected two radical assemblymen, they celebrated with a mock funeral of the fee proclamation. They took a copy, as they had taken the effigy of Zachariah Hood, and placed it in a coffin inscribed as follows: "*The Proclamation*, The Child of Folly and Oppression, born the 26th of November, 1770, departed this life the 14th of May, 1773, and Buried the same Day, by the Freemen of Annapolis." [68] Two flags preceded the coffin, one marked, "Liberty" and the other, "No Proclamation"; drummers and fifers played a dead march; and the delegates and citizens comprised a great concourse. Where patriotic sentiment ran so high, the candidate for the "court party" did not dare to show himself in public. Another coffin, like the one in Annapolis, but larger, was put to rest in Anne Arundel county. In Frederick, a thousand people were reported to have gathered for a similar performance.[69] In all, the election returned thirty-four of the fifty-eight delegates who had been elected in 1771. To judge by the policy of the new house, the only change was in the direction of stronger anti-proprietary feeling.

The assembly met three times before the year closed, and in the third meeting made the only possible practical arrangement of the inspection and fee issue: it enacted a tobacco law without a fee schedule, and let the fee question stand. The House of Delegates approached this conclusion with a maximum of publicity and of deference to popular feeling. During the first of the three meetings, held in June, the houses deadlocked as in 1771. For six successive weeks after the adjournment, the lower house had its old resolutions printed in the *Gazette*, condemning the proclamation as illegal, arbitrary, and unconstitutional. Newspaper discussion accompanied assembly debate; the question was picked up by more vulgar and less able writers than "First Citizen" and "Antilon." On one side or the other, "A Very Great Patriot," "A Customer,"

68. *Maryland Gazette*, May 20, 1773.
69. *Maryland Gazette*, May 27, 1773.

"A Voter," "Solon," "Lycurgus," and "Elector" brought invective and scurrility into the public decision.[70]

The October meeting of the assembly was cut short at the request of the lower house. The members wished to consult their constituents on the question whether or not they should proceed to other business before an inspection law were passed.[71] This expressed a degree of dependence on the voters which had never before been equalled, and which had been approached only in 1765, when the house had refused to advise the governor about receiving stamped paper because it had no instructions. The governor permitted an adjournment. On reconvening, the Delegates proceeded at once to pass an inspection bill; and, with the question of a fee schedule aside, the governor and council enacted it.[72] The assembly thus accomplished what had seemed altogether unlikely three years before: it had passed a tobacco law without extraneous conditions. For the life of the act, at least, the House of Delegates had sacrificed its principal source of bargaining power.

At first view, this seems a considerable victory for the council. If the upper house could not claim that the principle of the fee proclamation had been accepted, at least the resolutions of the lower house and the theories of the controversialists had proved insufficient to upset the proclamation. On the financial side, even more plainly, the upper house had the victory; the lower house had sought a reduction of fees, while the council had not asked for more than the old law allowed. This rate the proclamation now assured for the officers.

On the other hand, there were political advantages on the side of the "country party." The inspection law, which

70. *Maryland Gazette*, September 23, 30, October 7, 21, 28, November 4, 1773; *Maryland Journal*, November 6, 1773; Carroll to Carrollton, November 18, 1773, *Md. Hist. Mag.*, XV, 287.

71. *Votes and Proceedings*, October 28, 1773; Carroll to Carrollton, November 12, 1773, *Md. Hist. Mag.*, XV, 286.

72. Note on the law, in A. C. Hanson, editor, *Laws of Maryland, Made since MDCCLXIII* . . . (Annapolis, 1787), November, 1773, ch. 1.

both sides had wanted, had been passed only in terms of an unprecedented display of solidarity between the House of Delegates and the people. As the new inspection law was framed on the old pattern, which was always considered favorable to great landholders and unfavorable to small, the landed gentlemen of the House of Delegates did well to exert a political leadership and control over the mass of men at this moment. The wealthy Charles Carroll of Carrollton had pleaded, in the columns of the new Baltimore paper, for the separation of the inspection bill from the fee issue; he argued that such a maneuver would isolate the "court" in an untenable constitutional position —the reactionary defense of the prerogative evoked by the fee proclamation.[73] Legally, indeed, the proclamation of 1770 stood as effective in the courts in 1773, as the proclamation of 1733 had stood in 1736. But in terms of political energy and popularity, the lower house opposition of 1773 was an incomparably different thing.

Parallel and closely related to the issue over officers' fees was another issue, known as the "vestry question." It, too, arose automatically with the expiration of the tobacco-inspection law. The act of 1747 had reduced the church tax from forty pounds of tobacco per poll, the amount fixed in the permanent act of establishment of 1702, to thirty pounds. Accordingly, when the inspection act lapsed, the clergy maintained that the earlier provision again applied. The ministers thus presented a more challenging problem than the officers—they had a statutory claim for an actual increase of income. The general sentiment, however, that the clergy were overpaid and scandalously in need of supervision, made it inevitable that they should be attacked in the assembly.

The last session of Sharpe's administration, the short

73. Carroll was "A Voter," who made this plea in the *Maryland Journal*, November 6, 1773. Letter from his father, November 18, 1773, *Md. Hist. Mag.*, XV, 287. The approval with which Joshua Johnson wrote of the law, from London, indicates that his firm and their associates favored it. Letter of February, 1774, Wallace, Davidson, and Johnson Letterbook, 1771–1774, MHRecs.

session of 1768, had seen the beginning of a movement appropriate to the Bennet Allen period of church history. At that time the Delegates offered a bill which would have authorized the governor to appoint three clergymen and three laymen to sit with him in a sort of court, with visitatorial capacity over such ministers as might be accused of immorality., The upper house, with the Dulanys in favor of the measure, passed the bill; but Sharpe, although he felt the need and rather liked the lower-house plan, held it up because he thought that his instructions forbade it.[74] At the same time there was growing among the reformist clergymen themselves the old idea of an American bishopric. In 1767 two northern clergymen had visited Maryland in behalf of the plan; and the recently established Jonathan Boucher gave it such ardent support as to become estranged, for the moment, from the governor and even his patrons, the Dulanys.[75] When Sharpe reported this sentiment in behalf of an episcopate, he received a reply from Secretary Hamersley which was uncompromisingly opposed, as he expected.[76] In the proprietary view, an American diocese would have run counter to the charter of 1632.

But the proprietor did not persist in objecting to the assembly plan of clerical discipline. Before Governor Eden came to America, he and Lord Baltimore saw the Bishop of London and discussed the Maryland church; they learned that the present bishop, unlike his predecessors, would exercise no authority in the colonies. At this time Lord Baltimore expressed a definite willingness to pass such an act as the lower house had proposed and the upper house approved.[77]

74. Letters to Hamersley, June 15, 22, 1768, *Archives,* XIV, 504, 506–507; Walter Dulany to Hamersley, September 29, 1768, Dulany Papers, II, 51, MHS.

75. Boucher, *Reminiscences,* p. 65.

76. Sharpe to Hamersley, June 9, to Baltimore, June 11, 1767, Hamersley to Sharpe, November 10, 1767, *Archives,* XIV, 394–395, 401, 431.

77. Hamersley to Walter Dulany, August 1, 1769, Dulany Papers, I, 44, MHS.

In 1770, then, the political situation of the Maryland clergymen was a very complicated one. All were in a legal position to claim more income than they were receiving; and as a body they were threatened with what none of them liked, a measure of secular discipline. This seemed to them to be "presbyterian" and "puritanical," and contrary to the constitutions of the province and the church.[78] Aside from common opposition to assembly discipline, the ministers were divided. Boucher and his group—the "High Church (or rather No-Church) Ruffians," they were called—favored an American episcopate. Others opposed the idea, in line with the proprietary interest and the natural sentiment of the province. At the beginning of the Eden administration, as at the beginning of Sharpe's, the clergy took to general voluntary meetings, and to the discussion of their own affairs. But they were not to be able to control them.

The publication of a handbill, dated September 28, 1770, brought the question of the clergymen's incomes to the public notice. The writer, who signed himself as "The Church of England Planter," complained that the clergy rode him "like an ass." He proposed that their salaries be set by law at ten pounds per poll; and that the vestries be given authority over the ministers, with power to summon, to reprimand, and, on third offense, to discharge them from the parishes. He dismissed the obligation to pay forty pounds per poll as without basis; he built up a new and surprising argument to prove that the act of church establishment had no constitutional validity. He rested his case not on principle but on a technicality: the governor who had signed the law in 1702 had done so some weeks after the death of King William, the sovereign whose commission he held; to be valid the law should have been repassed and signed under a commission from Queen Anne. In the "Church of England Planter's" arguments, the obvious common-sense features in the matter received no

78. Hugh Neill to Bishop of London, September 20, 1768; clergy addresses to Eden and Baltimore, July, 1770, Allen, Synodalia, LC.

consideration; that the governor of 1702 could not possibly have known his error, that the law had stood for seventy years—such facts had no meaning in the argument.

The plain purpose of the handbill was to bring the Maryland church into public agitation, and it succeeded. "A Constitutionalist" wrote and published a twenty-two page pamphlet in reply;[79] and another writer upbraided the "Church of England Planter" in the *Gazette*, calling him a "Gentleman of the New Regulation" and an "Advocate of Anarchy."[80] The mere challenge excited the clergymen of the Maryland establishment. Thrown on the defensive and made fearful that a new inspection law would reduce their salaries, they were put in mind of an appeal to the Crown, as they had appealed, in 1728, against the tobacco "burning" law. Twenty ministers sent addresses to the governor and the two houses, asking that the church and the faith be preserved. They pointedly reminded Eden that an invasion of their revenues was an invasion of the proprietor's prerogative, and that the interests of church and government were the same.[81]

At this stage of the discussion of church affairs, the assembly enacted the measure of discipline proposed in 1768. The new law required each clergyman to take an oath of loyalty to the government, and swear that he had made no "simoniacal contract" for his appointment. It provided that, whenever a majority of the vestry and churchwardens of any parish should complain in writing to the governor in council of neglect on the part of its minister, the governor should appoint three clergymen and three laymen to sit with him in a special court. Under the terms of the statute, the court was given power to admonish the minister, or suspend or deprive him of his parish,

79. *A Reply to the Church of England Planter's First Letter Respecting the Clergy* (Annapolis, 1770, copy in Gilmor Papers, MHS). The original handbill is summarized in the pamphlet.

80. *Maryland Gazette*, June 27, 1771.

81. Address to Eden, October 5, 1771, Md. Dioc. Lib., Letters, I (also in Allen, Synodalia, LC).

according to the offense.[82] This law was alarming, in principle, to the high churchmen of the province; but it did not assume practical importance. The new court seems never to have been invoked.

Complaint against the clergy continued, however, and the political attack increased. The long interval between the sessions of 1771 and 1773 saw church affairs thrown into more desperate confusion, even, than the affairs of civil administration. In Boucher's judgment, the aim of the Delegates was "a total renversement"; and the councilors were so "cunning" as to place the clerical order "in front of the battle, that themselves might take shelter behind us." [83] Contributors to the newspaper pursued the question raised by the "Church of England Planter." Samuel Chase wrote a legal opinion which expressed doubt about the establishment; he did not try to express real certainty of judgment.[84] This was followed by a good deal of vulgar writing, pro and con; then Chase was supported, and more than supported, by the weighty words of William Paca. Paca traced and analyzed the act of establishment through three closely printed newspaper columns, and concluded as follows:

My opinion, then, is, that upon the demise of King William, the assembly of this province was dissolved: that the assembly which afterwards met and enacted the contested forty per poll law, being called without a fresh *writ of summons*, was *illegally* and *unconstitutionally* convened: That, therefore, no obligation can result from said forty per poll act as a law.[85]

In view of Paca's position as a leading delegate and lawyer, here was a very proposal of "renversement."

Notices in the *Gazette* showed that Paca and Chase had

82. Hanson, *Laws*, November, 1771, ch. 31; see Steiner, *Eden*, pp. 50–51.
83. Boucher, *Reminiscences*, p. 69.
84. *Maryland Gazette*, August 6, 1772.
85. *Maryland Gazette*, September 10, 1772.

many followers. On the question of the establishment, the provincial bar assumed that the courts would accept the radical arguments; lawyers offered to plead, gratis, for any one refusing to pay the clergy tax. A test case was actually tried before the justices of Charles county. Joseph Harrison, a delegate, appeared as plaintiff against Sheriff Richard Lee, a councilor, who had jailed him for refusal to pay the forty pounds per poll. Harrison claimed that the incarceration had been illegal, and Paca, Chase, and Johnson acted as his counsel. According to the *Maryland Gazette*, the idea of liberty held by the Charles county jury was such that it viewed the sheriff's demand for taxes as a violation of the rights of Englishmen. Verdict was given to the plaintiff, and sixty pounds sterling awarded as damages.[86] The law, and not the defendant, had been on trial; the case is a rough equivalent, in Maryland, of the famous Parson's Cause argued by Patrick Henry in Virginia.

The war on the poll tax was acutely felt within the church. Many people were encouraged by the lawyers not to pay; and the ministers' incomes dropped half or more than half, especially in the cases of those who made bold to speak for their rights under the act of establishment.[87] The crisis, however, produced an advocate in Jonathan Boucher, who became the "Antilon" of the Maryland church. Without the cover of a pseudonym, he debated with Paca and Chase in the *Gazette*, just at the time when Dulany and Carroll were carrying on their controversy over fees. Boucher's plea for the church establishment was the product of an ultra-conservative mind, for he was a

86. *Maryland Gazette*, March 4, 1773; Mr. W. M. Albrittain, clerk of the Circuit Court for Charles county, was so kind as to search the court proceedings for 1772 and 1773, but he found no record of the case. See Boucher, *Reminiscences*, p. 70.

87. *Idem;* Boucher to James, November 16, 1773, *Md. Hist. Mag.*, VIII, 183-184. See also Boucher's sermon "On Reducing the Revenue of the Clergy," in his *A View of the Causes and Consequences of the American Revolution* . . . (London, 1797), ch. V. Boucher's conservatism was perhaps more complete in theory than in practice; as a Virginia parson he had opposed the Stamp Act and the Townshend duties.

follower of Filmer. But he had the basis for a good case, and a considerable understanding of colonial affairs; he made his plea as logical and vigorous as any in Maryland history.[88]

An illustration from a single exchange early in the controversy will show that the issue between Boucher and the lawyers was fought along the same intellectual lines and in the same sort of terminology as all issues between the proprietary and the representative elements in Maryland. Boucher said that Paca and Chase were inconsistent in attacking the validity of the statute of 1702; while writing their opinions about it, they continued as vestrymen in parishes which would have no legal existence, if their opinions were correct. They themselves acted unconstitutionally if they took part in an unconstitutional arrangement.[89] But Paca and Chase argued less from the laws, more from the law, than did Boucher. They replied that the British common law was just and would protect them from all "infernal jurisdictions," whether ecclesiastical or civil. They asked: "What then is the common law? The law of right founded upon reason and ripened into perfection by the wisdom of the ages: a system of jurisprudence adored by Englishmen, as the palladium of their rights, liberties, and properties." [90] With all the freedom which the canons of right reason could justify, Chase and Paca continued the argument. Like the people of Coventry parish, they contended that the parishioners delegated their powers to the vestrymen, and that their own positions were dependent not on assembly statute but on a church compact.[91] Thus the stereotypes of liberal thought entered

88. The letters appeared in the *Maryland Gazette* as follows: Boucher to Paca and Chase, December 31, 1772, February 4, April 15, 29, 1773; Paca and Chase to Boucher, January 15, March 18, 1773; Paca to Boucher, February 25, March 11, 25, April 8, 1773; Boucher to Paca, March 4, 18, April 1, 1773. See Boucher, *Reminiscences*, pp. 70–71; and Marshall, "What Jonathan Boucher Preached," *Virginia Magazine of History and Biography*, XLVI, 1–12.

89. *Maryland Gazette*, December 31, 1772.

90. *Ibid.*, March 18, 1773.

91. From this line of thought the lawyers were able to take advantage

every department of the politics of protest. They assumed intellectual grounds which gave no space to the opposition; but those very assumptions placed those who used them far outside the institutions and establishments of provincial Maryland.

When the assembly met again, in 1773, this thorough publicizing and theorizing of church affairs achieved a practical meaning. In two years of agitation, the newspaper controversialists had gone beyond, rather than followed, the old declarations of the lower house; now, in the June session, the Delegates quickly adopted the position of Paca and Chase as their own. The house declared in formal resolutions that the act of establishment had been unconstitutionally passed, and was void; it resolved that it approved the custom of Virginia, to pay all ministers equally; and it framed a bill in just these terms. The upper house rejected so extreme a measure, but, in line with the new policy to reform the church, it did indicate that a moderate bill would be passed.[92] Finally, in the November session, the houses agreed on a new law for the church tax. Refusing to consider a proposal of the clergy, that the payment of ministers be partially equalized by diverting funds from the larger parishes to such purposes as religious education or the erection of new parishes,[93] the lower house offered a bill which provided thirty pounds of tobacco or four shillings per poll for the clergymen, the taxpayer to have the choice between tobacco and money payment. In a moment of weakness, according to Boucher, the governor and council, advised by some clergymen, enacted the bill.[94]

The victory of reform was a considerable one. The pay-

of Boucher's sentiment in favor of an American bishop. In speaking of it they led another writer, "Patuxent," to say that he had favored Boucher until he heard this, but could no longer go with a minister so unlike Jesus. *Ibid.*, March 25, 1773.

92. *Votes and Proceedings*, June 19, 25, 1773.

93. *Ibid.*, December 8, 1773.

94. *Ibid.*, December 14, 16, 1773; Hanson, *Laws*, November, 1773, ch. 28; Boucher, *Reminiscences*, p. 71.

ment of thirty pounds per poll was the same as under the old inspection law, and may be considered as anticipating a maximum church revenue at a rate equal to that before 1770, an arrangement quite parallel to the officers' fees. But the option of a money payment was intended to favor the taxpayer, and has been estimated as likely to have reduced clergy incomes from one-fifth to one-half.[95] A group of the ministers tried to get the law disallowed; it did meet with the disapproval of Secretary of State Dartmouth and the Bishop of London,[96] but it nevertheless remained on the statute books. For once, the House of Delegates had won a substantial financial concession—a concession on the edge, rather than at the center, of proprietary privilege.

In these years, just prior to the Revolution, the old strategy of appeal to the Crown, and the old affirmations of parliamentary rights and privileges, lost their immediacy. But they were not abandoned. Twice during Eden's administration, as during Sharpe's, the House of Delegates proposed a grant for a college, and both times the bill was rejected.[97] In 1769 and 1771, the house proposed laws to support an agent,[98] the recent failure of the Liberty Lottery and of Garth's agency to the contrary notwithstanding.

The great session of November and December, 1773, which passed the inspection law and clipped the clergymen's incomes, also settled the old contest over the payment of the clerk of the council. The upper house at first refused and then decided to make a concession. In the final compromise, the Delegates agreed to pass a journal with full appropriation to date, and the council waived the claim for the future.[99] At the same time the lower house

95. Allen, Synodalia, LC; Estimate, 1775, Perry, *Collections*, IV, 343–344.

96. Letter of David Love, May 23, 1774, British Museum, Additional MSS. 15,489, LC.

97. *Votes and Proceedings*, October 25, November 16, 1771, December 7, 1773.

98. *Ibid.*, December 20, 1769, November 5, 18, 1771.

99. *Ibid.*, December 22, 23, 1773.

carried on with restatements of its own authority. In 1773 and again in 1774, during the last pre-revolutionary session, the house resolved that it had the right to commit to jail anyone guilty of breach of privilege or contempt of the house; a recent bill had carried the suggestive title, "to preserve the independence of members of the lower house." [100] Meanwhile the assembly moved into its splendid new building, the Georgian structure which is still the central unit of the capitol of Maryland. The House of Delegates ended its provincial history active in the tradition of sovereign claims, as it was also active in the newer habit of direct reference to the people.

The agreements of 1773 represent a certain easing of tension within Maryland. It may be, if provincial event is conceivable apart from imperial, that Governor Eden's greater independence and flexibility than Sharpe's—represented by his willingness to sacrifice the clergy and to yield on the point of the clerk's allowance—would have ushered in a period of appeasement and small compromises between the proprietary and representative elements. Possibly, even with an aroused and newly-effective public opinion in the scales, a political equilibrium might have been struck; and tolerable conditions might have been restored, in place of the breakdown of normal procedures, civil and ecclesiastical, between 1771 and 1773.

Even so, provincial politics in Maryland had achieved no basis for enduring stability, and little disturbance was needed to renew the conditions of controversy and struggle. The liberal element was far from political exhaustion. Through long decades of controversy, indeed, the Delegates' attack on the proprietorship must have seemed endless and hopeless, especially to those of conservative mind. But in 1773, recent experience with radical politics was not discouraging; participation had been exciting to rich and poor alike. If few minds had moved so far as to contem-

100. *Ibid.*, July 2, 1773, April 15, 1774; *Maryland Gazette*, October 18, 1770; Steiner, *Eden*, pp. 79–80.

plate separation from England, Charles Carroll of Carrollton had anticipated it. Separation he conceived as historically necessary and morally desirable; his mind was troubled by no vision of a social conflict or a struggle of arms. There was no reason for pessimism. Radical out-of-door politics had come to Maryland to the accompaniment of economic gain: resistance to the Stamp Act had coincided with upturn from deep depression; and non-importation, against the Townshend duties, had perhaps contributed to improvement in the tobacco trade. Even when the province's own inspection system had fallen, by reason of politics, the people had carried on inspection, and then —through the Delegates—had restored the system, with show of power and without apparent economic loss. Leadership stood where it always had, in the hands of gentlemen of land, commerce, law, and learning. Carroll, Paca, Johnson, and Chase, of the new generation of leaders, were all men of wealth as well as brilliance, of dignity as well as daring.

According to their standards, the news which was to come from Boston and Westminster, in 1773 and 1774, could only be profoundly disturbing. For a considerable interval, outside affairs had had little public significance in Maryland. From the breakdown of non-importation, late in 1770, to December, 1773, when reports of the Tea Party reached Annapolis, the *Maryland Gazette* had carried almost no news of intercolonial and imperial affairs. The House of Delegates had taken only one action in that respect: in October, 1773, it had set up a standing committee of correspondence and inquiry, as the legislatures of Massachusetts, Connecticut, Rhode Island, and Virginia had invited it to do. Eleven members, including Speaker Tilghman and Chase, Paca, and Johnson, sat on the committee; but it reported little correspondence in 1774.[101] Even when the *Gazette* reported the enactment of the tea duty, in the summer issues of 1773,[102] there was

101. *Votes and Proceedings,* October 13, 15, 1773, April 11, 1774.
102. *Maryland Gazette,* July 15, 22, August 19, September 2, 7, 1773.

no alarm. No one discussed the matter in the newspaper; and, when it met, the lower house passed no resolutions. For three years, all political attention was centered on affairs within the province, and no one predicted trouble from outside.

Both the Annapolis *Gazette* and the new *Maryland Journal and Baltimore Advertiser* printed detailed and stirring narratives of the Tea Party in Boston. They had prepared their readers by accounts of the arrival of the tea, in Boston and the other ports; and they followed up with events in Boston and the mother country. Marylanders could read approving accounts of how Boston fixed the price of undutied tea, and the full texts of the addresses of the council and House of Representatives of Massachusetts to Governor Hutchinson.[103] The *Maryland Gazette* noted that the Privy Council rejected the petition of Massachusetts to remove Hutchinson from office.[104] On May 26, 1774, it printed the full text of the Boston Port Act.

This news galvanized Maryland. There was a sudden response that something should be done. Daniel Dulany is said to have shaken his head, saying that he dreaded the consequences but advised a new boycott of British trade. The radical leaders, Johnson, Carroll, and their group, at once consulted about steps to be taken. Carroll wrote to the English friend, to whom he had confided his thoughts about Britain playing the part of the decadent Roman empire. "If," he said, "the present measures should be obstinately pursued, we have no alternative, and you would despise us justly if we could hesitate a moment between slavery and freedom. To expose the injustice, the cruelty, the absurdity of the late acts would be misspending my time and yours: all these are self-evident. Hear what America is doing and tremble at the consequences." [105] The leaders of both parties were thoroughly shaken.

103. *Ibid.*, December 30, 1773, January 6, 13, 1774; *Maryland Journal,* November 20, 27, December 9, 18, 30, 1773, January 8, 20, 1774.
104. March 3, April 28, 1774.
105. Letter to Graves, August 15, 1774, *Md. Hist. Mag.,* XXXII, 224.

A circular letter had been received from Boston even before the Port Act could be printed in the paper. It asked for support against the tyranny of Great Britain, by means of a non-importation and non-exportation association. On May 24, within hours of receiving it, a number of merchants and "respectable mechanics" of Baltimore met, and took vigorous action. They selected a local committee to correspond with the neighboring colonies, as the "exigencies of affairs may make it occasionally necessary." [106] On the next day, about eighty of the inhabitants of Annapolis gathered and passed resolutions that the town of Boston was suffering in the common cause of America, and that all the colonies ought to unite in a single effort to obtain the repeal of the Port Act. They fell in with the suggestion of Boston, that a general non-importation and non-exportation agreement be arranged, and committed themselves to it. They proposed, for the first time in America, an even more radical step: that all lawyers be stopped from suing for debts to British creditors during the life of the Boston Port Act.[107] A committee consisting of John Hall, Charles Carroll of Carrollton, William Paca, Matthias Hammond, and Samuel Chase was named to join with other local committees and together form a large colony committee, "to effect such association as will best secure American liberty." [108] Within a fortnight Queen Anne's, Kent, Harford, Baltimore, and Frederick counties had fallen into line with the radicalism and unionism of Annapolis.[109] On June 22, 1774, the first provincial convention was held at Annapolis. Maryland had enthusiastically made the cause of Boston her own.

106. *Maryland Journal*, May 28, 1774.

107. This was at once opposed by an open letter signed by 160, including three Dulanys, three Stewarts, Eddis, and Aikman, the bookseller. They described the proposal as "pregnant with bankruptcy and treachery," as it condemned creditors unheard and was certain to injure Maryland credit. *Maryland Gazette*, June 2, 1774. See Schlesinger, *Colonial Merchants*, pp. 360–361.

108. *Maryland Gazette*, May 26, 1774.

109. *Ibid.*, June 9, 1774. There are many documents for this period in Scharf, *History of Maryland*, II, 144–158.

Spontaneous action set the province into an accelerating movement not to be stopped short of revolution and republicanism. Caught in the stream of intercolonial affairs, Maryland moved on, into association, Congress, war, independence, statehood, Confederation, and Union.

The sloughing off of the old—especially the feudal—aspects of the Maryland system was to mark the victory, at last, of the anti-proprietary movement. The demands of 1739, and more than those demands, were to be fulfilled by the Revolution in Maryland. Proprietary offices and fees, the duties and prerogatives, the old land system, the collection of quit-rents, and the tax-supported church—all these were to fall during the Revolution. Their destruction was to be the completion of generations of assembly protest.

On the constructive side, as well as the destructive, revolutionary Maryland was to build on the foundation of colonial politics. The erection of the state government was to be based on old usages and on the anti-proprietary movement, on its tradition, leadership, and principles. The lawyer-leaders of the provincial lower house and of public opinion in the fee and vestry struggle—Carroll, Johnson, Paca, Chase—were, with others of their class and type, to become signers of the association, signers of the Declaration of Independence, the authors of the constitution of 1776, and the first statesmen under it. That constitution was to be a perfect image of their leadership, at once revolutionary and conservative: it was to begin with an eloquent bill of rights; it was to fix high property qualifications for the offices of governor and member of the legislature; it was to modify hardly at all the old property qualifications for the vote.[110] In the Revolution, as before, the

110. The Revolution in Maryland waits broad study. The constitution of 1776 is in Thorpe, *Constitutions and Charters,* III, 1686–1701. See also Scharf, *History of Maryland,* II, chs. XX–XXXI; John A. Silver, *The Provisional Government of Maryland, 1774–1777,* JHUS, XIII (1895), no. 10; Beverly W. Bond, *State Government in Maryland, 1777–1781,* JHUS, XXIII (1905), nos. 3–4; Bernard C. Steiner, *Western Maryland in the Revolution,* JHUS, XX (1902), no. 1; Allan Nevins, *The American States During and After the Revolution, 1775–1789* (New York, 1927), pp. 95, 157, 308–323, 429–431, 443–444, *passim.*

leadership of wealthy men was to command the support of the smaller landholders. The leaders might do certain things which the very conservative would not: confuse "fees" with "taxes," in the arguments of 1773; prevent British creditors from suing Maryland debtors, in 1774; supplant the provincial with extra-legal government, in 1775; become patriots, not loyalists, in 1776; and speak always of the people's rights and powers. But the property-mindedness and aristocracy of their leadership was to remain; landholding, slave-ownership, commercial wealth, and classical and legal education were long to be the factors and tokens of power and prestige in Maryland.

This looks far beyond the Boston Port Act. Such a glance forward should aid perspective; it should help us see the proper limit of our own problem. Revolutions are not well bounded by calendar dates, but the events of May and June, 1774, do mark a change in emphasis in Maryland. From that last coming-to-terms with the old provincial order, expressed in the legislation of the autumn of 1773, to the forward movement which was to lead straight to American independence—this transition comes close to locating Maryland's step from the preliminaries into active revolution. After the spring of 1774 the politics of protest were to move far before they would again be stopped short, the ideals of the gentlemen of the lower house were to have great opportunity for translation into life.

Scholars have explained the coming of the American Revolution in terms of large historical movements. Many have accented nationalism and liberalism; they have variously emphasized the separation of American life from British, the drawing-together of the eighteenth-century colonies, the extent of colonial autonomy, the growth of democracy, and opposition to British mercantilism. Older writers have made much of heroism, exemplified by Samuel Adams and George Washington; and radical writers have spoken of a class struggle, in terms of an American middle class opposed to a ruling class in Britain. The frontier idea, with its significances of individualism and the breaking of traditions, has been made illuminating. In such terms, what of Maryland? Does this case throw any light, however local in focus, on the larger questions of interpretation?

In coming to conclusions, there are special reasons for being cautious. The very notion of "revolution," expressed in our own time, erects an obstacle to an understanding of the eighteenth century. We are conscious, these days, of order and disorder, as problems; of evolution and revolution, scarcely distinguishable in history. The men of the eighteenth century were conscious, instead, of rights. Members of the Maryland House of Delegates had a logical comprehension of the wide difference in assumption between their position and that of their government, as of 1739; they were ready to hold to their line. To us, relatively and historically, their position was an extreme one, it even denotes radicalism. But the men of the lower house did not think of themselves as radicals; they thought less of relative present differences from the proprietary council than of long-run similarities to the House of Commons—they were the Cokes and Hampdens of the true English tradition. In their own way they were conservative idealists, believers in a political absolute; they conceived a king and Privy Council which never existed, when they moved for the appeal against the proprietorship. To us their assembly struggle is one of many, an instance of political bargaining; to them it was the preservation of sacred inherited rights.

On a practical level, too, there are conditions which may easily be lost from view. A question of radicalism today leads at once to a second question, Who cares? Policeman? Employer? Priest? But when the delegate of Maryland accused the proprietor of usurpation and wrong, there was none to put a threat into the second question. If he were not a justice of the peace himself, his kinsman or his friend was. He—not his servant, slave, or tenant—could speak freely and loosely of his superior, nay in the end court popularity by disbelief in and by attack on the established government. The British Empire may have rested on naval strength, against its enemies; but the Maryland delegate did not know the threat of policeman or soldier. With the advantage of social superiority, the delegate's attitude of objection, his preparation for the American Revolution, was an easy process, untroubled by risk of Bastille or concentration camp.

In the longest view, what influences promoted political idealism, or radicalism? What gave force to the politics of discontent? Without desiring to reduce ten chapters to a phrase, the writer may suggest that certain elements in the pre-revolutionary situation weighed so powerfully in the scales of history that to remove them—in an experiment altogether hypothetical—would upset the balance of forces altogether. Without certain features of Maryland life, entrance into the American Revolution would seem to have been impossible. The task of interpretation is to single out influential forces, and estimate their strength.

The larger things which we have examined are of course indispensable to understanding: staple agriculture, government under the charter, the parliamentary tradition, the stratified society. Remove any one of these from the historical scales and the pointer moves so suddenly, beyond the dial, that even hypothetical measure is impossible; the object of study becomes too distorted for observation. On the other hand, almost any leader might be lifted from the political surface with little disturbance to the scales: Ogle or Bladen, Bordley or Dr. Carroll—the traditionalism of proprietary and anti-proprietary politics was so considerable that there could be few heroes of great historical influence.

The elements of middle weight are the ones which balance our crude scales. What was the importance of some of the features usually called decisive—the growth of American nationalism, the influence of the frontier? What the importance of the solidarity of the upper class, of commercial depression, of the democratizing process, of literary culture and parish radicalism?

1. Without the continental element, the emergent nationalism of 1774, there could have been no American Revolution. But the "Background" in Maryland would not have been very different. The anti-proprietary movement could have occurred on an Atlantic island, although it might not have become so boisterous at the end, lacking association with the intercolonial protest against the Stamp Act and Townshend duties. In Maryland, local struggle against the proprietary system was the schooling for the Revolution; the war destroyed that prerogative which had long been made unwelcome in the colony.

2. The frontier element, in the wide sense that Maryland and all the colonies were far removed from the seats of power and traditionalism, is hardly ponderable within our premises; life in Maryland was different from English life, separated by distance and by increasing years, but it was also imitative of England. Such differentiation and imitation was continental, not local, and invites intercolonial study. The frontier element, in the narrow sense of the settlement of the Maryland north and west, however, did have an influence in preparation for the Revolution, though not a conspicuous one. Cresap's Sons of Liberty at Frederick once threatened the clerk of the council, but they did not move on Annapolis; nor was there an element of western populism, or evangelical democracy, in the Delegates' critique of the proprietorship. Yet western settlement was a great part of the general growth of population and economic life of Maryland. Without it some of the dynamics of the eighteenth-century history of the province—the accumulation of wealth, the growth of confidence—could hardly have been possible.

3. Social class we have seen everywhere in Maryland; the "class struggle" is not so plain. The lord proprietor, his appointed clergymen, and his servants in the land system may, with historical justice, be spoken of as representative of the old feudal owning-class; and, in the language

of Marxian thought, the attack on his tenurial and ecclesiastical privileges may be called a middle-class struggle. But neither the land system nor the right of advowson was the center of the assembly conflict, and the struggle was rather within the upper class than between classes. Very often the politics of protest had an economic meaning, beyond any doubt, with fees, duties, and offices the object of jealousy and attack.

4. Without persistent depression in the tobacco trade, neither political discontent nor intercolonial connection would have been so great or prominent. Constitutional struggle could not have grown from English tradition alone, nor from legal-mindedness; its great dynamic was economic need, as the twinning of the fee issue with tobacco inspection amply illustrates. The parallelism between the growth of intercolonial routes of trade, when the staple was low, and the development of intercolonial politics, when imperial affairs became aggravated, is very plain; the influence of the one on the other is not so clear. The trade with the other colonies and southern Europe is nevertheless suggestive, the more so as it was largely in the hands of the provincial merchants, not the British, and as it anticipated adjustments to be made during the period of the Revolution itself.

5. The idea of democracy in any full sense did not dawn on colonial Maryland. Yet American democracy has rarely been complete, it has rather been a compromise between the people and the holders of political power. In pre-revolutionary Maryland, new compromises—election pledges, instructions to delegates, mass meetings, committees and associations—gave increasing force, from outside legislative doors, to the politics of protest. Such practices never placed plebeians in the assembly; they enlarged rather than narrowed the leadership of the gentry. Yet they brought the gentry into closer connection with the people, and gave practical rather than theoretical meaning to the phrases about popular rights, so widely held in the province.

6. The importance of liberal culture, with the emphasis Maryland knew on the emancipating ideas of the Enlightenment, is perhaps the most difficult feature of the whole situation to estimate. With the evidences of rationalism in the parishes—the deism of the skeptic and the congregational polity of the discontented—those ideas had a wide, it seems almost an exclusive, spread. In the mind of the present writer, such a frame of thinking was a powerful influence; it gave political and economic liberalism a friendly climate, and it had great vitality apart from public issues, the strength of consistency, of vision, of detachment, and of moral force.

The scales of history are at best inexact. They invite weighing and reweighing, in the hope of striking a just and useful balance of ideas.

APPENDIX

TABLE I

Population and Landholding in Maryland

COUNTY	Average holding in acres 1755 or year given[1]	Number of landholders 1755 or year given[1]	Number of free adult white males 1755[2]	Total population 1755[2]	Per cent of population landholders
Lower counties, Western Shore					
St. Mary's.....	282.0 (1754)	567 (1754)	1,561	11,254	5.0
Charles........	343.1	692	1,929	13,056	5.3
Calvert........	364.1	312	609	5,715	5.5
Anne Arundel ..	472.8	730	1,534	13,150	5.6
Lower counties, Eastern Shore					
Worcester......	255.3	1,203	1,768	10,125	11.8
Somerset.......	307.9	938	1,348	8,682	10.8
Talbot.........	329.5 (1756)	628 (1756)	1,223	8,533	7.4
Kent..........	279.6 (1760)	634 (1760)	1,454	9,443	6.7
Outlying counties, west and north					
Frederick......	370.1 (1752)	1,032 (1752)	2,775	13,969	7.5
Cecil..........	371.9 (1749)	348 (1749)	1,345	7,731	4.5

1. Gould, *The Land System in Maryland*, p. 77n.
2. *The Gentleman's Magazine and Historical Chronicle*, XXXIV, 261.

TABLE II

Proprietary Income: Revenues from Land[1]

Year Ending Michaelmas	Quit-Rents			Land-Office Income			Manor Rents			Alienation Fines		
	£	s.	d.	£	s.	d.	£	s.	d.	£	s.	d.
1731	5,204	9	0	964	9	1¼	135	19	10½	....	....	....
1733	6,515	8	1	660	14	3	170	13	11½	....	....	....
1748	4,339	11	7	2,522	19	5	703	18	9	130	16	6
1752	5,013	15	2½	3,048	16	3	1,058	11	2	150	2	9½
1753	5,752	4	8¼*	....	....	.:..	731	3	1¼	149	15	10
1754	5,325	12	9¼*	4,678	8	11	813	16	0	114	14	2
1755	5,126	2	4*	2,747	6	5½	374	10	5¾	145	17	3
1756	5,121	3	11¾*	1,993	13	11¼	900	17	2	143	10	10¼
1757	6,082	17	0¾	1,484	5	4	1,297	0	11¾	158	12	5
1758	8,593	16	4*	1,574	18	0	1,033	7	11¾	136	19	6
1759	5,814	10	11½	3,369	10	6¼	1,134	4	6	166	5	1
1760	6,093	19	7¾*	4,621	13	4¼	1,251	14	11¼	104	16	3
1761	8,383	5	11½*	6,113	15	6¾	958	2	11½	237	17	4¼
1768	7,416	4	4	1,548	9	0	78	12	6	85	10	11
1769	7,118	16	10	2,771	3	4	1,467	2	11	142	5	9
1770	7,067	7	5	2,428	7	1	986	15	0	317	15	9
1771	6,230	13	8	2,590	8	5	1,037	5	0	198	0	8
1772	7,604	4	8	2,221	13	3	345	7	6	168	14	4
1773	7,604	4	8	1,976	13	5	345	7	6	168	14	4
1774	7,499	14	8	1,939	9	7	322	11	6	186	17	8

1. The figures for the years 1731 through 1761, except those marked with an asterisk, are taken from the Calvert Papers, MHS; and the later figures from both the Calvert Papers and the Chalmers Papers, NYPL. For an exact designation of the materials used, see above, p. 139, n. 50. In the quit-rent column the figures for 1731 and 1733 represent returns from the tobacco duty equivalent for quit-rents; and the figures marked with asterisks are those from Bond, *The Quit-Rent System*, p. 216 n.

TABLE III

Proprietary Income: Duties and Minor Revenues[1]

Year Ending Michaelmas	Hogshead Duty			Combined Duties			Tonnage Duty			Minor Revenues		
	£	s.	d.	£	s.	d.	£	s.	d.	£	s.	d.
1731	1,478	13	6				768	5	8	9	1	0½
1731										13	10	0FR
1733	1,578	3	0				993	2	11	37	7	10½
1733										15	2	6FR
1748				2,314	6	8						
1752				2,347	15	2						
1753				1,290	11	7*				11	17	6
1754				2,544	3	1				28	12	9¾
1755				1,807	9	10				75	10	2c
1755										2	17	0FR
1756	1,340	7	0				1,012	0	6	71	4	11c
1757	1,102	8	2				723	14	8½	206	13	9½c
1758	1,428	5	5½				1,004	3	10	67	12	2¾c
1759	946	2	3				827	13	2¾	274	7	1¼c
1760	1,066	7	9¾				877	11	6	115	6	4c
1761	2,141	0	0				1,508	1	0	159	2	2¾c
1768	1,204	13	4				1,107	19	1	20	14	9
1769	1,197	1	6				1,328	2	8	137	9	8
1770	1,185	5	9				1,493	16	2	131	13	7
1771	1,457	14	0				1,382	14	9	30	12	9
1772	1,674	15	9				1,473	15	6	52	0	6
1773	1,674	15	9				1,473	15	6	52	0	6
1774	1,564	15	4				1,623	17	6	67	7	1

* Incomplete.

1. Figures for the years 1748 and 1752–1755 placed between the "Hogshead Duty" and "Tonnage Duty" columns represent the combined revenues from both duties. In these cases no statistics are available for the duties separately. The returns from the hogshead duty for 1731 and 1733 are computed as they would have been had they not been combined with the quit-rent equivalent. Figures in the "Minor Revenues" column when not followed by the capital letters "FR" all represent the incomes from fines and forfeitures in the law courts (which the lord proprietor received as governor rather than as proprietor, for they were withheld during the royal government), and a small "c" indicates receipt in provincial currency, about two-thirds as valuable as sterling. The figures followed by "FR" indicate income, noted for three years only, from the issue of ferry licenses and rangers' commissions.

These statistics are derived for the most part from the documents listed above, p. 139, n. 50; but Calvert Papers no. 930, 931, 933, 948, 949, 950, 951, 952, 978, 980, 981, 982, 983, 984, 1017 have also been used, MHS.

TABLE IV

Estimated Annual Sterling Value of the Patronage Offices.[1]

OFFICE	1745	1754	1761	1745–1752	1763–1769
Lieutenant governor and chancellor	1550	1000	1200	......	1861[c]
Deputy-secretary	800	842	300	781	1116
Commissary-general[a]	900	644	250	902	1000
Agent	......	200	....	......	100, 150, 500[d]
Two judges of the land office, each	......	298	300	453	865
Two treasurers, each	125	......	40	......	......
Attorney-general	......	106	50	......	......
Two surveyors-general, each	......	151, 86	130	......	......
Examiner-general	......	100	....	......	235[e]
Two rent-roll keepers, each	......	......	....	......	175[f]
Five naval officers, each	150	168	50 to 150	......	......
Three commissioners, paper currency office, each	40	53	50	......	......
County clerks, each	115	......	80 to 200	......	......
Sheriffs, each	200	......	80 to 200	......	......
Deputy-commissaries, each	......	......	10 to 20	......	......
Deputy-surveyors, each	......	......	10, 50 to 150[b]	......	......
Clerkships, average	......	......	50 to 130	......	......
of council	160	85	....	......	......
of upper house	......	76	....	......	9[e]
of lower house	50	......	....	......	......
of secretary's office	65	......	....	......	......
of provincial court	......	......	....	......	......
of paper currency office	40	......	....	......	......
Registerships					
of commissary's office	80	......	....	......	......
of land office	......	......	....	......	......
Armory keeper	40	......	....	......	......
	9550		8460		

1. The values given in the column headed "1745," the approximate date, are taken from "A List of the Several Public Offices . . . in . . . Maryland, with their Revenues . . .," Massachusetts Historical Society, *Collections*, ser. I, vol. VII, 202–203. Those in the column headed "1754" are from a List of the Civil Officers of Maryland, 1754, Portfolio no. 3, MHRecs; and those headed "1761" are in Answers to Queries, January 14, 1762, Board of Trade Papers, Proprieties, XXI (1), HSP. The two columns on the right, "1745–1752," and "1763–1769," indicate values calculated from tobacco fees reported to the lower house in 1753 and 1770, for the periods indicated. A few figures from scattered sources are included.

Many of the original figures are stated precisely, in pounds, shillings, and pence, but for convenience such figures are here reproduced only to the nearest pound. In the original estimate, reproduced in the 1754 column, only the salaries of the governor and agent are given in sterling. The others, given in provincial currency, have been evaluated in sterling at the prevailing rate, approximately £150 currency for £100 sterling. (See Gould, *Money and Transportation in Maryland*, pp. 33, 98.) In translating the tobacco-fee incomes of the deputy-secretary, the commissary-general, and the judges of the land office into sterling, tobacco has been rated at 8s. 6d. per hundredweight, a conservative value and the one used by Governor Sharpe for a similar purpose in preparing his "exact estimate" of 1767, at a time of low tobacco prices.

ᵃ The office of commissary-general was sometimes divided between two holders.

ᵇ Ten pounds was estimated as normal for the settled counties, £50 to £150 for the counties where new land was being granted.

ᶜ This estimate is made from figures in an important document, dated 1767, written in Governor Sharpe's own hand, and headed, "An exact Estimate of the Annual Charge of maintaining and supporting the entire Establishment of the Province of Maryland distinguishing the different Funds and the different Services to which those Funds are appropriated . . ." (Portfolio no. 3, MHRecs.). The "exact estimate" is evidently the original draft or a copy of the report on the Maryland establishment ordered by Lord Shelburne in 1766, sent in May, 1767, and cited by Professor Bond from Public Record Office materials as C.O. 5: 112. f. 155. (See Bond, *The Quit-Rent System*, p. 215 n, and letters, Shelburne to Sharpe, December 11, 1766, and Sharpe to Shelburne, May 14, 1767, *Archives*, XIV, 361, 387–388). According to this report, the governor's income consisted of the twelve-pence-per-hogshead tobacco duty, which normally yielded £1291 9s. 0d., of a three-pence-per-ton duty on all vessels not owned in Maryland, which normally yielded £228 15s. 9d., and of the customary revenues from a twelve-shilling fee for marriage licenses, which normally yielded £341 4s. 0d. Two points should be noted: first, the governor's three-pence tonnage duty was apart from the fourteen-pence tonnage duty, which was assigned to the lord proprietor, and was not even entered in the agent's accounts; and, second, the estimate of £1861 as the governor's income, from the three sources specified above, represents his income as governor only, and does not include his fees as chancellor and surveyor-general.

According to the agents' accounts, the following sums were paid the governor from the hogshead duty alone for the years indicated: £1000, for 1752, 1753, 1754, 1755, 1759; £1002 7s. 9¾d., for 1760; £1139 14s. 6½d., for 1756; £1371 0s. 7¼d., for 1773; £1427 15s. 5½d., for 1758; £1978 10s. 10½d. for thirteen months in 1771 and 1772; and £2117 7s. 8¾d., for 1761 (Calvert Papers, MHS).

ᵈ The agent's accounts show that his own salary was £100 in 1733, £150 from 1748 to 1761, and £500 from 1769 to 1774. He also received a 5 per cent commission on manor rents and alienation fines.

ᵉ These estimates are made from the only available figures, those for the years 1767, 1768, and 1769.

ᶠ The rent-roll keepers' commissions varied in exact proportion to the quit-rents, but £175 is representative.

TABLE V

Size of Landholdings

County	Average Size of Delegates' Holdings[1]			Average Size of All Freeholds about 1755[2]
	1740	1758	1771	
St. Mary's..............	....	2,557	1,323	282.0
Charles.................	....	2,018	1,331	343.1
Calvert.................	....	2,390	1,495	364.1
Prince George's........	....	1,801	1,931	....
Anne Arundel..........	....	6,699	6,877	472.8
Baltimore..............	....	993	1,687	....
Worcester..............	....	1,232	1,015	255.3
Somerset...............	2,447	1,056	1,160	307.9
Dorchester.............	....	2,854	3,375	....
Talbot.................	2,562	956	4,331	329.5
Queen Anne's..........	1,061	4,076	3,756	....
Kent..................	616	885	1,205	279.6
Cecil..................	2,113	1,087	1,349	371.9
Frederick..............	....	3,676	2,450	370.1
All counties	1,754.1	2,221.6	2,423.6	....

1. The average for the lower house should ideally be based on 132 estates, that is, the holdings of each of the four delegates from all the counties for which there are figures. The averages are actually based on 125 estates: 18 out of 20 (five counties) for 1740, 54 out of 56 for 1758, and 53 out of 56 for 1771. There is some liability to error. When, as in a few cases, an estate could not be identified for a given year, the figure for another year, shortly before or after, was substituted. Whole groups of none too legible figures, taken from the Debt Books of several counties, had to be assembled to determine certain of the estates. There may have been oversights of out-of-county holdings, but the search was a thorough one and I may hope that not many relevant figures escaped. The averages are more liable to understatement than overstatement.

2. Gould, *The Land System in Maryland*, p. 77 n.

BIBLIOGRAPHICAL NOTE
BIBLIOGRAPHIES

There is no guide to the materials of Maryland history. Until this need is filled, the investigator in any area will have to search for himself, with considerable risk of oversight. There is much help to be had, however, from partial lists which cut across various sections of the manuscript, documentary, and monographic materials.

Within the limits indicated in the title, Paul H. Giddens, "Bibliography on Maryland during the Time of Governor Horatio Sharpe, 1753–1769," in *Maryland Historical Magazine*, XXXI (1936), 6–16, provides a useful check list. It deals with all types of materials, manuscript and printed, primary and secondary, books and articles. It is accurate but incomplete, and not suggestive on the side of eighteenth-century printed materials. On this side, Lawrence C. Wroth's "Maryland Imprints," in his *A History of Printing in Colonial Maryland, 1686–1776* (Baltimore, 1922), pp. 157–256, is invaluable. It not only lists and locates, but also describes and comments on hundreds of printed items. There is also Bernard C. Steiner, *Descriptions of Maryland*, Johns Hopkins University Studies in Historical and Political Science, XXII (1904), nos. 11–12.

Other lists and guides, of narrower application, are given in the appropriate sections below.

MANUSCRIPTS

1. In the library of the Maryland Historical Society, Baltimore.
Until 1936, the Maryland Historical Society kept under one roof nearly all the important and usable collections of provincial manuscripts. In that year the Society began turning over to the new state Hall of Records, in Annapolis, the great collections of official colonial records which it had held as custodian. There is an account of the early holdings of the Society in Lewis Mayer, *Catalogue of Manuscripts, Maps, Medals, Coins, Statuary, Portraits, and Pictures; and an Account of the Library of the Maryland Historical Society, made in 1854* (Baltimore, 1854).

The Society's vault still contains the one most important unprinted manuscript collection of the colonial period, the Calvert Papers so frequently cited in this study. It is a very large miscellany of proprietary commissions, instructions, accounts, letters, and memoranda. The collection is not fully catalogued, as it should be, but *The Calvert Papers*, I (Maryland Historical Society, *Fund-Publications*, no. 28, Baltimore, 1889) gives a classification and a listing of the documents. *The Calvert Papers*, II (*Fund-Publications*, no. 34, 1894), contains most of the eighteenth-century correspondence in the collection, and is very valuable; vol. III (*Fund-Publications*, no. 35, 1899) has some seventeenth-century materials. The writer has examined all the eighteenth-century manuscripts of this collection except those dealing exclusively with the boundary dispute with the Penns. The most valuable have been the proprietary instructions and correspondence, and the accounts rendered the lords proprietors by the receivers-general. Without them much of the report on proprietary interests and policies would be very slender.

Related in interest to the Calvert Papers are the large Portfolios, boxes which contain a number of instructions to the colonial governors and a considerable body of letters, petitions, and miscellaneous papers. Originally twelve boxes in all, an important part of this collection has been transferred to the Hall of Records. Although not of contemporary making, the Goldsborough List of Civil Officers of Maryland is also of use to the student of pre-revolutionary institutions and politics. It is a manuscript list, in three volumes, of the holders of office, great and small. The volume marked "1749–1891" was the one most useful for this study.

The Society is not as rich in manuscripts in economic as in political history, but it has some of the port records and certain minor collections of commercial importance. There are two Annapolis Port of Entry Books, 1756–1775; the one covers the entries of vessels in, and the other covers clearances out, for the port and period indicated. A book marked as the Collector's Accounts of the Port of Oxford, Maryland, 1726–1811, gives entries in and clearances out, 1759–1775. These "port of entry books" are compiled naval officers' lists, and they give detailed information about each vessel clearing the ports, according to the forms prescribed by royal instruction. They are at once too fragmentary and too detailed to be readily subject to summary; but if not totals they do supply test samplings of provincial trade. Our statistical knowledge of the trade of all the colonies will be vastly extended by the compilations of naval-office materials made at the University of California under the leadership of Professor Lawrence Harper and Dr. John Cox.

The Historical Society has four or five other collections of some economic significance. The Hill Papers are account books, letters, and miscellaneous papers; they afford some information about mercantile usage and method, and about prices. The Hamilton Papers are those of a Scottish factor in Port Tobacco in correspondence with James Lawson of Glasgow, and they throw light on the position and status of the factor. The William H. Corner Collection contains bills, indentures, and notes; and the early boxes of the Scharf Papers have a good many manuscripts referring to paper money. A bound collection, Principio Papers, Letters and Deeds, 1723–1730, has twenty-one documents bearing on the early history of the most important iron company in Maryland.

The other useful collections of the Maryland Historical Society for this period are the following: the Dulany Papers, five boxes, partly Tuesday Club papers but otherwise disappointing; the Bordley Papers, five letter books, 1727–1759, suggestive as to lower-house politics, as to trade, and as to thought; and, finally, the Gilmor Papers. This collection is from the period of Sharpe's administration, and comes from the family of Sharpe's secretary and favorite, John Ridout. Besides a number of official documents, now printed in the *Archives of Maryland*, the Gilmor Papers contain rare handbills and certain papers of the Homony Club.

A number of the manuscripts and transcripts of the Maryland Historical Society have been printed in the *Maryland Historical Magazine*, notably the letters of Charles Carroll of Carrollton, those of Dr. Charles Carroll and Charles Carroll, Barrister, and the correspondence of Governor Eden. Citations in the footnotes, above, and bibliographical references, below, are made to the printed location of such materials, and not to the manuscript originals.

2. In other depositories in Baltimore.

The Maryland Diocesan Library of the Protestant Episcopal Church is located in the Peabody Institute. The Callister Papers comprise its most valuable colonial collection. They number about eight hundred documents, largely letters; they include Callister's own correspondence from 1742 to 1766, and there are some later papers. The Callister Papers give an incomparable insight into the social and economic life of Maryland below the level of the established gentry. In the same depository there are some interesting letters bearing on the established church before the Revolution; they are in a volume marked "Letters, I."

The Johns Hopkins University Library has three bound volumes of Dr. Hamilton's manuscript "History of the Tuesday Club."

3. In Annapolis.

The Maryland Hall of Records, under the direction of the state archivist, Dr. Morris L. Radoff, now has the originals of the official colonial records. The laws, the proceedings of the executive council, the proceedings of the two houses of assembly, and many court records are there. Many of these materials have been printed, however, either in the *Archives of Maryland* or in the contemporary *Votes and Proceedings* of the House of Delegates. Accordingly the smaller collections of the Hall of Records have been more useful for this study than the larger.

Of these collections the most valuable have been the proprietary papers in the Black Books. These manuscripts, bound in eleven volumes, are a part of the "Rainbow Series" of documents, which run on beyond the colonial period. The Black Books contain many documents now in print and many others which are scattered and trivial, but they also contain a number of valuable provincial papers of Sharpe's period. So too do Portfolios number 2, 3, and 4, recently brought from the Historical Society to the Hall of Records (see especially p. 257, n. 4). Both collections are essential to an understanding of proprietary policy.

The Hall of Records, like the Historical Society, has certain of the colonial port records. There are two folios, as follows: Port of Annapolis, Clearings Outward, 1748, which contains entries in and clearances out at Annapolis, 1748–1759, and at the port of Oxford, on the Eastern Shore, 1742–1746; and Entries Inward for Patuxent District, 1745–1757, which contains entries in at the ports of Patuxent, Annapolis, and Oxford, for the period indicated. These "port of entry books" have the same character as the similar books at the Maryland Historical Society. The Hall of Records has also the two Wallace, Davidson, and Johnson Letter Books. The first volume, for the years 1771–

1774, is the most revealing business correspondence for the last period of this study.

The Hall of Records has also a great number of testamentary materials and church records. The writer has sampled the inventories and wills to get indications of standards of living, but has no more than sampled them. The Hall of Records has begun to publish lists of its holdings of this type.

Another Annapolis depository of official manuscripts is the Maryland Land Office. It is under the active direction of the chief clerk, Mr. Arthur Trader, whose detailed knowledge is generously available to investigators. The office contains a vast number of manuscripts referring to titles, estates, and tenancies. For the needs of this study, principally to determine the landholdings of public men, the Debt Books, that is, the annual lists for the collection of quit-rents, have been invaluable. The Rent Rolls, or lists of grants, have also been of use.

The Annapolis depositories and the county courthouses contain many little-investigated volumes of court records and land records. Not only the legal historian but also the social historian, if he is willing to work much ore for rare metal, will find value in these records. The present writer has not attempted to search them. There is a suggestion of the amount of the material in Hester D. Richardson, "Report of the Public Records Commission of Maryland," American Historical Association, *Annual Report*, 1905 (Washington, 1906), I, 367–368. The Historical Records Survey of the Works Projects Administration has catalogued the materials in seven of the county courthouses. A real indication of what good historical work may be done in this area is to be found in the introductions to recent volumes of the *Archives of Maryland* (volumes XLIX, LI, LIII–LIV) in the *Court Series*. Behind much of the present effort in this field lies the influence and scholarship of Chief Judge Carroll T. Bond, of the Maryland Court of Appeals. When legal and social history is better known, by the single method of new spade work, many other aspects of colonial and revolutionary history will be illuminated.

4. In Washington and New York.

Outside Maryland, there are important manuscripts of the provincial period in the Library of Congress and in the New York Public Library.

The Library of Congress has two collections of first-class importance. The Galloway, Maxcy, Markoe Papers are a very large collection, the first dozen volumes of which refer to the colonial period. They contain the correspondence of Samuel Galloway of Tulip Hill from 1754 to 1775. Galloway was a Quaker merchant, near Annapolis, a man of wealth, and connected by business as well as blood with the Galloways of Philadelphia. His letters are largely mercantile letters, with correspondents in England, Ireland, Portugal, the Madeiras, the West Indies, and the continental colonies. There are also Maryland letters, some from Thomas Ringgold, a leading delegate of the Eastern Shore; but the collection is weak on the side of politics. The other important collection in the Library of Congress is the Maryland and Virginia Firm Accounts. The Firm Accounts are those of Scottish traders, and are more numerous and important for Virginia than for Maryland. In the form of ledgers, journals, and daybooks, their story is not a plain one. There are some inventories, however, and a few letters; and the very bulk of the collection testifies to the commercial aggressiveness of the Scots in penetrating the best tobacco country of the Potomac and Patuxent valleys.

The Library of Congress has other scattered Maryland manuscripts. Papers acquired before 1931 are indicated either in *Handbook of Manuscripts in the Library of Congress* (Washington, 1918), or in Curtis W. Garrison, "List of Manuscript Collections in the Library of Congress to July, 1931," American Historical Association, *Annual Report, 1930* (Washington, 1931), I, 123–233. The most useful of the minor items have been the small collection of the Papers of Charles Carroll of Doughoregan Manor, 1684–1771, and the photostat of the "Synodalia: Or Records of Clergy Meetings in Maryland between 1695–1773," a manuscript by Ethan Allen, D. D., Baltimore, 1864.

There are a few valuable Maryland papers in the New York Public Library. They are listed in Evarts B. Greene and Richard B. Morris, *A Guide to the Principal Sources for Early American History (1600–1800) in the City of New York* (New York, 1929), especially pp. 97–98. The most important are in the George Chalmers Collection, Papers Relating to Maryland, I–II, 1619–1812; some of them supplement the figures on proprietary revenues which are to be found in the Calvert Papers. In the same library is a small collection of Maryland Manuscripts, Miscellaneous. It contains items referring to the Liberty Lottery and to the social clubs. There is also a small collection of Samuel and John Galloway letters, which supplement those in the Library of Congress.

5. Transcripts of British Records, in Washington and Philadelphia.

The British records in the Public Record Office and the lesser archives have less importance for Maryland than for most of the colonies. The proprietary form of government insulated the province from full normal contact with the authorities of the Crown.

The standard and invaluable guides, by Professor Andrews and Miss Davenport—Charles M. Andrews and Frances G. Davenport, *Guide to the Manuscript Materials for the History of the United States to 1783, in the British Museum, in Minor London Archives, and in the Libraries of Oxford and Cambridge* (Washington, 1908), and Andrews, *Guide to the Materials for American History, to 1783, in the Public Record Office of Great Britain* (two volumes, Washington, 1912, 1914)—do lead, however, to materials essential for Maryland history. Most of these materials have been transcribed for the Library of Congress or for the Historical Society of Pennsylvania.

The following transcripts and photostats in the Library of Congress have been especially useful: Treasury Board Papers, of the Public Record Office, especially in-letters, class 1, which supply naval office lists, data on the customs establishment in Maryland, and on the Stamp Act period; certain of the Additional Manuscripts of the British Museum, and manuscripts in the House of Lords Library, which give statistics about trade; and Maryland papers in the Fulham Palace Manuscripts and in the records of the Society for the Propagation of the Gospel, which supply information about the established church in Maryland. These materials are cited in detail in the footnotes.

The Historical Society of Pennsylvania, with an interest to possess the full colonial record of Maryland's neighbor and sister proprietary province, has a complete transcription of the Journals of the Lords of Trade and Board of Trade, 1675–1782, and of the Board of Trade Papers, Proprieties, 1697–1776, under the old British classification. These transcripts supply ample material for examining the relationship of Maryland to the British commercial system. In all the fifty-eight volumes of the Journals (vols. XXVI–LXXXIII) and thirteen volumes of proprietary papers (vols. X–XXII) which cover the sixty years between the restoration of proprietary government in Maryland and the outbreak of the Revolution, there are relatively few Maryland items. Yet they represent a little-understood aspect of provincial history and one of real importance for this study. Although examination of the Journals was made by means of this transcript, footnote references are, for the convenience of the reader, to the printed *Journal of the Commissioners for Trade and Plantations, 1704–1783* (14 vols., London, 1920–1938), which has been completed since this study was begun.

PRINTED SOURCES

1. The "Archives of Maryland."

The principal source and foundation of this study has been the great printed collection of the *Archives of Maryland* (Baltimore, 1883–   ). It is the best of the modern issues of colonial documents. The series has been well edited, as follows: vols. I–XVII and XIX–XXXII by William H. Browne; vols. XXXIII–XXXV by Clayton C. Hall; vol. XVIII and vols. XXXVI–XLV by Bernard C. Steiner; and vols. XLVI–LVI by J. Hall Pleasants.

For the central questions of politics and assembly traditions and usage, I have drawn principally from vols. XXXV–XXXVII, XXXIX–XL, XLII, XLIV, XLVI, L, LII, LV, which comprise the *Proceedings and Acts of the General Assembly of Maryland*, from 1724 to 1758 (this series is still to be completed). Hardly less important, and essential for understanding proprietary policy, have been the volumes containing the executive archives. I have used especially the following: vols. XXV and XXVIII, *Proceedings of the Council of Maryland, 1698–1753;* vol. XXXI, *Proceedings of the Council of Maryland, 1753–1761, Letters to Governor Horatio Sharpe, 1754–1765;* and vol. XXXII, *Proceedings of the Council of Maryland, 1761–1770, Minutes of the Board of Revenue, Opinions on the Regulation of Fees, Instructions to Governor Eden.* The *Correspondence of Governor Horatio Sharpe, 1753–1771*, in vols. VI, IX, and XIV (with additional letters in vol. XXXI), makes possible an especially full knowledge of his administration.

2. Contemporary Maryland Documents.

For the period after 1758, not yet covered in the *Archives of Maryland*, the proceedings of the Delegates and the laws of the assembly may be found in contemporary imprints. For the laws before 1765, Thomas Bacon's splendid edition of the *Laws of Maryland at large, with proper indexes. Now first collected. . . . Together with notes and other matters, relative to the constitution. . . . To which is prefixed the charter* . . . (Annapolis, 1765), is very satisfactory. For the years from 1765 to the Revolution, I have relied on the *Laws of Maryland made since M,DCC,LXIII, consisting of acts of assembly under the proprietary government, resolves of convention, the declaration of rights, the constitution and form of government, the articles of confederation, and acts of assembly since the Revolution* (Annapolis, 1787), edited by A. C. Hanson. William Kilty's edition of *The Laws of Maryland, . . . the original charter, . . . the bill of rights and constitution of the state, . . . with an index* . . . (2 vols., Annapolis, 1799), covers the period from 1692 to 1799, but, for the pre-revolutionary years, it is not quite as full as the Hanson edition. Both editions give notes or abstracts, not the texts, of the laws or parts of laws which had expired at the time of compilation. The full texts of all the laws are to be found in the *Laws of the Province of Maryland* (the title varies) printed after each session by the provincial printer at Annapolis. For guidance to these imprints, see Wroth, *History of Printing in Colonial Maryland*, pp. 165–243.

For assembly affairs, after 1758, I have used the *Votes and Proceedings of the Lower House of Assembly of the Province of Maryland*, which were issued sessionally, as the *Laws* were, and which are listed and located in Wroth's "Imprints" (to find any item in the series, see the *History of Printing in Colonial Maryland*, pp. 172–243). In some instances, I have read the manuscript originals of the proceedings of both houses, but the fullness of the *Votes and Proceedings* makes such an investigation unnecessary. They contain the record of the Delegates; they also contain the addresses and messages of the upper house to the lower, and there is little beside these messages in the original record of the upper house. Our fuller knowledge of the council comes from its executive proceedings, now printed in the *Archives*, and not from the legislative proceedings.

3. Other Official Documents.

In a useful proportion, the *Maryland Historical Magazine* (Baltimore, 1906–   ) is a collection of miscellaneous official documents. Interspersed among a greater number of articles, reviews, and letters is a generous sprinkling of eighteenth-century materials not printed elsewhere. The most important for this study are the following: the "Correspondence of Governor Eden," vol. II (1907); "Maryland in 1773," *idem.;* and the "Stamp Act Papers," from the Public Record Office, vol. VI (1911). These, and less important documents, including a few printed in *The Pennsylvania Magazine of History and Biography* (Philadelphia, 1877–   ), are cited in detail in the footnotes.

This study has required the repeated use of William S. Perry, *Historical Collections of the American Colonial Church* (Hartford), IV, *Maryland* (1878). It is an admirable source for the history of the Anglican establishment in Maryland, and one which is only supplemented, not displaced, by the available British transcripts. The printed calendars of British Colonial Office and Treasury Papers have been of no real use for this study, for the reasons that the subject is late in time, where publication is incomplete, and that the proprietary government did not mesh closely enough with royal supervision to create a normal amount of such records. I have made use, however, of the *Acts of the Privy Council, Colonial* (six volumes, Hereford and London, 1908–1912), edited by W. L. Grant and James Munro. These volumes are indispensable for all the colonies, though not rich for Maryland.

4. Newspapers and Pamphlets.

Both the first *Maryland Gazette*, under William Parks, from 1727 to 1734, and the second, under Jonas Green and his family, beginning in 1745, are first-class historical sources. (For a discussion of their quality and content, see above, pp. 62–64, 82–83, 101–102, 168–171.) They are supplemented, from within the province, by William Goddard's *Maryland Journal and Baltimore Advertiser,* launched in Baltimore in 1773, and by the *Maryland Almanack,* printed in Annapolis. I have found valuable Maryland items scattered in the *Virginia Gazette* (Williamsburg), beginning in 1736; in the *Pennsylvania Gazette* (Philadelphia), beginning in 1728; and in the *Pennsylvania Chronicle and Universal Advertiser* (Philadelphia), beginning in 1767.

For a full listing and locating of Maryland colonial periodicals, see Wroth, *History of Printing in Colonial Maryland,* pp. 172–253; and George C. Keidel, "Early Maryland Newspapers," *Maryland Historica¹ Magazine,* XXVIII (1933), 119–120. For colonial newspapers generally, see Clarence S. Brigham, "Bibliography of American Newspapers, 1690–1820," *Proceedings of the American Antiquarian Society* (Worcester), New Series, XXIII–XXXVII (1913–1927); the Maryland papers are listed in vol. XXV (1915), 130–192. The complete file of Green's *Maryland Gazette*, in the Maryland State Library, has been film-copied and distributed by the Yale University Library.

The principal Maryland pamphlets of this period are three: Daniel Dulany, the elder, *The Right of the Inhabitants of Maryland to the Benefit of the English Laws* (Annapolis, 1728); Daniel Dulany, the younger, *Considerations on the Propriety of imposing Taxes in the British Colonies, for the Purpose of raising a Revenue, by Act of Parliament* (Annapolis, 1765); and, by the same writer, *The Right to the Tonnage, the Duty of Twelve Pence per Hogshead on all exported Tobacco, and the Fines and Forfeitures in the Province of Maryland* . . . (Annapolis, 1766). The first is reprinted, as an appendix, in St. George L. Sioussat, *The English Statutes in Maryland*, Johns Hopkins University Studies in Historical and Political Science, XXXI (1903), nos. 11–12; and the second is in the *Maryland Historical Magazine*, VI (1911), 374–406; VII (1912), 26–59. For full bibliographical discussions of these pamphlets, see Wroth, *History of Printing in Colonial Maryland*, pp. 173, 223–226, 227–228.

5. Memoirs and Letters.

By all means the most informing comment on pre-revolutionary Maryland is that in William Eddis, *Letters from America, Historical and Descriptive; Comprising Occurrences from 1769, to 1777, inclusive* (London, 1792). Eddis was a surveyor of the customs at Annapolis, a favorite and associate of Governor Eden, and a parvenu who naturally saw the province in a favorable light. But his comment is detailed and penetrating, and as fair to the tobacco-raising gentry as to his associates in appointive office. His report is supplemented by that in the *Reminiscences of an American Loyalist, 1738–1789, being the Autobiography of the Rev'd Jonathan Boucher* (Boston, 1925), edited by Jonathan Bouchier. Boucher's view of Maryland, where he lived for only a few years before the Revolution, reflects equally the favors and the conflicts to which the Anglican clergyman was subject. There are no other first-class reminiscences, but the e are two American travel-diaries which contain valuable passages descriptive of Maryland. The first, by Dr. Alexander Hamilton, the Scottish Marylander, is *Hamilton's Itinerarium, being a narrative of a journey from Annapolis, Maryland, through Delaware, Pennsylvania, New York, New Jersey, Connecticut, Rhode Island, Massachusetts and New Hampshire, from May to September, 1744* (St. Louis, 1907), edited by Albert B. Hart. The other account of special value here is that of the young tutor, Philip Fithian. His descriptions and comments, on both tidewater and back country, are to be found in two volumes, *Philip Vickers Fithian, Journal and Letters* (Princeton, 1900), edited by John R. Williams; and *Philip Vickers Fithian, Journal, 1775–1776* (Princeton, 1934), edited by Robert G. Albion and Leonidas Dodson.

The collected letters of a number of eighteenth-century Marylanders have been printed in the *Maryland Historical Magazine*. The most important are the following: "Letters of the Rev. Jonathan Boucher," in vols. VII–X (1912–1915); "Extracts from the Carroll [of Carrollton] Papers," and "A Lost Copybook of Charles Carroll of Carrollton," edited by J. G. D. Paul, in vols. X–XVI (1915–1921) and XXXII (1937); "Extracts from the Account and Letter Books of Dr. Charles Carroll of Annapolis," in vols. XVIII–XXVII (1923–1932); and "Letters of Charles Carroll, Barrister," beginning in vol. XXXI (1936) and not yet completely issued. The Charles Carroll of Carrollton papers in the *Maryland Historical Magazine* were preceded by the valuable *Unpublished Letters of Charles Carroll of Carrollton and of His Father, Charles Carroll of Doughoregan* (New York, 1902), edited by Thomas M. Field. This type of contemporary writing is of the highest value for social, economic, and intellectual history.

SELECTED SECONDARY WRITINGS

1. State and Local Histories.

A history of Maryland written according to the standards of modern scholarship and interest is still wanting, but there are two or three which are very helpful. The more than century-old work of the lawyer, John V. L. McMahon, *An Historical View of the Government of Maryland from its Colonization to the Present Day* (Baltimore, 1831), was written with a rare understanding of the proprietary system and the anti-proprietary impulse. There is also value in James McSherry, *History of Maryland; from its First Settlement in 1634, to the year 1848* (Baltimore, 1849); it was edited and continued in a new edition (Baltimore,

1904) by Dr. Bartlett B. James. John Thomas Scharf, *History of Maryland from the Earliest Period to the Present Day* (three volumes, Baltimore, 1879) is a labor of love for Maryland, its non-political as well as its political history. The work lacks system and form, but it is a useful compendium, especially because it includes many documents and newspaper items, reprinted in full. Matthew Page Andrews' large *History of Maryland: Province and State* (Garden City, 1929) undertakes a full-length narrative, but it has little value for the student.

Town and county histories are of unequal value and use. From two old histories, David Ridgely, *Annals of Annapolis* (Baltimore, 1841), and Thomas W. Griffith, *Annals of Baltimore* (Baltimore, 1833), it is possible to get a firmer picture of the principal colonial towns than from either the large compendia of local and biographical data, such as the Baltimore histories brought out by John Thomas Scharf in 1874 and 1879, or from breezy popular accounts of recent writing. The slender annals of a century ago were near enough to the eighteenth century to have a "feel" for colonial events; and they reprinted much from colonial newspaper and comment. This last merit is achieved also in Elihu S. Riley's compilation, *"The Ancient City." A history of Annapolis in Maryland, 1649–1887* (Annapolis, 1887).

Two county histories are outstanding. Oswald Tilghman, *History of Talbot County, Maryland, 1661–1861* (2 vols., Baltimore, 1915), is an informing work, based on much knowledge of local conditions and biography. George Johnston, *History of Cecil County, Maryland* . . . (Elkton, 1887), is more annalistic and less interesting, but it has local information not easily to be obtained elsewhere. The other county histories are mostly overlarge, and over-genealogical for much use to the student of history; there is little to be gleaned from them for this period which is not more readily available in the source materials.

2. Special Monographs.

Three excellent studies throw much light on difficult and complex aspects of Maryland's provincial history. Newton D. Mereness, *Maryland as a Proprietary Province* (New York, 1901), is the student's gateway to Maryland's colonial institutions. The work is analytical, a product of Professor Herbert L. Osgood's school of colonial history, and it lacks movement; but without it the half-feudal complexities of the proprietary government would present a serious obstacle to the study of provincial history. Of the Maryland section of the work of Beverly W. Bond, *The Quit-Rent System in the American Colonies* (New Haven, 1919), there is much the same thing to be said. Without the work of Bond, who has a preliminary study of Maryland quit-rents in the *Maryland Historical Magazine*, V (1910), this complex part of land system and land policy would be obscure. To be bracketed with the studies of Mereness and Bond, because it also strikes a salient into a little-known area, is Avery O. Craven, *Soil Exhaustion as a Factor in the Agricultural History of Virginia and Maryland, 1606–1860*, University of Illinois Studies in the Social Sciences, XIII (Urbana, 1926), no. 1. This book is based more largely on Virginia than on Maryland materials; but the achievement of its early chapters, in setting forth the historical connections between agricultural condition and other aspects of colonial history, is highly suggestive to the student of Maryland.

With the exception of these three studies, all the important monographs on provincial Maryland have been published in Maryland, in the Johns Hopkins University Studies in Historical and Political Science (Baltimore, 1883–   ). The most valuable are the economic studies by Clarence P. Gould, *The Land System of Maryland, 1720–1765*, vol. XXXI (1913), no. 1; and *Money and Transportation in Maryland, 1720–1765*, vol. XXXIII (1915), no. 1. The following are also essential: Margaret S. Morriss, *Colonial Trade of Maryland, 1689–1715*, vol. XXXII (1914), no. 3; Kathryn L. Behrens, *Paper Money in Maryland, 1727–1789*, vol. XLI (1923), no. 1; St. George L. Sioussat, *The English Statutes in Maryland*, and *Economics and Politics in Maryland, 1720–1750, and the Public Services of Daniel Dulany, the Elder*, vol. XXI (1903), nos. 11–12, 6–7; Vertrees J. Wyckoff, *Tobacco Regulation in Colonial Maryland*, Extra Volumes, New Series, no. 22 (1936); and Bernard C. Steiner, *The Life and Administration of Sir Robert Eden*, vol. XVI (1898), nos. 7–9.

3. Historical Articles.

There is no necessity to repeat from the footnotes the titles of the many articles which bear on pre-revolutionary Maryland and have been of use for this study. But the special value of the *Maryland Historical Magazine* must be credited in this respect as in others; any student of Maryland history should search the file for materials in his field of interest. For mid-eighteenth-century Maryland, the articles of Paul H. Giddens, on various aspects of the administration of Governor Sharpe, are scholarly and accurate. The earliest is in vol. XXVII (1932), and the series is listed in Giddens' own "Bibliography," in volume XXXI (1936), pp. 13–14.

Articles referring to Maryland are widely spread in many journals other than the *Maryland Historical Magazine*. The close student is referred especially to *The Pennsylvania Magazine of History and Biography* and to *The Virginia Magazine of History and Biography* (Richmond, 1893–   ).

4. Foundation Works in Revolutionary History.

There is no need to discuss the wider literature of the revolutionary impulse in America. Students will recognize that this book has been affected indirectly where not directly by the writings of the master-students of the present century. Without the works of Professors Charles M. Andrews, George L. Beer, Herbert L. Osgood, Claude H. Van Tyne, and Arthur M. Schlesinger, new writers would lack the foundation upon which it is their right and privilege to build as best they can.

INDEX

Acts of the Province, printing of begun, 167; increased, 246

Adams, Joseph, British merchant in trade agreement, 88

Addison, Rev. Henry, pleads for education, 52; favors church reform, 278

Agent, colonial, proprietor acts as, 194; proposed by Delegates, 218; issue in attack on proprietorship, 228–232, 235; opposed by proprietor, 238; issue re-opened, 242, 252, 304–305, 334, 337, 366; failure of, 338–340

See also Franklin, Benjamin; Garth, Charles; Paris, F. J.; Privy Council

Agent, proprietary revenue officer. *See* Receiver-general

Agriculture, in Frederick co., 11–12; in northern counties, 13–14; on Eastern Shore, 98, 106, 109, 110n; on Western Shore, 98–99, 106, 109

See also Diversification; Tobacco; Trade

Aikman, William, launches circulating library, 66

Albany Congress, appropriation for, 207

Alienation fines, collection of attempted, 260

See also Proprietary Revenues

Allen, Rev. Bennet, as receiver-general, 268, 286; personal history of, 281; church scandal of, 281–288; significance of, 288–289, 316

All Saints' parish, Allen at, 286–288

Almanac. *See Maryland Almanack*

Anderson, William and James, London firm, 74

Andrews, C. M., on Maryland government, 118; on constitutional conflict, 154

Anglican Church, in Baltimore co., 20; establishment contrary to dissenters' convictions, 25; establishment of, by statute, 43, 45–46, 358, 360–365; character of, 45–46; salaries in, 46–47, 92, 358, 366; evil conditions in, 47–50 (*see also* Allen, Bennet; Coventry parish); lack of authority of Bishop of London, 49, 359; proposal for reform in, 49, 216, 275–277, 358–360; political activities of, 92, 93, 359–360 (*see also* "Vestry question"); value of patronage in, 148; reforms in, 361–362, 365–366; disestablishment of, 371

See also Deism; Education; Rationalism; clergymen and parishes by name

Annapolis, 52; character and appearance of, 54–55; election activities in, 174, 176, 332, 355–356; troops billeted in, 209–210; Stamp Act demonstrations in, 299–301; non-importation at, 321, 324–326; activities of Wallace, Davidson, and Johnson at, 343; association of 1774 at, 370

See also Clubs; Delegates, House of; Libraries; Proprietary government

Anne Arundel county, 4, 6; landholding in, 31; gentry of, 36; center of politics, 176, 179–180 (*see also* Annapolis); petition of, to Delegates, 254; instructions to Delegates, 301; non-importation in, 320

Answer to the Queries, An, pamphlet, 252–253

Anti-Catholicism, 117; Carroll of Doughoregan on, 29; laws expressing, 43–44, 172, 240; during French and Indian War, 240, 254

See also Anglican Church; Catholics; Protestants

Architecture, of frontier, 12–13, 16; of towns, 21, 54–55; Georgian style, 38–39